This book makes a significant contribution to the literature on accountability for policing in three particular ways. First, it adopts much broader conceptions of both accountability and 'policing' than have been evident in almost all the previous literature on this topic. Second, it is historically grounded, which enhances understanding of where things stand today. Third, it is thoroughly up to date, exploring new conceptual frames, the most recent developments, and the most recent critiques. For all these reasons, it is a book that should be read by anyone who is interested, for whatever reasons, in its central subject.

Philip C. Stenning, *Professor of Criminology and Criminal Justice, Griffith University, Queensland, Australia*

*Accountability of Policing* is a sorely needed text in the policing research cannon. Lister and Rowe, along with a long list of well-respected scholars in this field, have compiled an informative and insightful text on a topic of great interest in policing. It will be a valuable resource for students, researchers and practitioners.

Megan O'Neill, *Lecturer in Human Geography, University of Dundee and the Scottish Institute of Policing Research, UK*

Focusing on such diverse subjects as corruption, complaints, and stop and search, and bringing together the leading authors in their respective fields, this impressive volume offers the most up-to-date analysis of the contemporary state of accountability in policing and private security. This will be essential reading for teachers and students of policing.

Tim Newburn, *Professor of Criminology and Social Policy, London School of Economics, UK*

# Accountability of Policing

*Accountability of Policing* provides a contemporary and wide-ranging examination of the accountability and governance of 'police' and 'policing'. Debates about 'who guards the guards' are among the oldest and most protracted in the history of democracy, but over the last decade we have witnessed important changes in how policing and security agencies are governed, regulated and held to account. Against a backdrop of increasing complexity in the local, national and transnational landscapes of 'policing', political, legal, administrative and technological developments have served to alter regimes of accountability. The extent and pace of these changes raises a pressing need for ongoing academic research, analysis and debate.

Bringing together contributions from a range of leading scholars, this book offers an authoritative and comprehensive analysis of the shifting themes of accountability within policing. The contributions explore questions of accountability across a range of dimensions, including those 'individuals' and 'institutions' responsible for its delivery, within and between the 'public' and 'private' sectors, and at 'local', 'national' and 'transnational' scales of jurisdiction. They also engage with the concept of 'accountability' in a broad sense, bringing to the surface the various meanings that have become associated with it and demonstrating how it is invoked and interpreted in different contexts.

*Accountability of Policing* is essential reading for academics and students involved in the study of policing, criminal justice and criminology and will also be of great interest to practitioners and policymakers.

**Stuart Lister** is Senior Lecturer in Criminal Justice at the University of Leeds. His research interests focus on exploring the changes and continuities in the arrangement, provision, accountability and effectiveness of contemporary policing and security endeavours. He has worked previously at the universities of Durham and Keele.

**Michael Rowe** is Professor of Criminology at Northumbria University. His research interests focus on the ethics and governance of policing, diversity in criminal justice, and offender desistance. He has taught at Victoria University, Wellington, and at the University of Leicester.

# Routledge Frontiers of Criminal Justice

# Accountability of Policing

**Edited by Stuart Lister and
Michael Rowe**

Routledge
Taylor & Francis Group

LONDON AND NEW YORK

First published 2016
by Routledge
2 Park Square, Milton Park, Abingdon, Oxon OX14 4RN

and by Routledge
711 Third Avenue, New York, NY 10017

*Routledge is an imprint of the Taylor & Francis Group, an informa business*

*British Library Cataloguing-in-Publication Data*
A catalogue record for this book is available from the British Library

*Library of Congress Cataloging-in-Publication Data*
Accountability in policing / edited by Stuart Lister and Michael Rowe.
    pages cm. – (Routledge frontiers of criminal justice ; 29)
    1. Police administration. 2. Police. 3. Responsibility. I. Lister, Stuart.
    II. Rowe, Michael
    HV7935.A25 2015
    363.2068'4–dc23                                                    2015007788

ISBN: 978-0-415-71533-1 (hbk)
ISBN: 978-1-3-1588189-8 (ebk)

Typeset in Times New Roman
by Wearset Ltd, Boldon, Tyne and Wear

# Contents

# Illustrations

**Figures**

**Tables**

# Contributors

**Ben Bowling** is Professor of Criminology and Criminal Justice, and Associate Dean of the School of Law, King's College London. He worked previously at John Jay College of Criminal Justice (New York), the Home Office Research Unit and the University of Cambridge. He has been a visiting professor at the University of the West Indies, Monash University (Melbourne) and the East China University of Political Science and Law (Shanghai). His books include *Violent Racism* (OUP 1998), *Racism, Crime and Justice* (with Coretta Phillips, Longman 2002), *Policing the Caribbean* (OUP 2010), *Global Policing* (with James Sheptycki, Sage 2012) and *Stop and Search: Police Power in Global Context* (edited with Leanne Weber, Routledge 2012).

**Gordon Boyce** is an interdisciplinary accounting scholar who works in the Department of Accounting at La Trobe University, Melbourne, Australia. Gordon's research agenda is concerned with critical and interpretive perspectives on accounting, with a particular focus on the social functioning of accounting. His published work encompasses social accounting and accountability; sustainability and environmental issues in accounting; public administration and accountability; professionalism and the public interest; and various dimensions of accounting education in its sociopolitical context. He serves on several journal Editorial Boards.

**Cindy Davids** is Associate Professor in the School of Law at Deakin University, Melbourne, Australia. Cindy has interdisciplinary research interests and publications across policing, legal regulation, professional and public sector accountability, conflict of interest, corruption and bribery. She has worked collaboratively with a number of police and oversight agencies including Victoria Police, Australian Federal Police, and the Victorian Ombudsman, and has advised various other agencies in Australia and the UK. She has taught across an array of areas in criminology and law and her current teaching is in the area of criminal procedure.

**Courtney Hougham** is Principal Planning Analyst with Hennepin County's Department of Community Corrections and Rehabilitation in Minneapolis, Minnesota. She graduated in 2011 from the City University of New York

Graduate Center with a PhD in Criminal Justice focusing on jury decision-making.

**Trevor Jones** is Professor of Criminology at the School of Social Sciences in Cardiff University. He has researched and published extensively in a range of the fields including policing and crime prevention, private security, comparative criminal justice policymaking, and workplace bullying and harassment. He is author/co-author of six research monographs, co-editor of two major edited collections, and author of large number of journal papers, research reports and book chapters.

**Stuart Lister** is Senior Lecturer in Criminal Justice at the Centre for Criminal Justice Studies in the School of Law, University of Leeds. His research interests come together around exploring the changes and continuities in the arrangement, provision, accountability and effectiveness of contemporary policing and security endeavours. He is co-author of *Bouncers: Violence and Governance in the Night-time economy* (with Hobbs, Hadfield and Winlow, OUP 2003), *Plural Policing: The Mixed Economy of Visible Security Patrols* (with Crawford, Blackburn and Burnett, Policy Press 2005) and *Street Policing of Problem Drug Users* (with Seddon, Wincup, Barrett and Traynor, Joseph Rowntree Foundation 2008).

**Louise Porter** is Lecturer in the School of Criminology and Criminal Justice, Griffith University, Brisbane, Australia. Louise is a British Psychological Society Chartered Psychologist, holding previous appointments at the University of Liverpool, University of Birmingham and, more recently, the ARC Centre of Excellence in Policing and Security at Griffith University. Her research applies social psychology to forensic contexts, including co-offending as well as police corruption and misconduct. Her work on police misconduct has focused on types of misconduct behaviour, its causes and the systems in place to address such behaviour.

**Tim Prenzler** is Chief Investigator in the Australian Research Council Centre of Excellence in Policing and Security (CEPS) and a Professor in the School of Criminology and Criminal Justice, Griffith University, Brisbane, Australia. In CEPS, he manages the Integrity Systems Project and works in the Frontline Policing Project. He teaches courses in situational crime prevention and security management, and criminal justice ethics and corruption prevention. He is the author of *Police Corruption: Preventing Misconduct and Maintaining Integrity* (CRC Press – Taylor & Francis 2009) and co-author, with Adam Graycar, of *Understanding and Preventing Corruption* (Palgrave Macmillan 2013).

**John W. Raine** is Professor of Management in Criminal Justice at the University of Birmingham, UK. His research interests centre on governance structures and processes within criminal justice, and over a 30-year period he has undertaken various projects on local police accountability and systems of governance before developing an interest in the new role of Police and Crime

Commissioners. He has worked in the Institute of Local Government Studies (INLOGOV) at Birmingham since 1979 (including eight years as Director) and his interests in local governance have led him into practice as both a county and district councillor for his home area in Worcestershire. He is also a member of the Criminal Justice Council for England and Wales.

**Robert Reiner** is Emeritus Professor of Criminology in the Law Department, London School of Economics. His books include *Law and Order: An Honest Citizen's Guide to Crime and Control* (Polity Press 2007); *The Politics of the Police* (OUP fourth edition 2010); *Policing, Popular Culture and Political Economy: Towards a Social Democratic Criminology* (Ashgate 2011); *The Oxford Handbook of Criminology* (edited with M. Maguire and R. Morgan; OUP fifth edition 2012).

**Michael Rowe** is Professor of Criminology at Northumbria University. His research and teaching interests focus on policing, race and crime. He has published widely on these and related topics, including *Race and Crime* (Sage 2013), *Introduction to Policing* (Sage 2014), *Race, Racism and Policing* (Willan 2004), and in many journal articles. He founded the Policing Network of the British Society of Criminology, is on the editorial board of *Policing and Society* and was previously Vice President of the Australian and New Zealand Society of Criminology.

**James Sheptycki** is Professor of Criminology at York University, Toronto, Canada. His research interests centre on policing and crime under conditions of transnationalisation. He has written on a variety of substantive criminological topics including domestic violence, serial killers, money laundering, drugs, public order policing, organised crime, police accountability, intelligence-led policing, witness protection, risk and insecurity.

**John Topping** is Lecturer in Criminology at the University of Ulster, specialising in community and public order policing, officer training and security governance. He sits on the board of directors of Community Restorative Justice Ireland (CRJI), as the leading restorative practices organisation across Ireland. John is also an independent member of the Belfast Policing and Community Safety Partnership, with a statutory responsibility to hold the Police Service of Northern Ireland (PSNI) to account and work in conjunction with a range of community and statutory providers in the delivery of community safety. He has also acted in consultancy and advisory roles for the PSNI and Office of the Police Ombudsman for Northern Ireland (OPONI).

**Louise Westmarland** is Senior Lecturer in Criminology at the Open University. Her areas of expertise are policing, police culture and ethics, gender and violence, and homicide investigations. Her research on gender and policing has informed equal opportunities training in the UK police and she has conducted studies in the US which involved interviewing and shadowing homicide detectives on live investigations. As a Home Office Accredited Domestic

Homicide Independent Reviewer, Dr Westmarland has investigated several murder inquiries and her work on police ethics and integrity has been widely cited in policy and academic arenas.

**Adam White** is Lecturer in Public Policy in the Department of Politics, University of York. His research focuses on three interconnected themes: (1) the rise of the private security and private military industries in the post-war era; (2) corresponding issues of governance, regulation and legitimacy in the contemporary security sector; and (3) the changing nature of state–market relations. These interests are multidisciplinary, lying at the intersection of politics, international relations, criminology and socio-legal studies. Recent publications include *The Politics of Private Security* (Palgrave Macmillan 2010) and *The Everyday Life of the State* (University of Washington Press 2013).

**Richard Young** is Professor of Law and Policy at the University of Birmingham. He has conducted empirical studies of neighbourhood mediation, restorative justice, the police complaints system and legal aid decision-making in England, Wales and Northern Ireland. He is co-author of *Criminal Justice*, now in its fourth edition (OUP 2010), and has co-edited four collections of essays, *Access to Criminal Justice* (1996), *New Visions of Crime Victims* (2002), *Regulating Policing* (2008) and *The Futures of Legal Education and the Legal Profession* (Hart 2015).

# Acknowledgements

The idea for this book took shape following a one-day symposium in January 2013, hosted by the School of Law, at the University of Leeds, which explored police accountability in the light of the introduction of Police and Crime Commissioners. The symposium was the inaugural event of the Policing Network of the British Society of Criminology, and was co-organised by the Network and the Centre for Criminal Justice Studies, University of Leeds. We wish to thank all those who participated in and helped to make that event such a success. In particular, we acknowledge the contributions of Megan O'Neill and Matt Jones from the Policing Network, Loraine Gelsthorpe and Charlotte Harris from the British Society of Criminology, Adam Crawford from the University of Leeds, and Fraser Sampson from the Office of the Police and Crime Commissioner for West Yorkshire.

We owe a tremendous debt of gratitude to Heidi Lee, our editorial contact at Routledge, who provided invaluable advice throughout the development of the book. Her tolerance and patience of our editorial and personal shortcomings have been greatly appreciated.

Finally, but probably most importantly, we would like to thank our contributors who responded promptly and diligently to our comments and feedback, and have provided excellent insight into the various topics addressed in the pages that follow.

# 1 Accountability of policing

*Stuart Lister and Michael Rowe*

Accountability, understood as a characteristic of governance, is a central tenet in the study of policing. At root this is because the task of policing is intrinsically political, a normative enterprise concerned with the use of authority to maintain a particular construction of social order. Self-evidently those who wield institutional power ought to be held accountable for how it is exercised. Debates about policing are thus never far removed from debates about accountability. As a concept, however, accountability requires rigorous academic enquiry. At base, it concerns a social relationship in which someone is required to explain or justify their (non)conduct in a forum that may lead to sanction (Bovens 2005). It would be a grand irony should those whose core role entails enforcing rules and bringing others to account for their normative transgressions, be themselves found wanting for accountability (Stenning 1995). Yet accountability is a hugely contested issue. It is, as Bovens (2005) reminds us, a 'hurrah' word, the fundamental purpose of which is difficult to oppose. As a consequence it can be rhetorically invoked to justify all manner of political or ideological reforms. It has also become something of a versatile and expansive concept, which has been pulled in various conceptual directions allowing it to be deployed in support of particular but often fleeting agendas (Mulgan 2000). This mutant characteristic, however, reaffirms the need for academic study. Its deployment raises a series of descriptive questions concerning the selective nature of accountability arrangements: who is accountable, to whom, for what, through what structures, what standards will be applied, and with what effects (Mashaw 2006)? These questions are important as they beget analytical or more sociological questions concerning the broader implications that arise from the pursuit of 'accountability'. Accountability regimes therefore – like policing systems – involve political choices. The power *to oblige* others to account for their actions, decisions and omissions can be understood as a means of control. It is therefore crucial within the study of policing that we understand how accountability regimes function, the changes and continuities apparent within and between them, as well as their causes and effects.

Broadly stated, it is apparent that political, legal, economic and technological developments have served to alter the contexts, methods and processes by which those involved in organised forms of policing are governed and rendered accountable. Principles of accountability rooted in liberal democratic systems of government have been tested by new demands emerging from a fast-changing policing environment, new challenges of crime, security, and shifting patterns of governance in society more broadly. Established mechanisms of accountability (never wholly effective in early periods) have struggled to adapt to these new landscapes. As a result, changes within accountability regimes are apparent across different dimensions of policing, including those 'individuals' and 'institutions' responsible for its delivery, within and between the 'public' and 'private' sectors, and at 'local', 'national' and 'transnational' scales of jurisdiction. The extent and pace of change raises a pressing need for ongoing academic research, analysis and debate.

In the recent period we have seen the burgeoning growth of private sector involvement in policing opening new fields for academic analysis, as well as a barrage of neo-liberal inspired reforms of state-organised policing institutions that demands descriptive and analytical enquiry. Such developments are at times a cause, at other times an effect of accountability challenges. Indeed, we never seem far from the latest scandal or crisis to hit policing, the political and media fallout from which almost invariably leads to concerns about perceived failures of accountability. This is no coincidence. It is well-documented in the political science literature how 'accountability' has become a container concept for public anxieties about all multitudes of sins (Mashaw 2006). Poor behaviour, wrong policy choices, ineffective performance, inefficient use of resources are commonly reduced to a lack of accountability. The risk is that reforms set in train may not only primarily serve a political function, but may also pull policing institutions in different, potentially competing directions. For instance, policing has been a key public policy arena in which the tensions of 'localism' and 'centralism' have been played out. In England and Wales, as in other Western countries, we have seen principles of 'community policing' advanced to enhance police 'responsiveness' to local publics, simultaneous to the institutionalisation of centrally determined performance targets intended to drive greater organisational efficiency and effectiveness. Contemporary policing institutions are subject to diverse and multifaceted accountability techniques, generating empirical, conceptual and normative questions concerning the nature, effect and implications of the accountability relationships to which they give rise.

This book contributes to scholarly debates by analysing emergent and existent accountability regimes of 'police' and 'policing'. It explores the key concepts of 'policing' and 'accountability' in broad terms. Hence, for example, its analytical gaze stretches beyond state-funded policing institutions, to include private providers of policing and plural policing networks. Emerging forms of constitutional and legal governance of 'high' policing are considered alongside internal and external procedures designed to regulate the activities of policing actors, such as public complaints systems, occupational licensing regimes and ethical codes and protocols. Equally, it engages with the concept of 'accountability' in a broad sense, bringing to the surface the various meanings that have become associated with it and demonstrating how it is invoked and interpreted in different contexts. Whilst the core focus of the book concerns developments in England and Wales, it includes original perspectives on developments in Europe, North America and Australasia. Emerging from the contributions it is clear that changes in the organisation of the social, economic, and political worlds have given rise to new approaches to rendering policing accountable. At the core of this collection of essays, then, is a related series of emerging concerns which explore how the focus, mechanisms and challenges of policing accountability have been rapidly transformed. Against this background, this collection of essays aims to undertake some of the necessary theoretical and empirical work to enhance the prospect of the effective accountability of policing. Before providing a summary of each of the contributions we contextualise some of the book's key themes. By definition many of these themes are not new in conceptual terms. While revisiting them, however, we seek to identify how certain features of policing in the twenty-first century pose new challenges that require innovative responses.

## Guarding the guards: why does accountability matter to policing?

Police officers have a paradoxical relationship with their fellow citizens. On the one hand, in common law liberal democratic societies, police have tended to be rhetorically regarded as 'citizens in uniform'. Describing the British model, Robillard and McEwan (1986: 2) summarised this conceptualisation in the following terms:

> The police of this country have never been recognized, either by the law or by tradition, as a force distinct from the general body of citizens. Despite the imposition of many extraneous duties on the police by legislation or administrative action, the principle remains that the policeman, in the view of the common law, is only a person paid to perform, as a matter of duty, acts which if he were so minded he might have done voluntarily.... Indeed a policeman possesses few powers not enjoyed by the ordinary citizen, and public opinion, expressed in Parliament and elsewhere, has shown great jealousy of any attempts to give increased authority to the police.

In the three decades since this account was written police powers and responsibilities – the 'extraneous duties' mentioned by Robillard and McEwan – have changed, but the underlying principle remains: in *de jure* terms, the police continue to have few legal powers unavailable to citizens and continue to be personally accountable for their actions. The paradox is, of course, that in de facto terms, the police do have considerable powers that are unavailable to civilians. Police officers have far-reaching powers to stop, detain and question citizens, famously characterised by former Metropolitan Police Commissioner Sir Robert Mark as the 'power to inconvenience' (Judge 1986: 175). Policing actors per se also have considerable tacit and symbolic power that frequently ensures citizens comply with requests and directives, either through recognition that negative consequences might otherwise ensue or, more positively, because of respect for authority figures. For public police officers this symbolic authority extends from the frontline officer on the street to more senior leaders who collectively and individually have considerable power to identify, articulate and define social problems. Loader and Mulcahy (2001a and 2001b) have described this as the 'power of legitimate naming' whereby elite police voices shape and define political and social agendas. The power of the police (and other elites) to act as 'primary definers' of deviance, and social problems more broadly, has been noted across a range of policy domains, including juvenile delinquency, urban unrest, drug use and prostitution, and is a capacity not readily available to private citizens (Hall *et al.* 1978).

Equally, the institutional power and resources of the police also constitute forms of power unavailable to the general public. While any member of the public might have the legal power to carry out a citizen's arrest, the police are one of the few institutions that have the resources and capacity to make this proposition viable. That capacity is contained and regulated through internal police management and oversight as well as external, more public-facing mechanisms. While most of the contributions in this collection are focused on political and regulatory practices it must be noted that the legal system also provides a forum for scrutinising policing activity and an avenue of redress. As Prenzler (2009) has noted, a fundamental cornerstone of democratic accountability is that police are subject to the rule of law such that operational decisions can be tested in court. Hence individuals can seek judicial review of discretionary police policy decisions and practice can be amended as a result of legal judgement. Moreover, citizens are able to bring civil law claims against police in circumstances where negligence or malpractice is alleged. Whether private law remedy actually serves as a mechanism of accountability is debateable as Chief Constables hold vicarious liability for the (non)actions of their officers when on duty (Smith 2003). Individual officers can though be subject to criminal prosecution, albeit they are not subject to the same criminal process as citizens (Smith 2001). In practice, however, the ability of private citizens to bring legal action against the police might be curtailed. The resources, and cultural and social capital, required are not equally available to all and many of those who might be most gravely exposed to police malfeasance might be among those sections of the public least able to access justice (Smith 2003). Prenzler (2009) also reminds us that citizens must have access to information if they are to be able to scrutinise effectively policing institutions: reliable information, transparent decision-making and access to senior managers and policymakers are some of the necessary precursors of democratic oversight.

The complex and institutionally embedded nature of police power means that external accountability mechanisms that extend beyond legal regulations are required for effective oversight consistent with broader principles of liberal democracy. Public accountability structures, widely seen as a hallmark of 'good governance', ensure the governance of public policing institutions is linked through a series of principal-agent relationships to political forums within the democratic polity (Bovens 2005). This transfer of citizen sovereignty to political representatives tasked with holding state-funded policing bodies to account signifies democratic control, a core function of public accountability. Yet as Reiner argues in his contribution to this volume, for policing to be considered 'democratic' it requires more than simply ensuring those who hold police to account have an electoral mandate. Whilst descriptively such a model might entail a legal framework, a democratic governance structure, systems to investigate complaints, codes of conduct to promote professional integrity, more broadly it also requires a normative commitment to advance human rights, civil liberties and notions of social justice. As Lister and Jones argue in their contribution, the concept of 'democracy' may imply certain structures and processes but ultimately these are underpinned by a range of democratic values that instil a normative foundation for critical assessment (see also Jones *et al.* 1996).

Robust accountability also functions to improve performance (Bovens 2005). In order to be effective in combatting crime and disorder organised modes of policing require public assistance and cooperation in a host of ways. Research evidence confirms the public police enjoy greater levels of public trust and confidence in circumstances where they are perceived to act on the basis of procedural justice (Hough *et al.* 2010). In this context, procedural justice needs to be done, and to be seen to be done, in order to deliver core aspects of the police mandate. Public reassurance and community safety depend in part on the 'communicative action' of policing, in which audiences interpret actions in various ways (e.g. as 'legitimate' or 'illegitimate'). That policing institutions are charged with delivering security and reassurance to citizens requires engagement with subjective perceptions of well-being and safety, and so accountability to the public needs to be demonstrated. In this way, accountability mechanisms that promote transparency and compliance with norms of democratic governance can serve to enhance public confidence in policing institutions.

As citizens are more likely to cooperate with requests for information and assistance if they perceive those delivering policing to have integrity and legitimacy, then accountability has an important role in delivering core policing functions of law enforcement, security and order maintenance. As Jones (2008) suggests, 'accountable' policing is not just morally and ethically desirable, but instrumentally superior to 'unaccountable policing'.

A key element of promoting effective policing in diverse communities has been to ensure meaningful 'community engagement' with groups that often might have had relations of tension and conflict with police. Although community engagement is often considered to be a direct form of public accountability, it is perhaps better considered as a form of 'answerability', particularly as there is no direct sanction for perceived failings. Further, it is often imperfectly conducted on terms established by the police rather than the community, following an established police agenda, and might not easily engage with 'difficult to hear' communities (Jones and Newburn 2001). When done effectively, though, police engagement with local communities can enable consultation and demonstrate transparency that encourages the public to report crimes and work to co-produce solutions to community problems. As Keith (1993) noted of police and public consultation committees set up in local areas within the Metropolitan Police in the 1980s, liaison of this kind can provide a useful conduit to promote communication and dialogue that can diffuse tensions and enhance relations with the public. Nonetheless, as we suggest conceptually, consultation is distinct from accountability, not least because the former does not disturb established power relations (Keith 1993).

Other more administrative forms of accountability offer the potential to improve performance through target setting, monitoring and evaluation. Moves to promote evidence-based policing seek to apply scientific methods to identify outcomes and the inputs and mechanisms that characterise effective interventions. Communication and dissemination, through, for example, in the UK, Her Majesty's Inspectorate of Constabulary or the College of Policing, seek to embed good practice throughout the public police. Scientific policing, however, remains contested terrain in terms of the blend of methodologies that can provide reliable data, the extent to which practice can be transplanted from one context to another, and the degree to which 'outcomes' can be appropriately identified and measured. While often not expressed in terms of governance and oversight these practices nonetheless feed into accountability regimes. Since the development of New Public Management and its extension into state-funded policing and criminal justice institutions much criticism has been made of the distorting impacts that can arise from managers chasing arbitrary targets rather than achieving more appropriate outcomes (McLaughlin 2007). Clearly there have been many examples of policing practice being skewed by a 'target management' culture. The core problem, however, has stemmed from the politicisation of policing rather than the fundamental analysis of effective performance on the basis of professional and scientific judgements (Hope 2009; Tilley 2009). Peer review, professional practice and scientific evaluation offer the possibility of developing greater efficiency and effectiveness in the delivery of policing. But the challenge of ensuring that this is done in an independent and objective manner is a real one.

The effectiveness of much policing practice has remained unquestioned and unexamined, with little having been subject to rigorous scientific analysis. Partly this may be due to the lack of expenditure on research. Weisburd and Neyroud (2011) noted that law enforcement contrasts very poorly with other public policy sectors such as agriculture and medicine when it comes to investment in technological innovation and evaluation. In the UK, they argued, government investment in medical research amounts to £600 million per year, whereas the annual Home Office budget for crime research amounted to just £2 million. Further, these authors argued that it is the political, institutional and cultural contexts of policing that make the development of a new paradigm of 'police science' challenging. It might also be that the contested and ambivalent mandate of policing makes a scientific evidence-based model difficult. If the role and function of the police, for instance, cannot easily be identified then it is difficult to imagine how it can be scientifically evaluated in overall terms. Clearly scientific innovations can contribute to the investigation of crime, enhance communications and provide for better health and safety of officers, but not all aspects of policing can easily be subjected to scientific evaluation or the rigours of the randomised control trial. Not only are there significant methodological challenges to be overcome in the development of scientific evaluation of policing interventions (Hope 2009) but many key functions of policing are inherently subjective, open to interpretation and fundamentally contested. This illustrates that an overarching challenge for accountability of policing concerns the mechanisms by which it is delivered and the standards against which it is judged. Alongside these very broad questions – that are reviewed through the chapters that follow – are some more specific challenges, and it is to those that the chapter now turns.

## The challenges for accountability

Inevitably, securing effective accountability within policing institutions presents enduring and complex governance challenges. The chapters in this collection explore overlapping dimensions of the challenges faced. These are considered in terms of trying to deal effectively with public complaints (see chapter by Prenzler and Porter), ensuring that policing which exists beyond the nation state, whether transnationally (see chapter by Bowling and Sheptycki) or in the private sector (see White's chapter), or the broader question of ensuring effective governance (see Reiner's chapter, and Lister and Jones's chapter). This broad catalogue of challenges – and this book does not claim to examine all possibilities – can be considered in terms of those intrinsic to policing functions and those that are external and relate instead to the broader operational environment. In the former category the paragraphs below consider challenges to accountability that relate to police operational independence (see Raine's chapter), the inevitability of police discretion and police operational subculture (Young's chapter), and exposure to 'invitational' opportunities for corruption or malpractice (see Rowe *et al.*'s chapter). External challenges relate to debates about the declining capacity of the state to provide for regulation in the light of market provisions of policing services, the political context of policing and public services, and advances in communication technology (see the chapter by Davids and Boyce) that transform the collection, transmission and analysis of data both by policing agencies, actors and citizens.

### *Operational independence*

The powers of the police are complex and extend beyond the 'black letter' of the law. To be effective, mechanisms of accountability need to be sufficiently robust to respond to the multifaceted exercise of police power in various forms and at various organisational levels. Several contributions to this collection reflect on problems of avoiding organisational capture such that those tasked with critical oversight become overly dependent on the police and therefore unable to exercise independent scrutiny. Another concern is that the long-established principle that police have 'operational independence' in discharging their duties and enforcing the law becomes very difficult to apply in practice. The boundary between appropriate oversight and inappropriate interference in operational policing tends to be very blurred (Lustgarten 1986). Well-rehearsed debates about the provision of equipment such as rubber bullets and water cannons illustrate these tensions. For some the debate is an operational one and so the decision ought to be made on the basis of the efficacy of these provisions for containing disorder. Others focus on the ethical and political questions of the right of the state to use 'less-than-lethal' weapons against the public and the balance between protecting the right to life, free assembly and the right to private property. Such debates raise questions of where responsibility ought to rest for deciding whether to deploy. If the argument is primarily about tactics and efficacy then this might be an operational matter for senior officers; if it is primarily a political or ethical one then it is more likely to be a matter of governance to be decided by political leaders or the courts. As several authors note in the chapters that follow, the principle of operational independence has been tested in the recent British context since the creation of Police and Crime Commissioners, but these are recent manifestations of an inherent challenge for police accountability.

### The peculiar nature of police discretion

A fundamental cornerstone of five decades of police research is that officers operate with considerable autonomy and discretion. Early studies of the police demonstrated that the law provided only a limited guide for how officers approached enforcement and that a host of cultural, political and sociological factors shaped the operational discharge of their duties (Banton 1964; Skolnick 1966; Wilson 1968). Among the many implications of the 'discovery' of police discretion is that officers might overturn or misapply laws that are authored through constitutional democratic means. The discretion available to officers risks the possibility that they effectively create law on their own terms as they attend to their routine operational duties (Neyroud and Beckley 2001). The challenges that discretion poses for accountability are exacerbated because it is a particular feature of the operational activity of the lower ranks, who tend to operate in conditions of relative invisibility. James Wilson's (1968: 7) famous observation that police 'discretion increases as one moves down the hierarchy' has clear implications for the capacity to monitor, control and hold officers to account for their (non)conduct. New technologies can help to make discretionary decisions more visible – officers' actions can be captured on 'head cam' technology or 'Body-Worn Video' devices, for example – but there has been little research or debate on the effects of such developments. Administrative procedures requiring officers to complete forms to record details and circumstances in which powers are exercised is another bureaucratic attempt to monitor how officers discharge their duties, albeit research findings have recurrently queried the efficacy of such regulatory endeavours (see Young, this collection). Even if such managerial techniques of internal accountability were highly effective, however, the nature of police discretion is routinely about officers deciding not to intervene. Monitoring these 'non-reviewable decisions' presents substantial challenges for designing effective accountability arrangements.

### Opportunities for unethical behaviour and cultural challenges

Not only do police officers often exercise considerable discretion in circumstances of low visibility, they often do so when interacting with 'service users' who are engaged in criminal activity – and who might wish to influence that discretion in corrupt ways. Although effective police governance is about much more than preventing corruption and promoting integrity, there are recurring problems of malfeasance and misconduct that arise from officers' exposure to crime and wrongdoing (Punch 2003). Many historical cases of corruption have arisen when officers have had close, long-term relations with 'professional criminals'. Moreover the exposure to such circumstances also shores up the internal solidarity, loyalty and sense of mission that are integral to police occupational culture (Reiner 1978). It is those experiences that define officers' sense that they are the 'thin blue line' protecting society from lawlessness. In part, these features of police subculture are derived from institutional and functional activities. In some ways they are desirable elements and in many respects they seem inevitable responses to the routine experiences that officers face (Chan 1997). Nonetheless, they have the potential to pose problems for governance and accountability in a number of ways. Not only can they foster circumstances in which officer misconduct can develop unchecked in an insular occupational subculture, they also pose challenges to efforts to investigate allegations of misconduct and hold officers to account through complaint processes. As a number of contributions to this collection consider, the challenge of developing effective mechanisms to respond to complaints about misconduct often relates to the difficulty of getting behind the 'blue curtain of silence': the strong cultural norm for officers not to report concerns about the problematic behaviour of their colleagues and not to cooperate with internal or external related enquiries (see Rowe *et al.*'s contribution).

The above discussion has explored three related sets of challenges to police accountability, each of which is presented as an internal feature of the policing role and environment. The following sections discuss a number of challenges that are related instead to the external social, economic and political context in which policing is delivered.

### The decreasing capacity of the regulatory state

Analysis of police governance and accountability tends to begin (and usually to end) with those mechanisms and regulations authored and delivered by the nation state. An important emphasis in this collection concerns 'policing beyond the state' and how this might be more effectively governed and brought into a framework of democratic accountability. Just as modern policing expanded as the nation state itself developed in a form that we still recognise, in the British context at least, so too the need to regulate and govern policing has largely been focused on the activities of the state. Offices, laws, regulations, inspectors, complaint investigations, codes of practice, targets, audits and a host of other techniques have been introduced either directly by the state, or have been delivered by agencies closely under its auspices. The capacity of the nation state to continue to deliver these functions has been subject to considerable scrutiny and swathes of public administration literature have reviewed the extent to which liberal democratic states have developed a role of 'steering' rather than 'rowing' in the delivery of public services (Osborne and Gaebler 1992; Milward and Provan 2000).

The growth of a state that focused on regulation of public services rather than direct delivery has been discussed in the context of the pluralisation of policing (Loader 2000; Wood and Shearing 2007; Crawford 2008). Collectively, the chapters contained here suggest that there are also significant challenges in terms of state systems for regulation. If the state is 'hollowed out' then the extent to which it is able to provide effective governance might be seriously reduced (Milward and Provan 2000). Although research has suggested that the extent to which the state has lost capacity might have been overemphasised (Pollitt and Bouckaert 2011; Ongaro 2009), the chapters below often suggest that regulatory capacity has been redistributed within state systems rather than abrogated. Nonetheless there are important concerns that a period in which policing has become pluralised and privatised (see White's chapter, and Lister and Jones's chapter) and increasingly occurs within transnational networks (see Bowling and Sheptycki's contribution) has made the need for effective accountability ever more pressing. At the same time, the very factors that have driven the reorganisation of policing threaten to render the democratic state less able, and perhaps less willing, to deliver that accountability.

### 'Anti-politics' and the police 'fall from grace'

Recent concern about unethical and corrupt behaviour within British policing has occurred against a background of scandal and controversy in respect of a number of other public agencies. Although the post-2010 Coalition Government couched its policies in terms of transforming a police service that was the 'last unreformed public-sector agency' it has been clear for several decades that the exalted political position that the police previously enjoyed has slipped away (Reiner 2010; Loader and Mulcahy 2003). Indeed, it is more than two decades since Waddington (1993) noted that the police service had 'fallen from grace' among political elites. The development of concern about the efficacy of accountability cannot be understood solely as a mechanistic response to identified problems. As such, the particular debates analysed in this book cannot be understood in isolation from broader critiques of police community relations, the quality of leadership, effectiveness in law enforcement, trends in crime and antisocial behaviour, and expenditure.

Against a context of neo-liberal ideological suspicion of public sector provision, institutions of civic society have been encouraged to take responsibility for their own welfare and well-being, an outcome of which has been a decline in the status of public provisions. In a society characterised by 'hyper-individualism' and self-reliance established relationships of collective provision, deference and trust are eroded in ways that affect a broad range of institutions, including but not limited to the police. Young (2011) argues that a growth in public demand for scrutiny of agencies represents a triumph for advocates of equality and social justice and as such is to be welcomed. What remains a challenge is to ensure that the capacity for citizens to exercise demands effectively is not limited only to those with the financial, social or political capital to articulate and press their case.

### Social media, direct democracy and policing

The death of Ian Tomlinson during a protest at the London G20 summit in 2009 has been a significant case in recent controversies about policing and its accountability. Following Tomlinson's death, a cell-phone video recording showed an officer pushing Tomlinson to the ground in the moments prior to his death. The officer concerned was subsequently charged and acquitted of criminal offences arising from Tomlinson's death, but was subsequently sacked by the Metropolitan Police for gross misconduct. In many respects this tragic incident was similar to others that have occurred periodically for many decades. The Tomlinson case, however, was distinct from earlier incidents owing to the role of social media and the growth of low-level forms of citizen-surveillance enabled by new technologies. During the long-running fallout from the case, the Metropolitan Police admitted that one of its officers had 'probably' been responsible for striking (and killing) Blair Peach during a public demonstration against fascism in 1979. Yet whereas it took nearly four decades for the police to acknowledge a degree of culpability in the death of Blair Peach, the video showing police use of force against Ian Tomlinson was disseminated widely within hours of his death (see Greer and McLaughlin 2012).

It would though be simplistic to suggest that the only difference between the death of Ian Tomlinson and that of Blair Peach was that the former was filmed and disseminated on the World Wide Web in a very short time frame. But the two cases illustrate yet another consequence of technological change in contemporary society. The criminogenic potential of social media and cyberspace are much debated, but what is less widely noted is the capacity for 'citizen journalists', campaigners and ordinary members of the public to record policing activity in authoritative ways that have strong evidential value. Mobile apps are available that enable information to be recorded about encounters with those delivering policing, including details of the type of evidence to record and advice on how incidents can be reported. The potential for information and communication technology to develop the 'technologically enabled officer', equipped with data, maps and other resources to respond more effectively to crime and public demands, is set to increase in future years (Innes 2013). Such technology will also bring to bear new challenges of governance and accountability, to ensure inter alia that it is employed in ways that serve not only the interests of those delivering, but also those receiving, policing.

The discussion above has identified a series of challenges for the governance and accountability of policing. The challenges faced were reviewed in terms of emerging internal changes within policing: these included operational independence, the significance of officer discretion, exposure to opportunities for officers to behave corruptly or unethically, and subcultures within policing that can encourage misconduct and inhibit internal and external procedures of oversight and investigation. These challenges develop in a wider context of concern about the capacity of the state to govern policing and other services, the broader politics of policing and criminal justice, and the transformations wrought more widely by communication technology and social media.

## Overview of chapters

The debates identified above, alongside others, are addressed through the contributions contained in this collection. Offered below is a brief résumé of each.

Young explores the use of police powers to 'stop and account' citizens as a means for considering broader debates about the nature of accountability. The experience of efforts to scrutinise police use of stop and account powers in the aftermath of the Macpherson Inquiry is reviewed by Young. The potential to enhance accountability by requiring officers to record details of stops with the public was significantly undermined by poor record-keeping and a failure to extend the recording requirement to all public encounters. Problematically, the confused rationale for the operational practice of 'stop and account' undermined efforts to gather information that might enhance accountability. In some cases the public were unwilling to provide information necessary for effective scrutiny because they had assumed it was being used for purposes of intelligence-gathering and crime control. For such reasons, Young argues, it is ineffective to require police officers to gather the information required to hold their own behaviour to account. A radical approach is proposed using citizen-recordings as part of a pluralistic regulatory strategy for stop and account. While this strategy will be challenging and requires resources and a robust system to oversee the investigation of material gathered by citizens, Young argues that it provides a creative basis for more effective democratic oversight of police work.

Similarly innovative responses are developed in Prenzler and Porter's analysis of systems to deal with complaints against police. Their chapter explores ways of addressing police behavioural issues through enhanced management of complaints and disciplinary systems. Complaints can be used as a key learning tool to inform improved policing practices by modifying training and managerial procedures in response to patterns of allegations in the context of a problem-solving and complaints reduction programme. Prenzler and Porter argue that accountability and fairness can also be improved by supplementing simple investigative and disciplinary approaches to complaints with more restorative responses, including informal resolution and mediation. The chapter includes consideration and analysis of a number of successful cases studies from a range of jurisdictions.

Rowe *et al.* explore emerging strategies designed to reduce police officer corruption and malfeasance. Codes of ethical conduct, disciplinary measures, cultural programmes, training, and professionalisation of policing have developed in response to various challenges to police integrity. Their chapter explores each of these – drawing on international examples – and considers how an array of initiatives operates in relation to dominant police subcultural values of loyalty and camaraderie. In so doing, they consider how policing institutions might seek to overcome the 'blue wall of silence' that is said to prevent officers reporting concerns about misconduct among their colleagues. The authors argue that responses to misconduct by police have been improved by recent developments but that significant problems still need to be addressed, particularly in a pluralised policing environment. Moreover, they argue the diverse cultural and institutional settings in which challenges to integrity emerge continue to be overlooked by analyses that continue to focus primarily on malfeasance in individualistic terms.

Davids and Boyce begin their analysis of police misuse of confidential information with a discussion of the UK's Leveson Inquiry, which highlighted significant ethical concerns over police and media relations. The Inquiry revealed that unauthorised use of confidential police files included, for instance, information passed to journalists about alleged criminal activity and members of the public (suspects, victims and others). In the ordinary course of their police duties, officers invariably receive or have access to a wide variety of such information, both from official police databases and other sources. Police officers may also use their position to solicit information (unrelated to official duties) in which they have a private interest. Davids and Boyce identify and analyse the problem of unauthorised access and disclosure of confidential information by police. They consider several forms of domestic or private/personal use of information by police officers or their associates. Problems associated with the disclosure of information to outside parties are also analysed (including situations where payment may be involved). In considering the types, sources and uses of information, Davids and Boyce examine the harms that can arise for individual officers, the community and the legal system itself. A range of materials are drawn upon to inform the analysis, including both academic and empirical data sources that evidence the nature and extent of the problem. The private disclosure of confidential information strikes at the heart of public confidence in, and the integrity of, the police. Their chapter explores these issues in the context of police accountability and its relationship with integrity and public trust in policing.

Raine considers the implications of the introduction in 2012 of Police and Crime Commissioners (PCCs). It is widely accepted that PCCs – one for each police area of England and Wales outside London – embody the most significant reform of police governance for at least a generation. The new arrangements were highly contested in Parliament during the legislative process and had an inauspicious start with disastrously low electoral turnout at the polls. Several chief constables left their posts prematurely in response to the reform and allegations of 'cronyism' were rife over the appointment of deputies. Raine examines the early impact of, and prospects for, the new police governance structure. He focuses on the nature of relationships within the new governance framework, between PCCs, chief constables, Police and Crime Panels, local communities, the Home Office and other crime-related agencies. Underlying Raine's analysis is the key question of whether in practice the introduction of PCCs has enhanced accountability of policing, as proponents of the reform intended, or created the conditions for more autocracy in police governance through concentrating too much power and responsibility in a single pair of hands.

The recent restructuring of police governance in England and Wales is further analysed in Reiner's chapter. He begins by noting that, unusually, a government's claim of significant reform of policing is not exaggerated. The Coalition's reforms of police governance are arguably the most radical since the development of the modern British police in the early nineteenth century. Reiner notes that although democratic policing has become a mantra to which lip service is paid around the world, the notion is seldom analysed. His chapter seeks to help rectify this lacuna through the application of T.H. Marshall's seminal analysis of citizenship. On this basis he suggests that democracy in general, and democratic policing in particular, has not one dimension (elections), but three: civil, political and socio-economic. The Coalition's reforms involve only one of these dimensions, the political, and in the narrowest sense. In the absence of strong civil and socio-economic rights, Reiner argues critically, voting alone does not achieve democracy in any meaningful interpretation.

Topping analyses how approaches to police accountability in Northern Ireland have played a central role in the broader development of the state in the post-conflict period. The Police Service of Northern Ireland (PSNI) has become governed by a host of statutory, governmental and other bodies, to the extent that it is widely conceived as the global 'gold standard' of police oversight. However, Topping identifies a number of 'mediating realities' that serve to undermine the mechanisms of police accountability. Centrally, Topping's argument is that accountability for both institutional and operational 'police action' in Northern Ireland is itself a 'site' of contest and that official 'accounts' of policing are but one version of reality. He further argues that the continuing need for robust anti-terrorism policing sits uncomfortably with the 'post-conflict' reimagining of the PSNI as a community neighbourhood police service. He suggests the promotion of police accountability, as part of the country's transition, has been used in partisan ways and weighted toward capturing the 'positive' realities of police activity. Problematically, he argues, this means that the harsh realities of the country as a post-conflict society have been conveniently 'ushered' to the side.

White examines debates about policing and accountability as they apply in the context of the sizeable growth of the private security industry during the last few decades. Accompanying this growth, both domestically and globally, has been an increasingly prominent debate about the nature of the accountability mechanisms to which they are subject, how these are implemented and to what effect. White examines four ways in which private security (actors and institutions) may be held to account: generic legal measures; specific legal measures applied directly to private security, through contract compliance; and via 'public ritual'. White argues that private security actors and institutions are not the passive subjects of accountability measures. Rather these four dimensions are spaces in which accountability is negotiated. This is an important point because it implies that these measures should not be regarded as the 'solution' to the pathologies of private security provision. Instead, White argues, they represent institutional structures through which public/private boundaries are made, unmade and remade.

Lister and Jones focus on the accountability of the mixed economy of public and private policing in England and Wales. Their starting point is the recognition that a variety of public, private and hybrid actors are engaged in the authorisation and provision of policing. As a consequence, they do not restrict their analytical gaze to how state power, as deployed by police forces, is made accountable. Rather, they consider how, under market conditions, networks of plural policing can be governed according to, and accommodated within, a set of democratic principles. In so doing, they argue that 'local security networks' comprising state, civil society and market actors, and whose governance and accountability mechanisms frequently stand outside of extant political structures, raise specific challenges if they are to be governed not only effectively but also democratically. They proceed to consider options for bringing democratically accountable governance to plural policing networks.

Bowling and Sheptycki scrutinise the diffuse phenomenon of global policing. This chapter explores the architecture of global policing and provides a sense of the occupational subculture which has built it up around it. The chapter shows how representations of global crime and disorder problems have been used to justify global policing in political, legal and social terms. The credibility of this account is sustained by the pervasiveness of certain cultural tropes that have their origins in the transnational subculture of policing, which are given a global reach through the subculture of transnational policing. Bowling and Sheptycki proceed to reflect upon how global policing is politically and legally accountable, and try to advance thinking by considering how it ought to be. The task is difficult, they argue, because our models for structuring police accountability are ill-fitting in the global context. Policing, in the broad sense of regulation, is an inherent feature of any community, Bowling and Sheptycki argue, and is an inevitable feature of transnational global society. Ensuring that it is made accountable is a necessity if global policing is to promote economic activity and respect cultural traditions and safeguard the environment.

## References

Banton, M. (1964) *The Policeman in the Community*, London: Tavistock Publications.

Bovens, M. (2005) 'Public Accountability', in E. Ferlie, L.E. Lynn and C. Pollitt (eds)

*The Oxford Handbook of Public Management*, Oxford: Oxford University Press, 182–208.

Chan, J. (1997) *Changing Police Culture: Policing in a Multicultural Society*, Melbourne: Cambridge University Press.

Crawford, A. (2008) 'The Pattern of Policing in the UK: Policing beyond the Police', in T. Newburn (ed.) *The Handbook of Policing* (2nd edn), Cullompton, Devon: Willan, 136–68.

Greer, C. and McLaughlin, E. (2012) '"This is not Justice" Ian Tomlinson, Institutional Failure and the Press Politics of Outrage', *British Journal of Criminology*, 52: 274–93.

Hall, S., Critcher, C., Jefferson, T., Clarke, J. and Roberts, B. (1978) *Policing the Crisis: Mugging, the State, and Law and Order*, London: Macmillan.

Hope, T. (2009) 'The Illusion of Control: A Response to Professor Sherman', *Criminology and Criminal Justice*, 9: 125–34.

Hough, M., Jackson, J., Bradford, B., Myhill, A. and Quinton, P. (2010) 'Procedural Justice, Trust, and Institutional Legitimacy', *Policing*, 4: 203–10.

Innes, M. (2013) 'Reinventing the Office of Constable: Progressive Policing in an Age of Austerity', in J. Brown (ed.) *Policing Futures*, London: Routledge.

Jones, T. (2008) 'The Accountability of Policing', in T. Newburn (ed.) *The Handbook of Policing* (2nd edn), Cullompton, Devon: Willan, 603–27.

Jones, T. and Newburn, T. (2001) *Widening Access: Improving Police Relations with Hard to Reach Groups*, Police Research Series Paper 138, London: Home Office.

Jones, T., Newburn, T. and Smith, D.J. (1996) 'Policing and the Idea of Democracy', *British Journal of Criminology*, 36(2): 182–98.

Judge, A. (1986) 'The Provisions in Practice', in J. Benyon and C. Bourn (eds) *Police: Powers, Proprieties and Procedures*, Oxford: Pergamon Press, 175–82.

Keith, M. (1993) *Race, Riots, and Policing: Lore and Disorder in a Multiracial Society*, London: Macmillan.

Loader, I. (2000) 'Plural Policing and Democratic Governance', *Social and Legal Studies*, 9: 323–45.

Loader, I. and Mulcahy, A. (2001a) 'The Power of Legitimate Naming: Part I – Chief Constables as Social Commentators in Post-War England', *British Journal of Criminology*, 41: 41–55.

Loader, I. and Mulcahy, A. (2001b) 'The Power of Legitimate Naming: Part II – Making Sense of the Elite Police Voice', *British Journal of Criminology*, 41: 22–65.

Loader, I. and Mulcahy, A. (2003) *Policing and the Condition of England: Memory, Politics and Culture*, Oxford: Oxford University Press.

Lustgarten, L. (1986) *The Governance of the Police*, London: Sweet & Maxwell.

McLaughlin, E. (2007) *The New Policing*, London: Sage.

Mashaw, J.L. (2006) 'Accountability and Institutional Design: Some Thoughts on the Grammar of Governance', in M.W. Dowdle (ed.) *Public Accountability: Designs, Dilemmas and Experiences*, Cambridge: Cambridge University Press, 115–57.

Milward, H.B. and Provan, K.G. (2000) 'Governing the Hollow State', *Journal of Public Administration Research and Theory*, 10: 359–79.

Mulgan, R. (2000) 'Accountability: An Ever-Expanding Concept?, *Public Administration*, 78(3): 555–73.

Neyroud, P. and Beckley, A. (2001) *Policing Ethics and Human Rights*, Cullompton, Devon: Willan.

Ongaro, E. (2009) *Public Management Reform and Modernization*, Cheltenham: Edward Elgar Publishing.

Osborne, D. and Gaebler, T. (1992) *Reinventing Government: How the Entrepreneurial Spirit is Transforming the Public Sector*, New York: Plume.

Pollitt, C. and Bouckaert, G. (2011) *Public Management Reform: A Comparative Analysis: New Public Management, Governance, and the Neo-Weberian State*, Oxford: Oxford University Press.

Prenzler, T. (2009) *Police Corruption: Preventing Misconduct and Maintaining Integrity*, Boca Raton, FL: CRC Press – Taylor & Francis.

Punch, M. (2003) 'Rotten Orchards: "Pestilence", Police Misconduct and System Failure', *Policing and Society*, 13(2): 171–96.

Reiner, R. (1978) *The Blue-Coated Worker*, Cambridge: Cambridge University Press.

Reiner, R. (2010) *The Politics of the Police* (4th edn), Oxford: Oxford University Press.

Robilliard, St. J. and McEwan, J. (1986) *Police Powers and the Individual*, Oxford: Basil Blackwell.

Skolnick, J. (1966) *Justice without Trial: Law Enforcement in Democratic Society*, London: Macmillan.

Smith, G. (2001), 'Police Complaints and Criminal Prosecutions', *Modern Law Review*, 64(3): 372–92.

Smith, G. (2003) 'Actions for Damages Against the Police and the Attitudes of Claimants', *Policing and Society*, 13(4): 413–22.

Stenning, P. (1995) 'Introduction', in P. Stenning (ed.) *Accountability for Criminal Justice*, Toronto: University of Toronto Press.

Tilley, N. (2009) 'Sherman vs Sherman: Realism vs Rhetoric', *Criminology and Criminal Justice*, 9: 135–44.

Waddington, P.A.J. (1993) 'The Case of the Hidden Agenda: The Latest Plans for Police Reform are Part of a Historical Process of Centralisation', *The Independent*, 31 July.

Weisburd, D. and Neyroud, P. (2011) 'Police Science: Toward a New Paradigm', *New Perspectives in Policing*, Washington, DC: National Institute of Justice/Harvard Kennedy School.

Wilson, J.Q. (1968) *Varieties of Police Behaviour*, Cambridge, MA: Harvard University Press.

Wood, J. and Shearing, C. (2007) *Imagining Security*, Cullompton, Devon: Willan.

Young, J. (2011) *The Criminological Imagination*, Cambridge: Polity Press.

# 2 The rise and fall of 'stop and account'

## Lessons for police accountability

*Richard Young*

The police in England and Wales have for many centuries engaged in the practice of stopping people in public spaces to ask such questions as 'What is your name?', 'What are you doing here?' and 'Where are you going?'. In most such situations the police lack a formal power to require people to answer and no formal safeguards or specific accountability measures apply. This situation changed as a result of the report by Macpherson (1999) which recommended that all stops should be recorded, including 'voluntary' ones. The Labour Government of the time accepted this recommendation but its ambit was restricted to encounters falling short of a search where someone was asked to account for themselves. Following localised pilot studies, and a process of gradual implementation, the law was duly amended to require the police to record such encounters on a national basis as from 1 April 2005. In January 2009 the recording requirement was watered down so that only the officer's identifying details and the ethnic group of the detainee needed to be recorded. The new Coalition Government abolished the recording requirement altogether in March 2011, leaving it up to individual forces to decide how, if at all, they wished to monitor this form of policing activity. Most police services subsequently abandoned any formal monitoring of stop and account.

This chapter reflects on the rise and fall of national policy concern about stop and account, and draws out more general lessons about the possibility of entrenching meaningful accountability measures where routine street policing is concerned. Its ambit is restricted to stops conducted by the public police of England and Wales, but the arguments may be applicable (with necessary modifications) to other types of policing in a variety of settings. The chapter is based on desk research but draws also on ad hoc contacts with police officers and police staff from three English police forces during 2013. These contacts do not amount to systematic research but they have nonetheless been useful in allowing the arguments presented here to be tested and sharpened. The core argument is that the recording of street policing for accountability purposes is only likely to be successful if citizens, rather than the police, create the relevant records.

## Accountability – some preliminary observations

As the meaning and use of 'accountability' can vary, it is important to specify how the term is understood in this chapter. Syrett (2011: 160) defines accountability as 'answering for, explaining or justifying one's actions or decisions, usually to some external body which is independent of the original decision maker'. This usefully highlights that while one mode of answering for one's actions may be internal and managerial in orientation, the more usual sense of accountability involves oversight by an external, independent body. In practice, the prospect of external accountability often provides the impetus for processes of internal accountability, as those in the police who have been involved in preparing for a visit by Her Majesty's Inspectorate of Constabulary (HMIC) readily testify. Syrett's definition might be criticised by those who favour a less literal reading of 'accountability' (e.g. Reiner 1995: 81) but the position taken here is that it is worth exploring the potential of a requirement that police officers should 'answer for' their actions. To appreciate why, it is worth briefly considering the main alternative, namely that accountability should be treated as a virtual synonym for either control or regulation.

Accountability is sometimes distinguished from control or regulation on the basis that the former is oriented towards explaining a decision or policy already made, while the latter involves an attempt to (respectively) direct or guide future behaviour. However, as Scott (2000: 39) observes, 'there is implicit in the capacity to call to account some element of control capacity'. Debates about accountability often turn on how great that element of control should be. At one end of the spectrum is the model of 'explanatory accountability' put forward by Marshall (1978). He argued that a simple requirement of providing explanations would exert a significant restraint on police behaviour and that this was preferable to subjecting them to external direction or control. There are some obvious objections to this model, and they have been forcefully expressed by those at the 'full democratic control of policing' end of the spectrum. Lustgarten (1986: 1) notes that: 'Accountability in the sense of after-the-fact explanation means acceptance of a sharply limited degree of control'. This is because the explanations themselves:

> may be defensive, dogmatic or simply unilluminating ... [and] present a partial and misleading account. Nor is it unknown even where full democratic control is supposed to operate, for information to be concealed or destroyed; under the explanatory mode, conduct of that kind is even less likely to be discovered. Moreover, explanations are often simply couched in vague generalities, with heavy reliance on terms like 'the public interest' which themselves embody controversial political choices.... Finally, the explanation may reveal a policy that is simply unacceptable.... Marshall's approach requires that the public must simply live with it.
>
> (Ibid.: 167–8; see also Reiner 1995: 81)

Lustgarten (1986: 1) observes that accountability is 'often used as a weasel word', by which he means that it can effectively mask the fact that there is little meaningful control. He accordingly avoids use of the term for the most part, advancing an argument in favour of local democratic control of policing policy (ibid.: 171–3). Other writers, however, use accountability as virtually synonymous with control. For example, Jefferson and Grimshaw (1984: 174–81) similarly advocate local democratic control of policing policy in an extended discussion labelled 'police accountability', but say very little about the role of explanation within such arrangements. It is surely possible to argue, however, that even in a system of full democratic control of policing that it would be sensible for explanations to be sought from Chief Constables and other officers prior to the formulation or amendment of policy, the expression of criticism or the imposition of sanction. To change behaviour effectively requires as full an understanding as possible of what shapes and motivates it. Moreover, it is not an unreasonable extrapolation from the procedural justice literature (e.g. Tyler 2007) to suggest that the police would be more likely to regard external direction or criticism as legitimate, and thus be more likely to respond constructively, if their views on the issues in question had been given prior consideration. For these reasons, the conflation of accountability with control is perhaps best resisted. More helpful is the position that control and accountability should be seen as linked concepts, operating on a continuum (Scott 2000: 39). In short, accountability mechanisms may form part of larger arrangements for the effective control of the police.

Under current constitutional arrangements in England and Wales, it is more accurate to see the police as subject to various forms of regulation rather than democratic control (see further the chapter by Reiner in this collection). The pithy definition by Black (2002: 26) is useful here:

> Regulation is the sustained and focused attempt to alter the behaviour of others according to defined standards or purposes with the intention of producing a broadly defined outcome or outcomes, which may involve mechanisms of standard-setting, information-gathering and behaviour modification.

Accountability is clearly intertwined with the regulatory endeavour (Seddon 2010: 264). Regulation provides a set of standards to which actors can be held accountable, and requiring explanations constitutes an important mode of information-gathering. Once that information is assessed, appropriate steps can be taken to secure any behaviour modification thought necessary to achieve the desired outcome. Accountability, then, seems to be more than just a relatively passive process of providing an explanation, but rather carries with it a sense of being 'called to account' with the possibility of criticism or remedial action where the explanation is found wanting against predefined standards. For accountability to be effective, the explanations must be accurate, illuminating and delivered to persons or bodies who can and will act on them appropriately.

Thus far we have established that accountability may form part of a strategy of control or regulation aimed at ensuring that holders of power live up to the authoritative standards set for them. But locating accountability as a kind of subset of regulation directs our attention to the possibility that holders of power may go beyond the required standards in ways that deserve praise rather than criticism. The most significant contribution to theory along these lines is that by Braithwaite *et al.* (2008) in their international study of the regulation of nursing homes. They argue that effective regulation requires not just critique and enforcement where things go wrong, but sharing and reinforcing of good practice where things go right. Regulators should therefore identify strengths of existing arrangements and facilitate a process of continuous improvement. A strengths-based approach will work better if there is effective accountability in the sense deployed in this essay – the provision of an honest and useful explanation for a decision taken. In this way regulators will be better able to identify strengths and opportunities to build on them.

As a final preliminary point, it is worth considering different ways of conceptualising the complex arrangements for accountability that currently pertain in criminal justice. Under a linear model, accountability is seen as a matter of particular institutions holding a service provider to account for a particular issue or value. So, in the case of the police, HMIC holds the police to account for the provision of an efficient and effective overall service, whereas the Independent Police Complaints Commission (IPCC) seeks to call to account particular officers for alleged infractions of law or codes of conduct. In practice, however, Scott (2000: 50) has demonstrated that closer examination of any policy domain in the United Kingdom reveals a non-linear structure which can be captured by two different models: *interdependence* and *redundancy*. Under the latter model, overlapping accountability mechanisms are deployed to ensure that the system works as it should. Each independent mechanism is redundant in the sense that were it to fail other mechanisms would 'prevent disaster' (Scott 2000: 53). One obvious example in criminal justice is the availability of civil actions against the police for aggrieved citizens who remain dissatisfied with the outcome of the police complaints system (Cohen 1985: 258).

Under Scott's interdependence model, the formal parliamentary, judicial and administrative methods of accountability are supplemented by an interactive form of accountability situated in the space where actors necessarily come together.

> Interdependent actors are dependent on each other in their actions because of the dispersal of key resources of authority ... information, expertise, and capacity to bestow legitimacy ... each of the principal actors has constantly to account for at least some of its actions to others within the space'.
>
> (Scott 2000: 53)

This sense of interdependence need not be seen as only applicable to relations between formal regulators (such as the HMIC) and the police, but could be extended to analyses of relations between the public and the police, a point to which we will return later in the chapter. Let us first turn to the question of what it is about 'stop and account' that requires police accountability, before considering the forms of accountability that have been, and might be, deployed to better regulate the use of this tactic.

## Models of stop and account

Arguments for the better regulation of stop and account are unlikely to persuade policymakers (a term which includes all levels of the police service – Reiner 1993: 8) unless rooted in a realistic appreciation of the current uses of the tactic. With that in mind, in this section three models of stop and account will be sketched.

### The crime detection model

Police officers will often encounter persons who may be committing, or have just committed, or be about to commit, a crime. To assess whether this is so, and whether they should be searched or arrested, officers will typically want to question such persons, for example to find out why they took evasive action on seeing the police, why they were ejected from a nightclub, why they are bleeding, etc. In the case of motorists, a precondition to putting questions is the exercise of the specific power to stop vehicles under s.163 of the Road Traffic Act 1988, but in the case of pedestrians the police usually rely on a more generalised notion of power (Sanders and Young 2003: 228) to ensure that people stop in one place long enough to provide the answers required (sometimes referred to as a 'voluntary stop'). An important source of this latter power is the (usually accurate) belief amongst those stopped that if they fail to provide a satisfactory account, or try to leave, the police will resort to coercion (e.g. Shiner 2006: 28), treating the lack of cooperation as helping to satisfy the precondition of reasonable suspicion which attaches to (most) powers of stop-search and arrest (Dixon 1997: 95–8; Ewing 2010: 20). Should the police invoke the power to stop-search they may continue to question (but cannot search if the answers dispel reasonable suspicion), whereas once a decision to arrest has been made the police should not question suspects any further until they are taken to a police station, at which point certain due process protections will apply (such as the right to legal advice).[1] The most common 'outcome' of being stopped, however, is 'just being asked questions' (Allen *et al.* 2006: 18; see also Moon *et al.* 2011: 23).

This model of stop and account has much to commend it, representing, as it does, a proportionate way of engaging in the investigation and detection of crime. The main alternative would be that (1) where reasonable suspicion was lacking, the police refrained from any questioning (leading them either to do nothing or to seek information in a less efficient and possibly more intrusive way, as by putting someone under surveillance in an attempt to firm up suspicion); and (2) whenever the (low) threshold of reasonable suspicion was met, the police stop-searched and arrested without first testing their suspicions through questioning (leading to substantial incursions on liberty with relatively little law enforcement pay-off). The model is also central to the police sense of mission as proactive law enforcers, has long historical antecedents, and is strongly endorsed through administrative and legal means.

That the police valorise action in the form of the skilful detection and arrest of 'good villains' (even though, and perhaps because, most of their time is spent on more mundane activities) is well established (e.g. Smith and Gray 1985: 346–7; McConville and Shepherd 1992: 149; Loftus 2010: 5; Reiner 2010: 120). The use of stop and account for detecting crime dates at least to the system of town watchmen stretching from medieval times to the early eighteenth century (Emsley 2010: 16–17). The watchmen were to be superseded by Peel's more bureaucratically organised 'New Police' of 1829 but the latter's instructions highlight the continuing important role of stop and account in legal provisions and police practice.[2] The current (2013) Code C of the Police and Criminal Evidence Act 1984 (PACE) reminds officers in note 1K that 'when police officers are trying to discover whether, or by whom, offences have been committed they are entitled to question any person from whom they think useful information can be obtained'. Stop and accounts aimed at crime detection need not be conducted in a confrontational manner in order to achieve their purpose. In practice, it will either be obvious why the police are questioning, or the police will usually explain their actions. Surveys indicate that many stop and accounts are perceived by those who were questioned as legitimate and conducted politely and fairly (e.g. Smith and Gray 1985: 279; Clancy *et al.* 2001: 68; Fitzgerald *et al.* 2002: 70; Moon *et al.* 2011: 23). The public generally understands the need for police questioning as a method of crime detection and is not opposed in principle to powers of stop and search (Stone and Pettigrew 2000: 52). When, however, the stop and account is conducted disrespectfully, or stereotyping is perceived to form part of the basis for police suspicion, then the person stopped may regard the encounter as illegitimate even if it is clear that the police goal is crime detection. There is no doubt that stereotyping does play a major role in the formation of police suspicion (e.g. Quinton *et al.* 2000: Ch. 3; Shiner 2006: 52; Quinton 2011: 364–6) and this no doubt partly explains why ethnic minority survey respondents report substantially less positive experiences of stops than their white counterparts (e.g. Clancy *et al.* 2001: 69).

### *The social disciplining model*

In this model, the police are not primarily oriented towards detecting specific crimes, but rather towards maintaining social order in the sense of keeping the 'criminal classes' in check (Brogden 1985; McConville and Shepherd 1992: 164; Choongh 1997; Shiner 2010: 945). Accordingly, the police use stop and account in an ongoing attempt to deter disorder and crime. In doing so they are concerned with maintaining control and their own authority at virtually all costs (Rawlings 2002: 216; Westmarland 2008: 268). Questions will often be framed in a way which communicates prejudice and disdain, as in 'been nicking any cars tonight lads?', and 'Don't fuck me about, right, and I won't fuck you about, where have you got your drugs?' (Bland *et al.* 2000: 82–3; see also MORI 2004: 10). In consequence, the stop and account will usually be a tense affair, with officers sensitive to any signs of resistance. Some will even seek to provoke such signs precisely in order to legitimise a tough disciplinary response to someone who has 'failed the attitude test' (Smith and Gray 1985: 352–3; Foster 1989: 133; McConville and Shepherd 1992: 182, 232; Bland *et al.* 2000: 82; Loftus 2010: 11). When oriented towards social disciplining it will be harder for the police to provide an acceptable reason for the stop (Bland *et al.* 2000: 84; MORI 2004: 18). Clancy *et al.* (2001: 61) found that black respondents were markedly less satisfied with the reason given for their foot-stop than any other ethnic group (54 per cent were satisfied, compared with 76 per cent of white respondents). Some officers may on occasion prefer to give no reason at all as a way of signalling to the other person that they have no interests or rights worthy of consideration. It appears that a fifth of adults stopped on foot are not given a reason (Clancy *et al.* 2001: 611; Scribbins *et al.* 2010: 42).

The police are here engaged in 'communicative surveillance' (Lister *et al.* 2008: 41) – letting people know that they are being watched, that they can be challenged at any time, and that their presence in an area is not wanted. Social disciplining is most likely to be deployed against groups stereotyped as criminogenic or disorderly, such as drug users, beggars, lower-class young males, some ethnic minorities, and, above all, those who are already known to the police through prior contact (Quinton 2011: 364), especially those with criminal records (Fitzgerald 1999) or those who associate with them (McAra and McVie 2005: 26). Again, this model is central to the police sense of their mission and has long historical antecedents but, unlike the crime detection model, lacks strong legal and administrative sanction.

It is clear, for example, that the medieval watchmen had a broad social control function centring on the exclusion of suspicious strangers (Rawlings 2002: 23) and the rural poor (Brogden and Brogden 1984: 48) from towns. The instructions to the 'New Police' in 1829 indicate that a large part of their mandate was similarly to control the 'criminal classes' through law enforcement processes that began with a stop and account.[3] However, these directives also emphasised that the constable should 'be civil and obliging to all people of every rank and class ... he must be particularly cautious not to interfere idly or unnecessarily, in order to make a display of his authority'.[4] No doubt these instructions were phrased with a view to maximising support for the new policing arrangements but there is nonetheless little explicit encouragement to be found in law or Home Office official guidance (either in 1829 or now) for a model of stop and account that emphasises actuarial-based suspicion, deterrence and confrontation. The current (2013) PACE Code A states in its very first paragraph that: 'Powers to stop and search must be used fairly, responsibly, with respect for people being searched and without unlawful discrimination' while para. 2.2 warns that the fact that someone has a previous conviction cannot provide the basis for searching someone.

Where this model of stop and account does find long-standing (Brogden 1985: 107), strong and explicit support is within the police service itself. Inspector Basil Griffiths told the Police Federation Conference in 1982 that 'in every urban area there's a large minority of people who are not fit to salvage. The only way in which the police can protect society is quite frankly by harassing these people' (cited in Rawlings 1985: 79). One can find similar comments within television 'reality' programmes such as *Brit Cops*, first shown on the now defunct Bravo channel in 2008. In 2009 the cameras followed the Hammersmith and Fulham robbery squad. Sergeant Jessop explained the ethos of the unit: 'We get out there … stopping people, searching people, and getting in people's faces basically. And we're not going to back down'. His colleague PC Jo Walsh added: 'In order to get the best out of a stop, you have to be clear, concise and robust, and show that you're not going to be walked over. And the best way to do that, sometimes, is force'. Whilst this model is in tension with PACE Code A, it finds some support from the broader political surround[5] and changes in the legal field – most notably the granting to the police of broad preventive powers to tackle terrorism and antisocial behaviour. The contemporary shift towards pre-emptive (Zedner 2007) and actuarial (Feeley and Simon 1994; Goldson 2010: 169) modes of criminal justice certainly coheres with the centrality within cop culture of keeping the usual suspects in check, as does the introduction of the National Intelligence Model with its emphasis on evidence-led deployment of policing resources to where they can achieve the maximum 'returns' (Tilley 2008: 383).[6] All of this results in some people being stopped or stop-searched several times a week or even repeatedly in one day (Bland *et al.* 2000: 80; MORI 2004: 9). Unsurprisingly, this model of stop and account is bitterly resented by those on the receiving end of such hostile police attention (Sissay 2013). Less obviously, it dismays the broader public who witness it in operation (McConville and Shepherd 1992: 172–6). The damage to police–community relations of such practices is enormous and needs no elaboration here (see further Sanders *et al.* 2010: 123–6; and Bradford 2012: 17–18).

### The criminal intelligence model

This model of stop and account is a kind of distorted subset of the practices that make up, or are supposed to make up, 'community policing'. The core idea in community policing is that the police should engage with the public in order better to understand their priorities, and, by being approachable and oriented towards service, encourage more frequent crime reporting and the provision of useful information. In practice, however, the orientation of the police has long tended to be not 'How can we help you?' but rather 'How can you help us?' (Whitfield 2004: 159). In other words, many police officers seek information from the community that will enable them better to pursue their cherished goals of maintaining (their sense of) good order and catching 'villains'. In practice, they learn little that they value from the general public, whether that be through attending formal public engagement events (such as Police/Partners and Communities Together

(PACT) meetings) or through more ad hoc contacts (McConville and Shepherd 1992: 143–6). Far more useful, in their eyes, is information gleaned from 'the usual suspects', particularly those with potential links to criminal gangs, drug dealers and so forth (Loftus 2010: 6; Sanders 2005: 109). This leads them to use stop and account as a way of gathering general criminal intelligence. The questions are not oriented primarily towards either attempting to detect a particular crime, or towards disciplining someone, but rather towards understanding patterns of behaviour and relationships that will help the police create a cognitive map of their 'patch' (Loftus 2010: 14), and meet the demand of management for measurable activity (through the submission of intelligence reports – Phillips 2008: 30). So while questions such as 'What are you up to?' and 'Have you had any contact with X?' may be put, it is not primarily suspicion, or hostility, that motivates the encounter, but rather the desire to cultivate and maintain ongoing relations with informal low-level informants such as sex workers (Sanders 2005: 106–12) and drug users (Bean and Billingsley 2001: 25–6). Nonetheless, it results in those 'known to the police' being questioned even more frequently than they otherwise would be, thus compounding stereotyping and the intrusive nature of stop and account. Moreover, while the police may trade favours (such as not arresting someone) for information during these encounters, the bargaining power of the two sides is lopsided, rendering the relationships involved essentially exploitative (Sanders 2005: 108–10).

### *The scope for accountability*

In practice these three models may be blurred or even fused together within the situated practices of patrol officers. In other words, a stop and account may offer the opportunity for crime detection, harassment and the gaining of criminal intelligence, and interactions will often move fluidly between these modes (Lister *et al.* 2008: 18). This renders attempts at accountability difficult, as the crime detection model can be invoked as a kind of smokescreen for social disciplining and intelligence-gathering. Similarly, encounters that might be presented after-the-fact as mere 'community engagement' might be initiated for subterranean reasons and can quickly morph into 'stop and account': one officer told me that he always said 'hello' to everyone he met because he wanted to see if they reacted nervously and thus merited closer examination.

The above discussion indicates that stop and account requires regulation because it involves the imposition of power, is often experienced as intrusive, exploitative and unfair, and is damaging to police–community relations. But the discussion also indicates that regulation is likely to be both difficult and resisted because the practice in all its forms is central to the traditional police mission. The police have a long history of fending off or subverting attempts to subject them to closer regulation and tighter accountability both at macro (e.g. Baxter and Koffman 1985: 2–3; Evans and Lewis 2013: 152–6) and micro (e.g. Loftus 2010: 12; Hough 2013: 190; Quinton and Olagundoye 2004: 14) levels, but they are not always successful in this endeavour, and there are even occasions when they have supported reform in a bid to regain legitimacy in the eyes of the public (e.g. Cohen 1985: 249–50). The strong links currently being drawn in the literature between fair stop procedures, police legitimacy and public support for the police (see Hough 2013) could form part of the 'business case' that typically motivates the police to accept the need for change (Holland 2007: 181–2). Moreover, the police are not mono-lithic: civilian police staff tend not to be so immersed in 'cop culture' as their sworn colleagues (Shiner 2010: 947), some officers (found especially amongst those who are female, ethnic minority or more experienced) are critical of sexist, racist and macho behaviour and more likely to accept the case for greater account-ability (ibid.; Loftus 2010: 6, 12; Walker 2012: 71), some front-line officers are committed to community policing, especially when this ethos is properly sup-ported by management (Fielding *et al.* 1989: 54–5; McConville and Shepherd 1992: 128–9), some officers are perceived by the public as conducting stop and account in a fair and respectful manner (MORI 2004: 10) and many police leaders have demonstrated commitment to bringing about change in policing (Savage 2007: 127–41). Is it possible to envisage a situation in which a critical mass within the police would welcome tighter regulation of stop and account and demonstrate the sustained commitment necessary to make it work? To answer that, we need to examine the rise and fall of the attempt by the Macpherson Inquiry to secure greater accountability for this core policing practice.

## The Macpherson Inquiry: promoting respect through explanatory accountability?

### *The Macpherson analysis*

The terms of reference of the Macpherson Inquiry focused on identifying the lessons to be learned from the murder of Stephen Lawrence for the investigation and prosecution of racially motivated crimes. But the Inquiry realised that it would be counterproductive to ignore the reasons for the evident 'lack of trust which exists between the police and the minority ethnic communities' (Macpher-son 1999: para. 45.6). This stemmed from 'institutional racism' resulting in ethnic minorities feeling over-policed and underprotected, a theme 'echoed by a simple but eloquent and clearly heartfelt plea.... "Please trust us with respect"' (para. 45.7). The Inquiry identified 'stop and search' as the subject of universal complaint, emphasising that the experience of ethnic minority communities was conditioned by their experience of stops which did not result in a search, includ-ing 'so called "voluntary stops"' (para. 45.8). Whilst acknowledging that it was not within their terms of reference to resolve the complex arguments surround-ing the inferences that could reasonably be drawn from the statistics relating to recorded stop-searches, they made a number of clear-cut observations:

(1) That black people were five times more likely than white people to be stop-searched, and also more likely to be arrested as a result, was in large part attributable to discrimination.

(2) That ethnic minority communities believed that if non-search stops were included in the figures the discrimination would be even more evident.

(3) That attempts to justify the disparities in the figures in terms of other factors, whilst not being seen to address the evident discrimination, would simply exacerbate the climate of distrust (paras 45.9–45.10).

The Inquiry accordingly made the following three recommendations:

> 61 That the Home Secretary, in consultation with Police Services, should ensure that a record is made by police officers of all 'stops' and 'stops and searches' made under any legislative provision.... Non-statutory or so called 'voluntary' stops must also be recorded. The record to include the reason for the stop, the outcome, and the self-defined ethnic identity of the person stopped. A copy of the record shall be given to the person stopped.

> 62 That these records should be monitored and analysed by Police Services and Police Authorities, and reviewed by HMIC on inspections. The information and analysis should be published.

> 63 That Police Authorities be given the duty to undertake publicity campaigns to ensure that the public is aware of 'stop and search' provisions and the right to receive a record in all circumstances.

Macpherson (1999: para 46.31) argued that these new requirements were 'essential to obtain a true picture of the interactions between the police and minority ethnic communities in this context'.

At first sight, this strategy seems promising, for we see here an example of the extended forms of accountability identified by Scott (2000). Redundancy is evident in the sense that three different organisations (police services, police authorities and HMIC) are given the job of analysing or reviewing the records of stops. If any one of them fails in this task, problems may still be brought to light and addressed through the action of one of the others. And interdependency is evident in the way that a national body (the HMIC) is given the job of overseeing how local monitoring is working in practice, through the potential scrutiny by the media of the published results of the monitoring, and also through the attempt to ensure that the public is aware of stop and search laws and of the right to receive a record containing the reason for the stop – a form of explanatory accountability. In theory this creates a regulatory space within which the public, the media and HMIC are empowered to confer or withhold legitimacy. It can be argued, however, that the Macpherson analysis of the problem and the possible solution was myopic, rudimentary and insufficiently evidence-based.

First, the problem of police stops was (understandably) couched above all in terms of racial discrimination. This misdiagnoses the problem in terms of ethnicity rather than seeing racial discrimination as one aspect of a much broader issue of the policing of subordinated groups in society (Delsol and Shiner 2006;

Shiner 2006: 60; Weber 2011: 466). Recording the ethnic identity of those stopped would, at best, reveal only one kind of disproportionate targeting, and the recording requirement would therefore be vulnerable to repeal as soon as concerns about the racialised nature of stops faded within policymaking circles.

Second, no attempt was made to understand how the police used and valued 'stops', with Macpherson simply accepting (without argument) 'their genuine usefulness in the prevention and detection of crime' (para. 46.31). Had Macpherson analysed the issues more carefully the different models of stop and account would have been brought to the surface, and the need for a more resilient regulatory approach might have been identified. In particular, the dangers that the police would be resistant to explaining themselves to those they wished to discipline, and that the form designed for recording stops might become a vehicle for the more efficient capture of intelligence was overlooked.

Third, the notion that a 'true picture' of stop interactions might be obtained by requiring police officers to record their own activities within the limited categories of reason for stop, ethnic identity of the person stopped and outcome of the stop was absurd. It was absurd partly because it assumed that police officers would keep accurate records of stop encounters, when analysis and research had long established the problems of under-recording and inaccurate recording of stop-searches (Koffman 1985: 16; Baxter 1985: 51; Brogden 1985: 95; Dixon *et al.* 1990: 349; Dixon 1997: 94–5; Fitzgerald, 1999: ch. 3). And it was absurd because Macpherson overlooked the implications of his own recognition that a central concern of ethnic minority people was a lack of respect. This lack of respect is partly manifested through racial discrimination infecting determinations of *who* to stop, but much of it is constituted by *how* police officers typically conduct a disciplinary stop encounter, where prejudice, hostility and deliberate provocation may be communicated by manner, inflexion or tone (McConville and Shepherd 1992: 179–80; Sissay 2013). Statistical record-keeping is incapable of capturing the dynamics and nuances of such encounters.

Fourth, the notion that a better informed public might exert some kind of regulatory restraint on the police by demonstrating knowledge of the limits to police powers, or by requesting a record of a stop, again evinces little understanding of the realities of street policing. Even leaving aside the impossibility of providing the public with a concise, clear and comprehensible statement of the complex network of stop and search laws (Baxter 1985; Sanders *et al.* 2010: 92–6, 104–5), research has amply demonstrated that to invoke one's rights on the street may result in the police becoming even more suspicious (Graham 2013: 16) or resorting to even more coercive measures as a way of reasserting their authority (Dixon 1997: 97–8). Certainly, those subjected to repeated social disciplining know only too well that an appearance of meek compliance is the best way to avoid further trouble (Sissay 2013; Bland *et al.* 2000: 83; MORI 2004: 10).

## Negating Macpherson: the devil in the detail

The first pilots of the Macpherson recommendations ran from late 1999 to May 2000. Whereas Macpherson had recommended that 'all stops' should be recorded, the pilot researchers, following discussions with the Metropolitan Police and HMIC, adopted a more restricted definition: 'When a police officer requests a person to account for their actions, behaviour or possession of anything the encounter will be regarded as a "stop" for the purposes of this pilot' (Bland *et al.* 2000: 14). Initial interviews with officers in London then led to a further narrowing of the ambit of the Macpherson recommendations:

> Officers working on community beats expressed particular concerns about the frequent informal 'low level' stops they conducted to gain community intelligence and also to monitor known prolific offenders. It was likely during the process of these encounters that some 'accounting' was called for by the person stopped. Officers were concerned about having to record them and how this might impact on their working practice.
>
> (Ibid.: 14–15)

In other words, the police were resistant to being held accountable when using 'stop and account' primarily for, or as part of, gathering criminal intelligence and/or social disciplining. Rather than seek to challenge or evaluate such practices, the pilot simply changed the 'rules of engagement' to make clear that such encounters were non-recordable (ibid.: 101). Even when restricted to the crime detection model of stop and account, however, officers were found to be unlikely to record the encounter. There was evidence that the required form was completed in just 22 per cent of the 118 recordable encounters that the researchers observed directly (ibid.: 31). Moreover, some of the reasons provided for a stop ('routine', 'traffic stop' – ibid.: 44) were distinctly uninformative. These recording problems obviously drastically limit the potential for supervisory control, and completely undermine the potential for any meaningful statistical analysis of ethnic disproportionality. The forms were particularly unlikely to be used in encounters where the 'accounting' questions put by the police were (to them) a relatively minor part of attempts at peacekeeping, 'routine checks' (e.g. of sex workers) or establishing the background to an incident (ibid.: 33).

That said, the rate of recording for even relatively straightforward suspicion-based stop and accounts was a mere 23 per cent (ibid.). Officers gave a variety of reasons for non-recording which might apply to this core kind of stop and account, including not wishing to delay the person further, reluctance to comply with the requirement in the case of brief or 'informal' encounters where there was no formal outcome, and the stop having no intelligence value (ibid.: 36). These explanations need to be seen in light of the fact that the recording requirement under the pilot extended considerably further than the 'Macpherson categories' of reason, outcome and self-defined ethnicity. The form used in Leicestershire, for example, prompted officers to record the following additional details: 'full name', address 'or description', sex, place and date of birth, height, place of stop, date and time of stop, power relied upon, and officer perception of ethnicity (ibid.: 116). It is difficult to see why members of the public should have details such as their height recorded unless the purpose is to garner 'criminal intelligence' that might later prove useful *to the police*. It is noteworthy that the majority of officers in all the pilot areas supported the design of the new stop and account form, in large part because it allowed 'improved recording of information or intelligence, particularly physical descriptions' (ibid.: 57), and could be used for both stop and account and stop-search processes.

The police have always recorded intelligence from stop and search processes when it suits them to do so (Sanders *et al.* 2010: 116–17). That makes good sense within the crime detection model of stop and account, but there are obvious problems from both the police and public's perspective with requiring such details to be recorded for *all* such encounters, however brief, and however quickly any suspicion was dispelled. From the frontline officer's perspective, completing a lengthy form makes little sense when the intelligence value of the stop is nil. From a stopped person's perspective, receiving a copy of a form dominated by one's personal information is more likely to signal entry into the 'suspect population' than that the police are accountable for their actions. As the pilot researchers noted, there were concerns expressed 'at the thought of a pile of forms with people's name on, sitting at the police station, even though they had never been charged with any offence' (Bland *et al.* 2000: 86). From a police management perspective, however, fusing the recording of intelligence with recording for accountability purposes not only appeared more efficient, but provided a way of marketing the reform to frontline officers sceptical about 'paperwork' and deeply resentful of the Macpherson verdict of 'institutional racism' which was seen as lying behind the new recording requirement (Shiner 2010: 948–9). In any event, once the decision had been made to structure the stop and account form in this way, it was virtually inevitable that the recording process would become time-consuming, intrusive and unsettling.

Officers wedded to using stop and account for criminal intelligence and social disciplining may have welcomed these effects when dealing with the 'usual suspects' (see MORI 2004: 17) but flouted the requirement to record when dealing with the 'respectable' on the basis that it was a waste of time or even counterproductive. Alternatively, they may have felt that the 'scrotes' were undeserving of the benefits of accountability, or would use the form to give the police 'a hard time' (Bland *et al.* 2000: 73–4). Either way, it seems unlikely that such officers would make much of an effort to explain the recording requirement in terms of police accountability, for that would run counter to their aim of imposing control and authority. This no doubt helps explain why in practice officers failed to provide an explanation for using the form in over half of the observed encounters where a record was made, and why some of the explanations given were hardly reassuring, as where those stopped were told that the form was for 'police records' (ibid.: 62). The poor level of explanation was associated with increased confusion and/or hostility from the person stopped (ibid.: 60–2), an effect that more confrontational officers may actually have intended.

Unsurprisingly, given this background, some members of the public in the pilot believed that they were asked to define their ethnicity for the purpose of gathering criminal intelligence rather than to aid accountability (ibid.: 57). Some officers were particularly reluctant to ask this question for fear that it would provoke hostility or accusations of racism (from black people) or ridicule (from white people), although those that provided a sensitive explanation for this requirement tended not to experience any adverse reaction (ibid.: 53–5). Again, one needs to bear in mind that for other officers, provoking an adverse reaction through putting this question without explanation may have been exactly what they intended.

Following the initial pilots, the Government's next iteration of PACE Code A circulated for consultation in March 2002 made provision for the national recording of stops, but the main police staff associations raised practical concerns about their implementation (Quinton and Olagundoye 2004: 3). Accordingly, it was decided to restrict implementation to just five police Basic Command Units from April/May 2002, with a view to finding out how best to introduce the recording requirement nationally. The requirement to record stops had narrowed further by this stage, e.g. by the exclusion of traffic stops where some other formal process was completed, such as issuing a 'producer' requiring presentation of driving documents at a later date (ibid.: 4, 14). The evaluation of this phased implementation largely confirmed the picture already presented above. Notably, the evaluation found a considerable level of under-recording related to difficulties in recognising when to apply the stop definition, the brevity of some encounters, and selective recording. It also confirmed that there was widespread support amongst the public for the recording of stops, once the purpose of doing so had been explained by the evaluators in terms of police accountability (ibid. 2004: 2; MORI 2004: 13). Compared to the earlier pilots, this evaluation placed greater emphasis on concerns about 'bureaucracy' but found that a recordable stop occurred only every 2.2 hours of patrol, and that three-quarters of stops were recorded in 'five minutes or less' with none taking longer than 10 minutes (Quinton and Olagundoye 2004: 13, 17). Some members of the public subjected to an unrecorded stop later told interviewers that they would not have wanted a form to be completed as this would have prolonged the encounter (MORI 2004: 16), which is an understandable reaction given that most people stopped found the experience unnecessarily hostile (ibid.: 9, and see also at 20).

Evaluation of the phased implementation also confirmed that local design of the stop forms was shaped by the police desire to use them to capture and use intelligence for investigative rather than accountability purposes (Quinton and Olagundoye 2004: 7–8). The use of the new form for capturing intelligence impeded public comprehension of its other function of aiding accountability. Interviews conducted by MORI (2004: 13) with those stopped found that no one thought the reason for recording the stop was to monitor police activity for ethnic disproportionality; those who were asked to self-define their ethnicity tended to think this was to help the police build up suspect descriptions, or to find terrorists or illegal immigrants, or to build up a statistical picture of which ethnic groups committed most crime (ibid.: 17). Sergeants and Inspectors responsible for checking the forms noted their value primarily in terms of capturing useful intelligence or as evidencing useful 'activity' by street-level officers (Quinton and Olagundoye 2004: 19).

Following consideration of the results of the evaluation, the Home Secretary required all police forces to implement the Macpherson recommendations on the recording of stops from 1 April 2005. The Home Office funded a further evaluation of the process of preparing for this implementation, which focused strongly on the police perspective. The main findings were that the recording of stops was 'highly contested' (Shiner 2006: iv) with many police resentful (ibid.: 47) of what they saw as 'just another piece of Home Office bureaucracy' (ibid.: 13) based on the faulty assumption that there was disproportionate policing of black communities (ibid.: 42–3). By this time, the 'rebranding' of the recording requirement as an intelligence-gathering mechanism had become pronounced amongst police leaders (ibid.: 24, 50–1). Frontline officers doubted the value of being forced to collect intelligence in each and every stop, however (ibid.: 52), and accordingly tended to record stops on a highly selective basis (ibid.: 50). When they did record, they did so at a time convenient to them (back at the station) which meant that the public did not receive a copy of the form at the time of the stop, as the official guidance required, other than in exceptional circumstances (ibid.: 50). Shiner argued that the study showed that 'internal police safeguards are a necessary but insufficient basis for effective regulation'; external scrutiny (including community monitoring) was needed to keep the police focused on effective implementation. He further argued that the focus of monitoring on race should be 'broadened to include other groups that may be susceptible to disproportionate policing' (ibid.: 63). Unfortunately, by this time the racial disproportionality horse had bolted, and the subsequent 'career' of the Macpherson recommendation remained shaped by a racialised meta-narrative.

For a few brief years, from 2005 to 2009, the recording requirement was implemented nationally, enabling statistics to be collated and published as part of the Ministry of Justice's series on Race and the Criminal Justice System. The total number of stop and accounts recorded rose from 1.4 million in 2005/6 to 2.2 million in 2008/9. Black people were around 2.5 times as likely to be subjected to a stop and account as white people, a disproportionality rate notably lower than for stop-search. Given the problems of under-recording documented earlier in this section, however, the significance of these statistics lies not in the 'trends' they reveal but rather in highlighting the practice as something worthy of national debate.

## Dismantling Macpherson

By the late 2000s it was clear that the political impetus in support of the Macpherson agenda was fading (Shiner 2010: 935). Concerns about police racism were now secondary to concerns about bureaucracy impeding police effectiveness. In April 2007, Sir Ronnie Flanagan, Chief Inspector of HMIC, was asked by the Government to carry out an independent review of policing in general. The terms of reference stipulated that unnecessary bureaucracy should be looked at as a priority. In his final report, published in February 2008, Flanagan argued that the police had gone further than Macpherson had intended by implementing a bureaucratic method of recording 'stop and account' lasting, he claimed, an average of seven minutes. Grossed up, this was said to consume 48,000 hours of officers' time in London alone (not including supervisors' checks or data entry) (Flanagan 2008: paras 5.56–5.57). In addition he contended that, however careful an officer was in explaining the purpose of this process, it engendered suspicion on the part of the person stopped (para. 5.57). This is a somewhat tendentious and partial analysis, however. It is tendentious in that the evidence from the pilots (reviewed earlier) indicated that interactions with the public tended to run smoothly when officers explained the purpose of the recording process properly. It is partial in that it fails to acknowledge that the process had only become so 'bureaucratic' (and liable to engender suspicion) because of the police's decision to capture intelligence through the standard form. Echoing their views about stop-search itself, the public had no objection to accountability in principle; they simply objected to the way the police were (mis)using it in practice. Regrettably, Flanagan demonstrated no appreciation of the criminal intelligence and social disciplining models of stop and account. Nonetheless, it is difficult to disagree with his assessment that what mattered to the public was courtesy, respect and a sense that the officer stopping them was accountable (para. 5.58; see also Bradford *et al.* 2009: 145–7). To achieve this whilst reducing 'bureaucracy', Flanagan recommended that the person stopped should be provided with a 'receipt', indicating the officer's identity, whilst making a digital record of the encounter (including the ethnicity of the person stopped) using the 'Airwave' radio communications system (Flanagan 2008: para. 5.62).

This new system was piloted briefly and the forces concerned reported that it had helped 'increase the quality of the encounter, reduced the amount of time that a person is detained in the street and helped free-up officers to spend more time on front line activity'.[7] PACE Code A was accordingly amended so that from January 2009 only a person's self-defined ethnicity had to be included in the record. It seems likely, however, that many forces continued to use a single form for both stop and account and stop-search and, therefore, continued to collect fuller information (StopWatch 2011: 6).

Then, in March 2011, the national requirement to record stop and account was simply abolished as part of the new Coalition Government's commitment to reduce 'police bureaucracy'. The Government argued that statistics on stop and account indicated that racial disproportionality was not a nationwide problem, and that it should therefore be left to local police forces to determine whether to continue recording.[8] A challenge to this decision by way of judicial review failed, partly because the High Court was impressed by the Secretary of State's evidence to the effect that both police officers and citizens found the requirement to ask for someone's self-defined ethnicity 'to be unnecessary, inappropriate and embarrassing', thus running the risk of actually damaging relations between the police and ethnic minority communities.[9] Here the High Court clearly had in mind only the criminal detection model of stop and account, overlooking the possibility that any embarrassment stemmed primarily from the confrontational attitude of some police officers when conducting stop and accounts. Supporting the abandonment of national recording on this basis flies in the face of the research findings reviewed above concerning public support for the recording requirement *when it was explained properly.*

Following local consultation, some forces, including, most importantly, the Metropolitan Police, decided to persevere with recording. By September 2012, however 35 out of 43 forces, including eight of the ten with the worst recorded disproportionality rates, were no longer keeping records for accountability purposes.[10] In early 2013 one of these forces indicated that it wished to facilitate research by academics into policing, but when I proposed a study of 'stop and account' the response was that there was no interest in that topic 'because it's no longer recorded'. It seems that stop and account is now falling below the radar at precisely the time when a huge amount of attention is being devoted to the fairness and effectiveness of stop-search powers, not least because they were implicated amongst the factors leading to the 2011 English riots.[11] To drive a wedge between different forms of street policing makes little analytical sense (Stop-Watch 2011: 31). This is not to argue that the monitoring of police-created records of stop-search encounters constitutes an effective mechanism for accountability, however. As we shall now see, there is a potentially far better way of promoting transparency and accountability in this arena.

## An alternative strategy – anchoring regulation by empowering the stopped population

### The visibility of stop and account

It is often said that street policing is inherently low visibility and thus difficult to regulate, particularly where decisions not to enforce law are concerned (e.g. Reiner 1993: 8). But there are a number of senses in which stop and account practices are highly visible. First, those stopped have provided ample first-hand accounts when interviewed to indicate that social disciplining is widespread, and the general perception is that 'the police use stops and searches to harass and annoy people, waste people's time and to exercise power' (MORI 2004: 6). Second, those not usually or ever stopped themselves but living in areas where they see the tactic frequently employed are similarly aware of the manner in which subordinated groups are singled out for repeated and hostile attention (McConville and Shepherd 1992: 172–6). Third, police officers are relatively open about these practices when interviewed by researchers, particularly if privately critical of their colleagues' observed actions (McConville and Shepherd 1992: 176–84). Fourth, researchers have observed many problematic stop and accounts, although (predictably) snapshot style studies tend to present a less disturbing picture (e.g. Quinton and Olagundoye 2004: 20) than does in-depth ethnography (e.g. Loftus 2010: 11). Fifth, as illustrated above, the television schedules are awash with 'reality' programmes which document (and applaud) aggressive and disrespectful stop philosophies and practices. Sixth, senior police leaders all have practical experience of low-level street policing at an earlier stage of their career, and have all attended the Senior Command Course prior to their elevation to the highest ranks of the service – a course in which they are required to study much of the research evidence referred to above.[12] Seventh, this is also true of chief and regional inspectors of HMIC as these are typically drawn from the highest ranks within the police service (Owers 2010: 243).

One might argue, therefore, that regulators know only too well that there is an enduring problem with stop and account. But knowing that there is a problem in general does not necessarily provide regulators with the necessary information or incentive to address the matter effectively, as the failure of the Macpherson strategy demonstrates. Thus, subjecting all stops to a recording requirement ran up against such difficulties as the exclusion from the scope of accountability of 'routine checks' of the 'usual suspects', the subordination of accountability to intelligence-gathering, and, above all, the subversion of accountability through inadequate recording and inadequate provision of explanations to those stopped.

The problem, then, is best not thought of as 'low visibility'. Rather, the issue is how to render stop and account encounters usefully and compellingly visible to those responsible for regulating them. It is not realistic to make street-level police solely responsible for rendering their own practices visible to regulators given the long-standing problems of inadequate recording, unwillingness to report concerns about the misconduct of fellow officers (see the chapter by Rowe *et al.* in this collection) and other evasions of accountability requirements. As some sergeants have noted, it is impossible for them to 'sign-off' encounters as conducted appropriately when all they have to go on is the officer's account (Quinton and Olagundoye 2004: 19). Moreover, statistical analyses of disproportionality are of little value when built upon the quicksand of police-created records. A further challenge is to establish a form of accountability that does not depend on the political impetus provided by a scandal such as that surrounding the murder of Stephen Lawrence (as that can dwindle over time, and comes with its own problems in terms of the shaping of understandings of why accountability is being introduced), but rather is stitched into the fabric of everyday policing. For so long as policing is organised on a localised basis, this requires that each police force is brought face to face with the reality of the routine practices engaged in by some of its own officers – expecting police services to act on examples of poor behaviour from outside their own 'patch' is not realistic (Shiner 2006: 44; Holland 2007: 183).

### *Rendering stop and account visible through pluralistic regulation*

At this point it is useful to extend our earlier discussion of regulation by suggesting that 'anchored pluralism' (Loader and Walker 2007: 193) may provide a fruitful way forward for the regulation of policing. As Sanders (2008: 72) argues: 'Applying the insights of the regulation literature shows that the best way of making regulation more effective would be to disperse it among those who have an interest in making it effective – that is, community and suspect representatives'. The state's role becomes one of anchoring such pluralistic arrangements, as by providing legal and other resources and through retaining a capacity to enforce obligations where necessary. Thus, for example, the state could empower defence solicitors, independent custody visitors and the friends of suspects to enter police stations at will armed with the power to require immediate explanations for the treatment of detainees. This would situate an accountability mechanism within the time and space where it is most needed. The position of such regulators could be further strengthened by locating them within networks of intersecting regulatory mechanisms (Shearing 2006). For example, the state might require that the concerns of custody visitors become a standing item on the agenda of the local Police and Crime Commissioner (PCC), who might in turn require the Professional Standards Department of the local force to take a more searching look at custody procedures and practices in the light of the reports received, or request an IPCC investigation. Bolstering the powers of custody visitors (especially their capacity to bestow or question legitimacy) should make police staff and officers based in custody suites more dependent on them and thus more willing to account to them on a continuing basis, as per Scott's interdependence model of regulation. It is much harder to see how regulatory pluralism would work in the case of street policing, however, and it is notable that Sanders is silent on this point, despite having identified stop-search as one of the areas where there is a need for more effective regulation. When a suspect is stopped on the street one can hardly expect a custody visitor or defence solicitor to be present.

Could we nonetheless conceive of the stopped population as an integral part of pluralistic interdependent regulation? To some extent, those stopped already have a form of regulatory power. They can, for example, make their views known by taking part in consultation arrangements (e.g. run by PCCs or police forces themselves), make complaints to the IPCC or bring actions in the civil courts. But those most likely to be stopped have fraught relations with the police and relatively little faith in, or representation within, standard consultation and complaint structures (MORI 2004: 12; Shiner 2006: 55, 58; HMIC 2013: 36–7; Graham 2013: 10). The research into the implementation of the Macpherson stop and account recording requirement found that while the 'usual suspects' thought that records might enable police managers to see that they were being harassed, they were sceptical that this potential would be realised in practice given the level of non-recording they had already experienced, with some also doubting the value of non-independent oversight of the records (Bland *et al.* 2000: 87–9; see also Shiner 2006: 38–9). Their scepticism partly stemmed from the limited nature of what will be recorded by a police officer about a stop and account, which does not extend to how the interaction was handled. Yet, according to the Home Office research, those stopped 'were clear that officers' attitude and the way they dealt with people was more important than the formal procedure they followed' (Bland *et al.* 2000: 90). One respondent said that: 'It's not what they say, but how they say it', while another explained that: 'Okay, so you've got a record of them giving this ... why they stopped you, but you don't know how their attitude was towards that stop' (ibid.: 87–8). They had, it may be argued, a realistic appreciation of the difficulties of convincing those in authority that they have been the victim of poor practice (see Sanders *et al.* 2010: ch. 12). From their perspective, the long-standing nature of problematic stop and account practices provided ample evidence that the officers concerned had nothing to fear from current accountability mechanisms.

To put this more analytically, at present the regulatory space within which police officers and the public come together lacks the quality of interdependence described by Scott (2000). Many street-level police officers do not currently see the need to constantly account for their actions 'as a precondition to action' where the usual targets of their suspicion are concerned – rather, as we have seen, power is often simply imposed and confrontation relished or even deliberately provoked. This does not mean that the interdependence model is inapplicable but rather it highlights the need for a shifting of the balance of power or reallocation of resources in order to change the way the model works in this particular case (Scott 2000: 52).

One possibility would be to change the nature of police records so that those stopped had a hand in creating them. Some of those that the Home Office researchers interviewed argued that the form should be amended to give the person stopped the right to sign it as a true record, with space provided for them to add additional comments about the encounter (Bland *et al.* 2000: 88–90). As one of those who took this view explained: 'it should be a new law saying that, explaining your reasons, half your story. They don't give you your story, it's just their story' (quoted in MORI 2004: 20). It seems doubtful, however, that merely adding a suspect's comments to a stop and account record will be sufficient to render more visible the reality of the relevant interaction on the street. As one of the 'usual suspects' observed:

> Really they [the police] can do whatever they want, they can take you in just for giving them a bad look, but they can say: 'Ah, I see him grabbing something.' It's your word against theirs and they are going to win at the end of the day.
>
> (Quoted in MORI 2004: 7)

A more radical alternative would be to encourage those stopped, and those who witness such stops, to make a digital recording of the interaction which could then form the basis for subsequent regulatory action. The ubiquitous presence in public space of smart phones, tablets and other recording devices has already led to ordinary members of the public, as well as more organised 'cop-watch' groups (Huey *et al.* 2006), 'hijacking surveillance' (Koskela 2009) by recording instances of serious police malpractice, most famously in the case of Ian

Tomlinson (Goldsmith 2010: 923–4). At present the products of this 'sousveil-lance' (Mann *et al.* 2003: 332) are usually disseminated via newspapers, tele-vision and Internet-based social media sites. Whilst such activity can be seen as an effective way of channelling critique, raising public concern and supporting democracy (Huey *et al.* 2006), one might also argue that it feeds into a narrative of police malpractice as consisting of the occasional scandalous act with dra-matic consequences rather than as ordinary everyday practice which gradually erodes public confidence in policing. It would be more productive to tackle the latter, not least because 'scandalous acts' are usually not a deviation from, but rather part and parcel of, established practices, often the only difference being whether people die as a result of them (Sanders *et al.* 2010: 223–8). It is not real-istic to expect the print and television media to take a close and critical interest in 'routine' stop and account processes, especially when their intrusive or con-frontational character is subtle in nature. But it is realistic to ask regulators such as the IPCC, Chief Constables, PCCs, HMIC and the Professional Standards Department of police services to take such an interest, and to be sensitive to the nuances of such interactions. The compelling nature of a direct recording is such that it would be difficult to deflect or deny the problem.[13] Academics have long understood the value of direct observation, and recording of practices, not to mention 'the power of the transcript' (Daly 2004: 505), which is why they have eagerly drawn on those recordings that the 'usual suspects' have occasionally made of their own treatment at the hands of the police (e.g. Sanders *et al.* 2010: 113–14). It would be important, however, to maximise the number of recordings made available to regulators as otherwise those that are received may be charac-terised and even dismissed as unrepresentative in nature.

Linked to this last point, it is not realistic to expect the traditional media to take an interest in routine forms of good practice by the police, whereas those whose mission it is to regulate the police can and should embrace the kind of strengths-based regulation referred to earlier (see also Shiner 2006: vi, 62). Access to recordings of actual stop and account interactions would enable regu-lators to identify, reward and share the effective practice of those police officers who typically conduct stop and account in an explanatory and respectful manner, eschewing social disciplining and intrusive forms of intelligence-gathering. The spreading of such good practice would mean that the stopped public would receive better explanations for police actions, with improved public confidence the likely result (Hough 2013). Moreover, encouraging the recording of 'good' as well as 'bad' stop interactions would be an effective way of tapping into the public's strong support of 'good policing' and 'good police officers' (e.g. Mann 2013: 5), and should help garner support for this new accountability initiative amongst the police themselves, particularly those who already take pride in behaving in an ethical and honest manner (see e.g. Shiner 2006: 13).

There would be two other beneficial effects within policing: first, it would dilute the long-dominant but profoundly counterproductive emphasis on assess-ing policing through quantitative measures such as the number of intelligence reports submitted or stop-searches carried out, rather than through the quality of interactions with the public (McConville and Shepherd 1992: 199–202); second, it would help counter the average police officer's sense that they are engaged in a 'thankless task', with little support from the public or 'management' (McConville and Shepherd 1992: 189; Loftus 2010: 8–9). It is not that police services currently fail completely to recognise good performance by their staff. But celebratory practices such as prize-giving ceremonies for 'PCSO of the year' tend to focus on eye-catching initiatives such as setting up a new youth club, rather than, say, the everyday respectful treatment of the stopped population.

Some other advantages of using citizen recordings as part of a pluralistic regulatory strategy for stop and account can be here only briefly enumerated. First, it would be up to those stopped rather than the police to determine whether the encounter (or the pattern of encounters of which it was a part) was of a kind that should be brought to the attention of regulators. Thus, for example, 'routine stops' of the usual suspects for social disciplining or intelligence-gathering would be opened up for review. Second, where the police have continued to record stop and account for accountability purposes, whether through paper forms or 'body-cams',[14] this new approach would provide a form of redundancy regulation, for should a police officer fail to record the encounter the citizen recording may remedy that omission, thus increasing the reliability of statistical and qualitative analysis of this form of street policing. Indeed, the very fact that citizens might report the encounter directly to a regulator should increase the likelihood that officers record properly themselves, as otherwise they might be held to account for this omission. Third, this type of record creation largely circumvents the problems of those stopped lacking credibility in the eyes of authority, as it will no longer be one person's word against another's. Rather than pitting indirect accounts against each other, the officer's account will be reviewed in the light of a direct recording of the interaction. Fourth, the member of the public would have initial control over the forms of oversight to which the record was subjected. Some of those stopped might wish to initiate the police complaints process, or to alert the local media, or to upload the recording to YouTube or Facebook to garner support from online communities (Goldsmith 2010: 928). Others might prefer to involve the PCC in addition to other regulatory bodies. Given the lack of confidence amongst the 'usual suspects' in authority figures, there should also be the possibility to send the recording to any policing-focused community-based groups, such as the Independent Advisory Groups set up in the wake of the Macpherson Report (see Braithwaite 2009). Sending the recording to multiple regulators (ideally via bespoke software such as a 'phone app') would help ensure, through the principles of redundancy and interdependence, that effective action was taken in response.

This accountability strategy, just like any other, is not free of the risks of subversion or evasion, and one must always be wary of placing too much faith in 'techno-solutions' to complex social problems (Zedner 2009: 265–7). The most obvious difficulties with this strategy can again be touched upon only briefly within the compass of this chapter. First, there is the possibility that street-level police officers will respond violently to the filming of their activities. There have been some high-profile examples of the police using force to undermine sous-veillance (Goldsmith 2010: 929), including one officer who responded to being filmed while conducting a stop-search by depositing a camera-wielding 15-year-old boy in a rubbish bin.[15] It is likely, however, that objections to the public filming of policing will fade as the beneficial use of increasingly unobtrusive recording devices to document all aspects of life continues to grow (Ali and Mann 2013: 253), and as individual officers come to accept the guidance of their forces that the public (except in exceptional circumstances) have a right to film their activities.[16] Moreover, if police regulators support (i.e. anchor) such filming then one can expect the resistance of street-level police to be further muted (Mann *et al.* 2003: 345).

Second, it might be objected that this accountability strategy assumes that the 'usual suspects' carry smart phones or other recording devices. That is an increasingly reasonable assumption to make in the case of most teenagers and young adults (Goldsmith 2010: 19), but not in the case of those who are poor or homeless. If police services and PCCs are serious, however, about improving the quality of their encounters with all sections of the public then the answer to this lies in their hands. It would not be difficult to identify from youth workers, community groups or stop-search records a way of contacting those who are repeatedly the focus of street policing. And it would not be that expensive to provide such people with basic recording devices and the training necessary to use them effectively – analytically, this could be thought of as part of their 'anchoring' role. The costs involved would be a reasonable price to pay for the service that these 'usual suspects' could then provide to the police by way of aiding their regulatory strategy.

Third, it would be important to guard against the possibility that the recordings transmitted by citizens would be used not for accountability purposes but rather to build up an intelligence picture for potential use against them. One safeguard here is to allow citizens to transmit the recording to an independent group only, on the basis that the latter would share the substance, but not the details, with other regulators. Citizens have the right not to give their name and address during a stop and account, and should equally have the right to transmit information to regulators on an anonymous basis if they so wish.

### The role of accountability within the anchored regulation of street policing

In this section the discussion has mostly focused on regulation rather than accountability. However, as noted earlier in the chapter, accountability can play an important part in the regulatory endeavour. There are at least two distinct ways in which the accountability of street-level police officers would be fostered by the strategy advocated here.

First, it would reduce the current massive power imbalance between the police and the stopped (Mann and Ferenbok 2012; Ali and Mann 2013: 250), thus making it more likely that regulatory interdependence would work. In other words, police officers would be provided with a clear incentive to explain themselves properly to those they stop. If they failed to account adequately for their actions then they would run the risk that the citizen would transmit a recording of their unsatisfactory behaviour to a variety of regulators. If, on the other hand, they provided a clear and legitimate explanation of their reasons for stopping and questioning then there would be a reasonable chance that citizens would bring their exemplary behaviour to the attention of those in a position to confer institutional praise and advance their careers. Communicative sousveillance might thus not only guard against the most negative aspects of the communicative surveillance inherent in much current stop and account activity but actively encourage positive forms of explanatory accountability.

Second, the direct recording of a stop and account would enable supervisory accountability to work much more effectively, as no longer would supervisors be relying merely on an indirect police record of what took place. Instead, officers could be required to listen to a recording of the interaction in the presence of a supervisor or regulator, and then be asked to explain themselves. There would still be a place for an officer's account in response to be taken seriously. A direct recording will not necessarily reveal the full range of factors that an officer took into account when deciding whether and how to conduct a stop, and there may be good reasons why this information was not shared with the person stopped (such as protecting a confidential source). Similarly, recordings will not capture every gesture of an interaction, which will in any case always be open to multiple interpretations (Koskela 2009: 153). Nonetheless, a citizen recording would greatly reduce the officer's '*account ability*: the capacity to provide a record of activities that explains them in a credible manner so that they appear to satisfy the rights and obligations of *accountability*' (Ericson 1995: 137 – emphasis in original). Poor practice would be more easily exposed and dealt with under these conditions. How it should be dealt with requires detailed analysis well beyond the scope of this chapter. The suggestion by Shiner (2006: 59) that some form of restorative justice process might be deployed is worth considering, however, not least because it could address differences of perception (Goldsmith 2010: 920–1). Bringing the officer and citizen together in controlled conditions, and asking them to reflect on the interaction in the light of the recording, could enable each to better understand the position of the other.[17] This might also be seen as providing a more discursive, richer form of accountability, perhaps better suited to bringing about long-term positive changes in behaviour (see also the chapter by Prenzler and Porter in this collection).

Accountability is not just for street-level officers, however. Rather officers at all levels of the policing organisation, as well as higher-level policymakers, should be held accountable for their part in facilitating intrusive stop and account practices. Aggressive policing flourishes at present in part because of permissive law (McBarnet 1983; Jefferson and Grimshaw 1984: 69; Quinton 2011: 360–1) and inadequate supervisory and accountability structures (Lustgarten 1986: 181). Above all else, however, it is senior police officers who determine where and when policing resources should be deployed, what style of policing should be pursued, and how much attention should be devoted to training, supervision, discipline and other matters bearing on individual officer behaviour. Issues of fairness and legality are clearly implicated when senior police officers decide, for example, to direct unusually large numbers of police officers to aggressively patrol areas with a high concentration of minority ethnic residents, as the lessons of the Brixton riot in 1981 show only too clearly (e.g. Jefferson and Grimshaw 1984: 85–102). Once actual recordings of stop encounters are systematically available for review (by the media, the Home Office, HMIC, PCCs, IPCC, local community groups and others), everyone within the police hierarchy right up to chief officers of police can reasonably be asked to account for problematic practice and to explain what they intend to do to ensure (and celebrate) fairer and more productive behaviour by 'their' officers in future. Perhaps Chief Constables might even become advocates for less permissive law, once they are brought face to face with the grim realities that some of those stopped face on a daily basis.

## Conclusion

When tackling issues of accountability, it can be helpful to pose a number of basic questions. Scott (2000: 41), for example, argues that: 'It is helpful to keep distinct the three sets of accountability questions: "who is accountable?"; "to whom?"; and "for what?"', while Reiner (1993: 20) refers to the principles of police accountability as 'For What? To Whom? How Much?' In this chapter I have argued that *the police at all levels* should be accountable *for* stop and account practices, that they should be accountable *to* both the public and official regulators, and that accountability should centre *much more* on citizen recordings of street-level interactions rather than police-created records. In this way we can at last begin to address the purpose, manner and style of policing, whilst not forgetting to pay equally careful attention to the linked disproportionality question of who gets stopped and how often. The scrapping of the national recording requirement is regrettable in many ways, but one might argue that it has at least opened up a space for local forces and their regulators to experiment with more creative, democratic forms of accountability, better suited to addressing the underlying problems. And on that metaphorical throwing down of the gauntlet, I cease.

## Notes

1 This is a necessarily simplified explanation of a complex legal position – for more detailed analysis see Sanders *et al.* (2010: chs 2–3) and StopWatch (2011: 12–18).
2 'New Police Instructions', *Morning Post*, 25 September 1829. See also Brogden and Brogden (1984: 51).
3 'New Police Instructions', *Morning Post*, 25 September 1829.
4 Ibid.
5 For example, in May 2008 the then Home Secretary urged police forces across the country to follow the example of a four-day operation by Essex Police in which 14

persistent offenders were confronted at their homes, openly filmed, followed by surveillance and other police officers, and repeatedly stopped and searched (a total of 60 times).

6　See also the comments of the Police Commander at HC Stdg Comm D, 13 April 2000, col. 27.

7　Explanatory Memorandum to the Police and Criminal Evidence Act 1984 (Codes of Practice) (Revisions to Code A) (No. 2) Order 2008 (2008 No. 3146), para. 7.

8　See Hansard, 1 December 2010, col. 295.

9　*Diedrick, R. (on The Application of)* v. *Chief Constable of Hampshire Constabulary and others* [2012] EWHC 2144 (Admin) at [33] and [42].

10　StopWatch, 'Stop and Account: Disproportionality and Recording', undated factsheet (www.stop-watch.org/get-informed/factsheet/stop-and-account – last accessed 24 September 2013).

11　See, for example, the Hansard debate on 2 July 2013 (col. 773), in which the Home Secretary announced a public consultation on stop-search powers, and HMIC (2013).

12　This is based on my experience of having taught on the Senior Command Course in 2001.

13　I am aware of one police service that recently reviewed its call-handling processes. It was only when senior police officers were brought together to listen to the mishandling of actual calls that they were sufficiently shocked into accepting the need for fundamental change.

14　The fact that by 2013 half of all police forces in England and Wales were reported to be requiring at least some of their officers to wear body cameras that would be capable of filming police–public interactions (www.bbc.co.uk/news/uk-23776839 – last accessed 29 September 2013) is not a satisfactory solution to the accountability problems documented in this chapter, because (1) individual officers would remain responsible for ensuring that problematic encounters were actually recorded (see HMIC 2013: 45–6), and the recordings preserved; (2) the police service would remain in control of who saw the digital footage; and (3) such footage would inevitably present matters from an officer's viewpoint, and thus not capture the nuances of the encounter from the citizen's perspective (see further Mann and Ferenbok 2012: 20). Body-cams should, however, assist strength-based regulation (as there will presumably be no reluctance amongst ethical officers to record and share well-handled stops), and they will further the redundancy principle of regulation given that not all encounters will be recorded by citizens.

15　This was filmed by the boy's friend on his mobile phone and then transmitted as part of a national television programme. The Metropolitan Police subsequently paid £4,000 in damages, and the officer received a written warning following investigation by the IPCC, thus illustrating the regulatory possibilities of such digital accountability. www.dailymail.co.uk/news/article-478725/Police-pay-4–000-boy-dumped-litter-bin-officer.html (last accessed 29 September 2013).

16　See the detailed advice provided by the Metropolitan Police at http://content.met.police.uk/Site/photographyadvice (last accessed 29 September 2013).

17　The difficulties of using restorative justice as part of handling complaints against the police are explored in Young *et al.* (2005), but note that the participants in the innovative process reviewed there did not have access to a direct recording of their earlier interaction – an element which should reduce the scope for unhelpful argument about what actually happened.

# References

Ali, M.A. and Mann, S. (2013) *The Inevitability of the Transition from a Surveillance-Society to a Veillance-Society: Moral and Economic Grounding for Sousveillance*, 2013 IEEE International Symposium on Technology and Society (ISTAS).

Allen, J., Edmonds, S., Patterson, A. and Smith, D. (2006) *Policing and the Criminal Justice System – Public Confidence and Perceptions: Findings from the 2004/05 British Crime Survey*, Home Office Online Report 7 June 2006, London: Home Office.

Baxter, J. (1985) 'Policing and the Rule of Law', in J. Baxter and L. Koffman (eds) *Police: The Constitution and the Community*, Abingdon: Professional Books.

Baxter, J. and Koffman, L. (1985) 'Introduction', in J. Baxter and L. Koffman (eds) *Police: The Constitution and the Community*, Abingdon: Professional Books.

Bean, P. and Billingsley, R. (2001) 'Drugs, Crime and Informers', in R. Billingsley, T. Nemitz and P. Bean (eds) *Informers: Policing, Policy, Practice*, Cullompton, Devon: Willan.

Black, J. (2002) 'Critical reflections on Regulation', *Australian Journal of Legal Philosophy*, 27: 1–35.

Bland, N., Miller, J. and Quinton, P. (2000) *Upping the PACE? An Evaluation of the Recommendations of the Stephen Lawrence Inquiry on Stops and Searches*, Police Research Series Paper 128, London: Home Office.

Bradford, B. (2012) 'Policing and Social Identity: Procedural Justice, Inclusion and Cooperation between Police and Public', *Policing and Society*, 1–22.

Bradford, B., Stanko, E. and Jackson J. (2009) 'Using Research to Inform Policy: The Role of Public Attitude Surveys in Understanding Public Confidence and Police Contact', *Policing*, 3(2): 139–48.

Braithwaite, J. (2009) 'Police Engagement with Communities Post-Lawrence', in N. Hall, J. Grieve and S. Savage (eds) *Policing and the Legacy of Lawrence*, Cullompton, Devon: Willan.

Braithwaite, J., Makkai, T. and Braithwaite, V. (2007) *Regulating Aged Care: Ritualism and the New Pyramid*, Cheltenham: Edward Elgar.

Brogden, M. (1985) 'Stopping the People – Crime Control Versus Social Control', in J. Baxter and L. Koffman (eds) *Police: The Constitution and the Community*, Abingdon: Professional Books.

Brogden, M. and Brogden, A. (1984) 'From Henry III to Liverpool 8: The Unity of Police Street Powers', *International Journal of the Sociology of Law*, 12: 37–58.

Choongh, S. (1997) *Policing as Social Discipline*, Oxford: Clarendon Press.

Clancy, A., Hough, M., Aust, R. and Kershaw, C. (2001) *Crime, Policing and Justice: the experience of ethnic minorities*, Home Office Research Study 223, London: Home Office.

Cohen, B. (1985) 'Police Complaints Procedure: Why and for Whom?', in J. Baxter and L. Koffman (eds) *Police: The Constitution and the Community*, Abingdon: Professional Books.

Daly, K. (2004) 'Pile it On: More Books on RJ', *Theoretical Criminology*, 8(4): 499–507.

Delsol, R. and Shiner, M. (2006) 'Regulating Stop and Search: A Challenge for Police and Community Relations in England and Wales', *Critical Criminology*, 14: 241–63.

Dixon, D. (1997) *Law in Policing: Legal Regulation and Police Practices*, Oxford: Clarendon Press.

Dixon, D., Coleman, C. and Bottomley, K. (1990) 'Consent and the Legal Regulation of Policing', *Journal of Law and Society*, 17(3): 345–62.

Emsley, C. (2010) *The Great British Bobby: A History of British Policing from the 18th Century to the Present*, London: Quercus.

Ericson R. (1995) 'The News Media and Account Ability in Criminal Justice', in P. Stenning (ed.) *Accountability for Criminal Justice*, Toronto: University of Toronto Press.

Evans, R. and Lewis, P. (2013) *Undercover: The True Story of Britain's Secret Police*, London: Faber and Faber.

Ewing, K. (2010) *Bonfire of the Liberties: New Labour, Human Rights, and the Rule of Law*, Oxford: Oxford University Press.

Feeley, M. and Simon, J. (1994) 'Actuarial Justice: The Emerging New Criminal Law' in D. Nelken (ed.) *The Futures of Criminology*, London: Sage.

Fielding, N., Kemp, C. and Norris, C. (1989) 'Constraints on the Practice of Community Policing', in R. Morgan and D. Smith (eds) *Coming to Terms with Policing*, London: Routledge.

Fitzgerald, M. (1999) *Stop and Search: Final Report*, London: Metropolitan Police.

Fitzgerald, M., Hough, M., Joseph, I. and Qureshi, T. (2002) *Policing for London*, Cullompton, Devon: Willan.

Flanagan, Sir R. (2008) *The Review of Policing: Final Report*, available at www.hmic.gov.uk/publication/flanagan-review-of-policing/ (last accessed 24 September 2013).

Foster, J. (1989) 'Two Stations: An Ethnographic Study of Policing in the Inner City', in D. Downes (ed.) *Crime and the City*, Basingstoke: Macmillan.

Goldsmith, A. (2010) 'Policing's New Visibility', *British Journal of Criminology*, 50: 914–34.

Goldson, B. (2010) 'The Sleep of (Criminological) Reason: Knowledge-Policy Rupture and New Labour's Youth Justice Legacy', *Criminology and Criminal Justice*, 10(1): 155–78.

Graham, J. (2013) *Policing Young Adults: A Scoping Study*, London: The Police Foundation.

Her Majesty's Inspectorate of Constabulary (HMIC) (2013) *Stop and Search Powers: Are the Police Using them Effectively and Fairly?*, London: HMIC.

Holland, B. (2007) 'View from Within: the Realities of Promoting Race and Diversity inside the Police Service', in M. Rowe (ed.) *Policing Beyond Macpherson: Issues in Policing, Race and Society*, Cullompton, Devon: Willan.

Hough, M. (2013) 'Procedural Justice and Professional Policing in Times of Austerity', *Criminology and Criminal Justice*, 13: 181–97.

Huey, L., Walby, K. and Doyle, A. (2006) 'Cop Watching in the Downtown Eastside: Exploring the Use of (Counter)Surveillance as a Tool of Resistance', in T. Monahan (ed.) *Surveillance and Security: Technological Politics and Power in Everyday Life*, New York: Routledge.

Jefferson, T. and Grimshaw, R. (1984) *Controlling the Constable: Police Accountability in England and Wales*, London: Frederick Muller.

Koffman, L. (1985) 'Safeguarding the Rights of the Citizen', in J. Baxter and L. Koffman (eds) *Police: The Constitution and the Community*, Abingdon: Professional Books.

Koskela, H. (2009) 'Hijacking Surveillance? The New Moral Landscapes of Amateur Photographing', in K.F. Aas, H.O. Gundhus and H.M. Lomell (eds) *Technologies of InSecurity*, Abingdon: Routledge Cavendish.

Lister, S., Seddon, T., Wincup, E., Barrett, S. and Traynor, P. (2008) *Street Policing of Problem Drug Users*, York: Joseph Rowntree Foundation.

Loader, I. and Walker, N. (2007) *Civilizing Security*, Cambridge: Cambridge University Press.

Loftus, B. (2010) 'Police Occupational Culture: Classic Themes, Altered Times', *Policing and Society*, 20(1): 1–20.

Lustgarten, L. (1986) *The Governance of Police*, London: Sweet & Maxwell.

McAra, L. and McVie, S. (2005) 'The Usual Suspects: Street Life, Young People and the Police', *Criminal Justice*, 5(1): 5–36.

McBarnet, D. (1983) *Conviction*, London: Macmillan.

McConville, M. and Shepherd, D. (1992) *Watching Police, Watching Communities*, London: Routledge.

Macpherson, Sir W. (1999) *The Stephen Lawrence Inquiry: Report of an Inquiry by Sir William Macpherson of Cluny*, CM 4262-I, London: The Stationery Office.

Mann, S. (2013) *Veillance and Reciprocal Transparency: Surveillance versus Sousveillance, AR Glass, Lifeglogging, and Wearable Computing*, 2013 IEEE International Symposium on Technology and Society.

Mann, S. and Ferenbok, J. (2012) 'New Media and the Power-Politics of Sousveillance in a Surveillance Dominated World', *Surveillance and Society*, 11(1/2) 18–34.

Mann, S., Nolan, J. and Wellman, B. (2003) 'Sousveillance: Investing and Using Wearable Computing Devices for Data Collection in Surveillance Environments', *Surveillance and Society*, 1(3) 331–55.

Marshall, G. (1978) 'Police Accountability Revisited', in D. Butler and A. Halsey (eds) *Policy and Politics*, London: Macmillan.

Moon, D. (ed.), Flatley, J. (ed.), Parfrement-Hopkins, J., Hall, P., Hoare, J., Lau, I. and Innes, J. (2011) *Perceptions of Crime, Engagement with the Police, Authorities Dealing with Anti-Social Behaviour and Community Payback: Findings from the 2010/11 British Crime Survey*, Home Office Statistical Bulletin 18/11, London: Home Office.

MORI (2004) *The Views of the Public on the Phased Implementation of Recording Police Stops*, Home Office Development and Practice Report 22, London: Home Office.

Owers, A. (2010) 'The Regulation of Criminal Justice: Inspectorates, Ombudsmen and Inquiries' in H. Quirk, T. Seddon and G. Smith (eds) *Regulation and Criminal Justice*, Cambridge: Cambridge University Press.

Phillips, Sir D. (2008) 'Police Intelligence Systems as a Strategic Response', in C. Harfield, A. MacVean, J. Grieve and Sir D. Phillips (eds) *The Handbook of Intelligent Policing*, Oxford: Oxford University Press.

Quinton, P. (2011) 'The Formation of Suspicions: Police Stop and Search Practice in England and Wales', *Policing and Society*, 21(4): 357–68.

Quinton, P. and Olagundoye, J. (2004) *An Evaluation of the Phased Implementation of the Recording of Police Stops*, Home Office Development and Practice Report 23, London: Home Office.

Quinton, P., Bland, N. and Miller, J. (2000) *Police Stops, Decision-making and Practice*, Police Research Series Paper 130, London: Home Office.

Rawlings, P. (1985) 'Bobbies, Aliens and Subversives: The Relationship between Community Policing and Coercive Policing', in J. Baxter and L. Koffman (eds) *Police: The Constitution and the Community*, Abingdon: Professional Books.

Rawlings, P. (2002) *Policing: A Short History*, Cullompton, Devon: Willan.

Reiner, R. (1993) 'Police Accountability: Principles, Patterns and Practices', in R. Reiner and S. Spencer (eds) *Accountable Policing*, London: Institute for Public Policy Research.

Reiner, R. (1995) 'Counting the Coppers: Antinomies of Accountability in Policing', in P. Stenning (ed.) *Accountability for Criminal Justice*, Toronto: University of Toronto Press.

Reiner, R. (2010) *The Politics of the Police* (4th edn), Oxford: Oxford University Press.

Sanders, A. (2008) 'Can Coercive Powers be Effectively Controlled or Regulated? The Case for Anchored Pluralism' in E. Cape and R. Young (eds) *Regulating Policing*, Oxford: Hart.

Sanders, T. (2005) *Sex Work: A Risky Business*, Cullompton, Devon: Willan.

Sanders, A. and Young, R. (2003) 'Police Powers' in T. Newburn (ed.) *Handbook of Policing*, Cullompton, Devon: Willan.

Sanders, A., Young, R. and Burton, M. (2010) *Criminal Justice* (4th edn), Oxford: Oxford University Press.

Savage, S. (2007) *Police Reform: Forces for Change*, Oxford: Oxford University Press.

Scott, C. (2000) 'Accountability in the Regulatory State', *Journal of Law and Society*, 27: 38–60.

Scribbins, M. (ed.), Flatley, J. (ed.), Parfrement-Hopkins, J. and Hall, P. (2010) *Public Perceptions of Policing, Engagement with the Police and Victimisation: Findings from the 2009/10 British Crime Survey*, Home Office Statistical Bulletin 19/10, London: Home Office.

Seddon, T. (2010) 'Rethinking Prison Inspection: Regulating Institutions of Confinement', in H. Quirk, T. Seddon and G. Smith (eds) *Regulation and Criminal Justice*, Cambridge: Cambridge University Press.

Shearing, D. (2006) 'Reflections on the Refusal to Acknowledge Private Governments', in J. Wood and B. Dupont (eds) *Democracy, Society and the Governance of Security*, Cambridge: Cambridge University Press.

Shiner, M. (2006) *National Implementation of the Recording of Police Stops*, London: Home Office.

Shiner, M. (2010) 'Post-Lawrence Policing in England and Wales: Guilt, Innocence and the Defence of Organizational Ego', *British Journal of Criminology*, 50: 935–53.

Sissay, L. (2013) 'Every 134 Days for 20 Years the Police Mistook me for a Crook', *Guardian*, 4 July.

Smith, D. and Gray, J. (1985) *Police and People in London*, Aldershot: Gower.

Stone, V. and Pettigrew, N. (2000) *The Views of the Public on Stops and Searches*, Police Research Series Paper 129, London: Home Office.

StopWatch (2011) 'StopWatch Statement on Police Stop and Account', available at www.stop-watch.org/get-informed/research/stopwatch-statement-on-police-stop-and-account (last accessed 28 September 2013).

Syrett, K. (2011) *The Foundations of Public Law*, Basingstoke: Palgrave Macmillan.

Tilley, N. (2008) 'Modern Approaches to Policing: Community, Problem-Oriented and Intelligence-Led', in T. Newburn (ed.) *The Handbook of Policing* (2nd edn), Cullompton, Devon: Willan.

Tyler, T. (2007) *Legitimacy and Criminal Justice*, New York: Russell Sage Foundation.

Walker, S. (2012) 'Institutionalizing Police Accountability Reforms: The Problem of Making Police Reforms Endure', *Saint Louis University Public Law Review*, 32: 57–91.

Weber, L. (2011) '"It Sounds Like They Shouldn't Be Here": Immigration Checks on the Streets of Sydney', *Policing and Society* 21(4): 456–67

Westmarland, L. (2008) 'Police Cultures', in T. Newburn (ed.) *The Handbook of Policing* (2nd edn), Cullompton, Devon: Willan.

Whitfield, J. (2004) *Unhappy Dialogue: The Metropolitan Police and Black Londoners in Post-War Britain*, Cullompton, Devon: Willan.

Young, R., Hoyle C., Cooper, K. and Hill, R. (2005) 'Informal Resolution of Complaints Against the Police: A Quasi-Experimental Test of Restorative Justice', *Criminal Justice*, 5(3): 279–317.

Zedner, L. (2007) 'Pre-Crime and Post-Criminology?', *Theoretical Criminology*, 11: 261–81.

Zedner, L. (2009) 'Epilogue: The Inescapable Insecurity of Security Technologies?', in K.F. Aas, H.O. Gundhus and H.M. Lomell (eds) *Technologies of InSecurity*, Abingdon: Routledge Cavendish.

# 3    Improving police behaviour and police–community relations through innovative responses to complaints

*Tim Prenzler and Louise Porter*

This chapter explores ways of addressing police accountability issues through enhanced management of complaints systems. Complaints systems provide accountability for police actions by providing (1) scrutiny of police action; (2) a voice to those who experience police action; and (3) consequences for inappropriate police action and poor performance. Complaints provide a rich and frequently underutilised source of information about conflict between officers and citizens. Formal investigations of complaints generally have very low substantiation rates in terms of conventional legal standards of proof. Nonetheless, studies indicate that problematic patterns of behaviour by police often lie behind complaints. Formal investigative processes also usually fail to address the genuine concerns of complainants and other stakeholders, including the general public and police officers themselves. In a democratic context, complaints need to be taken seriously to address possible injustices and patterns of undesirable behaviour, acting as both a deterrent and a system for learning and improvement.

The chapter begins by analysing the nature of complaints against police, inadequacies in traditional legalistic responses, and innovations in responding to complaints – including the creation of independent agencies to review or process complaints, informal resolution options and early intervention systems. This is followed by a review of perception and experience surveys of three key stakeholder groups in the police complaints and discipline process – the general public, complainants and police – indicating strong overall support for independent processing and for mediation options. The focus then shifts to emerging good practice. This section shows that accountability can be improved through a greater role for independent investigations, and by supplementing investigative and disciplinary approaches with more restorative responses, including informal resolution and mediation. Complaints can also be used as a key learning tool to inform improved policing practices by modifying training and procedures in response to patterns of allegations in the context of a problem-solving and complaints reduction programme. The chapter includes a number of successful case studies from a range of jurisdictions.

## The meaning of complaints against police

In many places, policing is characterised by large volumes of complaints, often at consistently high or increasingly high rates (Prenzler 2009). For example, in England and Wales, with approximately 132,000 police in 2011/12, there were 30,143 complaints made by 30,624 individuals, including 57,714 separate allegations (Home Office 2012; IPCC 2012b). These complaints involved 35,382 police employees, of whom 31,771 were police officers. There were also 6,339 appeals against police decisions on complaints, representing a 3 per cent increase on the previous year. Complaints fell by 9 per cent from the previous year, but the number almost doubled from 2002/03 to 2009/10. In Scotland, with approximately 17,400 police in 2011/12, there were 4,379 complaints, representing an increase of 4 per cent on the previous year (HMICS 2012: 17; PCCS 2012). The number of allegations rose by 13 per cent to 7,933.

Complaints against police represent a dilemma for policymakers and administrators. The purposes of complaints and discipline systems vary across a spectrum between redressing individual alleged wrongs and changing patterns of behaviour (Smith 2004). Finding the right focus is particularly difficult when complaints are variable and occur in large volumes, and when responses are likely to be resource-intensive. Within complaint figures, specific allegation types tend to be highly diverse, including assault and excessive force, financial and legal process corruption, wrongful arrest and detention, discrimination, intimidation, oppressive behaviour, inaction and rudeness. Complaints and allegations require an official response, but investigations generally fail to meet legal standards of proof – whether the criminal standard of 'beyond reasonable doubt' or the civil standard of 'the balance of probability'. Formal investigations, whether conducted internally or externally, typically only achieve substantiation rates of between 10 and 20 per cent (Smith 2004; Prenzler 2009). This might indicate that most complaints are vexatious or, at best, ill-informed. It could also be argued that complaints against police 'come with the territory', in that the exercise of state-sanctioned police powers, especially in restraining and arresting offenders, inevitably entails conflict and alienation (Bittner 1990). However, it is also likely that low substantiation rates for complaints are, at least in part, a function of the absence of independent witnesses or other evidence sources. Surveys of complainants indicate most are genuine in their belief that they suffered an injustice, and in wanting an apology or wanting to stop the same thing happening to other people (CJC 1994; Maguire and Corbett 1991; Schaible *et al.* 2012). Formal complaints are also indicative of a deeper problem of conflict between citizens and police. For example, surveys have shown that up to 90 per cent of people aggrieved by police actions do not make a complaint (e.g. Grace and Bucke 2009: 7).

Effective complaint reduction programmes add to the view that complaints can be indicative of problematic behaviours by officers. Large reductions in complaints have been achieved with interventions based on diagnoses of complaints – in areas such as modified procedures and training (Davis *et al.*

2005; Porter *et al.* 2012). Complaints analysis has also shown that a disproportionate number of officers attract multiple complaints. Closer examination usually shows these officers were engaging in patterns of abusive behaviour (Christopher 1991; Kolts 1992). Complaints are also often concentrated in particular units, such as public order response units involved in high-level applications of force. But controlling for different functions can also show concentrations of complaints that are best explained in terms of inappropriate tactics and poor management (Ede *et al.* 2002a). The issue of objective evidence in complaints is being addressed in some jurisdictions with police body-worn video. One recent evaluation found large reductions in the use of force and in citizen complaints as a result of the introduction of cameras, suggesting that police change their behaviour when placed under surveillance (Ariel 2013). Overall, then, it appears that complaints provide a very useful indicative measure of misconduct, which suggests they are also useful as a performance measure for testing interventions aimed at improving police conduct.

## Tradition and innovation in responding to complaints

For much of their history, police forces around the world have had primary control over complaints. In the main, the response involved token investigations and inaction or outright intimidation of complainants (McLaughlin and Johansen 2002). Judicial inquiries and government reviews around the world have repeatedly found internal investigations functioned to protect corrupt officers and limit damage to the organisation (Prenzler and Ronken 2001). Misconduct scandals were inevitably linked back to failures to take complaints seriously, including complaints or disclosures from police. From the 1990s, as indicated, there was also a growing awareness that 'problem officers' attracted large numbers of complaints, and engaged in excessive force, with management knowledge but no action (e.g. Christopher 1991; Kolts 1992). Complaints systems failed to function as a proper corrective to deviance, further compounding public distrust and alienation from police (Hayes 1997).

Police oversight agencies were one major innovation introduced in response to the problem of large volumes of complaints and failed internal processes. Many democracies now have some form of institutional oversight of police, including oversight of complaints (Porter and Prenzler 2012a). Oversight agencies range across a wide spectrum. The majority tend to be limited to review or audit roles in relation to police investigations and disciplinary decisions. Even those that conduct independent investigations often have their work undermined by the absence of an adjudicative function. While oversight agencies are widely seen as advancing police accountability, they frequently struggle to demonstrate effectiveness, either in making individual officers and managers accountable for specific wrongs or in contributing to improvements in police conduct. These dual internal/external systems are often characterised by high rates of complaints, a revolving door of complainants, large volumes of legal paperwork, and ongoing disputation between police and the oversight agency (Landau 1994; Maguire and Corbett 1991; Prenzler 2009).

There have been a number of other innovations in the management of police complaints, both in terms of addressing grievances and remediating misconduct. One major innovation involved the importation into policing of alternative dispute resolution practices (McLaughlin and Johansen 2002). 'Conciliation', 'informal resolution' and 'local resolution' were intended to address lower-level complaints, often related to customer service issues. On the whole, in comparison to adversarial and investigative processes, these approaches were found to be much faster, much cheaper and more satisfying for all parties (Ede and Barnes 2002). This was also consistent with a trend towards a two-tiered approach to police accountability, involving an early determination between more serious matters, largely of a criminal nature, that warranted an independent investigative and disciplinary process, and types of 'unprofessional behaviour' that warranted a more corrective managerial approach (Smith 2004: 21). In addition, the 'discovery' of the phenomenon of multiple complaints against individual officers led to the development of early intervention systems (Walker *et al.* 2001). Computer-based systems flagged officers (and work units) who registered complaints above a threshold. Interventions in the form of warnings, counselling or retraining triggered behavioural changes that often led to dramatic reductions in complaints (Macintyre *et al.* 2008; Porter *et al.* 2012). More complex systems now pull in numerous data about officers that can be used in early intervention to address a range of human resource management issues. More recently again, a number of oversight agencies have focused on specific 'lessons learnt' from complaints or significant adverse events. This includes reporting on changes in police procedures that have resulted from specific cases in which the oversight agencies worked with police to address systemic problems (Porter 2013).

## Stakeholder perspectives

The following section develops the idea of accountability to stakeholders by summarising the findings of a recent review of surveys of three key groups regarding the police complaints and discipline process: the public, complainants and police (Prenzler *et al.* 2013a). Survey topics included who should process complaints (focusing on the internal/external issue), experiences with different systems, and views on informal resolution and mediation. For the surveys of complainants and police, complaints systems were categorised as 'police-dominated', 'mixed' (generally involving limited review of internal processes) and 'independent'. A total of 94 surveys of the three stakeholder groups were included in the review, based on keyword searches of criminological databases, the Internet and police oversight agency websites up to August 2012. The large majority of surveys were from the United States, the British Isles, Canada and Australia, with one each from South Korea, Israel and the Philippines. A number of surveys were conducted in-house but a large number were conducted by independent survey firms.

## Public opinion

The researchers located 12 public opinion surveys with questions about complaints against police (Prenzler *et al.* 2013: 157–9). Very low or no support was expressed for purely internal systems, with the large majority of respondents supporting the principle of independent investigations. This included 89 per cent across six surveys in Queensland, Australia, and 91 per cent for 'serious complaints' across three surveys in Britain. High levels of support were also expressed for external 'oversight' and 'review'. A set of questions in five of the Queensland surveys included three types of complaints – with respondents supporting police management of lower-level complaints of rudeness, and majority support for an external body dealing with assault and bribery allegations. Reasons for these views were usually not asked in the surveys, but the general inference was that responses related to lack of trust in police to deal fairly and effectively with misconduct, and a belief that independent investigations or oversight would assist accountability.

## Complainants

The review included 26 surveys of complainants in police-dominated systems (Prenzler *et al.* 2013: 159–63). In all but one case, the large majority of complainants – averaging 70 per cent – were dissatisfied. The results were similar in nine complainant surveys involving mixed systems. In several surveys, lack of satisfaction appeared to be related to the fact that complaints were not substantiated, although respondents with substantiated complaints also tended to be dissatisfied. Lack of communication and slowness were key factors. Overall, however, the main factor appeared to be lack of trust in police investigating police. Nine of the surveys asked about the best agency to investigate complaints. The large majority of complainants – averaging 77 per cent – expressed a preference for independent investigations. Ten surveys of complainants in one independent system – the Police Ombudsman for Northern Ireland – showed overall satisfaction levels averaging 59 per cent. The majority satisfaction score for the Ombudsman was correlated with high scores on communication, timeliness, staff attitudes, and perceived fairness and impartiality. (More information on the NI Ombudsman is provided below.)

Five surveys of complainants who experienced some form of police-led informal resolution produced divided results. Satisfaction with the process reached 76 per cent in one survey and dissatisfaction reached 72 per cent in another. Reasons for dissatisfaction concerned lack of information, lack of an apology, lack of seriousness on the part of the target police officers, and lack of opportunity for a face-to-face meeting. Three surveys of complainants concerned experiences with mediation. In a police-led system in England and Wales, 61 per cent of complainants who experienced mediation were satisfied, compared to 33 per cent experiencing informal resolution. Two surveys of complainants who experienced independent mediation in US cities found satisfaction rates around

80 per cent on process. In four surveys of complainants, there was strong support for external management of informal resolution or mediation.

## *Police*

The review found much greater variation when it came to police experiences of complaints systems (Prenzler *et al.* 2013: 163–5). Seven surveys of officers with experience of police-dominated systems found most respondents were divided in their opinions, with less than a majority satisfied or dissatisfied. There was also wide variance in six surveys related to mixed systems. For example, the mixed system in the Philippines produced very high levels of officer satisfaction (80 per cent); whereas the Israeli system, which employed ex-police as investigators, produced very high levels of dissatisfaction (90 per cent). One survey in Denver showed an improvement in officer satisfaction when a police-dominated system was replaced with a mixed system (12 per cent to 37 per cent). In regard to independent processing of complaints in Northern Ireland, there were six surveys available, which showed overall satisfaction for police at 71 per cent.

Six surveys also showed wide variation in officers' general views on internal and external investigations. Support for internal systems tended towards just over 50 per cent, between 20 per cent and 70 per cent for mixed systems, and just under 50 per cent for external systems. Four surveys of police experiences of informal resolution of complaints showed wide variation, with satisfaction between 25 per cent and 83 per cent, but generally much more positive about informal resolution compared to formal investigations. Three surveys regarding experiences of mediation were very positive – registering between 73 per cent and 85 per cent satisfaction.

## Emerging good practice: complaint reduction and improving conduct

As stated earlier, policing typically attracts high numbers of complaints, and complaint numbers are increasingly used as a performance indicator for law enforcement agencies. Traditionally, high numbers of complaints have been taken to indicate problems within police agencies and tensions between police and the public. Conversely, low numbers of complaints can also represent problems; for example, inappropriate complaint handling (ignoring, misclassifying or covering up complaints) or lack of public confidence in a complaints system that deters potential complainants. Indeed, while there are documented cases of police complaint reduction, some police forces have set targets of increased numbers of complaints through increasing the accessibility of the complaints system to under-represented groups (Porter and Prenzler 2012a). In theory, one would expect that reform of a complaints system is likely to cause an initial increase in complaints, as the public gain confidence in the system, followed by a decline as police conduct and police–public relations improve.

Where complaints against police have reduced substantially, this has typically been the outcome of a targeted effort that has included a particular reduction objective and strategy (Davis *et al.* 2005; Walker *et al.* 2000). Strategies to reduce complaints can focus on both the system and the stakeholders. For example, systemic changes to the complaints management system may include increasing accessibility and transparency of the system, streamlining processes of complaint assessment and resolution, reducing time frames for resolving complaints, and increasing public reporting of complaint findings. Strategies focusing on improving stakeholder experiences can include improving communication to complainants and subject officers, improving the procedural fairness of the system, and seeking feedback from stakeholders on their expectations and experiences of the system (examples of which are outlined above). It is also necessary to focus on police behaviour associated with complaints, with systems to train officers, monitor and rectify poor performance, or punish or remove officers who display persistent or serious behavioural problems. Ultimately, though, the combination of strategies employed must be targeted towards a cultural shift to accepting responsibility for problems, and embracing learning at both the individual and organisational levels.

### Responses to complaints: targeting problems

Increasingly, police integrity systems are becoming more advanced and also more diverse, as a variety of potential integrity 'strategies' gain popularity. Integrity systems often evolve over time in a piecemeal approach that responds to emerging trends in the field, but with little systematic evaluative evidence about 'what works' (Porter and Prenzler 2012a). Further, due to the variety of forms of misconduct and opportunities for misconduct – not to mention cultural, economic and geographic differentiation between policing environments – a 'one size fits all' integrity system is unlikely to be effective.

One way to target a reduction in complaints is to first understand the nature of the complaints received. Understanding the underlying patterns of complaints across the organisation can help to inform where prevention or response efforts need to be targeted, as well as what might be most effective at identifying and removing the causes of complaints. For example, Ede *et al.* (2002a) used 'hot spot' analysis to examine the concentration and prevalence of police complaints across different units in the Queensland Police Service, Australia. By coding units according to duty type ('General Station', 'Criminal Investigation Branch', 'Traffic' and 'Other Duties'), they found areas of high concentration and prevalence of complaints, suggesting that prevention techniques should be tailored to address these 'hotspots'. Other variables shown to differentiate among 'types' of complaints include officer rank (Porter and Warrender 2009) indicating that, potentially, officer age and experience may also structure certain 'hotspots' of inappropriate conduct.

Complaints analysis can also highlight a particular type of problem, such as excessive force, which can be targeted for reduction. To illustrate, Prenzler *et al.*

(2013b) reviewed seven case studies of successful force reduction that involved identifying force-related problems (complaints, injuries, deaths) within police departments. They found a number of consistent reduction strategies across the case studies, including setting a specific complaint reduction agenda. Other strategies targeted individual officers (through profiling multiple complaints and remedial training) as well as organisational systems, such as policies and procedures, incident reporting systems, and analysis of cases to learn lessons. For example, in Australia, the Tasmania Police reduced assault complaints after patterns of multiple assault-related complaints were identified and provided to the districts involved, so they could target subject officers under their command (Porter *et al.* 2012). Recently in the UK, disproportionate complaints of racist conduct and excessive force by the Metropolitan Police Service's Tactical Support Group led to an intervention programme associated with large reductions in allegations. Interventions included better screening of applicants (including through complaints histories), specialist supervisor workshops, creation of a 'Professional Standards Team' within the group, and training development options for officers with multiple complaints (IPCC 2012a).

While the subject of complaints is typically categorised within police recording systems, such as 'assault' or 'criminal matter', a number of more sophisticated 'typologies' of misconduct have been explored in the literature to describe subtypes of misconduct. Such typologies could be used to identify particular misconduct problems, as evidenced through complaints, for targeted prevention. Early typologies, such as that offered by Roebuck and Barker (1974), outlined a number of categories of misconduct based upon the activity involved (for example, 'opportunistic theft', 'corruption of authority', 'kickbacks' and 'shakedowns'). Such a typology is often used by police oversight agencies to categorise matters received and investigated. In Australia, Ede *et al.* (2002b) examined police complaints data from the police oversight agency of that time in Queensland (the Criminal Justice Commission) and identified Roebuck and Barker's categories within the allegations. Examination of the allegations within categories, such as 'opportunistic thefts', led them to suggest particular prevention strategies that could be tailored to the patterns of activity involved. However, while typologies of this nature provide an idea of the variation of activity that can be regarded as misconduct, the specific categories reflect the trends of the time and, as opportunities evolve (for example, with new technology), such a typology could require an increasing number of categories that may be unwieldy for the purpose of identifying avenues for response and prevention.

More recent typologies have attempted to simplify misconduct activity to the underlying nature of the infraction. For example, Punch (2000) simply distinguishes between 'corruption', 'misconduct' and 'crime'. As noted above, Smith (2004) supported the differentiation between more serious matters, requiring formal investigation, and professional conduct matters amenable to more informal restorative responses. He also usefully proposed a third tier concerned with police policy matters. A number of recent efforts concerned with multidimensional typologies have built on Punch's work. Dean *et al.* (2010) and Dean and Gottschalk (2011) offered a typology incorporating both the type of behaviour and the level of seriousness. Specifically they drew distinctions between misconduct, corruption and 'predatory policing' on one dimension, and whether the behaviour is at the individual, group or organisational level on a second dimension. Further, Porter and Warrender (2009) explored misconduct cases for the existence of patterns between features describing 'who' and 'what' is involved and for what gains ('why'). The analysis uncovered three themes, or subtypes of cases, which were similar to Punch's (2000) typology, but which provide detail on the nature of those incidents and who was involved. Much like the earlier work of Ede *et al.* (2002b), Porter and Warrender (2009) argue that identifying 'types', and the common features of cases within these types, provides a useful framework for tailoring prevention efforts. Indeed, given the variation in misconduct cases, but the existence of some broad level similarities on certain features, prevention efforts might best be targeted towards themes of misconduct. Thus, prevention both avoids the one-size-fits-all model, and provides potential cost–benefit improvements over an individualistic case-by-case response model. Resources can, therefore, be targeted at multiple incidents, but specific features, to ensure the greatest impact.

### *Responses to complaints: targeting 'problem officers'*

Similar to targeting particular problem areas, strategies have also emerged for targeting 'problem officers'; that is, officers who are subject to above average numbers of complaints. Early Warning Systems, or Early Intervention Systems, are designed to monitor complaints, or indeed other behavioural indicators, to focus attention on recurring problems that need addressing. While an EIS can operate to monitor work units, the primary focus is typically on individual officers, with a system set up to create an alert when an individual meets a certain threshold (e.g. of complaints in a given period). This is similar to the ideas in the section above regarding profiling complaints across organisations, but with 'hotspots' of complaints being at the individual level.

Early Warning Systems were initially criticised for labelling officers as 'bad apples' and, in turn, fostering resentment and further misconduct (Walker *et al.* 2000). Indeed, organisational justice research informs us that feelings of unfair treatment can negatively affect job performance and rule adherence (Tyler *et al.* 2007). In contrast, perceptions of organisational justice have been positively linked to police officers' 'attitudes toward serving the public' (Myhill and Bradford 2013: 339) as well as a reduced likelihood of police officers supporting the code of silence or noble cause corruption (Wolfe and Piquero 2011). Similar to principles of organisational justice (Greenberg 1990), operant leadership (Komaki 1998) draws on the principles of operant conditioning to promote the effectiveness of providing antecedents for behaviour (clear guidance on expectations), monitoring of behaviour, and consistent performance-related feedback. Feedback, or consequences of behaviour, must be seen to be fair to be effective. Specifically, it is important that consequences are consistent, both within and between individuals (similar performance receives similar consequences), thus avoiding feelings of favouritism or discrimination as well as seeing value in performing well (receiving reward and avoiding punishment).

Recent developments in policing show several initiatives that can promote concepts such as leader visibility and fairness, and timeliness, consistency and proportionality of responses to performance throughout the organisation. For example, values statements, codes of conduct and ethics training can provide clear expectations of behaviour (antecedents). Management intervention models, devolution of complaints handling to local managers and Early Intervention Systems provide mechanisms for monitoring individual officer performance and providing responses to performance issues.

Modern Early Intervention Systems are increasingly designed with remedial measures in mind, serving to identify and correct behaviour before it leads to serious problems (Porter and Prenzler 2012a). From this perspective, the systems can be sold as a means of saving officers from career-damaging incidents and investigations (Porter *et al.* 2012; PERF 2011). Early Intervention Systems can provide an objective tool for highlighting potential 'problem' officers for supervisors to investigate. Adopting a process of procedural fairness in management also supports the process; for example, providing officers with the opportunity to discuss and explain performance issues. Further, disciplinary systems are increasingly incorporating initiatives for ensuring consistent responses that are commensurate with the severity of the infraction. For example, the Queensland Police Service introduced a recording system for disciplinary action that enables supervisors to view past responses to similar infractions within the organisation when making disciplinary decisions (Porter and Prenzler 2012a). Further, Shane (2012) proposes a disciplinary matrix that takes into account the level of seriousness, among other factors, and prescribes the appropriate discipline level to provide further objectivity to the decision. A combination of these initiatives, through incorporation of the leadership qualities mentioned above, can offer a complementary model for improving leadership, management and, ultimately, integrity (Porter and Prenzler 2012a).

## Emerging good practice: improving police–complainant relations

### *Independent investigations*

Public confidence in police, and positive police–community relations, are also likely to be enhanced by a more direct role for oversight agencies in the management of complaints – certainly for more serious complaints or as an option in a negotiated process with complainants. The evidence is overwhelming that police internal investigations compound the cynicism and distrust already felt by complainants. Oversight agencies that merely audit or review police investigations also aggravate the alienation felt by complainants. When oversight agencies refer matters back to police there is an added sense of betrayal on top of the sense of distrust (Landau 1994). Independent investigations free police from the stigma of bias and the hopeless task of convincing complainants they are impartial. This is a point conceded by police to some extent. Several surveys in Prenzler *et al.*'s review found police support for this proposition at about one-third (2013: 164). However, one survey in the UK put police agreement at 85 per cent. In Northern Ireland, 70 per cent of police who experienced the independent system supported the view that it 'makes police more accountable' (Table 3.1). What constitutes 'independence' is, however, far from a simple proposition (Savage 2013; McLaughlin and Johansen 2002). 'Civilian' investigators (and mediators) may be compromised by their relationships with police, and oversight agencies which are institutionally separate from police normally employ some former police officers. Consequently, organisational culture and public perceptions are important in judging the independence of police integrity agencies (Savage 2013; McLaughlin and Johansen 2002).

In addition, substantive independence on its own is not a panacea for stakeholder dissatisfaction (Savage 2013). External agencies will still need to pay close attention to process issues of communication and fair treatment; and seek to address the root causes of complaints, in part through working with police. The Office of the Police Ombudsman for Northern Ireland, established in 2000, presents as the best test case for independence (Savage 2013). The Police (Northern Ireland) Act 1998 requires the Ombudsman to determine how complaints against police will be handled. This includes discretion to refer matters to police for investigation, but it appears that all, or almost all, formal investigations are conducted by the Office (Savage 2013; Seneviratne 2004). The Office makes disciplinary recommendations to the Chief Constable, but also has an authority to direct disciplinary proceedings. A 2011 review found that some investigations into legacy cases may have lacked adequate independence (Criminal Justice Inspection Northern Ireland 2011). However, the review supported the Ombudsman's independence in processing contemporary complaints. The review noted that 'there is a substantial proportion of investigative staff (around 41%) from a former police background' (ibid.: 32), and there was an implication that this was above an appropriate threshold for public confidence. Nonetheless, when selection standards and 'operational protocols' were considered, the review found that, 'in the main, the necessary safeguards are in place to protect the operational independence of the Police Ombudsman' (ibid.).

As outlined above, the Ombudsman's Office has attracted relatively high levels of satisfaction from both complainants and police officers who were the subject of complaints. More detailed and updated figures for the last five years are provided in Table 3.1. The high satisfaction rates for police show clearly that officer concerns about bias can be alleviated by an independent system that is professional and responsive. If anything, comparatively lower satisfaction rates for complainants might suggest bias favouring police. However, this is more likely the effect of the evidence problem in complaints, given the high scores from complainants for impartiality, seriousness and fairness. It is also clear from

*Table 3.1* Per cent complainant and police satisfaction levels, Police Ombudsman for Northern Ireland

| Criteria | 2008/9 | | 2009/10 | | 2010/11 | | 2011/12 | | 2012/13 | |
|---|---|---|---|---|---|---|---|---|---|---|
| Complainant/Police | C | P | C | P | C | P | C | P | C | P |
| Overall | 59 | 68 | 65 | 68 | 59 | 74 | 52 | 72 | 52 | 73 |
| Outcome | 42 | 81 | 46 | 80 | 41 | 86 | 40 | 82 | 37 | 80 |
| Fairness | 73 | 83 | 74 | 82 | 70 | 85 | 66 | 83 | 62 | 85 |
| Timeliness | 58 | 47 | 60 | 52 | 58 | 56 | 53 | 57 | 51 | 61 |
| Frequency of updates | 65 | 48 | 67 | 57 | 63 | 58 | 55 | 56 | 58 | 60 |
| Seriousness | 61 | – | 66 | – | 63 | – | 55 | – | 55 | – |
| Staff polite | 96 | 98 | 97 | 96 | 96 | 96 | 95 | 98 | 94 | 96 |
| Staff professional | 89 | 93 | 91 | 92 | 89 | 93 | 89 | 94 | 84 | 92 |
| Staff not interested | 21 | 8 | 20 | 9 | 19 | 8 | 20 | 3 | 24 | 5 |
| Staff impartial | 67 | 91 | 67 | 88 | 78 | 93 | 76 | 93 | 75 | 91 |
| Staff easy to understand | 90 | – | 92 | – | 90 | – | 90 | – | 91 | – |
| Would use system again | 69 | – | 71 | – | 69 | – | 64 | – | 63 | – |
| Makes police more accountable | – | 69 | – | 68 | – | 68 | – | 69 | – | 73 |

Source: Police Ombudsman for Northern Ireland 2013: 43–5.

the data that complainants can be unhappy with the outcome while being satisfied with the fairness and responsiveness of the system.

The Northern Ireland Police Ombudsman appears to have gone a long way towards satisfying a number of key criteria for complaints investigations. Has it also improved complainants' view of police? This is a common question in complainant surveys, but not one used in the Northern Ireland surveys. The positive responses from complainants and police imply a degree of reconciliation, but more attention to this issue would be useful. There are very positive indicators in public perceptions of the Ombudsman. Over the last five years, on average, 83 per cent of respondents in public awareness surveys considered the Ombudsman independent of police, 79 per cent were confident that the Ombudsman dealt with complaints impartially, 85 per cent were confident they would be treated fairly if they made a complaint, and 85 per cent believed the Ombudsman would 'help ensure that the police do a good job' (PONI 2013: 42, 38–9, 41). Catholics and Protestants have similar positive views of the Ombudsman, and there are very few complaints against police concerning sectarian discrimination.

One assumption behind the creation of oversight agencies is that they will make police more accountable by substantiating complaints at a higher rate than occurs in police-dominated systems. In the Northern Ireland case, the evidence is unclear on this issue because of the absence of comparable data pre-Ombudsman (PONI 2010). Currently, about 40 per cent of allegations are 'not substantiated', 4 per cent are deemed 'ill founded', 20 per cent are not pursued due to complainant non-cooperation, and 1 per cent are 'substantiated – no action recommended' (PONI 2013: 32). On average, per year, approximately ten matters are referred to the public prosecutor with a recommendation for prosecution. Four per cent are sent to the police for 'recommended action' in the form of 'advice and guidance', 'management discussion', 'superintendent's written warning', 'formal disciplinary proceedings' or 'training/ops/supervision'. About 97 per cent of these recommendations were reported as 'accepted' in 2012/13 (ibid.: 33).

The effectiveness of oversight should also be evident in complaint trends. In Northern Ireland, complaints rose for two years following the establishment of the Ombudsman's Office – consistent with the view that a more open and independent system will attract more complaints. Complaints then fluctuated for eight years before trending down slightly over the last four years – from 3,542 in 2009/10 to 3,265 in 2012/13 (PONI 2013: 26). In a more promising trend, the number of allegations fell more sharply and consistently – from 6,501 in 2009/10 to 5,200 in 2012/13 – and the number of police attracting multiple complaints has also been falling (ibid.: 26).

Since 2010, the Ombudsman has been working with the Police Service on a 'focused PSNI Complaints Reduction Strategy', although a partnership approach to conduct issues predates this initiative (PONI 2013: 6). The Ombudsman's Office has documented a large number of areas of cooperation where police have implemented recommendations to improve procedures. Areas of agreed change have included search procedures, baton usage, firing of baton rounds, vehicle pursuits, handcuffing, and police responses to hate crimes and child abuse (PONI 2010). Two areas of cooperation that appear to have been particularly fruitful involved measures to address incivility allegations and duty failure allegations related to investigations (PONI 2010, 2013).

### *Alternative dispute resolution*

The review of stakeholder surveys by Prenzler *et al.* (2013) also found evidence that the interests of complainants and police can be more effectively addressed through carefully managed forms of informal resolution and, especially, mediation. Some systems of informal resolution operated by police received very high participant satisfaction scores. Complainants appreciated the personal communication, being able to have their say and receive an apology. Dissatisfaction related to lack of communication, non-receipt of an apology, and police managers being biased or not taking the process seriously. However, complainants who experienced informal resolution tended not to have a better view of police, and they had little faith that informal resolution would change police behaviour or improve accountability (e.g. CJC 1994; PONI 2005).

Informal resolution can function as a convenient 'bureaucratic suppression of a dispute' and complainants are alive to this possibility (Young *et al.* 2005: 300). Systems need to guard against misuse of alternative dispute resolution options as a quick and easy means of dispensing with complaints. One way to take the interests of complainants (and police) more seriously is to enhance the restorative capacity of the complaints system through mediation. This is a resource-intensive option, but one that attracts the highest rates of participant satisfaction. Both sides are allowed to have their say face-to-face in a managed environment with a skilled mediator who works towards a mutual agreement or understanding. However, despite high satisfaction rates, where data are available, they indicate that complainants are not likely to be convinced that mediation will lead to the kinds of changes in police behaviour that they expect (e.g. Young *et al.* 2005). It is likely that greater faith in the system will require evidence that the mediation process feeds into a larger system for improving police conduct (McLaughlin and Johansen 2002).

## Cooperation of police and oversight agencies: a problem-oriented policing approach

As outlined above, external oversight agencies were originally introduced to increase the accountability of police agencies in dealing with complaints, as well as to provide an independent investigative function to overcome problems, or perceptions, of police bias in internal investigations. However, this 'watchdog' role of oversight agencies is increasingly broadening to encompass functions that support internal reform and build capacity within police agencies. Many oversight agencies (with the exception of the PONI mentioned above) do not have the resources to investigate all complaints against police, but need to work with police agencies in managing the internal investigation process. The investigative function has always been a source of tensions between oversight agencies and police, as well as public concern regarding perceptions of independence and accountability. As noted, there is typically a strong preference among members of the public for independent investigations over internal or mixed models. However, the broader functions of oversight agencies, such as the prevention of misconduct/complaints, may benefit from closer inter-agency partnerships – subject to a watching brief against police capture of the process and the undermining of independence (Seneviratne 2004). In that regard, reducing complaints against police and reducing police–community conflict is likely to benefit from the 'Problem-Oriented Policing' framework that has successfully guided police efforts to reduce crime-related problems (Goldstein 2003).

### Case studies

Porter (2013) argued that the problem-oriented approach usefully describes ways in which oversight agencies can work with police to achieve internal reform, and reported on two case studies to illustrate this process. In the United States, in Portland, Oregon, beginning in 2006, a problem with excessive force by police was addressed by a task force consisting of the Portland Police Bureau, Portland's Independent Police Review Division and a Citizen Review Committee. The task force analysed a number of sources of information, including use of force data held by the police, and produced a report with 16 recommendations. The Police Chief agreed to an implementation programme, and the task force closely monitored the process and suggested refinements. Over a two-year period, the programme produced significant reductions in reported use of force, citizen complaints of excessive force, and injuries to both officers and citizens.

Second, in Queensland, Australia, the Queensland Police Service (QPS) and its oversight body the Crime and Misconduct Commission jointly undertook a review of the police Taser policy, following a number of adverse Tasering incidents. The review team analysed the international scientific literature and QPS data on Taser deployments. The 2009 report made 27 recommendations, emphasising the importance of ongoing collaboration between the two agencies in monitoring implementation and improving policy. A 2011 evaluation found that implementation of the recommendations led to major improvements in the use of Tasers, with less reliance on the weapons for control of suspects, and reductions in multiple and prolonged applications.

### Applying the SARA problem-solving model

The case studies illustrated the productive adoption of a problem-oriented prevention framework (Porter 2013). The key elements of the framework are that a problem is the basic unit of interest, rather than an individual complaint or case of misconduct, and that addressing problems means dealing with the causal conditions, rather than just reactively responding to the misconduct behaviour (e.g. through disciplinary means). It is, therefore, important for police to routinely and systematically analyse problems to identify and understand the issues, including the issues for various stakeholders. Central to the process is the importance of partnerships in solving problems, as well as evaluating the effectiveness of any implemented 'solution'. Evaluation is important for organisational learning, as well as providing an evidence base for future solutions, both for the agencies involved, and more widely. Specifically, Porter (2013) illustrates the approach through the application of the SARA problem-solving model, which describes a problem-solving process: Scan, Analyse, Respond and Assess (Eck and Spelman 1987).

The first two SARA stages are *scanning* the environment to identify the problem, and *analysing* the problem to understand the issues involved. These stages are similar to the concepts outlined above, which discussed ways to target problems through monitoring of complaints information and analysing complaints data for 'hotspots', or patterns of commonly occurring activity. Oversight agencies are in a prime position to scan for problems, having access to databases of complaints and investigation materials. The studies by Ede *et al.* (2002a, 2002b), mentioned above, illustrate how such data can be used in this way to identify problems, both in terms of problem units/divisions, and types of problems (activities/allegations). Increasingly, oversight agencies have their own internal capabilities for conducting such analyses, with many oversight agencies now including research areas in their portfolio.

After scanning and analysing the problem, the next stages are utilising this information to plan and implement a *response*, followed by *assessing*, or evaluating, the impact of that response. While oversight agencies can recommend responses, the implementation is typically the responsibility of the police. Tensions can arise where recommended responses are viewed by police as unrealistic, resource-intensive or unnecessary. Collaboration between oversight agencies and police agencies, within the boundaries of independence, to design and implement response strategies would facilitate acceptance and traction.

One concept continually highlighted in the field of police integrity is the existence of cycles of corruption, or 'scandal and reform' (Sherman 1978; Smith 2006). Agencies that do respond to problems can, over time, become complacent, or lack knowledge transfer mechanisms that are necessary for continued prevention. Central to this is the documentation and communication of knowledge – particularly in evaluating reform efforts and documenting successes or failures, or 'what works'. The final stage of the SARA model – Assess – is, therefore, vital in completing the problem-solving process and contributing to sustained improvement. Given their independence, and potential expertise, oversight agencies can be well placed to conduct or contribute to evaluations to assess the effectiveness of reforms. They can also produce public reports to document the results of their evaluations. However, such evaluations will often require the cooperation of the police agency, for example to provide feedback and data to assess the effects. Agencies, therefore, need to work together to implement and evaluate responses, and ensure knowledge is adequately captured and learning is not lost. Indeed, oversight agencies increasingly offer support services and capacity building to police agencies through provision of both informal advice and formal education/training, as well as promotion of values and lessons learned from their experience of investigations and analysis of complaints (Porter and Prenzler 2012a, 2012b).

## Conclusion

In traditional police complaints systems, large numbers of allegations are made by dissatisfied citizens and processed by police in an adversarial system ostensibly concerned with fact-finding and due process. Very few complaints are substantiated and there is a wide-ranging view that the system is biased against complainants and fails to provide proper democratic accountability for the exercise of police powers. Nothing much changes. The complaints continue at high volumes, and there is a failure to address questionable police behaviours that lie behind complaints. In response to this problem, innovation has occurred in a number of areas, including informal complaints resolution and civilian oversight. Some improvements are evidenced from these developments. However, informal resolution is generally too superficial to adequately address the aspirations of complainants or improve police behaviour. Civilian oversight is also often limited to a review role that fails to deliver appropriate levels of independence, input into disciplinary decisions and improvements in conduct.

This ongoing state of chronic failure is not inevitable. Support is slowly growing for an effective research-based approach to reform. The first step involves viewing complaints as providing a window on police conduct problems. Analysis of the factors behind complaints can then provide a guide to modifications in procedures and training that produce real changes in police behaviour, which in turn translate into large reductions in complaints. This process is likely to be significantly enhanced through a cooperative working relationship between police departments and oversight agencies aimed at problem-solving, using a standard POP methodology. At the same time, the enlargement of independent investigation and adjudication of complaints – properly managed – is likely to produce significant improvements in the experiences of both complainants and police; as well as satisfying the public interest around perceived impartiality in the management of complaints. These positive outcomes are likely to be further enhanced through opportunities for independent mediation. However, even the best managed system of independent investigations and mediation is unlikely to improve accountability and police–community relations unless it is combined with an explicit complaints reduction and problem-solving programme.

## References

Ariel, B. (2013) *Self-Awareness to Being Watched and Socially Desirable Behavior: A Field Experiment on the Effect of Body-Worn Cameras on Police Use-of-Force*, Washington, DC: Police Foundation.

Bittner, E. (1990) *Aspects of Police Work*, Boston: Northeastern University Press.

Christopher, W. (1991) *Report of the Independent Commission on the Los Angeles Police Department*, Los Angeles: Independent Commission on the LAPD.

CJC (1994) *Informal Complaint Resolution in the Queensland Police Service: An Evaluation*, Brisbane: Criminal Justice Commission.

Criminal Justice Inspection Northern Ireland (2011) *An Inspection into the Independence of the Office of the Police Ombudsman for Northern Ireland*, Belfast.

Davis, R., Mateu-Gelabert, P. and Miller, J. (2005) 'Can Effective Policing Also be Respectful? Two Examples in the South Bronx', *Police Quarterly*, 8: 229–47.

Dean, G. and Gottschalk, P. (2011) 'Continuum of Police Crime: An Empirical Study of Court Cases', *International Journal of Police Science and Management*, 13: 16–28.

Dean, G., Bell, P. and Lauchs, M. (2010) 'Conceptual Framework for Managing Knowledge of Police Deviance', *Policing and Society: An International Journal of Research and Policy*, 20: 204–22.

Eck, J. and Spelman, W. (1987) *Problem-Solving: Problem-Oriented Policing in Newport News*, Washington, DC: National Institute of Justice.

Ede, A. and Barnes, M. (2002) 'Alternative Strategies for Resolving Complaints', in T. Prenzler and J. Ransley (eds) *Police Reform: Building Integrity*, Sydney: Federation Press.

Ede, A., Homel, R. and Prenzler, T. (2002a) 'Reducing Complaints against Police and Preventing Misconduct: A Diagnostic Study Using Hot Spot Analysis', *Australian and New Zealand Journal of Criminology*, 35: 27–42.

Ede, A., Homel, R. and Prenzler, T. (2002b) 'Situational Corruption Prevention', in T. Prenzler and J. Ransley (eds) *Police Reform: Building Integrity*, Sydney: Federation Press.

Goldstein, H. (2003) 'On Further Developing Problem-oriented Policing: The Most Critical Need, the Major Impediments, and a Proposal', *Crime Prevention Studies*, 15: 13–47.

Grace, K. and Bucke, T. (2009) *Public Annoyance and Complaints about the Police: Findings from the 2006/07 British Crime Survey*, London: Independent Police Complaints Commission.

Greenberg, J. (1990) 'Organizational Justice: Yesterday, Today, and Tomorrow', *Journal of Management*, 16: 399–432.

Hayes, M. (1997) *A Police Ombudsman for Northern Ireland?* Belfast: Home Office Stationery Office.

Her Majesty's Inspector of Constabulary for Scotland (HMICS) (2012) *Annual Report 2011/12*, Edinburgh: HMICS.

Home Office (2012) *Police Service Strength, England and Wales, 30 September 2012*, London: Home Office.

IPCC (2012a) *Metropolitan Police Service Territorial Support Group: A Review of Complaints Data and IPCC Cases 2008–2012*, London: Independent Police Complaints Commission.

IPCC (2012b) *Police Complaints: Statistics for England and Wales, 2011/12*, London: Independent Police Complaints Commission.

Kolts, J. (1992) *Los Angeles County Sheriff's Department: Report by Special Counsel*, Los Angeles (s.n.).

Komaki, J. (1998) *Leadership from an Operant Perspective*, London: Routledge.

Landau, T. (1994) *Public Complaints against the Police: A View from Complainants*, Toronto: University of Toronto.

Macintyre, S., Prenzler, T. and Chapman, J. (2008) 'Early Intervention to Reduce Complaints: An Australian Victoria Police Initiative', *International Journal of Police Science and Management*, 10: 238–50.

McLaughlin, E. and Johansen, A. (2002) 'A Force for Change? The Prospects for Applying Restorative Justice to Citizen Complaints against the Police in England and Wales', *British Journal of Criminology*, 42(3): 635–53.

Maguire, M. and Corbett, C. (1991) *A Study of the Police Complaints System*, London: HMSO.

Myhill, A. and Bradford, B. (2013) 'Overcoming Cop Culture? Organizational Justice and Police Officers' Attitudes toward the Public', *Policing: An International Journal of Police Strategies and Management*, 36: 338–56.

PCCS (2012) *Police Complaints: Statistics for Scotland 2011–12*, Hamilton, Scotland: Police Complaints Commissioner for Scotland.

PERF (2011) *Review of Use of Force in the Albuquerque Police Department*, Washington, DC: Police Executive Research Forum.

PONI (2005) *An Evaluation of Police-Led Informal Resolution of Police Complaints in Northern Ireland: The Complainants' Perspective*, Belfast: Police Ombudsman for Northern Ireland.

PONI (2010) *Developments in Police Complaints – Ten Years On*, Belfast: Police Ombudsman for Northern Ireland.

PONI (2013) *Annual Statistical Bulletin 2012/13*, Belfast. Police Ombudsman for Northern Ireland.

Porter, L.E. (2013) 'Beyond "oversight": A Problem-oriented Approach to Police Reform', *Police Practice and Research. An International Journal*, 14: 169–81.

Porter, L.E. and Prenzler, T. (2012a) *Police Integrity Management in Australia: Global Lessons For Combating Police Misconduct*, Boca Raton, FL: CRC Press – Taylor & Francis.

Porter, L.E. and Prenzler, T. (2012b) 'Police Oversight in the United Kingdom: The Balance of Independence and Collaboration', *International Journal of Law, Crime and Justice*, 40: 152–71.

Porter, L.E. and Warrender, C. (2009) 'A Multivariate Model of Police Deviance: Examining the Nature of Corruption, Crime and Misconduct', *Policing and Society*, 19: 79–99.

Porter, L.E., Prenzler, T. and Fleming, J. (2012) 'Complaint Reduction in the Tasmania Police', *Policing and Society*, 22: 426–47.

Prenzler, T. (2009) *Police Corruption: Preventing Misconduct and Maintaining Integrity*, Boca Raton, FL: CRC Press – Taylor & Francis.

Prenzler, T. and Ronken, C. (2001) 'Models of Police Oversight: A Critique', *Policing and Society*, 11: 151–80.

Prenzler, T., Mihinjac, M. and Porter, L.E. (2013a) 'Reconciling Stakeholder Interests in Police Complaints and Discipline Systems', *Police Practice and Research: An International Journal*, 14: 155–68.

Prenzler, T., Porter, L. and Alpert, G. (2013b) 'Reducing Police Use of Force: Case Studies and Prospects', *Aggression and Violent Behavior: A Review Journal*, 18: 343–56.

Punch, M. (2000) 'Police Corruption and its Prevention', *European Journal on Criminal Policy and Research*, 8: 301–24.

Roebuck, J. and Barker, T. (1974) 'A Typology of Police Corruption', *Social Problems*, 21: 423–37.

Savage, S.P. (2013) 'Thinking Independence: Calling the Police to Account through the Independent Investigation of Police Complaints', *British Journal of Criminology*, 53: 94–112.

Schaible, L.M., De Angelis, J., Wolf, B. and Rosenthal, R. (2012) 'Denver's Citizen/Police Complaint Mediation Program: Officer and Complainant Satisfaction', *Criminal Justice Policy Review*, 24: 626–50.

Seneviratne, M. (2004) 'Policing the Police in the United Kingdom', *Policing and Society*, 14(4): 329–47.

Shane, J.M. (2012) 'Police Employee Disciplinary Matrix: An Emerging Concept', *Police Quarterly*, 15: 62–91.

Sherman, L.W. (1978) *Scandal and Reform: Reforming Police Corruption*, Berkeley and Los Angeles: University of California Press.

Smith, G. (2004) 'Rethinking Police Complaints', *British Journal of Criminology*, 44(1): 15–33.

Smith, G. (2006) 'A Most Enduring Problem: Police Complaints Reform in England and Wales', *Journal of Social Policy*, 35: 121–41.

Tyler, T.R., Callahan, P.E. and Frost, J. (2007) 'Armed, and Dangerous(?): Motivating Rule Adherence among Agents of Social Control', *Law and Society Review*, 41: 457–92.

Walker, S., Alpert, G.P. and Kenney, D.J. (2000) 'Early Warning Systems for Police: Concept, History, and Issues', *Police Quarterly*, 3: 132.

Walker, S., Alpert, G.P. and Kenney, D.J. (2001) *Early Warning Systems: Responding to the Problem Police Officer*, Washington, DC: National Institute of Justice.

Wolfe, S.E. and Piquero, A. (2011) 'Organizational Justice and Police Misconduct', *Criminal Justice and Behavior*, 38: 332–53.

Young, R., Hoyle, C., Cooper, K. and Hill, R. (2005) 'Informal Resolution of the Complaints against the Police: A Quasi-experimental Test of Restorative Justice', *Criminal Justice*, 5: 279–317.

# 4 Getting behind the blue curtain

## Managing police integrity

*Michael Rowe, Louise Westmarland and Courtney Hougham*

This chapter explores emerging strategies designed to reduce police officer corruption and malfeasance. Codes of ethical conduct, disciplinary measures, cultural programmes, training and professionalisation of policing have developed in response to various challenges to police integrity. The chapter explores each of these – drawing on international examples – and considers how they operate in relation to dominant police subcultural values of loyalty and camaraderie that have often amounted to a 'blue curtain' that prevents officers reporting concerns about the misconduct of their colleagues. It is concluded that although responses to misconduct by police have developed in useful ways, significant challenges remain. In terms of a future pluralised policing environment, the cultural and institutional contexts in which misconduct and corruption develop remain largely overlooked by policymakers, politicians, sections of the media and academic researchers.

## How did we get into this mess? The recent British experience of police malpractice

The police not only have to be accountable to their publics, but also have to be seen to be accountable. Open and transparent processes of accountability need to be maintained right across the range of police ranks and duties in order to be effective. In effect, one 'bad apple' may not really taint the barrel but in the eyes of the public, a chief constable who is sacked for corruption indicates an inability to maintain integrity across the force. Just as minor crimes might send powerful signals to communities, relatively minor (in legal or material terms) incidents of malfeasance can also have significant repercussions for police legitimacy (Murphy *et al.* 2008). Several recent high-profile scandals have made the police seem little better than a real-life version of the fictional television programme *Life on Mars*. The documentary *The Secret Policeman*, as McLaughlin argues (2007), showed them in an even worse light. In addition, numerous public reports into policing in the UK have unearthed a catalogue of inappropriate – and in some cases illegal – behaviour (see for example Ellison's report into the impact of corruption on the investigation of the murder of Stephen Lawrence, Home Office 2014). In the light of all of this, what place accountability for the police? In this chapter we review recent developments and analyse results from a survey of officer perspectives on integrity. We argue that management and leadership strategies have yet to develop necessary approaches to problems of corruption that are rooted in institutional practices and are not limited to the personal deviance of individual officers. A focus on the institutional context suggests that as the agencies delivering policing become more diverse, ranging across the public, private and third sectors, and transverse national and constabulary boundaries, the dynamics of misconduct will also become more complex. Existing approaches are woefully ill-prepared to respond.

Lord Leveson's 2012 inquiry into press misconduct suggested that 'guarding the guards' is an ongoing challenge for British policing. In part this might reflect more widespread concerns about standards in public life, not least those surrounding politicians in the wake of a series of 'expenses scandals' and public malfeasance in various institutions. For a range of reasons public confidence in policing is at the lowest level ever recorded, research by the Home Office (2011) suggested. In 2012 the Independent Police Complaints Commission (IPCC) highlighted substantial levels of complaints from the public about corruption and that few officers were ever charged with any offences. Much of the recent concern about the threat of police officer corruption remains anecdotal and circumstantial. Requests by journalists under Freedom of Information legislation in 2011 discovered that hundreds of police officers are formally charged and disciplined each year, but the process is closed to public scrutiny. Partly in response to these concerns the Home Secretary recently announced that the IPCC would be given greater resources to investigate police corruption (*Guardian* 2013a), although this is to be done by transferring existing capacity from local forces to the Commission. The College of Policing, which became operational in England and Wales in 2013, is committed to revising and strengthening a police Code of Ethics and to implementing greater coherence to in-service training for officers throughout their careers. Advantages and challenges associated with introducing police codes of ethics are reviewed below.

These debates have been fuelled by an extended series of revelations alleging police corruption or unethical behaviour. Since 2011 in England and Wales many of the revelations of police misconduct have focused on the personal morals and professional ethics of serving officers. A series of incidents has revealed the police service in less than exemplary light. Some of these have been historical, such as allegations that senior officers from South Yorkshire Police falsified information to denigrate victims of the 1989 Hillsborough disaster, that officers from West Yorkshire Police had inappropriate personal links with the celebrity Jimmy Savile which inhibited the proper investigation of his paedophilia, and that officers from the Metropolitan Police had spied on the family and friends of Stephen Lawrence. Other controversies have related to more contemporary events, such as those investigated by the enquiries of *Operation Elveden* into the misuse of confidential information and corrupt payments to police, the illicit use of undercover police to spy on peaceful protestors, and various claims of nepotism surrounding the appointment of staff. Despite the

Association of Chief Police Officers (ACPO) championing a published Code of Conduct since 2004, even police leaders still seem uncertain about what would be seen as ethically acceptable. When senior officers were recently questioned about their conduct by the Home Affairs Select Committee, some revealed what appear to be overly familiar relationships with journalists, and allegations arose of unethical activities, such as the leaking of sensitive information to the press (Home Affairs Committee 2011). Several other unrelated investigations into the integrity of senior officers were conducted in 2012 across the UK, one of which resulted in the dismissal of a Chief Constable after he was found guilty of gross misconduct (*BBC News* 2012).

From 2012 to 2013 the 'plebgate' saga continued to unfold as claim met counterclaim. Several investigations followed in the aftermath of a very brief encounter in September 2012 between a senior government minister, Andrew Mitchell, and police officers on duty at the security gates of Downing Street. Following an argument between Mitchell and the officers after they had refused to open the gates to allow him to cycle through, the officers claimed that Mitchell referred to them as 'fucking plebs'. The initial media scandal centred on the second rather than the first word in that phrase, which was presented as further evidence of an elitist government, disdainful of the general public. The controversy was rekindled by claims that other police officers misrepresented proceedings of their enquiries into the initial confrontation and that this was part of a politically motivated campaign by the Police Federation against the police reforms of the Coalition Government. More than a year later, the brief original exchange continued to provoke controversy; as a newspaper editorial stated, it 'context has transmuted an exchange that lasted less than a minute into a crisis that has been acutely damaging for an individual, a government, at least two police services, and the Independent Police Complaints Commission' (*Guardian* 2013b).

As Millie (2013) suggests, this episode pitched the police service into conflict with their traditional allies in the Conservative Party. In October 2013, two senior Conservative politicians intervened in the debate to suggest measures necessary to tackle corruption and unethical behaviour and to restore public confidence in the integrity of investigations into alleged malpractice. Chris Grayling MP, Secretary of State for Justice, argued that a new code of ethics introduced by the College of Policing would transform police culture and encourage officers to report concerns of unprofessional conduct by their colleagues. Several days later, David Davis (former Conservative Shadow Home Secretary) called for a Royal Commission into police ethics and proposed that police misconduct could be reduced by a tougher investigative regime coupled with greater surveillance of officers via body-worn video cameras. Although not proposed as 'either/or' options, these two perspectives represent different ends of a spectrum for regulating the behaviour of officers. Grayling's reliance on a code of ethics and transformation of culture seeks to affect officers' attitudes such that poor performance and a misplaced loyalty to colleagues are eroded in a new environment where officers place greater value on ethics and professionalism. At the other end of the spectrum, Davis's adopts a control model whereby officer behaviour is affected by enhancing the likelihood that unethical acts are detected, effectively investigated and subjected to disciplinary measures.

Despite their different approaches, a common theme in these proposals, and one that has emerged from many of these cases highlighted above, has been that individual officers who were concerned about a colleague's behaviour were reluctant to report perceived unethical actions to their superiors or to other responsible bodies. Although empirical research on police corruption is rare, some studies have shown that the problem of non-reporting of unethical or corrupt behaviour (or 'whistle-blowing') lies with organisational systems (Newburn 1999; Chan 2003; Punch 2009). The 'blue code of silence' (Westmarland 2005) is preserved because officers lack confidence in their management (Huberts *et al.* 2003). In effect they are worried that they will be blamed, stigmatised (Miller 2003) or ignored, and their information will have no effect on the organisation or the individual's behaviour. Some officers believe that any violations they report may not be investigated and that by pointing an accusatorial finger, whether at individuals or the institution, they may be treated unfairly and without impartiality (Kääriäinen *et al.* 2008).

It is in this context that we recently conducted a UK study (the first to question a large number of serving police officers, $n=520$) of police officers' attitudes to a range of unethical police behaviours. We detail the findings of this survey in the discussion below, but suffice to say here it found much uncertainty about the 'rules' of ethical behaviour (Westmarland *et al.* 2013). Additionally the results showed that many officers are unwilling to report colleagues' misdemeanours and that the notion of 'serious' corruption may not equate to what might be more widely viewed as harmful. Before the chapter reviews these results more fully, let us outline some changes to the nature of challenges to police integrity that have featured in recent debates about accountability and police integrity.

While in recent years there has been much concern raised about police misconduct it also appears that the nature of the problem is changing in the context of contemporary police work, which increasingly entails the collection, processing and communication of personal data. A review by Her Majesty's Inspectorate of Constabulary (2011) argued that police integrity is related to access to information, and the inappropriate disclosure of information, as well as more 'traditional' challenges relating to financial probity or the use of force. The crime investigation and prevention capacity of social media has been much discussed in recent times, and yet the prospect of officers using these new opportunities in ways that might raise concerns about ethics or operational effectiveness remains largely unexplored. Equally the use of intelligence to underpin the development of evidence-based policing requires that officers routinely use data in ways that might be of significant operational benefit but raise new challenges for ethics and integrity (Innes and Roberts 2011).

The role of data, intelligence and evidence about individuals, neighbourhoods and crime problems has become increasingly central to policing during the 15 years since Ericson and Haggerty (1997) characterised police officers as 'knowledge workers'. Innes (2013) outlined future working practices characterised by 'network enabled policing' based on real-time intelligence and information shaping officers operational practices. The development of new technologies of policing inevitably means a more central role for data and so a new context that will shape concerns about ethics and integrity. Challenges to police integrity evolve as the nature of policing is transformed.

## Findings

Issues of data protection and the misuse of personal information have emerged from formal and informal discussions that surrounded survey work done by the authors in 2012. Funded by an Open University grant, the study provided – for the first time in England and Wales – a robust body of independent evidence of officers' attitudes towards different forms of corruption and the appropriate legal, disciplinary and organisational responses. Our anonymous postal survey of officers from three forces in England and Wales asked respondents how they and their colleagues might respond to various scenarios relating to apparent misconduct. Approximately 3,000 questionnaires were distributed via the three forces, with 520 returned (in prepaid envelopes) directly to the researchers (a response rate of 17.3 per cent). Eleven hypothetical situations were described in which an officer acted in ways that might be interpreted as problematic, in relation to accepting gratuities, using force and interfering with the course of justice. Officers were asked whether they rated the described behaviour seriously in terms of misconduct, whether their colleagues would regard it as misconduct, whether the behaviour contravened force policy, and whether they would be prepared to report an officer whom they uncovered engaging in such activity. Officers were asked to rate each incident between one ('not at all serious') and five ('very serious'). Table 4.1 shows how respondents ranked the seriousness of the actions described in the scenarios.

The table shows the mean score for each of the 11 scenarios and that the theft of a watch from a burglary scene was regarded as the most serious example of misconduct. At the other end of the spectrum, accepting Christmas gifts from local traders was regarded as the least serious behaviour. Even this least serious example was rated only slightly below the median score of three, which suggests that officers tended to identify relatively commonplace gratuities as of potential concern for police integrity.

The data presented in Table 4.2 shows respondents' views on both their propensity to report problematic behaviour to the organisation, as well as that of their colleagues. It shows that even where officers were certain that behaviours were against force rules and thought them to be quite serious, they were often unwilling to report colleagues' actions. The most serious behaviour (theft of a watch from a burglary scene) was understood as 'against force policy' by 98.5 per cent of respondents and yet a smaller (albeit still very substantial) majority of 95 per cent of officers reported that they 'definitely' would report this

*Table 4.1* Officer perceptions of gravity of behaviour

| Case | Mean 'seriousness' rank |
| --- | --- |
| Officer pockets a watch from a burglary at a jeweller's shop | 4.994 |
| Officer keeps large sum of money from a wallet found in a car park | 4.981 |
| Accepting a gift from a speeding motorist to ignore offence | 4.944 |
| Cover up 'Driving under the Influence' by an off-duty officer | 4.741 |
| Financial kickback from garage recommended to those involved in car accidents | 4.627 |
| Free drinks at bar open beyond licence period | 4.551 |
| Officer punching a suspect as 'punishment' for attempt to flee | 4.474 |
| Supervisor authorises days off in return for an officer doing some repairs on his private car | 4.070 |
| Accepting gifts from shopkeepers | 3.463 |
| An officer running a security business while off duty | 3.023 |
| Christmas gifts to an officer from local traders | 2.829 |

behaviour to more senior officers. A smaller proportion (83 per cent) was 'definite' that their colleagues similarly would report it. As Table 4.2 indicates, 97.5 per cent of officers stated that they 'definitely' or 'maybe' would report this behaviour, and that a smaller majority of colleagues would do so. The propensity to report appears to be closely related to the perceived gravity of the behaviour. The rank order of the scenarios in Table 4.1, in descending order from most to least serious, is mirrored almost precisely by individual officers' personal propensity to report. The most serious behaviour is also that most likely to be reported and the least serious – accepting free gifts at Christmas – is also the least likely to be reported.

Another finding emerging from Table 4.2 is that officers consistently reported that their personal propensity to report problematic behaviour was greater than that of their colleagues. Of course, this might be an artefact of the survey methodology such that officers were keen to present themselves favourably, even though it was conducted anonymously. Additionally, it might suggest that respondents rated their own integrity as higher than the norm. Arising from Table 4.2 is a dilemma as to whether the apparent association between perceived gravity of the behaviour and the propensity to report might also reflect a desire to avoid 'in-the-job trouble' (Ianni and Ianni 1979). If this explains to some degree the finding then it might be that emphasising the gravity of certain actions and behaviour and introducing stronger sanctions on those who fail to report their concerns can increase the propensity to report. Kargin's (2009) study of police in Philadelphia found that the reporting of colleagues' misbehaviour was predominantly predicated upon the potential seriousness of the consequences for the reporting officer in cases of minor or moderate policy violations. In relation to major violations, however, the strongest predictor of reporting was officers' attitudes toward professional ethics. The demographic characteristics of officers, specifically of rank, age, ethnicity or gender, for example, were found to have no statistically significant bearing on

*Table 4.2* Personal and colleagues' propensity[1] to report problematic behaviour

| Case | You | Colleagues |
|---|---|---|
| Officer pockets a watch from a burglary at a jeweller's shop | 97.5 | 94.6 |
| Officer keeps large sum of money from a wallet found in a car park | 96.5 | 91.9 |
| Accepting a gift from a speeding motorist to ignore offence | 93.2 | 87.7 |
| Cover up 'Driving under the Influence' by an off-duty officer | 83.4 | 72.5 |
| Financial kickback from garage recommended to those involved in car accidents | 86.2 | 75.8 |
| Free drinks at bar open beyond licence period | 74.6 | 63.8 |
| Officer punching a suspect as 'punishment' for attempt to flee | 75.6 | 58.6 |
| Supervisor authorises days off in return for an officer doing some repairs on his private car | 65.6 | 49.4 |
| Accepting gifts from shopkeepers | 41.3 | 27.2 |
| An officer running a security business while off duty | 37.5 | 21.8 |
| Christmas gifts to an officer from local traders | 29.0 | 19.8 |

Note
1 Per cent stating 'maybe' or 'definitely' would report.

officer attitudes toward peer-reporting of misbehaviour, whatever the degree of seriousness. Instead Kargin (2009: 157) concluded that reporting of misbehaviour was shaped by the combination of other factors, beyond the individual characteristics of an officer: 'the main predictors of police officers' peer reporting intentions were individual attitudinal factors (ethical attitudes toward professional ethics codes and cynicism), organisational factors (peer association and reinforcement), and issue-related factors (seriousness of the ethical issue)'. This suggests that different strategies might be effective for addressing the diverse range of potentially unethical or unprofessional behaviour. In the light of this observation various approaches to officer discipline are reviewed below.

## Controlling the constable: strategies of accountability

A recurrent challenge to police accountability is that a great deal of policing is, whether intentionally or otherwise, conducted in conditions of low visibility and is therefore relatively difficult for managers or leaders to interrogate. Even if technological innovation and the introduction of stringent monitoring processes might mean that supervisors can capture information about officers' decision-making and behaviour – and therefore hold them to account – this capacity is inherently limited. In the exercise of officer discretion, decisions leading to positive interventions can be audited. Thus a police officer who decides to stop and search a member of the public can capture details of that discretionary intervention, perhaps in a contemporaneous record or on a 'headcam', as David Davis has recently advocated. On this basis a supervisor can subsequently monitor that officer's behaviour and identify potential problems of integrity. However, even if officers were wholly compliant with recording and monitoring requirements, it would remain the case that the exercise of discretion which did not lead to an intervention cannot, by definition, be monitored. In other words, it is unreviewable. An officer's decision not to stop and search an individual, for example, might raise questions about integrity but since no action or behaviour has unfolded opportunities for monitoring and accountability are highly curtailed.

These inherent problems are compounded by the 'blue curtain of silence': that component of police occupational culture which is based upon, and contrives to continue, a veil of secrecy. As others have argued (Reiner 2010; Waddington 1999) positive aspects of police occupational culture include teamwork, mutual dependency and loyalty. Such characteristics are functionally useful in a role that is structured by the risk of danger but become dysfunctional when assuming roles of 'covering' for colleagues or a reluctance to challenge their problematic behaviour. These negative aspects of police subculture have been widely noted in the research literature relating to integrity issues such as racism, sexism and homophobia as well as the unreasonable use of force or financial corruption.

Recognition of these problems has underpinned recent efforts to promote a new 'transparency' by the newly minted College of Policing. These efforts have been concerned with promoting ethics and professional integrity, developing a new code of conduct, and seeking to embed a form of professionalism that embraces ethical practice through transforming workplace culture. Similarly, proponents of direct entry of recruits from outside the police into the senior ranks have frequently accentuated the benefits claimed for challenging the ossified culture and practice in the service. Prime Minister David Cameron, for example, endorsed direct entry as a means of developing diversity and 'opening up police culture' (College of Policing 2014).

In October 2013 the College of Policing issued a draft Code of Conduct for police officers in England and Wales for consultation, which is based on a series of 'principles and standards of professional behaviour'. At the time of writing, the ten 'standards' of professional policing have been identified as follows (College of Policing 2013: 1):

- Honesty and integrity
- Authority, respect and courtesy
- Equality and diversity
- Use of force
- Orders and instructions
- Work and responsibilities
- Confidentiality
- Fitness for work
- Conduct
- Challenging and reporting improper conduct

The consultation document also included a further nine 'principles' of policing (College of Policing 2013: 15). These were derived from the Nolan Committee on Standards in Public Life, but with the addition of 'fairness' and 'respect':

- Accountability
- Fairness
- Honesty
- Integrity
- Leadership
- Objectivity
- Openness
- Respect
- Selflessness

The theme of principled policing articulated by the Code is not a new one, however. In 1998 former Chief Constable John Alderson stated that:

> Societies in which principled policing operates, it is contended, are less likely to suffer from policing injustices than those where policing is driven by political opportunism, professional caprice or just bad law.... There has to be a robust moral objectivity in the way in which policing operates if it is to avoid the worst misuses and abuses of power.
>
> (Alderson 1998: 15)

Aside from the problem of determining whose moral objectivity will form the baseline for police ethics, it seems likely that the new Code will be hampered by other inherent problems. As with other such documents, the Code is somewhat aspirational, describing an ideal type of behaviour and integrity with which it is difficult to disagree but which is testing to define in operational practice.

As Westmarland has previously argued (see, for example, 2000, 2004, 2005) codes of ethics can be interpreted in many ways and are mediated by the occupational culture. They do not remove officer discretion – and to do so would be both undesirable and impossible. The 'code of the street' is the rule of occupational cultural influences, and the standards and principles of the new code may be regarded as that of the management 'suites'. In a sense, therefore, the organisation sets out a series of 'rules' and 'cop culture' finds ways around them in a seemingly interminable game of cat and mouse. Despite strenuous efforts by police organisations around the world, the extent to which policy guides officer behaviour remains limited.

Ethical codes are often seen as an attempt to provide guidance in ambiguous situations for officers working in isolated and often 'heat of the moment' situations. Although well meant, one of the central problems in terms of shaping conduct is that police discretion, the ability to make decisions in these difficult situations, is difficult to regulate, predict and classify. In effect, the very ambiguity of the codes leads to difficulties (Westmarland 2000). In most cases, for instance, officers are asked to use their discretion ethically, to uphold the law and to behave in an honourable and professional manner. It is the interpretation of these codes that is problematic, however. As ethical codes continue to require individuals to reflect on their actions in the light of institutionally expressed moral principles, it remains very difficult to train officers to behave in certain ways or to 'do the right thing' in a given situation.

According to Cooper (2012), these sets of broad guidance may cause 'role conflict' in police officers arising from the communication of institutional roles and expectations. He argues that 'role behaviour' is the result of the complex interaction of the person 'receiving' the role, organisational factors, those 'sending' the role, and the relationships among senders and receivers. While broad in scope and application, one part of role theory pertinent to police corruption is that of role conflict. Role conflict is 'the simultaneous occurrence of two (or more) role sendings such that compliance with one would make more difficult compliance with the other' (Katz and Kahn 1966: 184). Applied to noble cause corruption, officers are 'sent' two roles. First, is the role of the protector, characterised by the desire to 'get ... bad guys off the street' (Crank and Caldero 2000: 35). Second, police officers are also exposed to another potentially competing role: that of agents of the state (Alpert and Dunham 2004). Cooper (2012: 170) suggests that:

> as agents of the state, police are bound by procedural law to protect the civil rights of individuals. Officers may see these guidelines as retarding their capacity to fulfil their role as protectors of the innocent (Roberg *et al.* 2008). Thus, police officers are set two roles by their organisation which at times may be perceived to be incompatible: that of the noble protector, and that of agent of the state bound by procedural requirements. This creates the potential for role conflict that may result in noble cause corruption: in their efforts to comply with the primary role (that of protector) they neglect or ignore the secondary role (that of agent of the state).

This tension may be exacerbated by political, cultural and social constructions of police work that valorise officers in their crime-fighting role, and apparently fail to recognise the complex service functions that are more central in terms of resource allocation and public interactions (Loader 2013).

Furthermore, it is the officers at the front line, often in the lowest position in the rank hierarchy, who have a great deal of power and discretion in immediate operational matters. These powers may include the ability to arrest a suspect – simple and commonplace in policing terms, but in reputational, career or personal terms to the individual arrested, potentially extremely detrimental. As a result, Waddington (1999: 129, emphasis in original) asks whether 'police rules made by superiors serve to insulate them from criticism by pushing responsibility *down* the hierarchy'. In effect police managers and senior policymakers draw up codes of ethics or 'principles' for guidance in certain situations, but officers may still have difficulty adhering to a set of professional ethical standards, as the example of the principles and standards outlined above illustrates. Furthermore, police recruits tend to be socialised by more experienced officers who teach them to be aware of 'insider' cultural rules (Fielding 1988). One of the most important of these is the need to be efficient and produce 'results' even if that means not following procedures (Skolnick 1966; Westmarland 2001,

2013). To add to this, police officers often work alone or with a close colleague, away from the public gaze, and come into contact with people who have reasons to corrupt them, making for what has sometimes been described as a 'morally dangerous occupation' (Barker 2006: 5).

## Ethical cultures – differences across the world

The only major international study of police ethics comparing attitudes in different countries revealed problems of moral relativity. Klockars *et al.*'s (2004) study explored attitudes towards police behaviour in 14 countries, and discovered that whilst police officers from most countries ranked the seriousness of the scenarios the study presented to them in 'remarkably similar' ways (ibid.: 13), there were some notable exceptions. For example, driving under the influence of alcohol is regarded differently in the countries studied, with the offence being regarded as the most serious in three countries and among the least serious in four of them. In the UK the study found that whilst over 90 per cent of officers thought the offence 'very serious', only around 50 per cent were prepared to 'definitely report' a colleague who, upon finding a police officer drunk in charge of a vehicle in the middle of the night having caused an accident, took the officer home without further action. In other words, the covering up of a police colleague's drink-driving, having caused an accident, is considered serious, but something they might well not report. At the same time, UK officers thought an officer taking money from a found wallet or taking a watch from a jeweller's shop that had been burgled was 'very serious' and around 99 per cent of respondents said they would report this behaviour. This indicates that propensity to report was not just influenced by the perceived seriousness of the incident but that other contextual factors are also significant.

This technique, which has become known as the 'Klockars Scale' allows researchers to investigate the issue of police integrity rather than actual instances of police corruption (Klockars 1999: 210–11). Klockars *et al.*'s international study also revealed other aspects of moral relativism, or as the authors described it, a 'difference in general cultural opinion' (2003:13). As they explained, the scenario describing the use of excessive force on a suspected car thief varies widely (ibid.: 13):

> In Hungary, it is regarded as the third most serious offense, worse than stealing from a crime scene or accepting a bribe; whereas in Pakistan, it is ranked as the tenth most serious offense and considered less serious than accepting a free cup of coffee.

In terms of this relativism, as the 'inventors' of modern policing, most UK officers can sit back and say that these 'less developed' police forces could benefit from training and that the international courses provided at Bramshill are very well attended. Critics might point out that UK officers in that original international study in 2003 were also unsure about reporting this offence (Klockars *et al.*

2003). Only 54 per cent said they would 'definitely report' a colleague who delivered a couple of punches to an already captured suspect, although 65.5 per cent thought it was 'very serious' (Westmarland 2005). In 2013, our study showed that only around three-quarters of the respondents would definitely report this behaviour (Westmarland *et al.* 2013).

A more recent study (Vito *et al.* 2011) using Klockars's original questions with a 'convenience sample' of 'management cops' from around the world found that police managers' perspectives on corruption echoed findings from a study of US officers in another follow-up to Klockars *et al.*'s initial study (Kutnjak Ivkovic 2005: 556). Regarding the covering up for a colleague's drink-driving, officers surveyed by this study found that with the exception of the Finland officers, who thought it represented a 'grievous ethical error' (Vito *et al.* 2011: 191), they thought officers would not report this behaviour. Indeed, Punch argues that there is a long tradition of 'institutionalised patterns of bribery' in US policing and a 'contrasting pattern in Europe' of noble cause corruption revealed by miscarriages of justice coming to light (2003: 173). As contextual differences influence the decision to report, not just the perceived gravity of ethical misconduct, so too national differences emerge from the wider literature on police integrity. The following section develops the core idea that the impact of ethical codes depends not just on their content but also on the context in which they are implemented, and that this requires consideration of the authorship or sponsorship of codes.

## Whose codes?

In terms of accountability, the use of professional standards and codes of conduct to control constables and those further up the rank structure, we might debate who propagates these principles or standards and how they are enforced. One of the final principles in the College of Policing's draft consultation code mentions that officers should challenge and report 'improper conduct'. It might be argued that officers ought to subscribe to the nine 'standards of professional policing' and the further nine 'principles' but these need to be embedded within the grass roots of police work rather than emanating remotely from above. Central to the key informal code of grass roots, 'boots on the street' policing is to maintain solidarity with colleagues, often even when to do so is in opposition to rules and regulations imposed top-down by police managers. Given this, we might ask, what benefit would rank-and-file officers expect from blowing the whistle on misbehaving colleagues? The 'code of the streets' is often highly prized by officers. The rules that occupational cultures develop cannot, given their longevity and persistence in the face of efforts at reform, be regarded as marginal to efforts to promote police integrity. Simply that to tell officers to behave with integrity and to present them with a code has much less purchase than to live, breathe and work with a set of morals in action, or a set of professional principles.

As in debates about leadership more generally, in policing it is problematic that efforts to promote integrity are often introduced without consideration of the concept of 'followership'. As Rowe (2006) has argued the perceptions and judgements that junior officers make of those in senior ranks can make a considerable difference to the success of initiatives and reforms. While the nature and quality of police leadership is subject to considerable debate, insufficient attention is paid to the view from the lower ranks. Given that the research evidence so strongly points to internal solidarity and the 'blue code of silence', more understanding is needed as to how officers respond to codes and policy initiatives. A potential contradiction here is that an ethical code can only succeed if a key obstacle to developing integrity (i.e. 'the blue curtain of silence') is tackled. At the same time achieving that outcome is a core goal of the code. Thus a significant tension remains such that 'opening the blue curtain' is both a prerequisite for the promotion of integrity as well as an outcome of codes intended to promote the same end.

## Conclusion

We have argued that international experience of developing and implementing police Codes of Ethics offer only limited grounds for optimism. While they might be normative, aspirational and ambiguous they do represent an essential condition to transform problematic police culture, respond to corruption and promote police integrity. As Shane (2013: 32) has noted recently policy statements represent an important symbolic contribution to transforming organisational behaviour:

> A comprehensive policy is an expression of how the agency intends to conduct its affairs and act in specific situations to minimize liability and errors at the agency, supervisory and line level, particularly when legal and ethical issues arise. Without guidance from the policy, officers do not have uniform procedures to follow, which invites deviance, inconsistency, and misconduct. When police misconduct does occur, it often originates with a failure to promulgate a clear written policy; misconduct is also likely to occur from failing to observe a published policy.

It seems unlikely that a Code of Ethics will, in itself, prevent a 'meat eating' (Punch 2009) corrupt police officer who seeks to exploit the peculiar opportunities that police work offers for bribes, violence and myriad forms of malfeasance. Rigorous and transparent investigations and disciplinary responses to alleged misconduct are required to ensure that the principles expressed in codes of conduct are translated into practice. However, in combination with other measures, including training and a wider discourse of professional practice, codes of ethics have the capacity to effect change to police subcultures that have been a stubborn obstacle to addressing integrity. Enhancing diversity within the police, a strong ethos of public service, and transparent engagement with the public can transform aspects of police subculture – such as isolation and unconditional group loyalty – that have made it more difficult to tackle corruption and other forms of unethical behaviour. Reshaping police culture in such ways will continue to be a hard task and will not be achieved either quickly or without opposition. As noted above, however, the imposition of a rules-based code of ethics in a top-down managerial form is unlikely to gain much traction if done in opposition to deeply embedded working cultures.

Even if such efforts do bear fruit, though, there will continue to be challenges to police integrity since decades of research demonstrate that organisational culture arises not just from the personal attributes of staff but also from the institutional arrangements of police work. Codes of ethics tend to focus on the occupational behaviour of individuals and do not speak to challenges for integrity that are institutional rather than personal in nature. Organisational pressures for officers to 'cut corners' or to engage in covert surveillance that extends to sexual relationships with members of the public, and the surveillance of peaceful and lawful political demonstrations all raise questions about integrity and ethics that are seldom addressed by codes of ethics.

The institutional arrangements of police work also mean that the nature of ethical challenges will change as the technologies and techniques of policing develop in response to new crime challenges, new financial environments and new forms of partnership delivery. As we have argued above, the increasing importance of data and information processing and communication opens new prospects for misconduct or malpractice. New policing environments include greater transnational global police work and the role of police in collecting, collating and disseminating information remains relatively overlooked both in terms of research and in relation to integrity. In relation to transnational police, cooperation challenges will arise in circumstances where ethical codes of practice are incommensurate across borders or where national police agencies interact with partner agencies that subscribe to lower or different ethical standards. Recent scandals about surveillance by the US National Security Agency and Britain's GCHQ might not have been focused upon the role of the public police in eavesdropping, monitoring email and telephone communication, or surveillance of citizens. Such practices can be understood, however, as aspects of policing in terms of social regulation and seem likely to form an increasing component of policing in the future and – as these controversies indicate – therein become more central to debates about integrity.

Moreover, the apparently unstoppable drive towards greater private sector delivery of policing functions also raises concerns about integrity and ethics since they rely on a contractual model of accountability that is distinct from democratic approaches outlined by codes of conduct. Many of the private corporations that have been contracted to deliver public services within the criminal justice sector (and more widely, for instance in delivery of welfare payments) have been embroiled in ethical scandals. In August 2013, for example, the Ministry of Justice (2013) announced that police had been asked to investigate claims that Serco staff had committed fraud in relation to the company's prisoner escort contract. A month earlier it was reported that G4S had overcharged the Ministry by claiming to supervise 18,000 offenders on electronic tags when actually supervising 15,000 (*Telegraph* 2013). And in October 2013 it was alleged that staff from G4S used electric shocks and forced injections to subdue prisoners at a Bloemfontein jail run by the company (*Guardian* 2013c). While these examples do not apply to private sector engagement in policing they do illustrate that challenges of ethics and integrity extend beyond the public sector. In each of the examples mentioned, the companies concerned have experienced, or been threatened with, commercial sanctions through loss of contracts or the withholding of payments. Such contractual accountability might be commercially effective but offers little in terms of ensuring justice or upholding public legitimacy. The difficulties of applying such principles to misconduct associated with police officers are often noted, and constitute the context against which codes of ethics and other mechanisms of accountability have been developed. Beyond the public sector, however, there is still less prospect that individuals and institutions afforded considerable power over their fellow citizens can be held to account. Addressing concerns about public policing is imperative, but the terms of the debate need to be broadened further to include the complex networks of public and private, national and international agencies engaged in the delivery of policing and social regulation.

## References

Alderson, J. (1998) *Principled Policing: Protecting the Public with Integrity*, Winchester: Waterside Press.

Alpert, G.P. and Dunham, R.G. (2004) *Understanding Police Use of Force: Officers, Suspects, and Reciprocity*, Cambridge: Cambridge University Press.

Barker, T. (2006) *Police Ethics: Crisis in Law Enforcement*, Springfield, IL: Charles C. Thomas.

*BBC News* (2012) 'Cleveland Police Chief Sean Price Sacked after Inquiry', 5 October, available at www.bbc.co.uk/news/uk-19840069 (last accessed 27 April 2015).

Chan, J. (2003) *Fair Cop: Learning the Art of Policing*, Toronto: University of Toronto.

College of Policing (2013) *Code of Ethics, Consultation Version*, London: College of Policing.

College of Policing (2014) 'College of Policing Launches New Recruitment Routes into Policing', 30 March, available at http://college.pressofficeadmin.com/component/content/category/45-press-releases (last accessed 27 April 2015).

Cooper, J.A. (2012) 'Noble Cause Corruption as a Consequence of Role Conflict in the Police Organisation', *Policing and Society*, 22: 169–84.

Crank, J.P. and Caldero, M.A. (2000) *Police Ethics: The Corruption of Noble Cause*, Cincinnati: Anderson Publishing.

Ericson, R. and Haggerty, K. (1997) *Policing the Risk Society*, Oxford: Clarendon.

Fielding, N. (1988) *Joining Forces: Police Training, Socialization, and Occupational Competence*, London and New York: Routledge.

*Guardian* (2013a) 'Theresa May to Expand IPCC in Crackdown on Police Corruption', 12 February, available at www.theguardian.com/politics/2013/feb/12/theresa-may-ipcc-police-corruption (last accessed 27 April 2015).

*Guardian* (2013b) 'Plebgate: The Ripple Effect', 15 October, available at www.theguardian.com/commentisfree/2013/oct/15/plebgate-ripple-effect-editorial-mitchell (last accessed 27 April 2015).

*Guardian* (2013c) 'G4S-Run Prison in South Africa Investigated over Abuse Claims', 28 October, available at www.theguardian.com/world/2013/oct/28/g4s-run-prison-south-africa-investigation (last accessed 27 April 2015).

Her Majesty's Inspectorate of Constabulary (HMIC) (2011) *Without Fear or Favour: A Review of Police Relationships*, London: HMIC.

Home Affairs Committee (2011) *Unauthorised Tapping into or Hacking of Mobile Communications, Part One*, London: House of Commons.

Home Office (2011) *Exploring Public Confidence in the Police and Local Councils in Tackling Crime and Anti-Social Behaviour*, London: Home Office.

Home Office (2014) *Stephen Lawrence Independent Review*, London: Home Office.

Huberts, L., Lamboo, T. and Punch, M. (2003) 'Police Integrity in the Netherlands and the United States: Awareness and Alertness', *Police Practice and Research*, 4: 217–32.

Ianni, E. and Ianni, F. (1979) *Street Cops vs. Management Cops – The Social Organization of the Police Precinct*, Washington, DC: National Institute of Justice.

Innes, M. (2013) 'Reinventing the Office of Constable: Progressive Policing in an Age of Austerity', in J. Brown (ed.) *The Future of Policing*, London: Routledge, 64–78.

Innes, M. and Roberts, C. (2011) *Policing, Situational Intelligence and the Information Environment*, London: HMIC.

Kääriäinen, J., Lintonen, T., Laitinen, A. and Pollock, J. (2008) 'The "Code of Silence": Are Self-Report Surveys a Viable Means for Studying Police Misconducts?', *Journal of Scandinavian Studies in Criminology and Crime Prevention*, 9: 86–96.

Kargin, V. (2009) *An Investigation of Factors Proposed to Influence Police Officers' Peer Reporting Intentions*, Doctoral Thesis, Philadelphia, PA: University of Pennsylvania.

Klockars, C. (1999) *Police Corruption in Thirty Agencies in the United States*, Washington, DC: National Institute of Justice.

Klockars, C.B., Haberfeld, M. and Kutjnak Ivkovich, S. (2003) *The Contours of Police Integrity*, Thousand Oaks, CA: Sage.

Kutnjak Ivkovic, S. (2005) 'Police (Mis)behavior: A Cross-Cultural Study of Corruption Seriousness', *Policing*, 28: 546–66.

Loader, I. (2013) 'Why do the Police Matter? Beyond the Myth of Crime Fighting', in J. Brown (ed.) *The Future of Policing*, London: Routledge, 40–51.

McLaughlin, E. (2007) *The New Policing*, London: Sage.

Miller, J. (2003) 'Police Corruption in England and Wales: An Assessment of Current Evidence', Home Office Online Report 11/03.

Millie, A. (2013) 'What are the Police for? Re-thinking Policing Post-Austerity', in J. Brown (ed.) *The Future of Policing*, London: Routledge, 52–63.

Ministry of Justice (2013) *MoJ Audit of SERCO contracts – Prison Escort Services*, press release, 28 August, available at www.gov.uk/government/news/moj-audit-of-serco-contracts-prison-escort-services (last accessed 27 April 2015).

Murphy, K., Hinds, L. and Fleming, J. (2008) 'Encouraging Public Cooperation and Support for Police', *Policing and Society*, 18: 136–55.

Newburn, T. (1999) *Understanding and Preventing Police Corruption: Lessons from the Literature*, London: Home Office.

Punch, M. (2003) 'Rotten Orchards: "Pestilence". Police Misconduct and System Failure', *Policing and Society*, 13: 171–96.

Punch, M. (2009) *Police Corruption*, Cullompton, Devon: Willan.

Reiner, R. (2010) *The Politics of the Police* (4th edn), Oxford: Oxford University Press.

Roberg, R., Novak, K. and Cordner, G. (2008) *Police and Society*, Oxford: Oxford University Press.

Rowe, M. (2006) 'Follow the Leader: Frontline Narratives on Police Leadership', *Policing: an International Journal of Police Strategies and Management*, 29(4): 757–67.

Shane, J. (2013) *Learning from Error in Policing*, London: Springer.

Skolnick, J. (1966) *Justice Without Trial*, New York: Wiley and Sons.

*Telegraph* (2013) 'G4S Faces Criminal Probe after Overcharging Taxpayer Millions for Electronic Tags', 11 July, available at www.telegraph.co.uk/news/uknews/crime/10174863/G4S-faces-criminal-probe-after-overcharging-taxpayer-millions-for-electronic-tags.html (last accessed 27 April 2015).

Vito, G.F., Wolfe, S., Higgins, G.E. and Walsh W.F. (2011) 'Police Integrity: Rankings of Scenarios on the Klockars Scale by "Management Cops"', *Criminal Justice Review*, 36(2): 152–64.

Waddington, P.A.J. (1999) 'Police (Canteen) Sub-Culture – an Appreciation', *British Journal of Criminology*, 39: 287–309.

Westmarland, L. (2000) 'Telling the Truth the Whole Truth and Nothing but the Truth? Ethics and the Enforcement of Law', *Journal of Ethical Sciences and Services*, 2(3): 193–202.

Westmarland, L. (2001) *Gender and Policing: Sex, Power and Police Culture*, Cullompton, Devon: Willan.

Westmarland, L. (2004) 'Policing Integrity: Britain's Thin Blue Line' in C.B. Klockars, M. Haberfeld and S. Kutjnak Ivkovich *The Contours of Police Integrity*, Thousand Oaks, CA: Sage, 75–94.

Westmarland, L. (2005) 'Police Ethics and Integrity: Breaking the Blue Code of Silence', *Policing and Society*, 15(2): 145–65.

Westmarland, L. (2013) 'Snitches get Stitches: Homicide Investigation in Downtown DC', *Policing and Society*, 23: 311–27

Westmarland, L., Rowe, M., Hougham, C. and Grimshaw, R. (2013) *Police Integrity Feedback Report*, Milton Keynes: Open University.

# 5 Integrity, accountability and public trust

## Issues raised by the unauthorised use of confidential police information

*Cindy Davids and Gordon Boyce*

In announcing the establishment of *An Inquiry into the Culture, Practices and Ethics of the Press* in July 2011 the UK Prime Minister David Cameron stated:

> the whole country has been shocked by the revelations of the phone hacking scandal ... an episode that is, frankly, disgraceful: accusations of widespread law breaking by parts of our press: alleged corruption by some police officers; and ... the failure of our political system over many, many years to tackle a problem that has been getting worse ... let me turn to the issue of ethics in the police, and in particular their relationship with the press. Of course it is important that there is a good relationship between the media and the police. Police often use newspapers and other media to hunt down wanted criminals and to appeal for information. However, allegations have been made that some corrupt police officers may have taken payments from newspapers. And there are wider concerns that the relationship between the police and the press can also be too close.
>
> (HC Deb 13 July 2011, vol. 531, cols 311, 313)

In conducting the Inquiry, Lord Justice Leveson was, in part, tasked with the responsibility of exploring the relationship between the media and police, reflecting widespread concerns in the UK that this relationship was 'inappropriately close and if not actually corrupt, very close to it' (Jay, quoted in Leveson 2012b: 743). Particular attention was drawn to this issue when it became known that police had failed to investigate properly allegations of illegal and improper phone hacking in 2006, 2009 and 2010. There were associated concerns about the unauthorised transmission of confidential information by police in the context of what Leveson found to be an 'arguably over-cosy relationship between the police and the press' (Leveson 2012b: 744). The Inquiry 'examined many facets of the way in which press and police interact ... looking at the overlapping issues of "tip offs", "taking media on operations", "off-the-record" briefings, leaks, whistleblowing, gifts and hospitality, entertainment etc.' (Leveson 2012b: 980). Leveson found that 'the best present analysis would suggest that although corruption is not widespread in the Police Service, where it does exist it has a corrosive effect on public confidence in the service as a whole' (ibid.: 943).

Concerns about misuse of police information are both long-standing and well founded. In one sense, the matters before the Leveson Inquiry highlighted the increased potential for inappropriate access to and use of information in an environment where significant amounts of information are stored in digital forms. On the other hand, the increased use of information and communication technologies (ICTs) within policing provides the potential for greater information security and tracking of use. In these circumstances, a sound understanding of the nature and dimensions of the problem of unauthorised use of police information is important to developing suitable systems for the collection, storage and use of information, detection of breaches and developing systems of accountability to deal with misuse.

Drawing on the academic literature and a number of data sources (complaints against police, prosecutions and a range of public reports including the Leveson Inquiry itself), this chapter examines what happens when police information gets into the wrong hands. Distinguishing inappropriate *private/personal* use of information from inappropriate *disclosure*, we consider types, sources and uses of information. Through an accountability lens, we seek to expound harms that can arise for individual officers, the community and the system of public administration. Our analysis suggests that viewing the problem of misuse of police information as part of the broader problem of conflict of interest facilitates a clearer perspective on the relationship between these concerns and issues of public trust, police integrity and accountability.

Following an outline of the nature of the problem and its relationship to the broader context of police accountability, we draw on empirical data and official reports from Australia and the UK in order to elaborate key dimensions of the problem providing an outline of a variety of types and sources of information. We subsequently analyse the range of circumstances involved in the unofficial uses to which that information can be put – in the context of both private or so-called domestic use of information and disclosure (or leaks) to outside parties. The range of scenarios canvassed is elucidated with original case data and a range of reports from Australia and the UK. We consider how this problem may be addressed as a part of the broader problem of conflict of interest and argue for a social accountability lens that attends to both accountability mechanisms and the need to develop accountability as virtue.

## Method and data sources

The analysis in the chapter draws on real case examples drawn from several key sources. First an original in-depth study that examined 377 internal investigations case files dealing with conflict of interest over a ten-year period in the Australian state of Victoria (Davids 2005, 2008; Cases from this data set are referred to throughout the chapter by their case number in the original study). The data set included all complaints against police for the ten-year period where conflict of interest was the primary element of complaint, as identified by the Victorian Ombudsman's office, which had oversight responsibility for complaints against police. The files were initiated by complaints from diverse sources including aggrieved members of the public, solicitors acting on behalf of members of the public, public sector agencies, private businesses, and by Victoria Police members who lodged against other police officers (Davids 2005: 12–16). Of the total sample examined, 58 matters (15 per cent) involved misuse of confidential police information.[1] We also utilise Victorian court cases involving prosecutions for matters related to misuse of police information.

The second key source is reports from public sector oversight and similar agencies in Australia and the UK, including:

- a British Home Office study that drew on interviews with staff in the professional standards units (PSUs) of eight UK police forces and the National Crime Squad (Miller 2003);[2]
- reports from police oversight and similar agencies including, in Australia, the Victorian Office of Police Integrity[3] and the New South Wales Police Integrity Commission, and in the UK, Her Majesty's Inspectorate of Constabulary;
- reports from the Leveson Inquiry in the UK (especially Leveson 2012a, 2012b).

## When police information gets into the wrong hands ...

### *A perennial problem*

The problem of inappropriate access and/or use of police information for private purposes is common to police forces across the world. It has long been recognised that '[i]nformation and intelligence is the lifeblood of policing', representing 'the most valuable commodity the Police Service needs to protect' (HMIC 1999: 39; Office of Police Integrity 2010a; Commissioner for Law Enforcement Data Security 2009; KPMG 2009). Police officers *necessarily* have access to a range of official information sources in the course of their usual duties, including formal records such as paper and digital files and documents, and various forms of verbal and similar 'intelligence'. The increased focus in contemporary policing on intelligence-led methods (Miller 2003: 13) and on the use of information technology (Chan *et al.* 2001) enhances both the amount of information available to police officers and the means to gain access to such data.

A 2003 British Home Office study of police corruption in England and Wales (Miller 2003) found that the compromise of police information was 'the single most common type of corrupt activity' in UK policing (ibid.: 10, iii). It was suggested that 'the picture of corruption [in England and Wales] is *dominated* by the leaking of information to those outside the organisation' (Miller

2003: 8, emphasis added). Misuse of information represents a major risk in contemporary policing, given that "[i]nformation, or law enforcement data, held by police can ... be extremely valuable to individuals or groups outside law enforcement agencies' (Office of Police Integrity 2010a: 8). Confidential police information may be 'what criminals most want to obtain, and is the currency corrupt officers have used when betraying their colleagues and their profession' (HMIC 1999: 39).

When police information gets into the wrong hands investigations may be compromised, criminals may evade justice and the policing function may be undermined in a number of ways:

> The consequences ... of information security and integrity failures can lead to catastrophic operational failures – complex investigations can be compromised, criminals can evade apprehension and conviction and the lives of law enforcement officers and others can be put at risk. Information security failures also lead to reputation damage. Other law enforcement agencies are less likely to share their sensitive information with an insecure and unreliable partner. Individuals and organisations are understandably reluctant to fully and frankly disclose information to a law enforcement agency that has a reputation for leaking. A law enforcement culture that is disrespectful of the security and integrity of law enforcement data is one that will fail to attract and retain the right law enforcement officers.
>
> (Commissioner for Law Enforcement Data Security 2009: 7; see also
> People 2008)

In a 2010 review of 'recurring themes' in the management of high-profile police investigations, the Victorian Office of Police Integrity noted how the 'possibly unforeseen and unintended consequences' of information disclosure can strike at the very heart of the policing function:

> In addition to compromising the privacy of individuals, the success of an operation or the integrity of an investigation or prosecution, other consequences of unauthorised disclosures may be even more serious. There are two high profile cases since 2004 where publication of leaked information immediately preceded the murder of key police witnesses in police corruption cases. There are other instances where leaked information has also:
>
> • put at risk the safety of operational police
> • created opportunities for suspects to collude, flee or destroy evidence
> • compelled a premature response by police requiring a covert operation to become overt
> • re-traumatised victims
> • caused witnesses to withdraw cooperation.
>
> (Office of Police Integrity 2012: 16; see also
> Office of Police Integrity 2010b)

It also stated that '[a]lthough many of our investigations indicate a reckless disregard for the consequences of "leaking", only a few indicate a deliberate self-interest or malicious motivation behind the leak' (Office of Police Integrity 2012: 15; see also People 2008). Nevertheless, it was suggested that '[t]he prevalence of "leaking" from within Victoria Police ... indicates that Victoria Police has a cultural problem' that manifests in 'a disturbing pattern of long-standing behaviour whereby police routinely leak confidential and sensitive information' (Office of Police Integrity 2010b: 16, 9).

Davids (2005, 2008) analysed the problem of inappropriate access and use of police information as part of a wider study of conflict of interest, noting that the problem of information misuse extends beyond mere *curiosity* or *interestedness*, with many cases involving active attempts to advance personal interests. Around many parts of the world, public awareness of the playing-out of conflicts of interest in public roles has contributed to a general decline in trust in public officials (Boyce and Davids 2009). Unauthorised access and disclosure of police information presents an archetypal conflict of interest because it unambiguously involves the placement of private interests ahead of the public interest. It also generally breaches police information access protocols and *ipso facto* may itself be classified as police misconduct or corruption as well as being a possible precursor to more serious breaches of duty (Davids 2008).

Unauthorised disclosure of information from a police database is a criminal offence in some jurisdictions.[4] In addition to statutory regimes, the behaviour may also be caught through a broad common law offence of 'misconduct in public office' or statutory codifications of the same offence.[5] The majority of misconduct in public office offences prosecuted at common law appear to involve public officials (but not necessarily police officers) who make improper use of information (Crime and Misconduct Commission 2008: 29). For the police, however, such matters are more commonly dealt with through internal discipline systems and recourse to criminal prosecution and sanctions is unusual (Director-Police Integrity 2005b: 23).[6]

### *Social accountability and public trust in policing*

Cultural problems that are manifested in an apparent normative acceptance of the misuse of police information represent a particular challenge for developing appropriate systems of accountability. In many respects, accountability is an elusive concept – 'one of those evocative political words that can be used to patch up a rambling argument, to evoke an image of trustworthiness, fidelity, and justice, or to hold critics at bay' (Bovens 2005: 182). Bovens notes that it therefore has rhetorical and iconic dimensions that evoke notions of 'good governance'. 'Public' accountability relates both to the status of both account-giving and account-giver – relating to the public sector, where the account-giving is done in some public way, to (or on behalf of) the public, and relating to public managers, spending public money, exercising public authority and/or managing under public law.

It may generally be agreed that public accountability includes both administrative forms manifest in the structures and organisational arrangements, and a moral or ethical sense that revolves around the need for public officials and public institutions to consistently demonstrate integrity and trustworthiness. Accountability has an inherent social dimension to the extent that an actor (individual or organisation) is obligated to explain and to justify their conduct to some forum, and to take responsibility for that conduct and its effects on others (Day and Klein 1987; Sinclair 1995; Bovens 1998). In this chapter we utilise the social accountability perspective enunciated by Boyce and Davids (2009, 2010). This is a broad-scope approach that incorporates multiple dimensions of answerability (to formal systems of accountability) and responsibility (in the sense of virtue – see Bovens 2010, 1998). Recognising that public officials who possess and exercise legal power and authority are accountable to the wider public for the exercise of that power, the social aspect adds a focus on the bottom-up dimension of responsibility that complements traditional top-down hierarchical perspectives (Roberts 1991).

A social accountability perspective can help to transcend the limitations of formal accountability mechanisms that 'may bypass central questions of moral responsibility that lie at the heart of corruption' (Boyce and Davids 2009: 632). It addresses both the need for appropriate accountability mechanisms, including regulation and enforcement, and the imperative to address ethical, organisational and cultural dimensions through a focus on accountability as virtue (Bovens 2010). Thus, social accountability seeks:

> to nurture proactive accountability through the development of responsibility as a personal and subjective sense of rightness and good conscience ... [as well as] accountab[ility] for the exercise of ... power. Accountability operates through organisational structures and hierarchies, but public officers must also be accountable to the broader community.
>
> (Boyce and Davids 2010: 283–4)

The pervasive, persistent and recurring nature of problems surrounding unauthorised access to or use of police information suggests that 'progress, over the long term, has been unacceptably slow' (Commissioner for Law Enforcement Data Security 2012: 4). The more recent revelations from the Leveson Inquiry suggest that both operational police and police management may have insufficient practical understanding of the nature and dimensions of the problem of inappropriate access to and use of information, and of the accountability issues involved. These matters are examined in the remainder of the chapter.

## Inappropriate access and use of information: the nature of the problem

Miller (2003) reported that abuse of the UK Police National Computer (PNC) database was said to be the subject of approximately 5 per cent of UK police disciplinary cases (ibid.: 13, fn 7). The Leveson Inquiry provided more recent evidence on this issue, with the Independent Police Complaints Commission reporting to the Inquiry that between 2006/7 and 2010/11 there were 5,179 recorded allegations relating to the improper disclosure of information, constituting around 2 per cent of all allegations recorded for the period (Furniss, quoted in Leveson 2012a: 810).

In Davids' Australian study, 15 per cent of all conflict of interest cases involved the misuse of confidential police information, with two-thirds of these cases involving disclosure of information to outside parties (see Davids 2008: 153). Contemporary concerns in Australia regarding unauthorised disclosure of police information are reflected in reports from various independent oversight agencies, which have identified the issue as a particular problem that often presents as a crucial dimension or common denominator in many flow-on issues for policing (e.g. Director-Police Integrity 2005c: 23; Crime and Misconduct Commission 2011). In addition, a number of high-profile official investigations examining the circulation of highly protected Police Information Reports or parts thereof to media, criminals and others underscores the need to protect confidential police information (Director-Police Integrity 2005d).

### *Information and communication technologies*

ICTs and official computer databases are increasingly important to policing. In Australia, which has separate police jurisdictions in each state, each police force holds its own computerised database; however, as in the UK, there is a National Police Reference System, which can link information for Australia's state-based police agencies (known as 'CrimTrac' – www.crimtrac.gov.au). Databases provide police officers with online access to information relating to crime reports and associated dealings between police and victims, offenders and members of the public. For example, the Victoria Police 'LEAP' (Law Enforcement Assistance Program) computer database is:

> used to record crime incidents and personal particulars and captures a range of information including details of lost and stolen property and vehicles of interest to law enforcement. LEAP provides an online interface to internal and external systems to facilitate name, vehicle and place searches. It is also used in relation to fingerprint classifications, case management and intelligence collation. Access to LEAP peaks at around 350,000 transactions daily and the system is lined to over 5,000 terminals 24 hours per day. The system is extensively used in support of operational policing and as a resource to provide management data.
> 
> Information stored on LEAP is, in large part, sensitive and personal.
>
> (Director -Police Integrity 2005b: 9–10)

The ease with which access can be gained often means that it is a relatively simple matter for a police officer or member of police staff to obtain information in which he or she has no *official* interest. Increasing use of ICTs has made the perpetration of ethical breaches easier because formerly bureaucratic processes have been replaced by technology accessible to all those working inside police institutions. Although ICTs also provide the possibility of tracking and monitoring police access to such information, recent history suggests that attempts at 'technological fixes' have been less than successful. Although access codes and audit trails provide a good source of evidence of database use, such evidence is not always conclusive or definitive and is generally only useful *ex post* – as a source of evidence after misconduct has occurred. Reliance on access codes has notable weaknesses; for example, police officers invariably know, or can guess, the access codes of colleagues (Independent Commission Against Corruption 1992: 13, 108–9) or steal them from other police officers (*R* v. *Bunning* [2007] VSCA 205). Further, allegations of inappropriate access to police databases commonly lead to a range of stock responses from officers, such as:

- They are unable to recall why they performed the transaction and their duty book, which might have assisted them to remember, cannot be located;
- There is a common practice to leave computer terminals open and it must have been someone else who used their ID; and
- They could have been using the computer and someone else requested them to perform a transaction on their behalf but they have no recollection as to who that person might have been.

(Kennedy Royal Commission, quoted by<br>Director-Police Integrity 2005b: 23)

Similarly, a Victorian Ombudsman's Report made the point that, when interviewed:

> members have commonly justified their access by reference to some police duty – for example, to avoid forming a possible undesirable personal association; to ascertain from car registration details seen in the vicinity of a person's home if the member or his family were under possible surveillance or to ascertain whether there were outstanding warrants against a family member.

(The Ombudsman 2001: 20)

Evidence to the Leveson Inquiry from various UK Constabularies did not paint a clear picture of computer database misuse, however some important evidence emerged relating to Britain's PNC database. The PNC (established in 1974) links a number of separate databases and holds a range of records including the details of individuals who are convicted, cautioned, arrested, wanted or missing; the registered keeper of vehicles; individuals with a driving licence entitlement or who are disqualified; certain types of stolen and recovered property including animals, firearms, trailers, plant machinery and engines; it supports enquiries against the national phone register and contains the details of individuals on the national Firearms Certificate Holders Register. The PNC is used by all UK police forces and other authorised agencies, including those with a brief to examine serious organised crime. Evidence to the Inquiry indicated that it has 'in excess of 250,000 users and handles in excess of 169 million transactions per annum, giving a daily average of just under 463,000 transactions' all of which were subjected to user activity and logging protocols (National Policing Improvement Agency Head of PNC Services, Karl Wissgott, quoted in Leveson 2012a: 812).

It is perhaps surprising, given the huge transaction rate of the system, that it was claimed that the PNC was only 'misused occasionally' for unlawful disclosure, with the associated belief expressed that the current security measures are 'effective and proportionate' and that there was no 'widespread systemic problem, nor that any particular and specific additional security measure would be effective' (Wissgott, quoted in Leveson 2012a: 813). By contrast, the Commissioner of the Metropolitan Police Service confirmed that over 200 officers and support staff had been disciplined for unlawful PNC access in the previous ten years, with 106 of these matters relating to the last three years; it suggested additional safeguards were required (Hogan-Howe, cited in Leveson 2012a: 813). These figures and the implicit trend represented therein provide an indication of the persistence of this problem – which is likely to be even more significant given the likelihood of additional undetected and unknown breaches.

There is some evidence to suggest that there is a tolerance for *accessing* database information, which is often regarded as a relatively minor offence. This seems particularly the case if access is motivated by professional curiosity rather than malicious intent or nefarious motives and if the information is not passed on, or disclosed, to third parties (Davids 2005).[7] The idea that police members are *entitled* to access information may be culturally ingrained within police forces (see Director-Police Integrity 2005b: 15).

It is clear that the increasing use of technologically mediated systems has brought a new series of challenges for systems of accountability in terms of their effectiveness and reach. In circumstances where information is ever more important to policing, it is vital to recognise that '[i]nformation security and integrity ... are the preconditions for effective information systems that empower police to do their jobs effectively and safely' (Commissioner for Law Enforcement Data Security 2009: 7). The technological tightening of audit trails may assist in identifying system users and provide proof of access, but debate about the legitimacy of individual actions often centres on the *justification* offered for accessing information. This emphasises the importance of ensuring that the design and implementation of information systems is intertwined with systems of accountability, such that all users of ICTs are cognisant of their responsibilities and accountabilities for the use of official information.

### Other sources

Whilst police databases provide a ready and convenient source of information, police officers may also make private use of information gleaned in the ordinary course of their duties – for example, during an investigation – or may actively use a police position to *obtain* information for private purposes. In the latter instance, information may be sought and obtained solely for private purposes that would not otherwise be obtained by the police officer either in an official or non-official capacity. Davids (2008: Ch. 6) identified two sources of police information that were significant in this regard: (1) information gleaned in the ordinary course of police duties and not necessarily entered into computerised databases; and (2) the *active* use of a police position and police channels to obtain information which would not otherwise be available to the police officer (either in an official or non-official capacity) (see also Miller 2003: iii).

## Dimensions of the problem: domestic use

Miller (2003: 13) characterised the typical 'domestic' use of information as involving inappropriate use of police databases for 'personal interest purposes' such as the conduct of checks on friends and neighbours or on motor vehicles that a police officer is considering purchasing. This type of abuse was said to be 'a common feature of misconduct cases'. Davids (2008) expanded Miller's categorisation to distinguish several other domestic uses of information: private commercial dealings; private business and secondary employment; to assist friends or family members in private commercial dealings; personal advantage in private, non-commercial matters; private family matters; intimate personal relationships; and professional curiosity.

Analysis of cases by Davids found that many problems arise in the context of private business, commercial and employment dealings and arrangements, where information itself is often an important 'currency'. Police information may be obtained from databases previously outlined, or the position of police officer may be used to obtain information (in relation to a private matter) that would not be available to an ordinary citizen.

The use of police information in such contexts may also be combined with injudicious behaviour towards those engaged in business with the officer. For example, a case where a police officer obtained personal details (home address, licence details) of a debt collector with a major finance company, who had contacted the officer in relation to monies owed on a vehicle (Case 69). In another case, a police officer used his position to obtain prior ownership and sale details of a motor vehicle he had purchased in a private sale, then used this information in an attempt to have the sale (to him) nullified and have his money returned (Case 121). Yet another matter involved a dispute over the parts used in repairs to a motor vehicle, where an officer pretended to be conducting an official investigation in order to obtain information that would assist him in this dispute (Case 64).

Police may also attempt to obtain a private benefit from the use of information in the context of their own private business or secondary employment arrangements. In this context, the use of police information may be associated with an apparent intention to derive a financial benefit that would not otherwise be available to the individual. There is significant potential for such interests to interfere with a police officer's impartial enforcement of the law. Case examples include:

- Allegations that a police officer used unreported crime information (not entered onto the police database, contrary to regulations) relating to an alleged robbery in order to assist in soliciting or securing private security business (Case 310);
- Intended use of information obtained in the course of police duties to assist in setting up a private business in police recruitment, education and training services (Case 234);
- A police officer, whilst on his way to work (on duty), conducted an ostensibly 'random' licence check of a driver; he subsequently obtained database details about the driver and contacted the person in an effort to recruit him into a work-from-home networking business opportunity (Case 236); and
- Secondary employment in the surveillance or private investigations industry and the use of official motor vehicle registration information in this context (Case 345).[8]

The use of police information in the manner described above may also extend to attempts to assist family members or associates of police in the context of their own private business and commercial dealings, such as debt collection matters or business/commercial disputes (Case 256) or tenancy disputes (Case 176).

Police officers may also seek to gain a personal advantage in private, non-commercial matters, including what would normally be regarded as relating to 'family' and relationship matters. For example, the use of a police database to track an ex-spouse in relation to problems concerning maintenance payments or other family law disputes (Cases 120, 152, 375), including child custody disputes (Case 360). There is also evidence that police officers may seek to use police information in the context of attempts to further intimate personal relationships, such as obtaining personal particulars of a person in whom the individual officer may be 'interested' (Cases 113, 111, 19), or personal information about a former domestic partner (Case 223). Information use in some circumstances may be easily (mis)interpreted as constituting harassment or stalking (Case 268). The 'domestic' uses of police information extend to police officers accessing personal details of members of the public and other matters on the basis of an apparent or claimed 'professional curiosity'. Evidence suggests that police accountability systems tend to deal with such matters on an ad hoc or reactive basis. For instance, following a 2003 public scandal over several police officers' access to the police files of a candidate standing in a state government election, the then Chief Commissioner of Victoria Police announced that much tougher rules and protocols over access to police information would be instituted. Under this approach, 'professional curiosity' would not be an acceptable reason for accessing any file, even where there was no malicious intent.[9] While this could be regarded as representing an appropriate response in relation to the formal rules for information use, such rule changes alone are insufficient to challenge the apparent *cultural* acceptance of domestic use of police information.

In 2005 in Western Australia, 580 police officers were censured and sanctioned for sending emails carrying confidential images of two young men who died in the Great Sandy Desert. Multiple graphic photographs of the men's bodies were circulated, with some ending up on a United States-based website featuring macabre events. Such was the public outrage that police management convened a 'restorative justice event that involved relatives of the dead men being invited to a forum in which they could tell 50 of the offending police officers of the pain and suffering they had experienced upon learning of the unauthorised circulation of the images.[10] Again, such a restorative justice event may be regarded as an appropriate response in the individual circumstances, perhaps producing some individual acceptance of personal responsibility, but the ad hoc nature of such an approach is likely to be insufficient to produce the kind of cultural change that is central to the acceptance of the broader responsibilities that attend to a police position and accompanying accountability for actions.

## Dimensions of the problem: disclosure

The release of confidential police information to outside parties has been an official concern for many years. As far back as 1993, the Victorian Deputy Ombudsman (Police Complaints) expressed concern over both the frequency of this type of complaint and the high substantiation rate (The Ombudsman 1993: 11).[11] The disclosures identified by the Deputy Ombudsman included 'purposeful, mischievous "leaks"' of several kinds of information:

> the names of people charged, criminal histories, police intelligence, police photographs and vehicle registration details. The types of information most commonly released have been criminal histories and registration details. The release has usually been to friends and relatives of the police involved and, more generally, to representatives of the media.
>
> (The Ombudsman 1993: 11)

As noted by the Victorian Commissioner for Law Enforcement Data Security, leaking of police information is particularly problematic on a number of fronts:

> As has been demonstrated in an international context, the actions of a single individual who releases sensitive information without authorisation can have a disproportionately large effect on organisational security and public trust and confidence in the institutions tasked with protecting community safety and security.
>
> (Commissioner for Law Enforcement Data Security 2012: 4)

Miller found that the 'leaking of information plays a central role' in the 'more common form' of 'individual corruption' in England and Wales, whereby 'members of police staff engaged in corrupt activities in isolation from colleagues' (2003: 10, iii). He outlined several types of leaks of police information to outside parties: ' "low-level" leaks' to friends or associates, such as carrying out police data checks for friends running businesses, which was described as 'common'; leaks of information, including 'sensitive operational police information' in relation to 'high profile cases', to journalists in the media – an activity that 'tended to involve payment of police staff by journalists' (clearly identifying this problem long before the Leveson Inquiry); and the deliberate leaking of police information to criminals, whether directly or through an intermediary – either as a favour or for payment (Miller 2003: 13). Davids' (2008) empirical study found several significant categories of leaks to outside parties: low-level leaks; leaks in the context of a business or commercial matter; leaks in the context of criminal investigations, legal or associated matters; and leaks to the media.[12]

### Low-level leaks

Many low-level leaks may be conceptualised as an extension of the 'domestic' use of information, where the personal or professional interests or curiosity of the police officer is replaced or supplemented by the curiosity or interest of another party to whom information is disclosed. Thus, a police officer may pass on police information in order to assist family members or associates of police in the context of their own private business and commercial dealings, such as tenancy disputes (Case 365), personal relationships (Case 237) and other family-related matters (Case 242).

Davids' analysis showed that the conflict of interest involved in low-level leaks is often evident on the facts, yet not acknowledged either by the police officers concerned or police management – both often see the problem as relatively innocuous. As with the apparent acceptance of domestic use of information (above), a police culture that accepts or marginalises the importance of 'low-level' breaches does not recognise how even seemingly minor breaches in such matters may impinge on police integrity and damage public trust. One prosecuted case in Victoria involved the disclosure by a serving police officer to a former police officer (friend) of a number of police manuals regarding the operation of speed detection devices – the context was the friend was intending to contest impending charges of exceeding the speed limit.[13] Although the defendant was acquitted because most of the material provided was also available on the Internet, questions about partiality and 'helping a mate' are problematic from a public accountability perspective. Accountability systems, and individual officers, must attend to both the action itself and 'political optics' (Davids and Boyce 2008).

### Leaks in the context of a business or commercial matter, or secondary employment

At what might be regarded as the 'high end' of low-level leaks are leaks in the context of a business or commercial matter – 'high' because disclosure is motivated by a quite specific type of business or commercial interest, and there may be particular damage to both the reputation of the Force and trust in the integrity of policing.

Problematic contexts include outside or secondary employment in the surveillance, private investigations and process serving industries, where intelligence about police operations or motor vehicle and other similar data is particularly valuable (Case 345; Case 380). A recognised problem exists in relation to 'ex-police officers working in the private investigation industry who requested information' from former colleagues who are still serving officers (Miller 2003: 13). The opportunities for networks of police colleagues and former colleagues are significant, as illustrated by an organised illicit trade in police information that came to light in New South Wales in the early 1990s (Independent Commission Against Corruption 1992). The trade included the provision of licence records and criminal histories to outside parties – often private inquiry agents, many of whom were former police officers, with the ultimate recipients of information, including insurance companies and financial institutions. These external parties were found to be a significant part of the problem insofar as they 'embraced' the trade and provided a ready market that contributed to its development.

Such cases illustrate the importance of police accountability systems dealing not just with the actions and activities of officers, but also with their personal relationships and involvements. Individual officers and police organisations must recognise the need to separate clearly private from personal interests and associations. Although problems with some kinds of personal relationships, such as associations with criminals or suspects, are well recognised and generally dealt with systematically within police accountability systems (through regulation, registration or prohibition of interests), the more general problems that can flow from private relationships and involvements must also be attended to (Davids 2006). Recognition of the 'shades of grey' in professional integrity and operational decision-making must be accompanied by enhanced understanding of the form of 'active accountability' that requires development of a sense of personal and collective responsibility in complex ethical situations.

### *Leaks in the context of criminal investigations, legal or associated matters*

Leaking of police information to criminals and others has been identified as a particular contemporary problem in Australia and the UK (Director-Police Integrity 2005a; Miller 2003; Davids 2008: 228–32). In Victoria, there has been much concern surrounding leaks of sensitive police information to criminals. Some of these leaks have compromised major drug-trafficking investigations, prosecutions and, in one instance, were believed to have resulted in the murders of a police informer and his wife (Director-Police Integrity 2005d; Taskforce Keel – see Victoria Police 2013).

Leaks of police information of this nature are much more serious than low-level leaks because of both the nature of the information and the context within which it may be used, which includes police investigation, criminal matters or in civil or criminal proceedings. This kind of conflict of interest may compromise the administration of justice in the matters concerned, hinder police operations, assist criminals to evade detection and/or prevent them being brought before the law (Cases 192, 241, 289). The impartiality of police overall may be called into question. Significant cases brought before the Victorian courts have included matters involving the disclosure of police database information to a drug-dealing friend and his associates regarding an ongoing investigation into the associates,[14] and the disclosure by a detective of confidential police information from various sources regarding police investigations, surveillance, telephone intercepts to a registered police informer and drug dealer.[15]

Other cases examined in Davids' study involved the supply of police evidence briefs, witness statements, criminal histories of individuals and other sensitive information. Most cases involved concerns about releases of information to alleged offenders but it can be equally problematic for the administration of justice to provide information to an alleged victim in a criminal matter (Case 212). The context of such leaks included pending or possible criminal charges (Cases 76, 15), civil proceedings (Cases 45, 115), employment law issues (Case 160), and family law and other family or relationship matters (Cases 255, 86, 18, 149, 247). In addition to concerns over conflict of interest, such matters could be regarded as attempts to pervert the course of justice and could impact on the viability of legal proceedings (Case 15). These cases also illustrate the potential for damage to be caused to individuals, which is present whether leaked information (e.g. about a criminal history) is accurate or not (e.g. about allegations or other unproven matters). This reiterates the importance of police officers being aware of their duty not to release confidential information, *and* the general injunction to not allow personal interests to interfere in official actions and decisions. Leaks of information may *seem* harmless from the perspective of the police officer involved, but the flow-on implications for public trust may be substantial.

Even more serious are deliberate leaks to criminals, which may be done as a favour to illicit associates of a police officer or in return for payment (Miller 2003: 13). Leaks to criminals may also be unintended, and may effectively result from what may be thought of as a low-level leak, as found in Miller's study:

> Leaked information can find its way to criminals even where this is not deliberately intended. In some cases, it is passed to associates, such as relatives, friends, social acquaintances or even ex-police colleagues, who, in turn, pass this information on to criminals. These types of arrangements apparently allow some criminals to network their way indirectly into police circles to obtain police information … some criminals [appear] to have a number of links of this kind with different members of police staff.
>
> (Miller 2003: 17)

Recent revelations in Victoria indicate a large volume of police records (including LEAP database records and sensitive information relating to police informers) have been provided to high-profile 'outlaw motorcycle gangs', resulting in criminal charges against one officer and investigations into other potentially corrupt police officers (Taskforce Keel – see Victoria Police 2013: 63). Allegations include the use of performance-enhancing drugs, leaked intelligence regarding crucial drug operations, and inappropriate social relations (police and organised crime figure friendships are particularly problematic) between serving police officers and senior motorcycle club members convicted of drug dealing.[16]

### Leaks to the media

The Leveson Inquiry in the UK reinforced the notion of policing by consent and drew attention to the important role of the media in shaping the relationship between police and citizens. It pointed out that public confidence in the police is axiomatic in the policing-by-consent model and noted the crucial role the media can play as a conduit for intelligence in relation to preventing and solving crime. Thus, effective and professional relationships between police and the media are important for successful policing. They can also prevent media stories from inadvertently scuppering investigations and in worse case scenarios jeopardising the safety of victims or highly sensitive case planning.

In its submissions to the Leveson Inquiry, the Commissioner of the Metropolitan Police Service (MPS) identified five areas in which 'keeping the media properly informed about policing and criminal matters was critical to the functioning' of the police (Leveson 2012b: 7465):

1  Police can communicate key messages associated with preventing and detecting crime;
2  A healthy relationship can increase public understanding of the work of policing;
3  Police can seek the assistance of the public, via the media;
4  Public confidence in the police may be enhanced, generating greater understanding of police policies and initiatives; and
5  The relationship provides a means whereby the public can scrutinise police actions and policies, and the police can 'test the persuasiveness of their strategies, policies and tactics'.

(Hogan-Howe, cited in Leveson 2012b 746–7)

The key concern outlined by Miller (2003) for the release of police information to the media was that it often involves the making of payments to police officers for information provided to journalists. Concern was also expressed that the disclosure of sensitive operational police information could directly impact on police sources. It was also noted that there could be an association between leaks to the media and to criminals: 'Certainly, where information is leaked to journalists it is likely to end up in the public domain, which will inevitably include criminals' (Miller 2003: 14).

In high-profile cases the release of confidential or sensitive police information to the media may directly impact on police sources by jeopardising the security of witnesses, informants and, on occasion, the operation itself (Miller 2003: 13; and see Director-Police Integrity 2005d). A 2013 prosecution in the Victorian Courts involved a senior detective in an antiterrorism operation who leaked advance information about the raid to a journalist.[17] There was no suggestion that the officer gained as a result of the leak; he and the journalist appeared to have had a long-standing relationship and shared some mutual professional interests. In another Victorian matter that was prosecuted through the courts, the issue was not a release of information to the media, but the publication of very sensitive police material in a book written by a serving detective. The material relating to a high-profile investigation was regarded by police management as possibly leading to the identification of police informers.[18]

Balanced against the general injunction against releasing information to the media is the notion that the release of police information to parties outside the organisation, including to the media, may form an important public accountability function, sometimes known as 'whistle-blowing'. A 1990s case in Victoria involved a prominent whistle-blower who made unauthorised public comments about internal police operations, primarily relating to a major internal investigation. These whistle-blower's comments were made to various media outlets, including mainstream and radical print media and radio (Case 318). An investigation of the underlying case by the State Ombudsman and Victoria Police internal investigations (1995–7) resulted in disciplinary charges against approximately 550 Victoria Police members (see The Ombudsman 2003: 72). The whistle-blower himself faced disciplinary proceedings for allegedly failing to comply with a lawful instruction from the Chief Commissioner to cease making public comments; it was argued that public comment could compromise a specific police operation.

Taking a different perspective, Sandra Laville, Crime Correspondent for the *Guardian* newspaper, identified to the Leveson Inquiry (2012b: 747) how journalism plays an important role in maintaining the media as the 'people's "eyes and ears"' in relation to the coercive powers afforded to the police. On this basis, a proper public interest and democratic function of the media is to challenge, interrogate and question police actions. The Inquiry noted the possibility of tension in the relationship between media and police, pointing to the differing needs of each party in relation to high-profile investigations (Leveson 2012b: 748–50). It is broadly recognised that:

> [b]oth police and the media have an important role in serving the public interest.... Media attention can assist police to solve crimes and convey important messages about emergency evacuations in natural disasters, road safety or alcohol-related violence. The media is also used to hold police accountable to the public they serve.
>
> (Office of Police Integrity 2012: 25)

As the Leveson Inquiry demonstrated, however, police–media relations are fraught with difficulty and it is not only the public image of integrity and impartiality in policing that is at stake:

> In addition to breaching the privacy of individuals, public airing of details from an investigation before it is finalised compromises the integrity of the investigation. When details of offences are publicly aired there is a real risk other evidence gathering processes will be tainted. For example, leaked details can trigger a witness to provide an account that is influenced by what he or she has read or heard in the media, rather than providing details from the person's own knowledge. Furthermore, if only one version of an incident under investigation is publicly aired, public opinion about the case can be determined without access to a full set of accurate data. This can give rise to public expectations that police will act in a particular way, for example charge a person. This places pressure on police to meet those expectations.
>
> (Office of Police Integrity 2012: 17)

## Buttressing integrity through accountability

### *Conflict of interest and police integrity*

The public impact of ethical breaches relating to disclosure and/or use of police information is high. The failure of honesty and impartiality on the part of individual public officials can have a particularly damaging effect on public trust in the integrity and impartiality of police. When integrity is not evident, public trust and confidence in the whole police organisation is affected. In part, public trust relates to the extent to which individuals expect others to be constrained by the duties and requirements attached to their roles, and to act to prevent abuses of official positions. It relies on a belief in the integrity of both individual police officers and police organisations as a whole. In addition to directly compromising investigations, unauthorised disclosure may negatively impact many practical aspects of policing. For instance, it may lead to reluctance on the part of those who supply information to police to do so in the future, which may undermine the continued supply of information essential to the policing function (see Billingsley *et al.* 2001).

In terms of conflict of interest, the leaking or use of official information for non-official purposes involves private interests (including the interests of family, friends and associates of a police officer) prevailing over public ethics and public duty. Notions of friendship and mateship, which may motivate leaks, are equally misguided in situations where a police officer is asked by a friend, relative, acquaintance, former colleague or private inquiry agent to make unofficial inquiries on their behalf. Even though low-level leaks may be regarded as minor, police officers can be caught in a conflict between loyalty to family or friends and their obligation to keep confidential those matters coming to their attention as a police member. It may also be that 'officers do not appreciate the seriousness of unauthorised disclosure at any time' (HMIC 1999: 42). Effective management lies in the responses that police make to these requests and in recognising that this area presents a problem that police officers may reasonably expect to have to confront.

### *Accountability*

Earlier in the chapter, it was suggested that public accountability includes both administrative dimensions (structural, organisational, regulatory) and a moral or ethical sense that relates to the *demonstration* of integrity and trustworthiness. Bovens (2005, 2010) highlights several key functions of public accountability:

1   democratic control within institutional arrangements, which may be regarded as including hierarchical accountability within organisations and agencies, ultimately proceeding up to ministerial and governmental levels;
2   enhancement of the integrity of public governance by preventing and detecting corruption, nepotism, abuse of power and other forms of unauthorised and inappropriate behaviour, particularly in the context of the application of delegated powers;
3   maintaining and enhancing the legitimacy of public governance – a particular challenge in light of a general decline in public confidence in public institutions and an absence of automatic deference to public authority;
4   ritual and purifying functions that may provide some form of public catharsis in response to tragedies, fiascos, scandals and failures;
5   fostering individual and organisational learning in ways that discourage or prevent future misconduct and enhance future performance – often through the development and reinforcement of appropriate norms and organisational culture that induce reflexivity and openness.

Dealing with the multiple challenges of accountability that are reflected in these functions implicates 'a whole series of flows, circuits, connections, disconnections, selections, favourings, accounts, holding to account and attempts at analysis' that means accountability in action involves a certain degree of 'messiness' (Neyland and Woolgar 2002: 272). As Bovens (2005) comments, '[p]ublic accountability may be the complement of public management – it certainly is the predicament of public managers' (Bovens 2005: 202).

The traditional concept of accountability in the public sector involves answerability to the community for, and exercise of, legal power and authority by a public official. The broader concept of *social* accountability invoked in this chapter takes a bottom-up social, rather than a top-down organisational, perspective in order to address ethical, organisational and cultural dimensions of organisational management. Thus, it also encapsulates both an:

> ex post answering for past decisions and actions and the need to have mechanisms in place that seek to deal with neglects of duty before they happen

... [including] some level of attention to political optics in terms of 'how things look' to reasonable members of the public.

(Boyce and Davids 2009: 604)

The inclusion of this latter element recognises the importance of public confidence in public institutions. There is an implicit recognition here that social accountability involves more than 'internalizing the values, processes and practices of accountability' that may produce rule-bound approaches that obviate the need to address how 'performance ... establishes the moral order that can be seen to provide the reference point for the mess and flows of connections' (Neyland and Woolgar 2002: 272).

Formal mechanisms of accountability embodied in organisational structures, rules, procedures and the like are vital to the first four functions of accountability outlined above and are instrumental to good governance. Just as important, and vital to the development of accountable organisational cultures that underpin the operation of accountability mechanisms, is the nurturing of accountability as individual and organisational virtue – an active sense of goodness and rightness that reflects a commitment to integrity and development of public trust.

Accountability as a mechanism and accountability as virtue are complementary and mutually reinforcing, but must be separately recognised and addressed (Bovens 2010). The social accountability framework for public sector conflict of interest developed by Boyce and Davids (2009, 2010) tackles the three core dimensions of the problem via three key elements of social accountability, with a 'reasonable person' standard (see Figure 5.1).

It is possible for an accountability system to deal with unauthorised use of confidential police information as an aspect of the broader problem of conflict of interest. Thus, problematic *interests* are attended to by limiting or prohibiting certain private interests that are inherently problematic. Such interests may be defined for this purpose as identifiable types of private interest that are deemed to be especially problematic, and therefore unacceptable, due to inherent incompatibility with police roles. The analysis in this chapter suggests that this is likely to include interests such as associations with criminals, commercial or off-the-record relations with journalists, and identifiably problematic forms of outside or secondary employment or business arrangements (including in the private inquiry industry).

Nevertheless, it is recognised that not all potentially conflicting interests can be effectively or reasonably regulated, such as those associated with familial and friendship relationships. These interests are recognised as giving rise to possible conflicts in certain circumstances only, and may be dealt with through the structuring of roles and functions so that officers are not involved in matters that may give rise to a conflict of interest. This requires both awareness of the potential problems and a preparedness to manage them in a situation-specific manner. These two elements – dealing with problematic interests and potential and actual conflicts – are buttressed and underpinned by ethical and accountable organisational cultures. Finally, appearances, or public perceptions, are an essential consideration in dealing with conflict of interest issues. The key aspect of

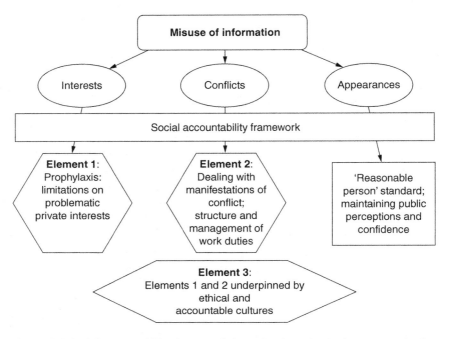

*Figure 5.1* Social accountability framework for police integrity in the context of private interests (source: adapted from Boyce and Davids 2009, 2010).

conflict of interest that undermines public trust and confidence in police relates to perceptions that a public position has been used for private advantage, challenging the ostensible commitment to serve the public rather than private interest. This is therefore destabilising for the policing function itself.

Understanding, managing and responding to conflicts of interest generated by unauthorised and inappropriate use of confidential information requires consideration of the intersection of subjective and objective elements. The subjective element relates to whether an individual has *actually* sought to gain a private advantage for themselves or others from the inappropriate use of a public position. The objective element revolves around application of a 'reasonable person' test that considers how things, in a particular circumstance, would *appear* to a reasonable member of the public. Because subjective concerns cannot be determined without 'knowing' the mind of the individual, effective management of conflicts of interest focuses on the objective element, which provides the standard or test against which judgements about conflict of interest may be made. This involves considering how things would look to a reasonable observer. Judgements about the appropriateness of particular classes of interests, and about the structuring of work duties to deal with conflicts, may also be made with reference to this standard.

Overall, a social accountability framework seeks to nurture proactive accountability through the development of responsibility as both a shared and personal and subjective sense of rightness and good conscience (see also Chapter 4), while accountability judgements can be made by applying an objective standard (Bovens 1998; Boyce and Davids 2009). As in any domain, public officials who hold power and authority must be accountable for their exercise of power. While accountability as a *mechanism* operates through organisational structures and hierarchies, broader social accountability and accountability to the community is a concept of accountability as *virtue* (Bovens 2010) that must consider both facts and appearances. Both forms of accountability are central to effective policing, because '[p]olicing is accountability, and without it the police have no legitimacy and hence cannot function effectively in a democratic society' (Punch 2010: 315).

## Conclusion

> Changing the police culture of 'leaking' has proven to be difficult, it requires a two pronged attack – an education program to drive home an understanding of the risks and consequences of an unauthorised disclosure of information, together with a highly visible sanctions program which will demonstrate that such disclosures will not be tolerated.
>
> (Office of Police Integrity 2012: 17)

The issue of 'leaks' of police information demonstrates how the power and position of police officers may be used to obtain information that is not required for official purposes, but which may be used to further the private interests of the police officer and associates. The conflict with official police duties is clear and unambiguous. When such matters come to light, they have the potential to severely damage the reputation of a police force, and to diminish the willingness and propensity of members of the public to trust police officers who rely on them to support the policing function. Although a range of harms can result, in worst case scenarios they can jeopardise investigations and lead to the injury or death of witnesses and informers. Failure to respect the trust that is placed in police to protect confidential information is also likely to have serious consequences for operational policing and for the reputation of a police force and the public trust that is placed in it.

Effectively dealing with the issues canvassed in this chapter requires some reflection on the nature and purposes of the public sector and of policing within the public realm. A clear 'commitment to integrity and ethics in the pursuit of the public interest is a bedrock of a socially accountable approach' (Boyce and Davids 2009: 633), but effective accountability requires both the assurance provided by rigorous mechanisms and a commitment to embrace an active sense of responsibility and adherence to public values by individuals, managers and their organisations.

## Notes

1 See Davids (2005: 105) for an explanation of the methodology for counting allegations or instances of conflict of interest. Space limitations mean that only brief case
   information can be provided in this chapter (see Davids 2005 for detailed case
   description and analyses; and a sumamarised analysis in Davids 2008: ch. 6).
2 These PSUs 'proactively cultivate and analyse information or "intelligence" on
   unethical police activity from a range of sources (e.g. police colleagues, informants,
   the public, other agencies, audits, and surveillance) and mount formal investigations
   into suspects identified' (Miller 2003: i).
3 The Victorian Office of Police Integrity was absorbed into a new Independent Broad-
   based Anti-corruption Commission established in 2012.
4 For example, *Police Regulation Act 1979* (Vic) s.127; *Crimes (Controlled Operations) Act 2004* (Vic), s.36; *Crimes (Assumed Identities) Act 2004* (Vic), s.30.
5 For example, *Criminal Law Consolidation Act 1935* (SA), ss251, 238; *Commonwealth
   Criminal Code* (Australia), s.142.2.
6 As this chapter identifies, there have, though, been several recent Victorian cases of police
   officers being prosecuted for offences involving disclosure of confidential information.
7 Cases 268 and 372.
8 In this case, the police officers also used police vehicles, radios and mobile telephones
   in the private surveillance work (see Davids 2008).
9 Silvester and Baker (2003), 'Police will face sack for improper use of files', *The Age*,
   24 October: 3.
10 ABC (2005), 'Relatives confront police about emailed photos', *ABC Online* 9 December
   (www.abc.net.au/news/2005–12–09/relatives-confront-police-about-emailed-photos/
   758420, last accessed 12 November 2013).
11 From 1991 to 1993, 78 complaints relating to disclosure of information were investigated, and 25 of these (32 per cent) were found to be substantiated. Davids' study
   covered 1988–98; 39 cases files included an allegation of disclosure of police
   information to outside parties; 38.5 per cent of these matters were found to be
   substantiated.
12 For the purposes of the present analysis, Davids' category of 'trading in police
   information for financial or commercial benefit' has been combined with 'leaks in the
   context of criminal investigations, legal, or associated matters'; 'inadvertent leaks'
   have been omitted.
13 *DPP* v. *Zierk* [2008] VSC 184.
14 *DPP* v. *Marks* [2005] VSCA 277.
15 *R* v. *Bunning* [2007] VSCA.
16 McKenzie and Baker (2013a), 'Bikies infiltrate police', *The Age* (Melbourne), 27
   March: 1–3; and McKenzie and Baker (2013b), 'Friends in all the wrong places', *The
   Age* (Melbourne), 27 March: 18–19.
17 *DPP* v. *Artz* [2013] VCC 56.
18 *D'Alo* v. *Nolan* [2006] VSC 362.

## References

*ABC* (2005) 'Relatives Confront Police about Emailed Photos', *ABC Online*, 9 December,
   available at www.abc.net.au/news/2005–12–09/relatives-confront-police-about-emailed-
   photos/758420 (last accessed 8 November 2013).
Billingsley, R., Nimitz, T. and Bean, P. (eds) (2001) *Informers: Policing, Policy, Practice*, Cullompton, Devon: Willan.
Bovens, M. (1998) *The Quest for Responsibility: Accountability and Citizenship in
   Complex Organisations*, Cambridge: Cambridge University Press.

Bovens, M. (2005) 'Public Accountability', in E. Ferlie, L.E. Lynn and C. Pollitt (eds) *Oxford Handbook of Public Management*, Oxford and New York: Oxford University Press, 182–208.

Bovens, M. (2010) 'Two Concepts of Accountability: Accountability as a Virtue and as a Mechanism', *West European Politics*, 33: 946–67.

Boyce, G. and Davids, C. (2009) 'Conflict of Interest in Policing and the Public Sector: Ethics, Integrity, and Social Accountability', *Public Management Review*, 11: 601–40.

Boyce, G. and Davids, C. (2010) 'A Social Accountability Framework for Public Sector Conflict of Interest: Private Interests, Public Duties, and Ethical Cultures', in A. Ball and S.P. Osborne (eds) *Social Accounting and Public Management: Accountability for the Public Good*, New York and Abingdon: Routledge, 275–86.

Chan, J., Brereton, D., Legosz, M. and Doran, S. (2001) *E-policing: The Impact of Information Technology on Police Practices*, Brisbane: Queensland Criminal Justice Commission.

Commissioner for Law Enforcement Data Security (2009) *Annual Report 2008–2009*, Melbourne: Commission for Law Enforcement Data Security.

Commissioner for Law Enforcement Data Security (2012) *Annual Report 2012–2013*, Melbourne: Commission for Law Enforcement Data Security.

Crime and Misconduct Commission (2008) *Public Duty, Private Interests: Issues in Pre-Separation Conduct and Post-Separation Employment for the Queensland Public Sector*, Brisbane: Crime and Misconduct Commission (Queensland).

Crime and Misconduct Commission (2011) *Operation Tesco: Report of an Investigation into Allegations of Police Misconduct on the Gold Coast*, Brisbane: Crime and Misconduct Commission (Queensland).

Davids, C. (2005) *Police Misconduct, Regulation, and Accountability: Conflict of Interest Complaints Against Victoria Police Officers 1988–1998*, Sydney: Faculty of Law, University of New South Wales.

Davids, C. (2006) 'Conflict of Interest and the Private Lives of Police Officers: Friendships, Civic and Political Activities', *Journal of Policing, Intelligence and Counter Terrorism*, 1: 14–35.

Davids, C. (2008) *Conflict of Interest in Policing: Problems, Practices, and Principles*, Sydney: Institute of Criminology Press.

Davids, C. and Boyce, G. (2008) 'The Perennial Problem of Police Gratuities: Public Concerns, Political Optics, and an Accountability Ethos', *Journal of Policing, Intelligence and Counter Terrorism*, 3: 44–69.

Day, P. and Klein, R. (1987) *Accountabilities: Five Public Services*, London and New York: Tavistock Publications.

Director-Police Integrity (2005a) *Investigation into the Publication of 'One Down, One Missing'*, Melbourne: Office of Police Integrity.

Director-Police Integrity (2005b) *Investigation into Victoria Police's Management of the Law Enforcement Assistance Program (LEAP)*, Melbourne: Office of Police Integrity.

Director-Police Integrity (2005c) *Office of Police Integrity Annual Report 30 June 2005, Edition 01*, Melbourne: Office of Police Integrity.

Director-Police Integrity (2005d) *Report on the Leak of a Sensitive Victoria Police Information Report*, Melbourne: Office of Police Integrity.

HC Deb, 13 July 2011, vol. 531, cols 311, 313.

Her Majesty's Inspectorate of Constabulary (HMIC) (1999) *Police Integrity, England, Wales and Northern Ireland: Securing and Maintaining Public Confidence*, London: Home Office/HMIC.

Independent Commission Against Corruption (1992) *Report on Unauthorised Release of Government Information: Volume I*, Sydney: Independent Commission Against Corruption.

KPMG (2009) *Review of Information Governance within Victoria Police: Final Report*, Victoria: KPMG (for the Commissioner for Law Enforcement Data Security).

Leveson, B. (2012a) *An Inquiry Into the Culture, Practices and Ethics of the Press. Report (Volume I)*, London: The Stationery Office.

Leveson, B. (2012b) *An Inquiry Into the Culture, Practices and Ethics of the Press. Report (Volume II)*, London: The Stationery Office.

McKenzie, N. and Baker, R. (2013a) 'Bikies Infiltrate Police', *The Age*, 27 March: 1–3.

McKenzie, N. and Baker, R. (2013b) 'Friends in All the Wrong Places', *The Age*, 27 March: 18–19.

Miller, J. (2003) *Police Corruption in England and Wales: An Assessment of Current Evidence*, London: Home Office.

Neyland, D. and Woolgar, S. (2002) 'Accountability in Action? The Case of a Database Purchasing Decision', *British Journal of Sociology*, 53: 259–74.

Office of Police Integrity (2010a) *Information Security and the Victoria Police State Surveillance Unit*, Melbourne: OPI Victoria.

Office of Police Integrity (2010b) *Sensitive and Confidential Information in a Police Environment: Discussion Paper no. 2*, Melbourne: OPI Victoria.

Office of Police Integrity (2012) 'Victoria Police: Recurring Themes in the Management of High Profile Investigations', Melbourne: OPI Victoria.

People, J. (2008) *Unauthorised Disclosure of Confidential Information by NSW Police Officers*, Research and Issues Papers, Sydney: NSW Police Integrity Commission.

Punch, M. (2010) 'Police Corruption: Deviance, Accountability and Reform in Policing', *Policing*, 4: 315–21.

Roberts, J. (1991) 'The Possibilities of Accountability', *Accounting, Organizations and Society*, 16: 355–68.

Silvester, J. and Baker, R. (2003) 'Police Will Face Sack for Improper Use of Files', *The Age*, 24 October: 3.

Sinclair, A. (1995) 'The Chameleon of Accountability: Forms and Discourses', *Accounting, Organizations and Society*, 20: 219–37.

The Ombudsman (1993) *Annual Reports: Report of the Deputy Ombudsman (Police Complaints) for Years Ending 30 June 1992 and 30 June 1993*, Melbourne: Office of the Ombudsman, Victoria.

The Ombudsman (2001) *Annual Report: Twenty-Eighth Report of The Ombudsman, 2000/2001*, Melbourne: Office of the Ombudsman, Victoria.

The Ombudsman (2003) *Annual Report*, Melbourne: Office of the Ombudsman, Victoria.

Victoria Police (2013) *Annual Report 2012–2013*, Melbourne: Victoria Police.

# 6 Electocracy with accountabilities?

## The novel governance model of Police and Crime Commissioners

*John W. Raine*

The election across England and Wales on 15 November 2012 of 41 Police and Crime Commissioners (PCCs) marked the launch of a novel governance model for policing, crime prevention and community safety at the local level. It was, however, a particularly inauspicious start. An embarrassingly low turnout at the polls – among the lowest in British electoral history, with an average of just 14.7 per cent – only seemed to fuel the wave of scepticism that had accompanied the parliamentary debate on the Government's proposals and which had also been rife within professional policing and criminal justice circles, including the police authorities that the directly elected PCCs were to replace (Amman 2013).

Paradoxically, such an underwhelming show of enthusiasm and democratic support for PCCs in the elections seemed to have amplified media interest in the new model. In the ensuing months, a spate of media reports provided several of the new commissioners with much unexpected, albeit mostly negative, publicity. Initially at least, much of this focused on allegations of cronyism in the appointment of deputies and assistants to PCCs, and also on the higher-than-expected costs to the public purse of the new teams that the commissioners were establishing. In the West Midlands, for example, the PCC chose to make eight senior appointments – a Deputy Commissioner, three Assistant Commissioners and four Non-Executive Members – to form a Strategic Policing and Crime Board that appeared, to the critics at least, to recreate the former police authority in a new guise. Meanwhile, the Lincolnshire PCC made the national media headlines when his decision to suspend his acting chief constable for alleged misconduct ended up in the High Court with the quashing of the suspension (the allegation subsequently being withdrawn) and a bill for legal fees amounting to some £58,000 (*Guardian* 2013a). Similarly profiled was the saga of 17-year-old Paris Brown, appointed as Youth Commissioner to assist the Kent PCC, but then resigning just a few days later in response to revelations about inappropriate 'tweets' she had posted two years earlier (*BBC News* 9 April 2013). There was also wide reporting of the conflict between the Gwent PCC and his chief constable, Carmel Napier, who, it was reported, had been pressurised into resigning (*Guardian* 2013b).

Such reports may have made uncomfortable reading for the Home Secretary, since the proposals for the new governance model had so recently and narrowly survived a challenging parliamentary process to reach the statute book. Further negative headlines followed as PCCs soon found themselves having to implement significant cuts in police budgets (HM Treasury 2013) leading to reductions in police personnel and the closure of police stations. Around the first anniversary of their election, a further low note was sounded as the Stevens Report (Independent Police Commission 2013: 81) concluded that 'the PCC model is systemically flawed as a method of democratic governance' and recommended its abolition. But then, as Newburn (2013) subsequently argued, since their impact had not yet become apparent it seemed 'too early ... for the Steven's Commission's attempt to bury them'.

Against this background, this chapter provides evidence of the work and contribution of PCCs in their first year of office. In so doing, it takes stock of the key changes that the new model has introduced, but stops short of attempting to assess its overall merits and limitations. In particular, the various, and competing, accountability relations that characterise the PCC governance model are articulated. At face value at least, the model might seem to conform closely to the concept of 'electocracy' – a descriptor first used by Dawisha and Parrott (1997). They use the term to describe political systems offering citizens the opportunity to vote for their preferred candidate (or party group) but where the elected office holder then assumes all authority to govern until the next ballot. The term has subsequently been applied by others (see, for example, Prasirtsuk 2007; Kryshtanovskaya 2008; Guinier 2008; Walker 2008; and Tierney 2009) mostly to portray more autocratic (post-election) styles of leadership, for instance, in various East European and Asian political settings, most notably in post-Soviet Russia and Thailand. The chapter explores the concept by drawing on evidence from interviews with a sample of nine PCCs which examined the nature and strength of their different accountability relationships.

The nine were selected from across England and Wales; three from the north of the country; three from the Midlands, and three from southern counties. The sample was further stratified by selecting from each such region one PCC sponsored by the Conservative Party, one by the Labour Party and one independent PCC (i.e. without affiliation to a formally recognised political party). At the same time, care was taken in the selection process to ensure a reasonable cross section of urban and rural police force areas (the final sample comprising PCCs for two metropolitan force areas, four for more mixed urban/rural force areas, and three for force areas of more rural character). Two members of the sample were female while all nine were white (as, indeed, are all 41 PCCs).

While the overall representativeness of this sample, or indeed, of the pattern of responses derived from it, is uncertain,[1] it seems likely that the key findings and broad messages at least hold good for the wider picture across the country. The interviews were conducted (by the author) on a one-to-one basis and in a semi-structured format,[2] discussing in turn eight accountability relationships for PCCs, each hypothesised to be of potential significance in shaping the patterns of influence and impact of the new governance model. These were respectively accountability with (1) the public; (2) Police and Crime Panels; (3) political sponsors; (4) chief constables; (5) central government; (6) local community safety partnerships; (7) agencies providing local criminal justice services; and (8) other statutory criminal justice agencies.[3] The research also involved reviewing a range of documentary information published on each PCC's website around the time of the interview (including Annual Reports, Police and Crime Plans, budgetary and commissioning reports, policy statements, minutes of meetings, formal decisions, blogs and other such communications).

Before turning to the key findings from this research, however, it should be helpful to describe in more detail the nature of the change in the governance model that was heralded by the first PCC elections in November 2012, and about the framework of relationships and hypothesised accountabilities that underpinned the research itself.

## From police authorities to Police and Crime Commissioners

Several observers, for example Raine and Keasey (2012), Lister (2014) and Davies (2014), have suggested that a strong motive for introducing directly elected PCCs was a general dissatisfaction with police authorities. Although operative for half a century, since the Police Act 1964, those bodies – one per police force area – each comprising a mix of local councillors (nominated by their respective local authorities), magistrates and other appointed 'independent' members,[4] had largely failed to achieve a strong public profile (Flanagan 2008). Nor did they enjoy a strong reputation within policing and criminal justice circles for providing effective governance of policing, whether in shaping policy or holding senior police officers to account. This state of affairs may have been a consequence of the lay and part-time status of their membership, which promoted deference towards the chief constable and senior commanders with their specialist policing knowledge and expertise. Perhaps, too, it reflected a weakness of 'committee-style' governance – with 15 to 20 individuals supposedly sharing responsibility – compared with the 'strong leader' model (or the elected mayor model) that successive recent governments felt would invigorate local government (Game 2003).

Some years earlier a White Paper from the New Labour Government had rehearsed the arguments about the weakness of police authorities (Home Office 2008), but no alternative mechanism emerged. The succeeding Coalition Government in 2010 returned to the issue and developed its own approach – that of the PCC. As so often in public policy, the model was seen to draw upon the experience of the US, specifically from 'city police commissioners'. However, the parallel is not strong since, across the Atlantic, commissioners are not directly elected but are either professional police officers or civilian administrators appointed by city mayors to undertake an oversight role for policing.

Also important for understanding the genesis of the new model was the growing enthusiasm in both national and local political circles for greater pluralism in public service delivery through 'commissioning' from the private and third sector organisations as an alternative to 'in-house' provision (Bovaird *et al.*

2013). Related, another argument in favour of the PCC model was the Coalition Government's avowed commitment to the polity of 'new localism' and an end to the centralism that had come to be seen as a hallmark of the preceding New Labour Government. In fact, as Lowndes and Pratchett (2012) noted, the roots of new localism were already well established in Labour's 'developing communities' agenda. However, the Coalition Government's much vaunted Localism Act 2011 was an eclectic mix of new statutes (ironically which created many additional powers for the centre as well as for local authorities) which signalled that local leadership and local choice were the preferred approaches wherever possible (Jones and Stewart 2011), and for which the opportunity for reforming police governance was seen as particularly timely and significant.

In a similar vein was the Coalition Government's enthusiasm for directly elected leaders at local level and for a more decisive and efficient form of decision-making that it was presumed to invoke. Like New Labour before it, the Coalition Government promoted the concept of directly elected mayors in local government and legislated to require local referenda on the issue in the 12 largest cities, albeit with little evidence of a body of public support for the idea.

The confluence of these various political currents provided the momentum for the idea of directly elected Police and Crime Commissioners to be taken forward as an early legislative priority for the Coalition Government, despite the arguments of the many critics, particularly about the risks of politicising policing. Above all, the model implied three main changes. First, from an indirect to a direct electoral process for selecting 'the governors'. Second, from a collective and largely part-time approach to governorship, to a more individualistic and essentially full-time one. Third, from a relatively narrow and specific remit for governing the police, to a wider-reaching responsibility that included crime reduction, prevention and community safety services. Importantly, too, the framework of accountabilities would change. While elements of the traditional 'tripartite relationship' would continue (now between the PCC, the chief constable and the Home Secretary), the introduction of a direct electoral process was particularly designed to build stronger local accountability with the voting public (Raine and Keasey 2012).

## A complex framework of accountability

In addition to the considerable literature on police accountability (see, for example, Reiner and Spencer 1993; McLaughlin 1994; Loveday 2001: Leishman *et al.* 2000; and Reiner 2010) there is a rich body of scholarly writing on the theme of accountability in public services more generally; the subject of accountability having long been of interest to students of public administration and public management (see, for example, Romzek and Dubnick 1987; Day and Klein 1987; Hood 1991; Ranson and Stewart 1994; Sinclair 1995: Pollitt 1996; Mulgan 2000; Lynn 2006; Romzek 2000; Behn 2001; Dubnick 2005; Bovens 2005; and Dubnick and Yang 2009). Much of this literature charts how, from its historic roots in relation to the 'keeping of accounts', the term 'accountability' has broadened in conception to embrace the reporting, scrutiny and third-party assessment of performance and, in so doing, has established itself as one of the watchwords of contemporary management (Harlow 2002). Various public administrative scholars have sought to categorise different forms of account-ability (for example, Stewart 1984; Dubnick 2002; Bovens 2007; and Erkkila 2007) with key distinctions being drawn between, on the one hand, more mana-gerialist forms of accountability centring on technical and professional perform-ance and, on the other, more democratic or political forms, with greater concern for public reporting and feedback. Much academic interest has also focused on accountability as a 'process', with Ranson and Stewart (1994), for instance, dis-cussing the relational nature of the subject in terms of 'bonds of accountability' and of the potential duality involved, on the one hand, with 'the giving of account', while on the other 'being held to account' (see also Ashworth and Skelcher 2005 for a discussion about the processes of 'taking into account' and of 'redress').

The discipline of economics has also contributed much to contemporary understanding of the processes of accountability and the behaviours involved, particularly through the application of Principal-Agent Theory (see, for example, Wood and Waterman 1994; Waterman and Meier 1998; Mayston 1993; Besley 2006; and Bertelli 2012). This is a theory that focuses, in its most simple form, on the relationship between the 'commissioner' of a task (or service provision activity) – 'the principal'– and the 'contractor' who undertakes the work – 'the agent'. A familiar problem in such relationships, however, is that of 'informa-tional asymmetry'; when the 'agent' (as contractor) knows more about the tasks involved than the 'principal' (Ferris and Graddy 1998). A consequence of this situation is that the agent may seek to exploit their greater knowledge to their own advantage, for instance by suggesting a larger-scale job than is really needed, and/or by charging more than is reasonable. The key challenge, then, for the 'principal' is to ensure that appropriate incentives are in place to serve their interests rather than those of the contractor. Carrying this general line of think-ing into police governance, then, one key question concerns the ability of PCCs to ensure that their chief constables (as their agents) do the necessary work (as asked of them) in the most effective and efficient manner.

The situation, however, with police governance, (as indeed, with regard to many public service contexts) proves rather more complex in practice and raises further interesting questions as a result. In particular, the complexities relate to the existence of 'multiple principals' (Knott and Miller 2006) or to chains of competing principal-agent relationships. Thus, for example, while PCCs may be 'principals' to chief constables, they must also be regarded as 'agents' to the public, 'agents' to their sponsoring political parties, and 'agents' to the Home Secretary too, at least for national policing responsibilities. Moreover, further complexity is to be found in the PCC framework because, as well as a commis-sioner for each police area, the Government decided also to establish a Police and Crime Panel – comprising nominated councillors from the various local authorities in the area – to act as a scrutiny body, holding the PCC to account on behalf of the public. Thus, the PCC might also be thought of as 'agent' to the Panel. Taken as a whole, therefore, the governance framework can be understood as comprising a number of different, potentially competing, principal-agent relationships, the interplay between, and implications of which could have a profound impact on the developing nature of policing policy and practice in England and Wales. In the succeeding sections of this chapter we will consider in turn the different accountability relationships involving PCCs, their relative strengths and the tensions between them, at least so far as they have manifested themselves to date.

Figure 6.1 depicts the key accountability relationships to be explored in this respect. Those with shaded arrows can perhaps be considered the primary relationships – those that also carry accountabilities, in the sense of either or both 'the giving of account and 'being held to account' (Ranson and Stewart 1994). First is the PCC's accountability relationship (as agent) towards the voters and the public at the local level, this stemming from the direct election process. Second is the accountability relationship of the PCC to the Police and Crime Panel. Third is the accountability relationship of the PCC to central government (particularly the Home Secretary in relation to national strategic policing issues, though also to other ministers with interests in relevant local public services). Fourth is the accountability relationship of those PCCs who

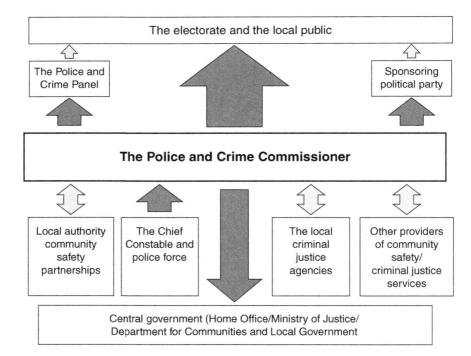

*Figure 6.1* PCC relationships and accountabilities.

stood as candidates for particular political parties towards their sponsoring parties (or branch constituency parties). Fifth (and facing the other way) is the accountability relationship of the PCC (as principal) to the chief constable (as agent for the implementation of the agreed policies and priorities for policing).

There are then further relationships to be considered (and depicted in Figure 6.1 without shading), notably, with the local community safety partnerships (principally comprising the police, local authorities and fire and rescue services) which are now funded by the PCC, and with the various agencies providing local criminal justice and community safety services which are currently (or which might in future be) 'commissioned' by PCCs, for example victim support services, women's aid centres, rehabilitative probation projects for offenders, and drug and alcohol treatment programmes. And while without involving direct accountabilities, there are also important relationships for PCCs in relation to the wider network of criminal justice agencies at the local level – particularly with the Crown Prosecution Service (CPS), HM Courts and Tribunals Service, and probation services.

Other relationships for PCCs might also perhaps be considered, for example with local media, but which, for reasons of retaining clarity, have not been included in Figure 6.1. Instead, the main focus here is on the relationships that potentially involve an element of accountability, and on the implications of such accountability for the nature of the governance process in practice. In the succeeding sections, then, we examine the eight relationships depicted in Figure 6.1 in turn, doing so by drawing on the evidence gathered in the round of interviews with nine PCCs from around the country.

## Accountability to the public and voters

Probably the most significant finding from the nine interviews concerned the large commitment of time and effort that each PCC had been devoting since the elections to building their profiles with the public and local communities. Perhaps, in part, a reaction to the very poor turnout at the polls and the very low level of public understanding of the new role, all nine PCCs had made it their first priority to pursue as many opportunities as possible for public engagement and for building relationships with local institutions and groups across their areas as well as with officers and staff at each of the police stations.

Interestingly, one of the nine who had previously served as a member of the (former) police authority for the area, suggested that 'police authorities hadn't thought of themselves as having a public profile' – a viewpoint that, if fair, would help to explain the very low level of public awareness of their existence. Yet within a matter of days of taking office, all nine PCCs had begun a circuit of public appearances, making presentations and answering questions at public meetings, arranging regular 'surgeries' in local communities, and 'pitching up' in market squares on Saturday mornings to meet shoppers, just as they had done during their election campaigns. Each had also begun a round of attendances at county, district and parish/town council meetings and had accepted a variety of invitations to speak at meetings of other community bodies such as Women's Institutes, Rotary and Volunteer Centres. They were also spending much time visiting different policing and criminal justice-related projects, including many community-based and volunteer-run initiatives undertaking community safety work or supporting criminal justice, for example victim support groups, domestic abuse projects, drug-treatment centres and various offender management projects. Indeed, all nine indicated spending at least a day per week away from their offices meeting community-based staff and volunteers involved in criminal justice-related project work of one kind or another, or addressing open meetings, community councils and the like. Many of their evenings were also taken up with speaking engagements and each was frequently writing articles for local magazines, community newsletters and bulletins. All were also making extensive use of social media – with near daily tweets and regular blogs on policing and crime issues arising from their work.

Clearly, then, the new PCCs have, without exception prioritised their relationships with their local public(s) and sought to provide a significantly more outward-facing governance profile than had been the case with police authorities. Moreover, and no doubt a consequence of such profile-raising efforts, each confirmed having seen the volume of direct communications from members of the public (via email, letter or phone calls) increase significantly. One commented that 'PCCs are set to become some of the most recognised public leaders in the country – more so than most local councillors and many members of parliament', while another pointed out that 'the police themselves are amazed at what this is all producing by way of complaints from public'.

Several interviewees also emphasised the importance they attached to hearing from all sections of the community, not just those who had made contact to complain about something or who had spoken up at a public meeting or other event. One, for example, talked at length about actively seeking out the perspectives of those who were perhaps unlikely to attend such meetings or to initiate contact – 'the quiet ones; the NEETs, ethnic groups and others below the radar'. And such proactivity certainly suggested a further positive dimension to the 'listening and learning' approach to which all nine referred. Also highlighted was the contact with frontline policing teams; each having already visited, or being in the process of visiting, every police station within their areas, and from which they similarly indicated gaining highly valuable learning, not least about the issues and problems of most concern locally.

> Listening is what this job is all about.... Only by listening and talking to frontline police and the public do you get a sense of whether or not resources are being satisfactorily deployed within the Force. .. being out and about and listening is how you learn about how the force is working.

Evidently, then, 'listening and learning' has clearly formed a highly significant dimension of the work of PCCs. And while this of course would not by itself necessarily amount to strong accountability, it would at least form a key element of such a process. Indeed, insofar as all the interviewees talked about the lively exchanges in which they were frequently engaged in public meetings, it seemed that the twin processes of 'giving account' and 'being held to account' were very much a part of this ongoing public engagement process.

## Accountability to the Police and Crime Panels

As indicated, the same legislation instituting PCCs also introduced Police and Crime Panels to undertake a scrutiny role and hold commissioners to account on behalf of the public. However, the legitimate roles of such panels are quite tightly defined in the statutes and relate particularly to the annual budget setting, the approval of the Police and Crime Plan (a five-year strategy document that each PCC was required to prepare and publish within four months of taking office) and approval of the appointment of chief constables. As Lister (2014: 24) has explained, the Panels' scrutiny roles are also balanced by more general 'supportive' functions that 'must be exercised with a view to supporting the effective exercise of the functions of the police and crime commissioner'. This, as Lister has suggested, implies some tension at the heart of the legislation, although, to be fair, this was also inherent in the role (and behaviour) of the former police authorities which similarly could be understood as 'critical friends' (in their case to the chief constable). But whereas the former police authorities had a clear oversight and scrutiny role for policing performance, the focus of Police and Crime Panels is much more narrowly drawn in relation to the work of the PCC, who, in turn, is solely responsible for holding the chief constable to account.

From the interviews the evidence as to the nature of accountability at work here seemed quite mixed. All nine acknowledged the difficulties that both the limited statutory powers and the tight (government-imposed) timetable had created in the first year for panel members in their consideration of the budgets and the Police and Crime Plans and more generally in the process of holding the PCC to account. Two PCCs specifically commented on the shift they had observed in the outlook of their Panels – from initial scepticism and negativity to becoming generally supportive once they had heard the Commissioner's explanations and had understood better the thinking behind the choices and decisions. Two others observed that panel members with previous experience on their respective police authorities had seemed to struggle to come to terms with their new role as 'scrutineers' of the Commissioner's (personally taken) decisions. Others again recognised the difficulties in this regard for panels of part-time councillors (from across the area) in scrutinising the decisions of a full-time PCC (and with considerably greater officer support and informational resources to call upon) – in other words, the 'principal-agent' problem of 'information asymmetry'.

Even so, three PCCs were quite critical of the quality of scrutiny offered by their Panels; one describing the process as 'a bit tokenistic', another as 'without real teeth' and 'not very dynamic', and a third, more bluntly still, as 'a wholly inadequate way of holding you to account'. Indeed, none felt the holding to account process to have been particularly onerous, and none had been asked by their Panels to provide additional information or to consider particular actions (as the statutes allow). On the contrary, in three instances, it had been the PCCs who had taken the initiative and invited the Panels to assist them by undertaking additional work – of a supportive nature. In one instance, the Panel had been in two minds about whether to accept such an invitation although in the other two instances, there had been willingness to assist and become more actively engaged with their PCCs as a result.

It would have been helpful in this context to have been able to compare the perspectives of PCCs on the accountability provided by Police and Crime Panels with those of panellists themselves, though to do so was beyond the scope of the particular research project. But it was interesting that, from the commissioners' viewpoints at least, the contribution of the Panels was seen very much along the lines that Lister (2014) had predicted – with a somewhat uneasy tension between the respective roles of providing scrutiny on the one hand, and support on the other, or what Coulson and Whiteman (2012) have summarised as a 'critical friend' relationship. One PCC suggested the difficulty here was partly compounded by the tendency for the constituent local authorities to prefer to nominate a senior political leader as their representative on the Panel (in most instances, the council leader or a cabinet member for community safety) rather than a councillor with particular aptitude for scrutiny work and with the analytical skills by which to hold executive personnel to account. Worse, as pointed out by one PCC, because of diary congestion of such senior political leaders, substitutes were often asked to attend the meetings in place of the official nominees with consequential discontinuity effects for the membership of the Panels.

## Accountability to central government

The third accountability relationship for PCCs (as depicted in Figure 6.1) is to central government, particularly in relation to national strategic policing requirements. Beyond the statutory position here, however, is a wider question about the extent of influence by the Home Office and Home Secretary upon PCCs, especially given the long-prevailing centralist culture of that department of state (Newburn 2012). This trend might be exacerbated by the political capital the Coalition Government invested in the PCC model. This leads to a paradox since the PCC model was devised, promoted and launched within the context of the Coalition Government's policy commitment to 'new localism' (Taylor-Gooby and Stoker 2011; Lowndes and Pratchett 2012). Indeed, it had been much cited by ministers as a key exemplar of the commitment to localism.

The research found that each of the PCCs felt that they had been largely left to carry out their responsibilities at the local level free of Home Office interference. Although recognising their obligations in support of the national 'strategic policing requirement', none saw this as presenting contentious pressures for them, or creating particular conflicts with their own local commitments and priorities. On the contrary, all nine commented positively on the constructive balance they felt the Home Office had struck between providing support, if and when requested (including good access to the Home Secretary in person), and allowing each to go about their role in their own way, for example organising and staffing their offices, determining their own policing priorities, and establishing working relations with chief constables as they felt most fitting. Two PCCs, however, aired concerns at the prospect of their autonomy being compromised should Her Majesty's Inspectorate of Constabulary (HMIC) reviews and reports be extended to cover strategic governance issues as well as operational policing matters.

Interestingly, however, several PCCs contrasted this state of affairs in relation to the Home Office – the lead department of government for policing – with what they saw as a very different stance of the Ministry of Justice, the other key department of state with which they had interactions. Of particular concern was the Ministry's decision to implement its new 'regional commissioning framework' for probation services, which breaks with the territorial structure of the PCCs' areas.

## Accountability to political sponsors

The fourth accountability relationship identified in Figure 6.1 applies only to those PCCs who stood for election as candidates for a particular political party. Consideration of the relationship here between PCC and the sponsoring political party (or local branch) brings us to one of the key criticisms levelled at the new police governance model when it was first elaborated and debated in Parliament, namely that it would risk introducing partisan politics into policing. In fact, out of 192 candidates who stood for election in November 2012, just 54 stood as 'independents' (i.e. without affiliation to a political party). Of the 41 successfully elected, 12 were 'independents'; while 16 were Conservative Party candidates and 13 were sponsored by the Labour Party. No Liberal Democrat, UKIP or other party candidates were successful at the polls in November 2012.[5] As Lister and Rowe (2014) have suggested, the relatively strong showing of the 'independent' candidates in the ballot rather suggested that many voters also shared the concern about potential politicisation of policing (and indeed most of the 'independent' candidates had focused on this concern as part of their own election campaigns).

Perhaps unsurprisingly, all six party-sponsored PCCs were keen to emphasise their commitment to a non-partisan approach, to serving all interests within their areas, and to pursuing policing priorities that would be reflective of the needs and aspirations of all communities. As one (Conservative) PCC commented, 'a clear message from the [election] campaign was that the public don't want politics in policing – so the rosettes are off'. In much the same vein, all six also claimed to have had little or no contact with their sponsoring party headquarters (or constituency branch) since the elections. None indicated feeling under any particular obligation or sense of accountability in this respect beyond recognising that their prospects for reselection in 2016 would depend on their sponsors' assessment of performance over the current period of office. On the other hand the interviews did reveal some interesting differences between the PCCs in their overarching perspectives, outlooks and ambitions, and which could be understood in macro-political terms. The three Conservative PCCs, for instance, each conveyed a strong managerialist polity in expressing their determination to improve efficiency and value for money in policing. They also spoke at length about their ambitions to 'get upstream' by investing more strongly in crime prevention and to support families where there were perceived risks of antisocial behaviour or involvement in crime. The three Labour PCCs talked much more about local issues in their areas; about some of the casework arising from their surgeries, and about their prioritisation of particular crime and antisocial behaviour problems in particular neighbourhoods or afflicting particular social groups. In short, there seemed to be a rather different polity from that of their Conservative counterparts – one much more about 'problem-solving' in the shorter term.

Probably such contrasting polities would also reflect differences of geography – and particularly the socio-economic and criminogenic contrasts between the more suburban/rural police force areas on the one hand (which had elected Conservative and Independent PCCs), and the more densely populated urban/metropolitan areas on the other (which had elected Labour candidates). At the same time, however, the respective career backgrounds of the PCCs seemed also to be a relevant factor here. For example, the three Labour PCCs had each been active in politics for a significant period of their careers, and indeed, within much the same geographical area. All had served as councillors, and two had been MPs for their local constituencies. Perhaps, then, the commitment they each articulated towards problem-solving on behalf of communities, groups and individuals had its roots in their previous experience as constituency and ward-level politicians.

All three Conservative PCCs, on the other hand, came not only from a business management background, but had also, more recently, served in political leadership roles within their (Conservative-controlled) local authorities (settings where the strategic objectives of achieving better value for money through more integrated public service provision have been particularly strongly emphasised in the past few years). Two of the three Conservative PCCs identified a stark contrast between the limited inter-agency collaboration and coordination within policing and criminal justice compared with the more integrative developments now taking place in the local authorities with which they were familiar. 'The police talk endlessly about strategy but are not good at it. Most of their work is about meeting deadlines in minutes and hours, and they struggle to lift their sights towards the longer term', suggested one of them. The other expressed particular frustration at what he saw as the huge scope for achieving greater efficiency through more collaboration with neighbouring forces and other local public service providers, for example in pooling budgets 'to prevent crime rather than having to react to it afterwards'. Both spoke critically of what they regarded to be outdated police practices, some of which they felt to be 'self-serving'. One commented that 'I hadn't prepared myself for the shambolic state of the business side of policing – not policing itself – but the systems and processes by which it is managed'.

That said, more complex differences between the three groups of PCCs (Conservative, Labour and Independent) were highlighted in an analysis of the priorities formally adopted by each of the nine PCCs in their Police and Crime Plans. The three Labour-sponsored PCCs had each proposed significantly more priorities than those of either their Conservative or Independent counterparts (an average of nine compared with one of fewer than four per PCC). However, there appeared little obvious group-based patterning in the chosen priorities. Indeed, rather than differences, the two most notable features from the analysis seemed to be, on the one hand, the degree of commonality across the three groups and, on the other, the shared commitment to very generalised pledges such as: 'reducing and preventing crime', 'protecting the public', 'customer care', and 'better value for money'.

## Holding the chief constable to account

Thus far the focus has been on four accountability relationships in which PCCs could be understood as the 'agent' – respectively to the public and voters, to the Police and Crime Panels, to the Home Office/central government, and to political sponsors. But in the relationship with the chief constable, as indicated earlier, the PCC is the 'principal'. Here, however, the simple principal-agent relationship is complicated by the 'operational independence' that is afforded in statute to the chief constable and which denies the PCC authority to provide directions on matters of day-to-day policing work – a complication not made any easier by the lack of formal or detailed guidance on what might exactly constitute 'operational' responsibility (Lister 2013). This arguably increases the potential for tension in the principle-agent relationship, which was highlighted in the first few months after the elections, as discussed at the outset of this chapter. But, in the context of accountability, such tension could of course be a positive facet while relationships of a close and comfortable nature could be regarded as potentially problematical.

Among the nine interviewees there was keen awareness of the significance of the less-than-clearly defined 'boundary line' between their own more strategic area of responsibility and that for operational policing of their chief constable. Indeed, from the comments and examples proffered it seemed that boundary line had been (gently) 'tested' on more than one occasion during the course of the first year. Mostly, however, relationships with chief constables were described in positive terms, with very few ongoing disagreements highlighted over division of responsibilities. Two of the nine had in fact made their own new chief constable appointment since the election following the resignation or non-reappointment of a predecessor, so were (unsurprisingly) content with the relationship. Another described their working relationship as 'good', but emphasised the importance of the 'keeping of distance' and 'retaining a certain formality'. For two others again, 'very positive working relationships' were explained as having resulted from a working relationship at local level that had preceded the elections. Meanwhile, another, who similarly knew the chief well from having served on the former police authority, indicated having had some differences of opinion on some key strategic issues, and described the position somewhat diplomatically as 'an appropriate working relationship'. Of the other three commissioners, two described their relationships with their chief constables as 'good' although, in both instances, adding that it was still 'early days'; both regarding it as 'an evolving relationship' with 'learning taking place on both sides as to the other's expectations'. In another instance, an initially 'difficult relationship' had, after several fraught months, begun to resolve itself to the extent that the chief constable had been awarded a new contract for a further term.

All nine interviewees reported holding regular formal meetings with their chief constables for the purpose of 'holding to account' (and with official minutes taken of such meetings). Such meetings were mostly held either weekly or fortnightly, though in one case it was twice weekly, and in another every six weeks (having initially been monthly). In each case, however, it was emphasised that interactions with the chief constable of a less formal nature took place on a near daily basis, either face-to-face or by telephone, and usually to discuss a particular issue that had arisen, or in the form of a briefing on a new development.

Such patterns of contact would undoubtedly be much facilitated by the choice made by six of the PCCs to establish their offices within the confines of police headquarters. However, particularly in light of all the comments about the importance of public profile and accountability to local people, it was perhaps a little surprising that most had prioritised proximity to the chief constable and senior officers over more publicly accessible locations. But in each case, the reason for the decision was explained in terms of saving office costs by making use of available (and free) police accommodation. In fact, of the three PCCs who had located themselves away from their force headquarters, two had actually chosen to occupy part of a local police station (in one case a former one) within their areas, so again making use of available space. The third was occupying city centre accommodation that had previously provided the headquarters of the former police authority (although the PCC indicated a desire to sell the building and relocate to less expensive premises in a more centrally positioned location within the police area as a whole).

## Accountability with local community safety partners and criminal justice agencies

In the final three sets of relationships for PCCs depicted in Figure 6.1 the focus is on the various bodies engaged at local level in the planning, provision and management of community safety and criminal justice services of one form or another. The three such relationships, which are discussed together here, are respectively: local community safety partnerships; other statutory criminal justice agencies at local level (notably prosecution, courts and probation); and the various 'provider' agencies for community safety and criminal justice services (e.g. women's refuges, victim support organisations, drug and alcohol teams, and youth offending teams).

The advent of PCCs has not materially affected the role of community safety partnerships – the statutory partnerships created under the Crime and Disorder Act 1998 to promote joint working between 'responsible authorities' at the local level (i.e. police, local authorities, fire and rescue services, probation and health authorities) in relation to offending, reoffending and antisocial behaviour. However, a key change has been that central government financial support for community safety has been devolved to the PCCs as the new 'commissioners' of such partnership activity. This, in turn, has implied a further accountability relationship, with PCCs again as 'principals' in supporting the partners as 'agents'. In the first year, in fact, most PCCs chose to fund the different CSPs within their areas on the same basis as in previous years (under central government funding), doing so partly to retain goodwill and partly because there was insufficient time for a thorough assessment of priorities and of the impacts of previous funding commitments. However, in future years there is every prospect of PCCs seeking closer alignment between the CSP activity that they commission and their own Police and Crime Plan priorities. A foretaste of this new commissioning approach, and the associated accountabilities, could be seen in the Home Office's decision in 2013 to require CSPs in future to submit their annual community safety plans and strategies to their local PCCs.

The second set of criminal justice provider/partner relationships (in Figure 6.1) comprises the range of agencies providing criminal justice and community safety services at local level, and which similarly involve direct commissioning and funding-dependency relationship with PCCs. Under the new governance model, indeed, PCCs have been given the principal 'commissioning' role for a wide range of criminal justice-related services. These include drug testing at police custody suites, drug and alcohol treatment programmes available as sentencing options for the courts, youth diversionary projects, the Independent Domestic Violence and Sexual Violence Adviser services (IDVAs/ISVAs), victim support services, restorative justice projects and the like.

There are potentially profound implications of such commissioning by PCCs for the future operation of criminal justice at the local level. This is especially so for the national organisation Victim Support. From 2015 the Ministry of Justice will cease direct funding of the organisation and instead disburse its budget to the PCCs for 'local commissioning' of services for victims (Ministry of Justice 2013). In doing so, the way will open for other victim-serving groups to compete for funding with the national agency. More generally, however, such a change in favour of local commissioning places PCCs in a particularly strong position to hold 'provider organisations' to account for service delivery that not only represents value for money but aligns closely with their own targets and priorities as expressed in the Police and Crime Plans for their areas.

The third set of provider/partner relationships for PCCs depicted in Figure 6.1 is the group of other public sector agencies with which police work, comprising the core of the local criminal justice system, notably the CPS, the probation service and the courts service. Of particular interest here is the impact and influence of the newly elected PCCs on Local Criminal Justice Boards (LCJBs), the established forums for coordinating and developing local criminal justice. Although these are non-statutory, they have been regarded since their establishment by government more than a decade ago as having a vital role in raising inter-agency efficiencies and effectiveness across the criminal justice sector at the local level, doing so by bringing together senior representatives of each of the main agencies – the police, the CPS, the probation service, the courts and the prison service. How might the new directly elected PCCs, with their significant commissioning roles in the sector, relate to this established executive structure?

In fact the interviews highlighted just how similar the PCCs saw their own role and objectives to those of the LCJBs in wishing to bring greater efficiency to local criminal justice processes through stronger coordination and integration. Several interviewees had begun to build relations with the senior professionals in the other agencies and were attending meetings of their LCJB. One talked of his ambition to effect 'a fundamental shift in policing and in criminal justice to a position … where offenders pay back to the communities they have harmed'. Another spoke of his plans to find 'ways of recovering from offenders the costs of police time and case preparation'. Yet another described the key challenge for PCCs as:

> getting the 'whole system' to work better for all of us … the role [of the PCC] is not the answer in itself, but the statutory influence the PCC carries across policing, criminal justice and community safety means that there is power to raise ambitions, provide a consistently joined up approach that serves people better and uses shrinking resources more effectively.

Time, of course, will tell the extent to which such ambitions will be achieved and how much they transform the wider local criminal justice system. A measure of this will be the extent to which the LCJBs – not just chief constables – become 'agents' of PCCs as they pursue such whole-system reform.

## Conclusion

At the outset of this chapter the question was posed as to whether the novel governance model of Police and Crime Commissioners might fairly be understood in terms of Dawisha and Parrott's (1997) concept of electocracy. The key argument here was that, at face value at least, the statutory requirements of the PCC role, which vests considerable powers and authority in the office holder, and with few limiting conditions, once elected, do tend to suggest a strongly monocratic form of governance for policing. Indeed, as discussed, critics of the PCC model have from the outset been greatly concerned at the concentration of authority and governance responsibility in the hands of one individual.

Be that as it may, the series of interviews informing this chapter reveal that, in reality, rather than practising autocracy, PCCs have gone to considerable lengths to build relationships with their local public and so foster an ongoing process of public accountability. Significantly, the interviews found that the other potential accountabilities and system checks on autocratic conduct by PCCs were mostly quite weak. Police and Crime Panels, in the first year at least, were said to play a fairly marginal role in holding the commissioners to account; the Home Office, it was pointed out, had resisted controlling and standardising temptations and, for the most part, left PCCs to develop the role as they individually felt best. The political party sponsors, the interviewees all agreed, were similarly unimportant in directing or pressuring their chosen candidate once elected. Instead, it has been the PCCs' own efforts at public engagement that have been providing the real counterbalance to any potential for electocracy to prevail.

While no doubt such efforts would, in part, be motivated by self-interest to build a strong personal profile and so ensure future re-electoral success, the research particularly highlighted the impact of such profile-building in creating the conditions for stronger public accountability. In this respect, it was also very clear that PCCs have been investing significant amounts of their time to ensure that they personally had good understandings of public expectations about policing and crime reduction and to ensure that such understandings would be reflected in the prioritisation and allocation of policing resources and in their approach to the role, more broadly. In this respect, for sure, they have been demonstrating much keener public accountability than was ever apparent under the previous regime of police authorities. And the spirit of such public accountability was very evident in the phraseology of all nine of the Police and Crime Plans of the PCCs, for example:

> In determining my priorities I have listened to the views that the public have expressed through engagement events and feedback questionnaires. I have also spoken to partner agencies, such as community safety partnerships and the Criminal Justice Board, as well as considering the professional judgement of the Chief Constable.

> This plan sets out our Police and Crime priorities for 2013–2017 which are based on the issues you have raised. You have told me that your concerns are anti-social behaviour, burglary and domestic and sexual violence. I will ensure that wherever you live – rural, suburban, town or city – your police will work with you and have the flexibility to deliver these priorities.

> I have listened to your experiences, concerns, and suggestions; I have met hundreds of you face-to-face and corresponded with hundreds more. It's a continuing and essential dialogue that means you help to decide where money and manpower can do most good. So in a very real sense, this is your Police and Crime Plan. You are my co-authors because you know your

communities better than anyone else. And together we can ensure that tax-payers' money – YOUR money – is spent where it can genuinely benefit the public.

It is, as Newburn (2013) has suggested, too early to draw firm conclusions about the impacts of the new model of police governance or, more specifically, to say anything definitively about its effect in strengthening democratic accountability in policing and local criminal justice. But, to date at least, it seems that the worst fears of critics of the model have not materialised to any significant extent while police governance in England and Wales has surely become more visible, more consultative and, by implication, more publicly accountable.

Ahead of the next scheduled PCC elections (which, as a result, should attract many more voters to the polls than in 2012) will come a general election in 2015, and with it the possibility of further change to police governance. As indicated, the Stevens Report (2013) recommended abolition of the PCC model; although perhaps more likely would be some amendment of the legislative framework in the light of experience. In this respect, for example, one possible step might be to enshrine into the relevant statutes more specific duties on PCCs for public engagement and associated public accountabilities rather than, as now, relying on volunteered commitment. Another possibility – and one that has already been considered in governmental circles – is the widening of powers of PCCs, notably to bring other 'blue-light services' under the commissioners' control (i.e. fire and ambulance governance as well). And then, were there to be fresh enthusiasm for restructuring and rationalising local government, another possibility might lie in the recreation of co-terminosity between police and local authority areas, in which case, we might envisage a significantly more integrated form of local public service governance – with directly elected mayors (rather than PCCs) overseeing a comprehensive portfolio of local public services which would include policing and associated community safety and criminal justice services.

## Notes

1  For example, the sample did not include a PCC who had previously served as a police officer, although nationally, about one in five of the 41 who were elected had done so.
2  In three of the nine cases, a senior assistant to the commissioner was also present for the interview.
3  To protect and respect confidentiality no personal names or force areas are cited in this chapter.
4  Police Authorities, as amended by the Police and Magistrates' Courts Act 1994, comprised 'independent members' appointed for their experience and skills from the local community, as well as representatives of the magistracy and local councillors nominated by their local authorities.
5  It is noteworthy that just 15 per cent of the successfully elected PCCs were female and none were from black and minority ethnic (BME) backgrounds, although 18 per cent of the candidates were female and 7 per cent from BME backgrounds.

# References

Amann, R. (2013) 'On the Receiving End: The Governance of Policing in Britain', *The Political Quarterly*, 84: 1–19.

Ashworth, R. and Skelcher, C. (2005) *Meta-Evaluation of the Local Government Modernisation Agenda: Progress Report on Accountability in Local Government*, London: Office of the Deputy Prime Minister.

*BBC News* (2013) 'Paris Brown: Kent Youth PCC Resigns After Twitter Row', available at www.bbc.co.uk/news/uk-england-22083032 (last accessed 31 October 2013).

Behn, R. (2001) *Rethinking Democratic Accountability*, Washington, DC: Brooking Institution Press.

Bertelli, A.M. (2012) *The Political Economy of Public Sector Governance*, New York: Cambridge University Press.

Besley, T. (2006) *Principled Agents? The Politcial Economy of Good Government*, Oxford: Oxford University Press.

Bovaird, T., Briggs, I. and Willis, M. (2013) 'Strategic Commissioning in the UK: Service Improvement Cycle or Just Going Round in Circles?', *Local Government Studies*, 40: 23–36.

Bovens, M. (2005) 'Public Accountability: A Framework for the Analysis and Assessment of Accountability Arrangements in the Public Domain', unpublished paper for *Democracy and Accountability in the EU*, Uppsala: Connex Research Group 2.

Bovens, M. (2007) 'Analysing and Assessing Accountability: A Conceptual Framework', *European Law Journal*, 13: 447–68.

Coulson, A. and Whiteman, P. (2012) 'Holding Politicians to Account? Overview and Scrutiny in English Local Government', *Public Money and Management*, 32: 185–92.

Dawisha, K. and Parrott, B. (eds) (1997) *The End of Empire? The Transformation of the USSR in Comparative Perspective*, Cambridge: Cambridge University Press.

Davies, M. (2014) 'The Path to Police and Crime Commissioners', *Safer Communities*, 13: 3–12.

Day, P. and Klein, R. (1987) *Accountabilities: Five Public Service*, London: Tavistock Publications.

Dubnick, M.J. (2002) 'Seeking Salvation for Accountability', *The 2002 Annual Meeting of the American Political Science Association*, Boston: American Political Science Association.

Dubnick, M.J. (2005) 'Accountability and the Promise of Performance: In Search of the Mechanisms', *Public Performance and Management Review*, 28: 376–417.

Dubnick, M.J. and Yang, K. (2009) 'The Pursuit of Accountability: Promise, Problems, and Prospects', *2009 American Society for Public Administration Annual Conference*, New York: The State of Public Administration.

Erkkila, T. (2007) 'Governance and Accountability – a Shift in Conceptualisation', *Public Administration Quarterly*, 31: 1–38.

Ferris, J.M. and Graddy, E.A. (1998) 'A Contractual Framework for New Public Management Theory', *International Public Management Journal*, 1: 225–40.

Flanagan, R. (2008) *The Review of Policing: Final Report*, London: Home Office.

Game, C. (2003) 'Elected Mayors: More Distraction than Attraction?', *Public Policy and Administration*, 18: 13–28.

*Guardian* (2013a) 'Court Overturns "Irrational" Decision to Suspend Lincolnshire Chief Constable', available at www.theguardian.com/uk/2013/mar/28/lincolnshire-chief-constable-suspension-overturned (last accessed 31 October 2013).

*Guardian* (2013b) 'Gwent Police Chief "Told to Retire or be Humiliated" by Crime Commissioner', available at www.theguardian.com/uk-news/2013/jul/02/gwent-police-chief-crime-commissioner (last accessed 31 October 2013).

Guinier, L. (2008) 'Beyond Electocracy: Rethinking the Political Representative as Powerful Stranger', *The Modern Law Review*, 71: 1–35.

Harlow, C. (2002) *Accountability in the European Union*, Oxford: Oxford University Press.

HM Treasury (2013) *The 2013–14 Budget*, London: The Stationery Office.

Home Office (2008) *From the Neighbourhood to the National: Policing our Communities Together*, White Paper Cm 7448, London: The Stationery Office.

Hood, C. (1991) 'A Public Management For All Seasons?', *Public Administration*, 69: 3–19.

Independent Police Commission (2013) *Policing for a Better Britain: Report of the Independent Police Commission* (The Stevens Report), London: Independent Police Commission.

Jones, G. and Stewart, J.D. (2011) 'Reflections on the Localism Act 2011', in J.W. Raine and C. Staite (eds) *The World Will be Your Oyster?*, INLOGOV: University of Birmingham.

Knott, J.H. and Miller, G.J. (2006) 'Social Welfare, Corruption and Credibility: Public Management's Role in Economic Development', *Public Management Review*, 8: 227–52.

Kryshtanovskaya, O. (2008) 'The Russian Elite in Transition', *Journal of Communist Studies and Transition Politics*, 24: 585–603.

Leishman, F., Loveday, B. and Savage, S. (eds) (2000) *Core Issues in Policing*, Harlow: Pearson Education.

Lister, S. (2013) 'The New Politics of the Police: Police and Crime Commissioners and the "Operational Independence" of the Police', *Policing*, 7: 239–47.

Lister, S. (2014) 'Scrutinising the Role of the Police and Crime Panel in the New Era of Police Governance in England and Wales', *Safer Communities*, 13: 1–16.

Lister, S. and Rowe, M. (2014) 'Electing Police and Crime Commissioners in England and Wales: Prospecting for the Democratisation of Policing', *Policing and Society*, 1: 1–20.

Loveday, B. (2001) 'Police Accountability in the Provinces: The Changing Role of the Police Authority', *Crime Prevention and Community Safety*, 3: 49–63.

Lowndes, V. and Pratchett, L. (2012) 'Local Governance Under the Coalition Government: Austerity, Localism and the Big Society', *Local Government Studies*, 38: 21–40.

Lynn, L.E. (2006) *Public Management: Old and New*, Abingdon: Routledge.

McLaughlin, E. (1994) *Community, Policing and Accountability: The Politics of Policing in Manchester in the 1980s*, Aldershot: Avebury Publishing.

Mayston, D. (1993) 'Principal, Agents, and the Economics of Accountability in the New Public Sector', *Accounting, Auditing and Accountability Journal*, 6: 68–96.

Ministry of Justice (2013) *Victims' Services Commissioning Framework*, London: Ministry of Justice.

Mulgan, R. (2000) 'Accountability: An Ever-Expanding Concept', *Public Administration*, 78: 555–73.

Newburn, T. (2012) 'Police and Crime Commissioners: The Americanization of Policing or a Very British Reform?', *International Journal of Law, Crime and Justice*, 40: 31–46.

Newburn, T. (2013) *The Stevens Report*, British Politics and Policy at LSE, blog, November 2013, available at http://eprints.lse.ac.uk/54786/ (last accessed 6 January 2014), London: London School of Economics.

Pollitt, C. (1996) 'Anti-Statist Reforms and New Administrative Directions, Public Administration in the United Kingdom', *Public Administration Review*, 15: 37–45.

Prasirtsuk, K. (2007) 'From Political Reform and Economic Crisis to Coup D'état in Thailand: The Twists and Turns of the Political Economy, 1997–2006', *Asian Survey*, 47: 872–93.

Raine, J.W. and Keasey, P. (2012) 'From Police Authorities to Police and Crime Commissioners: Might Policing become More Publicly Accountable?', *International Journal of Emergency Services*, 1: 122–34.

Ranson, S. and Stewart, J.D. (1994) *Management for the Public Domain*, London: Macmillan.

Reiner, R. (2010) *The Politics of the Police* (4th edn), Oxford: Oxford University Press.

Reiner, R. and Spencer, S. (1993) *Accountable Policing*, London: Institute for Public Policy Research.

Romzek, B.S. (2000) 'Dynamics of Public Sector Accountability in an Era of Reform', *International Review of Administrative Sciences*, 66: 21–44.

Romzek, B.S. and Dubnick, M.J. (1987) 'Accountability in the Public Sector: Lessons from the Challenger Tragedy', *Public Administration Review*, 47: 227–38.

Sinclair, A. (1995) 'The Chameleon of Accountability: Forms and Discourses', *Accounting, Organisations and Society*, 20: 219–37.

Stewart, J.D. (1984) *Management in the Public Domain*, London: Macmillan.

Taylor-Gooby, P. and Stoker, G. (2011) 'The Coalition Programme: A New Vision for Britain or Politics as Usual?', *The Political Quarterly*, 82(1): 4–15.

Tierney, S. (2009) 'Constitutional Referendums: A Theoretical Enquiry', *The Modern Law Review*, 72: 360–83.

Walker, A. (2008) 'The Rural Constitution and the Everyday Politics of Elections in Northern Thailand', *Journal of Contemporary Asia*, 38: 84–105.

Waterman, R.W. and Meier, K.J. (1998) 'Principal-Agent Models: An Expansion?', *Journal of Public Administration Research and Theory*, 8: 173–202.

Wood, D. and Waterman, R. (1994) *Bureaucratic Dynamics: The Role of Bureaucracy in a Democracy*, Oxford: Westview Press.

# 7   Power to the people?

## A social democratic critique of the Coalition Government's police reforms

*Robert Reiner*

For once a government's claim to profound reform of policing is not exaggerated. The recent Coalition Government's restructuring of the arrangements for police governance in England and Wales, centred on the establishment of elected Police and Crime Commissioners, are certainly the most radical since the 1964 Police Act, and arguably since the development of the modern British police in the early nineteenth century. The fundamental claim behind the policy is that it will make the police democratically accountable, and thus ensure policing that is in line with public wishes. Although democratic policing has become a mantra to which lip service is paid around the world, the notion is seldom analysed.

This chapter argues for the application of T.H. Marshall's seminal analysis of citizenship (Marshall 1950) to the analysis of police governance, suggesting that democracy in general, and democratic policing in particular, has not one dimension (elections), but three: civil, political and socio-economic. The Coalition's reforms involved only one of these dimensions, the political, and in the narrowest sense. In the absence of strong civil and socio-economic rights voting alone does not achieve democracy in any meaningful interpretation.

Policing controversies usually raise issues of police accountability at some point. If they involve policy conflicts or failures the cry 'who governs?' will be invoked; if they stem from specific instances of malpractice, bringing the culpable people to book will be a critical concern. The perpetual recurrence of accountability problems and disputes suggests it is a tough nut to crack, although successive reformers (not least the Coalition Government) have claimed to have the answer. This chapter will examine why police accountability has proved to be such a riddle. It will offer a brief history of the police accountability debate in England and Wales in order to contextualise the Coalition's reforms. Their policies will be critically analysed in relation to a model of the elements of democratic policing, arguing that elections are necessary but not sufficient, in particular in a context of massively widening socio-economic inequality.

### Riddles of police accountability

The ancient pedigree of the problem of police accountability is often underlined by citing Juvenal's question: '*Quis custodiet ipsos custodes?*' – who guards the guardians? This was not originally a reference to a conundrum of statecraft, but to the predicament of a husband worried about his wife's fidelity, and more particularly the fidelity of those entrusted with safeguarding it. Nonetheless it does point to a fundamental problem of governance. Relying on any agents to deal with deviance or preserve peace potentially leads to an infinite redress. Who or what protects against the guards' deviance or unreliability? And then how is that line of security itself secured, and so on – a potentially infinite regress. There are special problems, both practical and principled, in rendering *police* accountable, in addition to those involved in achieving the accountability of any organisation or agents.

The special practical problems include the low visibility of everyday police work, which has been noted since the very early days of police research (Goldstein 1960). Low visibility stems in part from the practical exigencies of police work, which is necessarily conducted largely out on the streets, beyond the gaze of supervisors. The police hierarchy has always sought to penetrate everyday policing, and indeed the history of police management can be told in terms of an arms race between new techniques of control and new rank-and-file strategies of evasion. In recent decades this has intensified with the increasing use of high-tech methods of recording police operations, from the tape-recording of interviews to current experimentation with 'Body-Worn Video' cameras (Rieken 2013). A truly new twist in this tale, however, is the proliferation in the last 25 years of citizen recording technology, culminating in the ubiquity of mobile phones. These have captured on video or audio many notorious cases of police abuse, from the beating of Rodney King in Los Angeles in 1991 to such recent British cases as the death of Ian Tomlinson. This profound shift has been analysed as 'synopticon' (Mathiesen 1997) or 'sousveillance' (Mann *et al.* 2003): the capacity of the masses to parallel the gaze of the powerful, the top-down surveillance of the 'panopticon'. There can be no doubt that such developments have brought to light police malpractice that would otherwise have remained hidden, creating an impression of greater police wrongdoing and hence accentuating the search for further technological ways to penetrate everyday policing. Whether this qualitatively transforms the low visibility of policing, making the degree of control analogous to most other occupations, where employees' activities are open and observed continuously by management, is yet to be established.

Physical 'low visibility' is bolstered by the socially contingent fact that most street encounters are with relatively powerless, low-status groups. These 'police property' groups stand lower in the politics of creditability in a hierarchical society, and their accounts are liable to be rejected in favour of the police officers' versions of events in any adjudicating forum, although with a decline of deference in recent decades 'police property' groups have gained greater 'voice' and creditability to some extent (Box and Russell 1975; Lee 1981). Thus the formally lowest ranks of the police become 'street-corner' politicians, making the effective policy decisions in practice, frustrating the nominal control of those higher ranked in the organisation, and *a fortiori* of external agents of accountability (Wilson 1968; Muir 1977; Punch 1983). Furthermore, the craft of policing also inculcates great ability to avoid discovery of police wrongdoing: detectives learn skills of covering as well as uncovering deviance. A crucial factor aiding this is a 'blue curtain' of silence against prying governors that arises from the solidarity developed by doing a job that is sometimes dangerous and frequently controversial (Punch 2009). (See Rowe *et al.*'s chapter in this book which discusses various strategies aimed at drawing open the 'blue curtain' within police culture.)

Even more fundamental problems of governance are due to the very nature of policing, as indicated by ongoing debates about what their role is or should be (service or force, crime-fighting or peacekeeping, etc. cf. Banton 1964; Punch 1979; Reiner 2010 ch. 5, 2012; Innes 2013; Millie 2013; Loader 2013; Bradford *et al.* 2013, Turner 2014: 14–16). Policing is 'dirty work' (à la Everett Hughes 1961); the 'fire to fight fire' (Brodeur 2012: 107); a necessary evil not an unequivocal good. This is analysed most acutely in two classic papers: Bittner's 'Florence Nightingale in Pursuit of Willie Sutton' (Bittner 1974), and Otwin Marenin's 'Parking Tickets and Class Repression' (Marenin 1983). As Bittner famously defined it, policing is 'a mechanism for the distribution of non-negotiable coercive force' that is 'situationally justified' (Bittner 1970: 131).

This immediately triggers the query: justified by and to whom, by what principles of justice? Whose law, what order? As Marenin argued, policing is Janus-faced, simultaneously reproducing 'general' (the universally beneficial protection of the prerequisites of cooperation and coexistence) and 'particular' order: a structure of power and privileges that oppresses as well as serves. In core policing contexts there is always an explicit or implicit conflict of viewpoints and interests. 'You're right from your side, I'm right from mine' as Bob Dylan taught.

Thus a special riddle of police accountability arises in principle as well as practice, although it is obfuscated by the CSI myth of policing as an objective appliance of science or at least craft and organisational skills, which (mis) informs most media representations and contemporary policy. Other public service bureaucracies have to meet two dimensions of accountability: effectiveness and fairness. How can we ensure effective health, education and so on; and is this 'good' fairly distributed? But a third dimension makes defining, let alone delivering or regulating, 'good' policing a deeper riddle. Policing inherently involves intervening in conflicts, so 'good' service to some must mean 'bad' outcomes for others (even if the latter, 'police property', are denied legitimacy, voice or credibility in much public debate). Policing itself, and hence any processes of accountability, is clogged by the fallout from socio-economic and power inequalities, shaping what counts as 'crime' or 'disorder', and what are appropriate tactics for responding to them.

There is also a semantic dimension adding to the conundrums of police accountability. 'Accountability' is a weasel word, implying a desirable state of affairs but without clear and agreed meaning. The Oxford English Dictionary offers a number of different (albeit related) definitions, but with two fundamental versions: (1) the obligation to give reports (often in the form of numerical statements of receipts and expenditure); and (2) the duty to 'settle' these, a responsibility

to meet the expectations of those to whom account is given. These variants under-
lie the two models of police accountability that were distinguished by Geoffrey
Marshall in his classic analysis: 'explanatory and co-operative' as distinct from
'subordinate and obedient' (Marshall 1978). In the former model, enshrined in the
1964 Police Act (at any rate as it turned out in practice), accountability is merely
the obligation to tell stories, with chief constables being obliged to give reports to
local police authorities but without any corresponding requirement to take account
of their responses. In the latter model, espoused by many radical critics of the
impotence of locally elected authorities to do more than comment on chief constables' accounts of their activities, accountability was a euphemism for control.
The police, in common with all other public services, should be governed by
democratically elected authorities. The conflict between these models of accountability has been perennial throughout police history.

## The historical context of police accountability debates in England and Wales

In view of these conceptual and practical riddles, it is no wonder that debates
about accountability have raged ever since proposals first emerged for creating
professional police forces more than two centuries ago. Given the extensive literature on police accountability the debates will only be sketched here. This literature has traced the complex and shifting arguments about what aspects of
policing should be made accountable, to whom, and how this should be accomplished (analytic overviews include: Jefferson and Grimshaw 1984; Lustgarten
1986; Reiner and Spencer 1993; Jones *et al.* 1994; Stenning 1995; Walker 2000;
Jones 2008, 2012; Reiner 2010 Ch. 7; Manning 2010; Stenson and Silverstone
2013). But a key change that has perhaps not been emphasised sufficiently is that
the driving concern of accountability, the conception of the mischief that
accountability processes are aimed at, has shifted implicitly but fundamentally in
the last three decades.

This change in the subject of accountability occurred as part and parcel of the
more general rise of the politics of law and order (Reiner 2007 ch. 5; Downes
and Morgan 2012). The criminal justice revolutions marched hand in hand with
the growing hegemony of neo-liberalism, destroying the social democratic and
welfarist consensus that had flourished in particular during the post-Second
World War decades. In a nutshell, accountability became synonymous with
accountancy. Until the early 1980s regulating police power was the primary
concern that animated accountability debates. The guarding the guardians riddle
has not disappeared of course, and continues to generate scandals and reforms.
But since the 1980s it has been overshadowed increasingly by crime control concerns. Accountability has been reconceptualised as a managerial (and most
recently a populist) quest for effective, efficient, economic security – or more
specifically security's symbolic synecdoche, criminal catching.

Before the *bouleversement* of the 1980s, debates had flourished about the dis-
tinctiveness of police accountability, who should be responsible for it and with

what degree of power, and whether some aspects of policing were off limits. In the nineteenth century most historians suggest that no fundamental distinction was made between the accountability of the police and other local services (although this has been disputed cf. Brogden 1982; Jefferson and Grimshaw 1984). In general they were governed by the same authorities (although the precise arrangements varied between areas and over time). Until the 1920s the doctrine of 'constabulary independence', that police should be insulated from political control in 'operational' matters, functioned as a shield for Home Secretaries to dodge sharp parliamentary questions. It was not yet used for the police to shelter from local government. The strong constabulary independence doctrine developed in late 1920s, spearheaded by the seminal 1930 judgement in *Fisher* v. *Oldham* that constables exercised an original authority under the Crown so did not stand in a master–servant relationship with police authorities of any kind. The consolidation of the doctrine, probably not accidentally, followed in the wake of the universal franchise and the election of several radical Labour-controlled local authorities (Lustgarten 1986). *Fisher* specifically concerned the liability in tort of watch committees for the wrongful acts of the constables they employed. In this regard it was reversed by the 1964 Police Act, which made forces vicariously liable for the malpractices of individuals. The survival of the broader doctrine of constabulary independence, however, was confirmed by a subsequent series of cases cementing it as law (for all its flaws in legal logic or constitutional principle).

The 1964 Police Act was *the* landmark legislation in the twentieth-century history of police governance, consolidating the tripartite governance structure that had developed from the mid-nineteenth century in different ways in provincial forces (Marshall 1965). The Act grew out of the 1960/2 Report of the Royal Commission on the Police, which had been a response to a variety of police abuse scandals in the late 1950s. The tripartite system in practice operated as the acme of what Marshall dubbed the 'explanatory and co-operative' model (Marshall 1978), which several commentators criticised as not only unacceptable in principle but not what the Act intended or indeed had enacted. Nonetheless, a tacit 'gentleman's agreement' rapidly emerged whereby the (primarily elected) local police authorities deferred on operational matters to the professional chief constable, and the Home Office hovered over both as the potentially dominant party in the triangle.

This cosy consensus came under growing pressure during the late 1970s as policing became an increasingly politicised arena of conflict. Labour politicians at central and local level advocated the 'subordinate and obedient' model as appropriate for a democracy, putting elected authorities in the driving seat as with other services. The police themselves, at all levels from the Police Federation to the Association of Chief Police Officers (ACPO), resisted this, as did the Tories, pushing the doctrine of constabulary independence. The conflict became especially acute after 1981 when several cities elected radical Labour authorities that championed control of the police by elected authorities. In the mid-1980s, especially during the Miners' Strike, this party political debate about police accountability was at its height. Tory rhetoric resisted the Labour call for democratic control of policing, invoking the threat of politicisation and defending the strong independence doctrine.

As Labour became 'New' in the early 1990s, in the era of Howard vs Blair as respectively Home Secretary and Shadow, a brittle consensus around tough 'law and order' developed, and this has reigned ever since. The police mission came to be seen entirely as crime control, and the focus was on 'general' order as an unequivocal, unproblematic good. Old Labour concerns about 'particular', i.e. partisan, order and abuse of police power were suppressed. The accountability agenda became reinterpreted as accountancy. The New Public Management model, a 'calculative and contractual' version of accountability, supplanted the old Punch and Judy debate between Marshall's 'explanatory and co-operative' and 'subordinate and obedient' models (Reiner and Spencer 1993; McLaughlin 2007 ch. 7).

This consensus has now itself been supplanted. Paradoxically the Conservative-led Coalition have been tougher on the police in the name of 'austerity' than any 'old' Labour Government would ever have dared to be, and relations with the police, the Tories' erstwhile pet institution, are at an all-time low (Brogden and Ellison 2012). The Coalition between the Conservatives and the Liberal Democrats, formed after the 2010 general election impasse (the Con-alition), purported to provide a radical new model, 'restoring' democracy. But does it?

## Coalition reform of police governance: an enigma in a mystery in a riddle

The Coalition accountability model, enshrined in the 2011 Police Reform and Social Responsibility Act, is reminiscent of the King Midas lesson: 'Be careful what you wish for'. At first blush, the heart of the project appears to be the achievement of the old Labour ambition of subjecting police to elected control, defying the old Conservative apprehensions about politicisation. The case for this has long been accepted in principle by this author and by many if not most academic commentators on policing (Reiner 1985: 181, 1995; Reiner and Spencer 1993: 14–16, 172–89; Marshall 1965 – partially recanted in Marshall 1978; Lustgarten 1986; Jones *et al.* 2011).

A central pillar of the Coalition Government rhetoric presenting the reforms is that they achieve democratic policing. Theresa May (2012) referred to them as 'the most significant democratic reform of policing in our lifetime'. David Cameron (*Liverpool Echo* 2012) claimed there 'will be a democratic voice speaking out for people'. The claim rests of course on the election of the Police and Crime Commissioners (PCCs), who are placed in pole position in the new governance structure. The other elements are the Home Secretary, the Chief Constables, and the Police and Crime Panels, a concession to the Liberal Democrats. The latter are selected in a similar way to the old police authorities, but with an explicitly advisory rather than even a nominally powerful role (see Lister 2014). Tripartism has become a square.

Constabulary independence is formally retained, through the tenuous operational/policy distinction elaborated in the 2011 Policing Protocol Order (Home

Office 2011; Home Affairs Committee 2013; Winsor 2013). But with PCCs having formidable powers to set objectives and budgets, hire and fire, what is really reproduced is the 'calculative and contractual' mode of shaping 'independence', albeit at local rather than national level. And the driving agenda remains crime control. The concerns about malpractice and discrimination which drove the old agenda of accountability receive no mention. The purpose of electoral input is to keep policing tough and on its toes. As the Prime Minister put it:

> People are going to be voting in their own law and order champion: one person who sets the budgets, sets the priorities; hires and fires the chief constable; bangs heads together to get things done.... If you want more tough policing, you can get it.
>
> (Cameron 2012: 5)

But is the new system really democratic?

## Democracy, policing and PCCs

### *Democracy and the arrival of PCCs: practical issues*

The Coalition Government claimed that its novel system of elected Police and Crime Commissioners (PCCs) achieves democratic governance of policing. This identifies democracy solely and wholly with voting, a common, albeit mistaken, trope. Even on that limited interpretation there are problems in the democratic legitimacy of the new PCCs. The actual conduct of the elections was a notorious omnishambles, poorly publicised, meagrely financed, and inconveniently timed, so it was hardly surprising that very few people (only 14.7 per cent of the electorate) actually voted. The claim that the current crop of PCCs enjoys democratic legitimacy is tenuous in the light of this (Barton and Johns 2013). However, these are arguably teething problems, and the next elections in four years' time may well produce PCCs with a stronger claim to a popular mandate.

Although wrapped in a mantle of making the police locally accountable to democratic processes like other public services, and supposedly borrowing from US models (notably New York City) that had achieved great success in crime control, the PCC system is an unprecedented innovation in public administration, in the UK or elsewhere. It is fundamentally different from the governance arrangements for other public services in the UK.

> What is new about PCCs is that their remit covers a specific and narrow field. By creating PCCs, Parliament gives birth to a multitude of dogs that didn't bark. Where is the directly elected commissioner for primary schools, for example? For health services? For children's services? To pose the question is to show that this new structure directs attention to one specific field of policy at the expense of others.
>
> (Jones *et al.* 2012: 232)

The origins of the PCC model hark back to a decade-long quest by right-leaning think-tanks for ways to make the police more responsive to local popular opinion (Loveday and Reid 2003; Davies 2014).

> By connecting the proposal to US governance arrangements, its political proponents were able to draw on the rich vein of law and order rhetoric that surrounds 'zero-tolerance policing' and its intimate association in the public imagination with the 'miracle' of the New York crime fall.
>
> (Lister 2013: 241)

But the PCC model does not match any of the various US models for making police democratically accountable (Newburn 2012), such as directly elected sheriffs or other chiefs of police, or the common big-city model of chiefs appointed by elected mayors (as in New York City or Los Angeles) who have more general city governance responsibilities (similar to the contemporary London position, but not the 41 provincial forces subject to the PCC system).

The novel structure reflects the view that crime is an exceptionally tough and threatening problem, unrelated to any other social, economic or cultural processes, and needs its own tough and smart specialists to tackle it and to bring retributive justice to victims. It is a quintessential embodiment of the politics of law and order that has become hegemonic over the last three decades. As I have argued in detail elsewhere, this entails five core assumptions: that crime is public enemy number one; that individuals are solely responsible for crime, with social explanations sidelined or denied; the interests of victims (the iconic centre of law and order discourse) are diametrically opposed to those of offenders, in a zero-sum conflict; criminal justice agencies, especially the police, can be effective provided they are smart and tough (contrary to the 'nothing works' pessimism of the 1970s and 1980s) and; social routines and popular culture are predicated upon a perpetual threat of crime. This perspective is the product of the broader neo-liberal hegemony that has developed since the 1970s, displacing the welfarist, Keynesian, essentially social democratic consensus that had prevailed particularly in the post-Second World War decades (Reiner 2007: 124–9).

### *Democracy and the arrival of PCCs: issues of principle*

There are much more fundamental and principled problems with the Government's claim that the PCC system achieves democratic policing. Opening up a process of selecting office holders to a public vote is clearly one aspect of what is understood by democracy. But the concept of democracy has a long and tortuous history, and there are many conflicting views of what it means and how it can or should be constituted (for recent surveys of the long and tortuous history of the concept of democracy in general, and in criminal justice, see Dunn 2005; Keane 2009; Karstedt and LaFree 2006). Free and fair elections are a necessary but not a sufficient condition of democracy.

The most obvious problems with identifying democracy with pure majoritarianism, highly germane to policing, which deals with actual or potential social and political conflicts, is the danger of a tyranny of the majority. This concept was most famously discussed by de Toqueville in *Democracy in America* (1835–40), and J.S. Mill (1851) in *On Liberty* (for a recent critical analysis of the issues see Guinier 1994). Unmitigated majoritarianism can and sometimes has (as in the Jim Crow South) produced unbridled oppression of vulnerable minorities, who become 'police property' (Lee 1981). The tripartite system of governance, at least in principle, guarded against this by dividing power between its three elements – although in practice the local police authority leg, the role of which was to symbolise and represent 'community interests', was virtually powerless.

Legal rights and access to independent courts have often been seen as a key protection against the danger of tyranny of the majority, and an essential component of democracy alongside elections. PCCs are of course subject to the law, as are Chief Constables and Home Secretaries. However, in the past the courts have been reluctant to intervene in police policy decisions because of the doctrine of constabulary independence. It will have to be seen how this plays out with the new structure. But PCCs do not hold the office of constable so judges will probably feel freer to review their conduct. Further, there is a tension on this issue in the legislation itself. Section 38 of the 2011 Police Reform and Social Responsibility Act gives the PCC power to require the chief constable to retire or resign, and this has been invoked or mooted in several cases within the first year of the Act's passage (Home Affairs Committee 2013). On the other hand, the legislation, and all government commentary surrounding it, rehearses the mantra that the doctrine of constabulary independence remains sacrosanct (Lister 2013). This is spelled out in detail by Policing Protocol Order 2011 (2011), issued in accord with the requirement specified by s.79 of the Act. It has been argued vigorously by the first civilian HM Chief Inspector of Constabulary that the courts will follow their earlier commitment to the constabulary independence doctrine, and not allow unfettered exercises of the s.38 power of PCCs to remove chief constables (Winsor 2013). However, the first few *causes célèbres* that have already occurred do not support this, if only because chiefs are likely to be reluctant to risk going to court and may well accept deals to go quietly at least as long as the courts' attitudes remain uncertain (Home Affairs Committee 2013).

In any event, as argued earlier, constabulary independence had already become something of a hollow shell with the accretion of market-based sanctions shaping chief constables' exercise of their nominal autonomy under the 'calculative and contractual' mode of governance. It is probable that the courts will only provide a sanction against criminal or flagrantly illegal conduct by PCCs, and will not challenge policy decisions except against the extreme standard of complete ('Wednesbury') unreasonableness ('so absurd that no sensible person could ever dream that it lay within the powers of the authority' as articulated by Lord Greene in the *Wednesbury* case). Whilst PCCs do not have the shelter of the quasi-sacred 'office of constable' to dazzle the courts, they do have a veneer of electoral legitimacy that may partly shield them from judicial review.

Elected authorities, like PCCs, may threaten the legal and civil rights of minorities, and indeed all individuals. Basic rights must be protected and preserved for a system to be called democratic. Again, the courts provide a potential remedy for illegal violations of rights, but not against policies or practices that may be grossly disproportionate in their impact on particular sections of the community, such as stop and search, if these are carried out within the very permissive limits of the law. Legislative institutions representative of the majority may formulate substantive criminal and other laws that whilst formally impartial end up reproducing the domination of particular minorities because of the way they play out in unequal and hierarchical societies. Stop and search powers such as those in the Police and Criminal Evidence Act 1984 s.1 apply equally to everyone in public space, and are subject to safeguards explicitly formulated to protect ethnic and other minorities from discriminatory use. However, they impact vastly disproportionately on certain minorities, because of their disproportionate 'availability' in public space as a transmitted effect of socio-economic opportunities. As Stinchcombe pointed out many decades ago, the institution of 'privacy' which structures the legal use of police powers reflects class and other inequalities (Stinchcombe 1963).

Unequal resources to affect the political process may result in plutocracy, the 'finest government money can buy' (Palast 2004), a clear and present danger in contemporary Britain, the USA and elsewhere. There is mounting evidence that we are moving towards a plutocracy: government of the rich, by the rich, for the rich. The massive increase in inequality engendered by neo-liberalism since the late 1970s, reversing two centuries of slow movement towards greater social inclusion, endangers the democratic process in a variety of ways. The process is far more advanced and evident in the USA, where distinguished political scientists have for many years charted the increasing takeover of the political process by the power of capital (Jacobs and Skocpol 2005; Wolin 2008). This trend towards plutocracy was hugely strengthened by a notorious 2009 US Supreme Court case, *Citizens United* v. Federal Election Commission, which decided that big corporations can spend unlimited funds on political advertising in any political election (Dworkin 2010).

The same processes are happening in Britain, although so far to a lesser extent, and less studied by academics (although radical journalists have assembled evidence of the march of plutocracy, e.g. Monbiot 2001). However, the growing conflicts about the role of political lobbying, and the revelations about the intimate interconnections between the right-wing press, politicians and the police that produced the Leveson Inquiry (Leveson 2013; Watson and Hickman 2013), point in the same direction. All underline the threat posed to democracy (based on the principle one person, one vote) by the neo-liberal unshackling of corporations and markets (in which one pound carries one vote, Reiner 2007: 5). Power is increasingly concentrated in the hands of the mega-rich few, whom the Occupy Movement called the 1 per cent (Graeber 2013: xi). This increasingly renders the outcome of elections irrelevant because of the constraints on the actions of national governments, especially because of their vulnerability to the dynamics of international capital markets. A further consequence for policing in particular is that the new system is likely to further encourage the 'mixed economy' of policing through the PCCs' power to commission private services. Whatever the immediate (but dubious) economic attractions of privatisation, it considerably hampers democratic accountability, which becomes dependent on the contractual link to the PCC (Innes 2011; Lister 2013: 244; Lister and Rowe 2014; Crawford 2014: 182–8; Manning 2014; Stenson and Silverstone 2013).

Related to this is unequal access to relevant knowledge about political and economic issues, and in particular criminal justice and policing matters. Most people see the mass media as their prime source of information, but a considerable body of research has shown how this largely amounts to *mis*information that disarms democracy (Dean 2012). This problem has been hugely accentuated in recent decades by the growing corporate domination of the mass media (Davies 2008). Public debate about criminal justice and policing matters in particular is hugely distorted by how the issues are framed in the media (Cavender 2004; Silverman 2011). Most people's conceptions of policing are drawn from the media. The 2002 survey on policing and people in London, for example, found that 80 per cent of respondents cited media news as their prime source of 'knowledge' of policing, and 29 per cent saw 'media fiction' as their crucial source – 9 per cent more than mentioned 'personal experience' (Fitzgerald *et al.* 2002). Given that a plethora of evidence shows that media representations of crime, criminal justice and policing follow a 'law of opposites' (Surette 1998), portraying crimes, offenders and victims in ways that are usually the inverse of official statistics (Greer and Reiner 2012), there is a massive educational job facing PCCs if they are to be swayed by anything but misinformed public opinion. Even what Ian Blair sarcastically dubbed an 'NVQ' on policing (Blair 2005), *The Bill*, became increasingly less concerned with verisimilitude as commercial pressures intensified (Colbran 2011).

The plutocratic threat to democracy marches in line with the digging-in deep of the post-1970s neo-liberal hegemony, despite the potential but as yet unrealised threat to this posed by the economic crisis since 2007/8. The overall problems of democracy reverberate with particular force in relation to criminal justice and especially policing, the arena in which social conflicts are most rapidly manifested. Obvious examples where this affects policing include dealing with trade union activities or political protests against neo-liberal economic policies such as the demonstrations at G20 meetings, against 'austerity' programmes with their savage cuts, or environmental campaigns. There is much evidence of apparently partisan policing of protest at several incidents in recent years (Gilmore 2012; Power 2011a, 2011b, 2011c, 2012; Monbiot 2013). Increasingly tough, sometimes illegal, policing of public disorder, biased towards the powerful interests of the corporate and conservative elites (as for so much of police history), is evident in other countries suffering from the neo-liberal 'austerity' bitter pill, such as Greece (Xenakis and Cheliotis 2013).

# The idea(l) of democratic policing

Democratic policing has become a worldwide mantra in recent years, aspired to or claimed for their systems by police leaders and policymakers around the globe (Bayley 2005; Marenin and Das 2010; Baker and Das 2013). In its increasing ubiquity as a brand, and its feel-good yet amorphous appeal, it is reminiscent of community policing, for some decades the label of choice for would-be police progressives. Both are impossible to be against in principle, but vague enough to mean anything or nothing in practice (Klockars 1988; Brogden 1999). Usually in international police discourse 'democratic policing' signifies primarily the ideal of policing that accords with principles of due process legality, rather than identifying democracy solely with elections as in current British Coalition Government rhetoric. Whilst civil rights and due legal process are indeed vital and necessary aspects of democratic policing, they too are not sufficient, even in conjunction with electoral democracy.

Peter Manning's recent book, *Democratic Policing in a Changing World*, asks for more (Manning 2010). Democratic policing must satisfy the Rawlsian conception of justice, Manning argues cogently, deploying a welter of sophisticated analysis and evidence. Famously, Rawls's two principles of justice call for equality of civil rights/liberties *and* of economic distribution, subject only to what he calls the 'difference' principle, i.e. not reducing the absolute welfare of the least well-off (Rawls 1971).

Rawls identified himself as a liberal, although his principles of justice (and the arguments underpinning them) amount to the tightest available foundation for a social democratic conception of fairness (Reiner 2012: x–xii, ch. 14, 2013). This can be spelled out in more explicitly social democratic terms (that I believe are entirely congruent with Rawls's analysis), by drawing on T.H. Marshall's celebrated account of citizenship (Marshall 1950). Democratic citizenship, Marshall suggests, requires not merely political rights but also civil, *and* social/economic. The achievement of these in modern Britain started with the civil/legal dimension (beginning in the seventeenth and eighteenth centuries), and then the gradual spread of political rights in the nineteenth and twentieth centuries. The third dimension of socio-economic inclusion was only being finally accomplished at the time Marshall wrote his classic lectures, with the post-second World War welfarist and Keynesian consensus. Socio-economic citizenship is a necessary condition for making legal and political rights more than formal (as Rawls also recognised), especially in the arena of criminal justice and policing because of their intricate involvement in conflicts (Reiner 2012 ch. 18). The trajectory of socio-economic incorporation has now been put into reverse with the neo-liberal hegemony since the 1970s, threatening the substance if not yet the shell of civil and political rights too.

The lesson of Marshall (and Rawls) is that liberal democracy must be accompanied by social democracy to prevent plutocracy, the penetration and covert undermining of legal, civil and political rights by the power of the purse. Elections in a context of vast and accelerating inequality of condition and resources cannot provide real power to the people, in policing or any other policy arena.

The new system of police governance, with PCCs as the lynchpin, moves policing further away from democratic governance than what it replaces, disguised by a fig leaf of populism (Turner 2014). The tripartite system at least in principle balanced the powers of the local and the national, of elected politicians and of professional experts. It also placed police governance firmly within the same model as the governance of other services. Its fundamental flaw was the uneven division of power, in particular the effective impotence of the local police authority. It was a mask for creeping centralised control (Reiner 1991), and that obfuscation was certainly a democratic deficit. But the problem was not the reality of central dominance; it was its concealment behind a façade of checks and balances that had no traction, so that there could be no adequate accountability for the real sinews of power. As Goodhart argued in a much admired dissent from the 1962 Report of the Royal Commission on Police, none of the standard arguments against a national force are sustainable – provided the locus of control is transparent (Royal Commission 1962). Scotland and the Netherlands have recently moved to a national structure, and there is no reason to believe they will not be at least as democratically accountable as the pretend localism of the old tripartite structure in England and Wales or its majoritarian successor (Fyfe 2014).

In the 1980s, when empowering fully elected authorities to govern policing was Labour policy, the Tories wielded vigorous arguments against it. In particular they stressed the dangers of politicising policing, with local tyrannies of the majority and restricted operational independence. These threats apply at least as much to the PCC structure (especially had the Liberal Democrats not been able to graft on to the legislation the supposedly balancing but weakly empowered Police and Crime Panels to whom PCCs must report, cf. Lister 2014). And the initial examples of PCCs flexing their muscles in apparently arbitrary ways indicate that such fears might be realised (Lister 2013; Lister and Rowe 2014).

## Conclusion

The Lenin question 'What is to be done?' is always the hardest to address. Rick Muir and Ian Loader have written an inspiring piece setting out an agenda seeking to rescue what is now a fait accompli. They identify some positive prospects for making policing more effective, fair and humane in the new system (Muir and Loader 2011), but this depends on persuading PCCs to adopt evidence-led policing styles, and hoping that these will prove visibly more effective than others before the next PCC elections.

One thing we should all be able to agree on is that the Coalition reforms will be subject to the same law of unintended consequences that has frustrated the intentions of police reformers so often in the past. In particular, a fundamental lesson of the sociology of policing is that there is little fit between policy formulated by any governance structure at the top of the organisation (even locally) and practice in the streets and cells. Nonetheless, although they may work out well in certain respects, the current changes are unacceptable in principle. They have, however, shattered the key plank of the old Conservative argument: that electoral control of policing is wrong. So when the next moment for change comes, I would argue for a back-to-basics approach: a truly balanced tripartism, the 1964 Police Act model with adequately empowered local police authorities. This would come closer to a system that could legitimately claim to be democratic.

But, in the final analysis, the problems facing democracy lie outside policing structures (Turner 2014). As Tawney suggested in the 1930s, at the start of the last great depression, democracy is more than a matter of elections: 'Is the reality behind the decorous drapery of political democracy to continue to be the economic power wielded by a few thousand – or ... a few hundred thousand – bankers, industrialists, and landowners?' (Tawney 1964 [1931]: 197). If this does remain the reality, then the prospects of democracy in one institution, especially the police, are dim. Democratic policing is not just a matter of elections, or indeed legality, though these are vital. It also requires the further element of universal citizenship and justice that was identified by T.H. Marshall and by John Rawls and others – a fair distribution of economic and social power.

## References

Baker, B. and Das, D. (2013) *Trends in Policing: Interviews with Police Leaders Across the Globe, Volume Four*, London: Routledge.

Banton, M. (1964) *The Policeman in the Community*. London: Tavistock Publications.

Barton, A. and Johns, N. (2013) 'Engaging the Citizen', in J. Brown (ed.) *The Future of Policing*, London: Routledge.

Bayley, D. (2005) *Changing the Guard: Developing Democratic Police Abroad*, Oxford: Oxford University Press.

Bittner, E. (1970) *The Functions of the Police in Modern Society*. Chevy Chase, MD: National Institute of Mental Health.

Bittner, E. (1974) 'Florence Nightingale in Pursuit of Willie Sutton: A Theory of the Police', in H. Jacob (ed.) *The Potential for Reform of Criminal Justice*, Los Angeles: Sage.

Blair, I. (2005) BBC Dimbleby Lecture, available at http://news.bbc.co.uk/1/hi/uk/4443386.stm (last accessed 20 October 2013).

Box, S. and Russell, K. (1975) 'The Politics of Discreditability', *Sociological Review*, 23(2): 315–46.

Bradford, B., Jackson, J. and Hough, M. (2013) 'Police Futures and Legitimacy: Redefining "Good Policing"', in J. Brown (ed.) *The Future of Policing*, London: Routledge.

Brodeur, J.-P. (2010) *The Policing Web*, New York: Oxford University Press.

Brogden, M. (1982) *The Police: Autonomy and Consent*, London: Academic Press.

Brogden, M. (1999) 'Community Policing as Cherry Pie', in R. Mawby (ed.) *Policing across the World*, London: UCL Press.

Brogden, M. and Ellison, G. (2012) *Policing in an Age of Austerity: A Postcolonial Perspective*, London: Routledge.

Cameron, D. (2012) *Speech to Centre for Social Justice*, 22 October, available at www.gov.uk/government/speeches/crime-and-justice-speech (last accessed 28 April 2015).

Cavender, G. (2004) 'Media and Crime Policy', *Punishment and Society*, 6(3): 335–48.

Colbran, M. (2011) *Watching the Detectives: A Case Study of Production Processes on 'The Bill'*, PhD thesis, London: LSE.

Crawford, A. (2014) 'The Police, Policing, and the Future of the Police Extended Family', in J. Brown (ed.) *The Future of Policing*, London: Routledge.

Davies, M. (2014) 'The Path to Police and Crime Commissioners', *Safer Communities*, 13(1): 3–12.

Davies, N. (2008) *Flat Earth News*, London: Chatto & Windus.

Dean, M. (2012) *Democracy Under Attack: How the Media Distort Policy and Politics*, Bristol: Policy Press.

Downes, D. and Morgan, R. (2012) 'Overtaking on the Left? The Politics of Law and Order in the "Big Society" ', in M. Maguire, R. Morgan and R. Reiner (eds) *The Oxford Handbook of Criminology*, Oxford: Oxford University Press.

Dunn, J. (2006) *Setting the People Free: The Story of Democracy*, London: Atlantic.

Dworkin, R. (2010) 'The "Devastating" Decision', *New York Review of Books*, 25 February, available at www.nybooks.com/articles/archives/2010/feb/25/the-devastating-decision/?insrc=toc (last accessed 5 October 2013).

Fitzgerald, M., Hough, M., Joseph, I. and Quereshi, T. (2002) *Policing for London*, Cullompton, Devon: Willan.

Fyfe, N. (2014) 'A Different and Divergent Trajectory? Reforming the Structure, Governance and Narrative of Policing in Scotland', in J. Brown (ed.) *The Future of Policing*, London: Routledge.

Gilmore, J. (2012) *'This is Not a Riot!' Regulation of Public Protest and the Impact of the Human Rights Act 1998*, PhD thesis, Manchester: University of Manchester School of Law.

Goldstein, J. (1960) 'Police Discretion not to Invoke the Criminal Process: Low Visibility Decisions in the Administration of Justice', *Yale Law Journal*, 69: 543–94.

Graeber, D. (2013) *The Democracy Project: A History, a Crisis, a Movement*, London: Allen Lane.

Greer, C. and Reiner, R. (2012) 'Mediated Mayhem: Media, Crime and Criminal Justice', in M. Maguire, R. Morgan and R. Reiner (eds) *The Oxford Handbook of Criminology* (5th edn), Oxford: Oxford University Press.

Guinier, L. (1994) *The Tyranny of the Majority: Fundamental Fairness in Representative Democracy*, New York: Free Press.

Home Affairs Committee (2011) *Police and Crime Commissioners: Power to Remove Chief Constables*, available at www.publications.parliament.uk/pa/cm201314/cmselect/cmhaff/487/487.pdf (last accessed 22 October 2013).

Home Office (2011) *Policing Protocol Order*, available at www.gov.uk/government/publications/policing-protocol-order-2011-statutory-instrument (last accessed 4 October 2013).

Hughes, E.C. (1961) 'Good People and Dirty Work', *Social Problems*, 10(1): 3–11.

Innes, M. (2011) 'Doing Less With More: The "New" Politics of Policing', *Public Policy Research*, June/August: 73–80.

Innes, M. (2013) 'Reinventing the Office of Constable: Progressive Policing in an Age of Austerity', in J. Brown (ed.) *The Future of Policing*, London: Routledge.

Jacobs, L. and Skocpol, T. (eds) (2005) *Inequality and American Democracy*, New York: Russell Sage.

Jefferson, T. and Grimshaw, R. (1984) *Controlling the Constable: Police Accountability in England and Wales*, London: Muller.

Jones, T. (2008) 'The Accountability of Policing', in T. Newburn (ed.) *Handbook of Policing*, Cullompton, Devon: Willan.

Jones, T. (2012) 'The Governance of Security', in M. Maguire, R. Morgan and R. Reiner (eds) *The Oxford Handbook of Criminology* (5th edn), Oxford: Oxford University Press.

Jones, T., Newburn, T. and Smith, D. (1994) *Democracy and Policing*, London: Policy Studies Institute.

Jones, T., Newburn, T. and Smith, D. (2012) 'Democracy and Police and Crime Commissioners', in J. Peay and T. Newburn (eds) *Policing: Politics, Culture and Control*, Oxford: Hart.

Karstedt, S. and LaFree, G. (eds) (2006) 'Democracy, Crime, and Justice', Special Issue of *The Annals of the American Academy of Political and Social Science*, May, Vol. 605.

Keane, J. (2009) *The Life and Death of Democracy*, London: Simon & Schuster.

Klockars, C. (1988) 'The Rhetoric of Community Policing', in J.R. Greene and S.D. Mastrofski (eds) *Community Policing: Rhetoric or Reality?*, New York: Praeger.

Lee, J.A. (1981) 'Some Structural Aspects of Police Deviance in Relations with Minority Groups', in C. Shearing (ed.) *Organizational Police Deviance*, Toronto: Butterworth.

Leveson, Lord Justice (2013) *The Report into the Culture, Practices and Ethics of the Press*, available at www.official-documents.gov.uk/document/hc1213/hc07/0780/0780. asp (last accessed 22 October 2012).

Lister, S. (2013) 'The New Politics of the Police: Police and Crime Commissioners and the "Operational Independence" of the Police', *Policing*, 7(3): 239–47.

Lister, S. (2014) 'Scrutinising the Role of the Police and Crime Panel in the New era of Police Governance in England and Wales', *Safer Communities*, 13(1): 22–31.

Lister, S. and Rowe, M. (2014) 'Electing Police and Crime Commissioners in England and Wales: Prospecting for the Democratisation of Policing', *Policing and Society* Advance access at www.tandfonline.com/doi/abs/10.1080/10439463.2013.868461?tab =permissions#tabModule (last accessed 1 April 2014).

*Liverpool Echo* (2012) 'David Cameron Thinks Police and Crime Commissioner Will Keep Liverpool's Streets Safe', 25 May, available at www.liverpoolecho.co.uk/news/liverpool-news/david-cameron-thinks-crime-commissioner-3345794 (last accessed 4 October 2013).

Loader, I. (2013) 'Why Do the Police Matter? Beyond the Myth of Crime-fighting', in J. Brown (ed.) *The Future of Policing*, London: Routledge.

Loveday, B. and Reid, B. (2003) *Going Local. Who Should Run Britain's Police?*, London: Policy Exchange.

Lustgarten, L. (1986) *The Governance of the Police*, London: Sweet & Maxwell.

Mann, S., Nolan, J. and Wellman, B. (2003) 'Sousveillance: Inventing and Using Wearable Computing Devices for Data Collection in Surveillance Environments', *Surveillance and Society*, 1(3): 331–55.

Manning, P. (2010) *Democratic Policing in a Changing World*, Boulder, CO: Paradigm.

Manning, P. (2014) 'Policing, Privatising, and Changes in the Policing Web', in J. Brown (ed.) *The Future of Policing*, London: Routledge

Marenin, O. (1983) 'Parking Tickets and Class Repression: The Concept of Policing in Critical Theories of Criminal Justice', *Contemporary Crises*, 6(2): 241–66.

Marenin, O. and Das, D. (2010) *Trends in Policing: Interviews with Police Leaders Across the Globe, Volume Three*, London: Routledge.

Marshall, G. (1965) *Police and Government*, London: Methuen.

Marshall, G. (1978) 'Police Accountability Revisited', in D. Butler and A.H. Halsey (eds) *Policy and Politics*, London: Macmillan.

Marshall, T.H. (1950) *Citizenship and Social Class*, Cambridge: Cambridge University Press.

Mathiesen, T. (1997) 'The Viewer Society: Michel Foucault's "Panopticon" Revisited' *Theoretical Criminology*, 1(2): 215–34.

May, T. (2012) 'Police Reform', speech to ACPO conference, 22 May, available at www. gov.uk/government/speeches/police-reform-home-secretarys-speech-to-acpo-conference (last accessed 3 October 2013).

McLaughlin, E. (2007) *The New Policing*, London: Sage.

Mill, J.S. (1991 [1851]) *On Liberty*, Oxford: Oxford University Press.

Millie, A. (2013) 'What Are the Police for? Rethinking Policing Post-Austerity', in J. Brown (ed.) *The Future of Policing*, London: Routledge.

Monbiot, G. (2001) *Captive State: The Corporate Takeover of Britain*, London: Pan.

Monbiot, G. (2013) 'Do the Police Act at the Behest of the UK's Rich and Powerful?', available at www.theguardian.com/environment/georgemonbiot/2013/sep/19/police-uk-powerful (last accessed 1 April 2014).

Muir, K.W., Jr (1977) *Police: Streetcorner Politicians*, Chicago: Chicago University Press.

Muir, R. and Loader, I. (2011) 'Why Labour Has it Wrong on Elected Police', *New Statesman*, available at www.newstatesman.com/blogs/the-staggers/2011/09/crime-commissioners-police (last accessed 28 April 2015).

Newburn, T. (2012) 'Police and Crime Commissioners: The Americanisation of Policing or a Very British Reform?', *International Journal of Law, Crime and Justice*, 40(1): 31–46.

Palast, G. (2004) *The Best Democracy Money Can Buy*, New York: Plume.

Policing Protocol Order (2011) available at www.essex.pcc.police.uk/wp-content/uploads/2012/11/20121126-PCC-Constitution-S6-Policing-Protocol-Order.pdf (last accessed 22 October 2013).

Power, N. (2011a) 'There is a Context to London's Riots that Can't be Ignored', available at www.theguardian.com/commentisfree/2011/aug/08/context-london-riots (last accessed 1 April 2014).

Power, N. (2011b) 'Let's Stop Assuming the Police are on Our Side', available at www.theguardian.com/commentisfree/2011/jul/26/metropolitan-police-arrests-hacking (last accessed 1 April 2014).

Power, N. (2011c) 'Sir Paul Stephenson's Strange Definition of "Restraint"', available at www.theguardian.com/commentisfree/2011/jul/18/sir-paul-stephenson-metropolitan-police (last accessed 1 April 2014).

Power, N. (2012) 'The Criminalisation of Protest is Part of the Elite's Class War', available at www.theguardian.com/commentisfree/2012/oct/19/boat-race-protest-class-war (last accessed 1 April 2014).

Punch, M. (1979) 'The Secret Social Service', in S. Holdaway (ed.) *The British Police*, London: Edward Arnold.

Punch, M. (ed.) (1983) *Control in the Police Organisation*, Cambridge, MA: MIT Press.

Punch, M. (2009) *Police Corruption: Deviance, Accountability and Reform in Policing*, Cullompton, Devon: Willan.

Rawls, J. (1971) *A Theory of Justice*, Cambridge, MA: Harvard University Press.

Reiner, R. (1985) *The Politics of the Police* (1st edn), Brighton: Wheatsheaf.

Reiner, R. (1991) *Chief Constables*, Oxford: Oxford University Press.

Reiner, R. (1995) 'Counting the Coppers: Antinomies of Accountability in Policing', in P. Stenning (ed.) *Accountability for Criminal Justice*, Toronto: University of Toronto Press, 74–92.

Reiner, R. (2007) *Law and Order: An Honest Citizen's Guide to Crime and Control*, Cambridge: Polity.

Reiner, R. (2010) *The Politics of the Police* (4th edn), Oxford: Oxford University Press.

Reiner, R. (2012) 'What's Left? The Prospects for Social Democratic Criminology', *Crime, Media, Culture*, 8(2): 135–50.

Reiner, R. (2013) 'Who Governs? Democracy, Plutocracy, Science and Prophecy in Policing', *Criminology and Criminal Justice*, 13(2): 161–80.

Reiner, R. and Spencer, S. (1993) *Accountable Policing: Effectiveness, Empowerment and Equity*, London: Institute for Public Policy Research.

Rieken, J. (2013) *Making Situated Police Practice Visible: A Study Examining Professional Activity For the Maintenance of Social Control With Video Data From the Field*, PhD thesis, London: LSE.

Royal Commission on the Police (1962) *Final Report*, London: HMSO. Cmnd 1728.

Silverman, J. (2011) *Crime, Policy and the Media: The Shaping of Criminal Justice, 1989–2010*, Oxford: Routledge

Stenning, P. (ed.) (1995) *Accountability in Criminal Justice*, Toronto: University of Toronto Press.

Stenson, K. and Silverstone, D. (2013) 'Making Police Accountable: Governance and Legitimacy', in J. Brown (ed.) *The Future of Policing*, London: Routledge.

Stinchcombe, A. (1963) 'Institutions of Privacy in the Determination of Police Administrative Practice', *American Journal of Sociology*, 69(2): 150–60.

Surette, R. (1998) *Media, Crime and Criminal Justice*, Belmont, CA: Wadsworth.

Tawney, R.H. (1964 [1931]) *Equality*, London: Unwin.

Turner, L. (2014) 'PCCs, Neo-liberal Hegemony and Democratic Policing', *Safer Communities*, 13(1): 13–21.

Walker, N. (2000) *Policing in a Changing Constitutional Order*, London: Sweet & Maxwell.

Watson, T. and Hickman, M. (2013) *Dial M for Murdoch: News Corporation and the Corruption of Britain*, London: Allen Lane.

Wilson, J.Q. (1968) *Varieties of Police Behavior*, Cambridge, MA: Harvard University Press.

Winsor, T. (2013) *Operational Independence and the New Accountability of Policing*, John Harris Memorial Lecture, London: HMIC, available at www.hmic.gov.uk/media/hmcic-tom-winsor-john-harris-memorial-lecture.pdf (last accessed 22 October 2013).

Wolin, S. (2008) *Democracy Inc*, Princeton: Princeton University Press.

Xenakis, S. and Cheliotis, L. (2013) 'Crime and Economic Downturn: The Complexity of Crime and Crime Politics in Greece since 2009', *British Journal of Criminology*, 53(5): 719–45.

# 8 Accountability, policing and the Police Service of Northern Ireland

## Local practice, global standards?

*John Topping*

Almost without exception, both the development and operationalisation of police accountability in Northern Ireland have gone hand in hand with the much lauded and complex reform process set in motion by the far-reaching recommendations of the Independent Commission for Policing in Northern Ireland (ICP 1999), known as 'The Patten Report'. Beneath the international attention focused upon the polity's policing affairs over nearly four decades, it may be observed that 'knowing' and 'overseeing' what the police 'do' have become integral to the country's contemporary policing (and political) landscape.

As part of the implicit ICP policy of 'wrestling' policing from the state and giving it 'back to the people' (Topping 2008b), creating one of the world's most accountable police services has become the bedrock of community trust and legitimacy not just in the police, but so too the state – notwithstanding the importance of policing to the wider political settlement and stability in the country (O'Rawe 2003). Thus, on both vertical (structural) and horizontal (sociopolitical) plains, the Police Service of Northern Ireland (PSNI) has become governed by a host of statutory, governmental and other bodies – generally conceived as the global 'gold standard' of police oversight, not limited to operational policing, human rights, public order policing and organisational governance (Ellison 2007; Office of the Oversight Commissioner 2007; Topping 2008a).

Yet in spite of the embedded nature of accountability mechanisms in terms of their legal and policy status, it may be argued that function has not necessarily followed form with regard to the outworking of police accountability – and especially so when set within the transitional and shifting context of the policing landscape of Northern Ireland. As will be observed below, a number of 'mediating realities' serve to challenge both the efficacy of the various mechanisms in place to hold the police to account. Indeed, the evidence would suggest the policing and security environment is something *other* than that which is conducive to the delivery of 'normal' policing, with a continuing terrorist threat, social and religious segregation, ritual public disorder and 'alternative' policing provision variously coalescing to challenge the outward projection of policing in the country as 'mission successful' – and accounts thereof (Topping and Byrne 2012c). With Northern Ireland further described as a 'criminological netherworld', police accountability thus remains as a subjective and flexible assessment of policing – rather than an objective metric of police performance and oversight (Ellison and Mulcahy 2001). In this regard, accountability for policing by PSNI in terms of what it 'does', what it delivers and what it is responsible for on the ground remains far from clear-cut (Topping and Byrne 2012a).

Against this backdrop, this chapter examines the key junctures of police accountability within a Northern Ireland context. Indeed, the intention is not to detail nor assess the efficacy of police oversight and monitoring as 'encoded' through the police governance structures per se. Rather, it sets out to explore the limits of police accountability as a function of the environment in which it is conceived. Ultimately, the chapter argues that accountability for both institutional and operational 'police action' in the country has become a 'site' of contest in and of itself – of which the official 'accounts' of policing are but one version of reality.

## The value of accountability in transition

When considering the value of police accountability within conflicted settings such as Northern Ireland, a key starting point must be to consider what precisely accountability stands for. While much of the country's international (academic) attention has been focused upon the past 15 years, concern over policing practice (and laterally oversight) extends far beyond the halo of the ICP and the 'modern reach' of police reforms (Ellison 2007). Indeed, looking back to the formation of the Northern Irish state in 1921 and the PSNI's predecessor – the Royal Ulster Constabulary (RUC), created in 1922 – policing has never been far from controversy as a function of the country's troubled domestic affairs (McGloin 2003; Ryder 1997). With the RUC during this period as the most visible manifestation of law, order and politics, the de facto conflict in which it operated only served to heighten the symbolism of policing and subsequent action as delivered on the ground (O'Leary and McGarry 1996). From the introduction of various draconian and discriminatory legislation since 1921 through to the close association of police command and control with a partisan Unionist Government, the empirical evidence points to the RUC having played a significant role in both precipitating and holding what may be described as the 'thin green line' between the triumvirate of British Government, Loyalist/Unionist and Republican/Nationals factions (Buckland 1979; Scorer and Hewitt 1981; Hillyard 1988, 1994; Ni Aolain 2000; Moran 2008). It is not, however, the intention of this chapter to recount the historical antecedents of the Northern Ireland conflict, nor the actions of the police during that period. Rather, it is instructive to turn to the parallel processes of police accountability and oversight (as broadly conceived) as the precursor for the *need* to ensure that state transgressions through the police did not go unchecked.

Turning to O'Leary and McGarry (1996), they point to early forms of police accountability insofar as the Labour Government's interventions in Northern Irish affairs during the 1960s left them 'stunned' by the lack of police independence from the dominant Ulster Unionist Party at the time. And it is from that point where a 30-year process of 'inquiry' into police practice and operations may be viewed. Among many, these included the Hunt Report (1969), which examined the structure of the RUC (and their reserve, the 'B-Specials') regarding their exclusively Protestant makeup (O'Rawe 2003); the Cameron (1969) and Scarman Reports (1972), exploring the civil disturbances associated with the beginning of the Troubles in the country; the Widgery Report (1972) that examined the deaths at the civil rights march in Derry, otherwise known as 'Bloody Sunday'; and the Bennett Committee (1979) which undertook an investigation into the interrogation practices of the RUC.

It is therefore the cumulative picture painted by these various reports and inquiries which points to the fact – both organisationally and operationally – that policing needed to move away from its centralised, militaristic and partisan approach (Weitzer 1999). Euphemistically known as the 'Barbed Wire Act' (the strict and often arbitrary enforcement of the law), this period of oversight may also be viewed as the foundation from which the necessarily robust and new forms of accountability needed to be created as part of the ICP's vision. And at its core, this 'new accountability' was about creating a whole new set of structures capable of changing the RUC into an acceptable policing service for the entire community which was to be: professional; effective and efficient; fair and impartial; free from partisan control; accountable, both under the law and to the community; and operate within a coherent and cooperative criminal justice system which conforms with human rights norms (O'Rawe 2003: 1017).

Before moving to consider the infrastructure of police accountability developed as part of the ICP, however, it is important to consider the value of accountability as part of the wider policing transition in Northern Ireland. In terms of introducing meaningful social, democratic, community and political oversight into policing, it was the ICP which stated:

> [I]n a democracy, policing, in order to be effective must be based on consent across the community ... [where the] community recognises the legitimacy of the policing task, confers authority on police personnel carrying out their role in police and actively support them. Consent is not unconditional, but depends on proper accountability.
>
> (ICP 1999: 22)

Though beyond the visible, structural level, it is interesting to observe that accountability as envisaged by the ICP consisted of three additional strands as part of 'getting policing right' (O'Rawe 2003). First, it advanced creating an accountability system for policing premised upon *minimising* the space in which police transgression could take place or become justified. In spite of the weight of evidence highlighting the need for external police oversight (as noted above cf. Ellison and Smyth 2000), it was police officers themselves during the conflict who often failed to see the damaging consequences of their actions and omissions. As characterised by the former Chief Constable Hugh Annesly when defending the actions of the organisation during the conflict: 'I do not accept the change argument. I do not believe that there is anything inherently wrong with the RUC that needs to be changed. I do not accept the organisation is wrong and must be fixed' (RTE Television Interview 1995, cited in O'Rawe 2003: 1030). Thus, police accountability flowing out of the post-conflict era necessarily had to be created as a neutral, independent and effective 'space' – not just for getting the police to account for their activities, but to allow actions to be publicly scrutinised as an attempt to build community and political trust and legitimacy. It may be further observed this was an a priori minimum starting point from which political and community trust in policing could even be conceived in the context of that which went before in terms of police action and activity (O'Rawe 2003).

The second key strand to the ICP's notion of 'proper accountability' also lay with the need to take accountability beyond fundamental cultural and structural policing issues (as noted above) and embed accountability for what may be conceived as 'everyday' policing (Topping 2008a). Reflecting wider societal changes away from the worst excesses of conflict-related violence, it was imagined that once fully developed, police accountability structures would allow oversight of the police to shift metaphorically from being the ambulance at the bottom of the cliff, to the fence at the top (O'Hara 1996; Hayes and McAllister 2005). As part of the ICP's central community policing ethos, this strand would further allow accountability to act as a conduit for building trust at the level of locale – while simultaneously displaying that policing was more than simply holding the 'thin green line' associated with the 'big' issues of conflict-related policing, such as communal violence, bombings and shootings (Ellison 2000).

The third strand of the ICP's accountability agenda may be viewed as a vehicle through which both Loyalist/Unionist and Nationalist/Republican communities could also be 're-educated' about the 'new' policing landscape following the creation of the PSNI in 2001. As Topping (2008b) contends, it is important to set accountability for policing within the context of those communities in which it is delivered – and especially so within the (still) divided and polarised society of Northern Ireland (Shirlow and Murtagh 2006). With the ICP reforms radically altering the policing landscape, evidence would point to the fact this has impacted on public expectations and perceptions of the police, regardless of operational activity (Byrne and Monaghan 2008). Within Loyalist communities – as those traditionally more supportive of the police – the disbandment of the RUC, as a police force comprising officers seen as 'theirs', combined with significant reductions in police numbers – currently 6,900 compared to the 13,500 officers during the RUC 'heyday' – has created a distinct and substantial sense of 'loss' and reduced sense of service delivery (Mulcahy 2000, 2006; Topping 2008b; PSNI 2014).

Conversely, within many Republican communities – as those traditionally opposed to policing and criminal justice system more broadly – police accountability has on the one hand become a means through which to 'measure' and 'signpost' the steps taken by the PSNI to distance itself from the style of policing associated with the RUC at a community level (Weitzer 1999). On the other hand, due to the historical separation between Republican communities and the state more generally, police accountability during the post-ICP era has become the medium through which those communities practically learn and understand about the limits of 'normal' policing – having in many cases never consensually engaged with the police in the past (Mulcahy 1999). In this regard, accountability as effected through the ICP can be seen as both a neutral and mediating vehicle through which to redefine and redraw the boundaries of police activity and operations as part of the ever 'normalising' policing environment. Furthermore, as part of developing trust and legitimacy in the PSNI within both Loyalist and Republican communities, this process necessarily needed a new 'space' within which communities could reimagine accountability as a connection *with* the police beyond merely *to* them.

In terms of the value of police accountability within the conflicted and transitional setting of Northern Ireland, it is clear that the concept of accountable policing extends well beyond that which can be defined as part of 'standard' police performance metrics. Indeed, in this context police accountability has become as much a symbol of the changing police and political order as it has a sophisticated set of oversight structures. As captured by Ellison (2007), the value of accountability set within the country's wider police reform process may thus be viewed as a central tenet contributing 'to the very foundations of political order upon which democratic freedoms so often depend' (ibid.: 243–4).

## The mechanics of police accountability

Before considering the collective of structures that comprise police accountability in Northern Ireland, it may be argued that both their strength and capacity are drawn from the stringency of the ICP reform process itself. Not only did the final ICP report make 175 recommendations for policing change in the country, but so too these were overseen by the Office of the Oversight Commissioner (OOC), established to ensure the 'faithful and comprehensive' implementation of those recommendations (ICP 1999: para. 19.2). Across 19 reports and 772 performance indicators, the final OOC report noted that virtually all recommendations had been completed – as part of one the most complex and far-reaching experiments in police reform ever attempted in the world (OOC 2007).

At a basic level, much of the attention related to police accountability in the country rests with the much vaunted legal accountability of the PSNI to the Office of the Police Ombudsman for Northern Ireland (OPONI). Established prior to the ICP under the Police (Northern Ireland) Act 1998, OPONI is considered to be one of the most robust and independent bodies in the world tasked with adjudicating on PSNI operational and disciplinary matters where the prospect of police misconduct exists, including discrimination, malpractice, incivility, failure in duty and oppressive behaviour (Mulcahy 2006; OPONI 2010–12). As a means of building core, community-wide legitimacy in the 'new' PSNI, 'without the establishment of the OPONI, the entire [ICP] reform process would have stalled ... and its role in enhancing the legitimacy of the PSNI should not be underestimated' (Ellison 2007: 261). At an annual operating cost of approximately £9 million, the OPONI has no financial targets, in line with the ICP's attempts to avoid 'false economies' in the delivery of its role (OPONI 2013). Indeed, with 8,465 complaint allegations dealt with during 2012/13, the return on the investment in the OPONI as part of cementing independence is incalculable in terms of its worth to societal trust and confidence in the police (Ellison and Smyth 2000; Mulcahy 2006; OPONI 2013).

Below the level of police complaints per se, the next key and necessary oversight body created through the ICP was the Northern Ireland Policing Board (NIPB). As a body designed to provide a procedurally 'thick' police authority for the country (Black 2000; Ellison 2007), the vision of the ICP was 'to go beyond the supervision of the police service itself, extend to the wider issues of policing the contributions that people and organisations other that the police can make towards public safety'(ICP 1999: 29). Across a series of performance, audit, risk, partnership and resources committees – as well as the full Board of the authority itself – the NIPB is charged with holding PSNI to account across a range of 'everyday', operational and financial policing matters, not limited to crime levels, human rights, community policing, public order, recruitment and equality issues (NIPB 2013). It must also be noted that the NIPB additionally acts as a key intersection of police operational matters for sociopolitical accountability and oversight. With the NIPB itself comprising 19 independent and political members, it provides the main platform upon which both cross-party and cross-community policing issues can be debated.

Yet in spite of what appears to be a robust structure it is important to note that the NIPB is not unique in terms of its flaws as a police authority (cf. Raine and Keasey 2012). On a broad level, the cyclical issues of violence, disorder and legacy of the conflict in Northern Ireland continue to pervade its oversight role on 'normal' policing matters (Byrne *et al.* 2014; Clarke 2014). Furthermore, the Northern Ireland Audit Office (NIAO) have, for the past two years, strongly criticised the NIPB for the lack of meaningful target-setting as part of the performance management of police operations (NIAO 2013, 2014). With the Board obliged under s.28 of the Police (Northern Ireland) Act 2000 to make arrangements to secure continuous improvement of policing, the NIAO have indicatively stated:

> the performance indicators included within the Policing Plan 2012–13 are reasonable. However, 40 of the 44 performance standards included in the Plan lack sufficient clarity as to the degree of improvement required and the timeframe within which it is to be achieved.
>
> (NIAO 2013: 4)

Thus, the evidence would suggest that in spite of the ICP's vision for the NIPB, the reality of police accountability is that of a procedurally 'thinner' version of the 'thick' aspiration set forth by the ICP (Ellison 2007; Topping 2008a). The implication being that the 'measuring' of policing has become a superficial rather than a substantive process. This is especially so where PSNI can satisfy such accountability regimes as a distinct and separate goal in and of itself without significantly impacting on operational policing delivery.

The final piece of the main police accountability 'architecture' in Northern Ireland is the establishment of Policing and Community Safety Partnerships (PCSPs). Formed under the Justice Act (NI) 2011, these statutory partnerships are the key community 'bridge' between the PSNI, the NIPB and local policing matters. With one PCSP for each of the country's 26 council areas, they comprise political and independent members for the purposes of consulting and engaging, identifying and prioritising, and monitoring and delivering on policing issues of community concern (Topping and Byrne 2012a).

On the one hand, the PCSPs were created to replace their much criticised predecessors – the District Policing Partnerships (DPPs) – summarily described as 'talking shops staged managed to avoid controversy' (CAJ 2005: 16; cf. Mulcahy 2006; Ellison 2007; Byrne and Monaghan 2008; Topping 2008a; Topping and Byrne 2012a). But on the other hand, evidence would suggest that little has changed to improve their effectiveness, efficiency or 'politicking' on policing under the new PCSP regime. In reference to the latter, with wider (often sectarian) politics often dominating debates at the expense of 'everyday' policing matters, it is of note that current figures indicate that 41 per cent of 'independent' members in fact have political affiliations; with only 3 per cent of PCSPs comprising any members from ethnic minority backgrounds; and no members under 18 (Topping and Byrne 2012a). Thus, the practicable degree of community input into local policing matters remains notional, rather than substantive – with recent research by the principle Belfast PCSP, for example, indicating that 54 per cent of the public do not know what the function of the PCSP is; and only 5 per cent indicating they would contact their PCSP on policing and community safety issues (Belfast City Council 2014). Additionally, they lack the potential for critical engagement and oversight on local policing matters insofar as they may be viewed as forums that do little more than provide PSNI a platform upon which 'they are better able to voice the feelings of the community than elected local councillors ... either by operationalising the biases of the community forums ... or by inter-personal gleanings from the "respectable" public' (Brogden 2006: 15). While current space precludes a fuller critique of the broad police accountability structures in Northern Ireland, their collective 'swarm' would certainly point to a system which (in spite of its flaws) has facilitated a societal 'leap' in terms of full social, political and democratic participation in policing matters – a position unthinkable 15 year ago (Mulcahy 2006; Ellison 2007). It must also be noted that the 'layers' of police accountability (as detailed) are additionally supplemented by an assemblage of statutory and non-government oversight bodies and structures, including: the Northern Ireland Human Rights Commission; the Equality Commission for Northern Ireland; Her Majesty's Inspectorate of Constabulary; the Criminal Justice Inspection Northern Ireland; and the Committee on the Administration of Justice. With each variously reporting thematically and via an ad hoc basis, as far back as 2007, it was the then Deputy Chief Constable of the PSNI who noted that together, these bodies had further generated approximately 1,070 recommendations above and beyond those of the ICP (Topping 2008a). In this respect, the current position on police accountability structures is detailed by Ellison (2007: 265), stating:

Arguably, Northern Ireland has some of the more farsighted and robust structures for police governance ... that exist anywhere, not to mention the normative and statutory emphasis on human rights, which is placed center stage in terms of police operational policies, strategies, and procedures.

## Accounting for what? The conflicted picture of policing and security in Northern Ireland

Having considered some of the normative and structural issues of police accountability in Northern Ireland, it is important to consider wider evidence related to what *precisely* these structures hold the police to account for. It may be observed that the structures and processes put in place under the ICP were predicated upon Northern Ireland becoming a settled, inclusive and peaceful society (Ellison 2007; Topping 2008b). To that extent, the current suite of accountability measures have, therefore, been oriented towards dealing with 'normal' policing matters – such as reducing levels of crime, building police confidence and delivering community policing. However, as shall be explored below, the environment in which the PSNI deliver policing is anything other than conducive to that vision of normality, with the accountability structures functionally remote from the 'realpolitik' of policing on the ground. Thus, the remainder of this section seeks to define the 'edges' of police accountability as part of operational policing as part of this environment.

It may be observed that the criminological 'netherworld' of Northern Ireland presents a number of counterfactual narratives around the official notions of policing and crime. This in turn helps to provide both an understanding of, and insight into, the complex dynamics underpinning the 'positive peace' in the country as it emerges from a protracted, internal armed conflict – and as a means for understanding the limits of police accountability more fully (Ellison and Mulcahy 2001; Eide and Holm 2000; Topping 2009).

To begin with, evidence would point to the fact that in spite of the transition from conflict to (relative) peace, Northern Ireland suffers from low levels of crime. Unlike the violent transitional democracy of South Africa (Altebeker 2005) – often compared to Northern Ireland – the 'official' projection of the country as a low-crime society has both been cemented and bolstered by the significant political progress which has itself facilitated the historical devolution of policing and justice powers to Stormont for the first time since 1972 (McDonald and Townsend 2011). On the one hand, such low crime levels have tended to be explained through a Durkheimian school of 'solidarity in conflict' as part of sociological accounts of close-knit communities and 'grapevines' prevalent across the country (Brewer 2001; Shaw and Shearing 1998). On the other hand, 'official' measures of, and processes of accounting for, crime and security confirm the conception of Northern Ireland as a low-crime, transitional 'netherworld'. From the first International Victim Survey in 1989 reporting Northern Ireland as Europe's low-crime comparator (Brogden 2000; Van Dijk *et al.* 1990), contemporary evidence points to the lowest levels of conflict-related violence on record; the lowest levels of recorded crime in the past 12 years; along with victimisation rates at approximately 13 per cent – the lowest since records began in 1998, which also compares favourably to England and Wales (Lyness *et al.* 2004). Furthermore, the Northern Ireland Policing Board (NIPB) continues to claim that satisfaction levels with the PSNI remain at record high levels (Toner and Freel 2010; NIPB 2014). However, beyond simple attributions and correlations of police activity to this status quo, a range of other evidence must be considered as part of the accountability debate in terms of considering what the PSNI are held to account for.

First, it is notable from research by NIPB that crime rates within what can be defined as predominantly Protestant or Catholic wards vary significantly – with higher crime rates generally within Catholic wards in comparison both to Protestant wards and the country as a whole (NIPB 2007). Second, relating to accountability for the delivery of 'normal' policing – and specifically looking at violent dissident Republicanism – while their terrorist capabilities are far lower than the threat posed by mainstream Republican paramilitaries at the height of the conflict, evidently dissident factions are still engaged in an armed campaign, along with the delivery of 'civil policing' within certain areas of Northern Ireland. This agenda has manifested itself through the planting of viable explosive devices and concerted efforts to kill members of the security forces across the country (*Belfast Telegraph* 2008a, 2008b, 2008c, 2010; *The Irish News* 2008, 2009) – resulting in the deaths of British soldiers Patrick Azimkar and Mark Quinsey outside the Massereene Barracks in Co. Antrim on 8 March 2009, and the murders of Constable Stephen Carroll on 10 March 2009 and Constable Ronan Kerr on 12 April 2011 (McDonald and Townsend 2011). Indeed, it is a continuing feature of the post-conflict landscape that the threat of politically motivated violence remains at 'severe' as defined by MI5 (Independent Monitoring Commission 2010; Kearney 2010; Owen and Dutta 2011). And this is notwithstanding the fact that HMIC (2011) have recently criticised the PSNI for only classifying 25 per cent of terrorist incidents in the country as such within the technical definition of the term – suggesting the levels of terrorist activity are in fact significantly higher than officially recorded.

It is also important to recognise that paramilitary activity has not been limited solely to those from a Republican background. Within many Loyalist working-class communities paramilitary structures remain in place and able to control communities and orchestrate widespread violence – as witnessed in East Belfast during June 2011 and December 2012. In terms of the former, with approximately 500 people involved in violence over 3 nights, it included gun battles between Loyalist and Republican paramilitary groupings along with the shooting of a Press Association photographer. And in reference to the latter, these more recent outbreaks of public disorder – referred to as the 'flag protests' – resulted in approximately 500 arrests, 700 PSNI officers injured and a cost to the public purse of approximately £20 million (McDonald 2012; Mulgrew and Erwin 2014). It may therefore be seen that as part of any account of policing in the country, the PSNI and the services it delivers cannot be divorced from these wider realities – where the presence of proscribed organisations at the community level along with their terrorist capacity remain far from being consigned to the annals of Northern Irish history (McDonald 2011a, 2011b).

Turning to the organisational arrangement of the PSNI, in contrast to the ICP's vision of normality and its focus on community policing, it still retains a structure mainly suited to the delivery of public order and security-focused policing (Topping 2008a). As identified by HMIC, in comparison with 'most similar forces' in England and Wales, the PSNI's retention of (necessary) public order and counter-insurgency capabilities is stark. Within the PSNI, the immediate post-ICP period was characterised by the fact that only 35 per cent of its District Command Units (DCUs) (at least up to 2006) claimed to be carrying out operational policing under 'normal' conditions (HMIC 2007). Furthermore, there are approximately six times as many officers dedicated to public order policing, with four times as many officers dedicated to intelligence duties than 'most similar forces'. Thus, when combined, for example, with a total of 86,073 overtime hours undertaken by PSNI officers in 2005/6 alone over the same period to cope with the extra public order demands, the significant overtime in the aftermath of over 40 days of public disorder as a result of recent Loyalist/Unionist disputes over the 'flag protests' (*Telegraph* 2013), and the fact over 1,200 officers have been injured in public order situations between 2005 and 2012, it gives a clear indication that accountability for policing matters in the country stretches far beyond the simplicity of crime levels (McDonald 2012).

Continuing on the theme of public disorder, it is also vital to outline current 'levels' of public order incidents and events, at least as mediated by those in charge of delivery and oversight – namely the PSNI, the Police Ombudsman for Northern Ireland (OPONI) and the Parades Commission. Turning first to the Parades Commission, as the statutory body set up to provide determinations and direction on parades and protests in Northern Ireland, it may be evidenced that parades, as the more traditional focus of public order policing in Northern Ireland, remain a constant feature of the country's sociopolitical fabric in addition to 'normal' crime and criminality. With an average of 3,641 notified parades per year from 2003/4 to 2010/11, there has been a steady increase in the number of parades over this period, indicating both the popularity and cultural sustainability of this particular form of expression and assembly – albeit with approximately two-thirds of all parades identified as 'Loyal Order/broad Unionist' (Bryan 2000; Parades Commission 2012).

Related to accounts of public order policing, the post-Patten era has, however, been demarcated by a significant shift away from the use of force by the PSNI, especially those associated with parades and protests (Ni Aolain 2000; Committee on the Administration of Justice 1996, 1997). This has been especially illustrated by the use of Plastic Baton Rounds (PBRs) and since 2005 of their replacement by Attenuating Energy Projectiles (AEPs). Since 2005 the PSNI have fired 1,723 AEPs, although the annual figures range from none in 2006/7 to 350 in 2011/12. This is in contrast to the late 1990s, when the RUC fired 6,949 PBRs in 1996, with more than 6,000 of these being fired in a single week at the height of the Drumcree dispute (Mulcahy 2006). More recently, turning to the serious public disorder which spread across Northern Ireland in 2011 from 20 June to 16 July, of the 350 AEPs fired during this period, approximately 85 per cent of those were discharged under the auspices of protecting officers or members of the public (PSNI Freedom of Information Request F-2011–023272). Thus, in parallel with the central prominence of community policing within PSNI, use of force remains a significant concern to the country's peacetime narrative (Topping 2008a; Byrne *et al.* 2013).

Within this contested environment, additional empirical evidence outside that of the NIPB's much vaunted confidence statistics in PSNI points to significant dissociation of many Republican/Nationalist, and to a lesser extent Unionist/Loyalist communities, from the vagaries of normal crime issues and interaction with the police, not necessarily as result of PSNI themselves (Ellison and Mulcahy 2001; Mulcahy 2006; Byrne and Monaghan 2008; Topping 2008a; Topping and Byrne 2012a). And when overlaid with continuing police legitimacy issues associated with the legacy of the conflict and parades/protests as noted above, it is clear that the accountability function of the NIPB and PCSPs becomes a negotiated process – pulled between their statutory obligations and procedures related to 'normal' police metrics – and the reality of the landscape outlined, which sits outside the traditional police accountability boxes to be 'ticked' (Byrne and Monaghan 2008; Lundy 2011).

In overview of the conflicted and often contradictory picture of policing in Northern Ireland, it is therefore clear that a significant lacuna exists. On the one hand, the very nature of accountability measures and metrics are focused upon monitoring PSNI for 'everyday' policing matters. Yet on the other hand, the empirical reality of the post-ICP landscape would suggest that many fundamental dynamics related to the delivery of policing are not considered – publicly or in policy – as part of any official discourse or 'measure' of the policing environment. Thus, in terms of accounting for what the police 'do' and in spite of wider evidence considered, the default position for PSNI operational accountability remains that all problems 'are frequently identified as police problems to which there are police solutions. Any change is attributed to police causes ignoring changes in the wider social system' (Fielding and Innes 2006: 136–7).

## Community policing and the PSNI: accounting for 'core' service?

Aside from the architecture and reality of that which comprises police accountability in Northern Ireland, an equally important focus of inquiry relates to accountability for what PSNI delivers as part of its core service. In terms of the ICP, a key goal was to move PSNI from counter-insurgency to a community orientation, with ICP recommendation 44 stating that community policing (or 'policing with the community' under the ICP rubric) 'should be the core function of the police service' (ICP 1999: para. 7.9). Thus, as part of considering accountability for what PSNI 'do' within a transitional context, it must be remembered that community policing is 'not an independent variable, but must be located within a wider mesh of social and political change' (Clegg *et al.*, cited in Brogden 2005: 90).

A key proposition for the delivery of community policing in Northern Ireland relates not just to its technical delivery (discussed below), but also the symbolism of that which it represents. As the foundation for a 'shift' in wider police–community relations in the country, community policing as mandated by the ICP represents the 'staged death' of 'traditional', conflict-related policing by the RUC; and the ushering in of a new era of effective, democratic and community-anchored service by the PSNI (Kappeler and Kraska 1998; Loader 2000; Topping 2008a). Yet in spite of a continuous 'stream' of PSNI policy and 'self-certification' as to the delivery of community policing in the post-ICP era (and empirically unsustainable claims about its relation to reductions in crime and police confidence), a range of additional evidence would suggest that accountability for its delivery is more complex than simple claims of its implementation (PSNI 2012; Byrne and Monaghan 2008; Topping 2008a, 2008b, 2012; Topping and Byrne 2012c).

As argued by Brogden, one of the first key stumbling blocks to wider accountability narratives about the 'success' of community policing by the PSNI is the fact that:

> police organisations with no tradition of decentralised decision making encounter major problems. The decentralisation required by community policing, and the resultant increased autonomy of the rank-and-file, may have three effects ... it may mean a loss in effective management controls as a consequence of decentralisation ... it may result in a loss of wider accountability and control. Finally, loss of external and internal supervision may lead to a breakdown of professional standards of behaviour by police officers.
>
> (1999: 180)

At least structurally, it has already been noted (above) that during the post-ICP era, the PSNI have (necessarily due to the terrorist threat) retained a relatively militaristic, hierarchical and counter-insurgency structure (HMIC 2007). Claims of the PSNI to have community policing as a core mission are further stretched when evidence also points to the fact only 10 per cent of the organisation (or approximately 700 officers for a population of 1.8 million) are actually dedicated community/neighbourhood officers (Topping and Byrne 2012c). Additionally, the problem of measuring community policing 'as something that never was' is further complicated as part of the post-conflict landscape in Northern Ireland (Innes 2005). At a basic level, measures of 'success' for community policing practice vary greatly in their scope. From its ability to maintain peace and order in transitional societies, through to reducing fear of crime, community policing creates an infinite pool of approaches that ultimately generates a need for an infinite pool of measures upon which police organisations could be held to account (Jesilow and Parsons 2000; Fielding and Innes 2006). And no less in this jurisdictional context, reductions in sectarian violence, terrorism and hostility towards the PSNI, for example, are often held to be blunt indicators for the 'successes' of community policing (Topping and Byrne 2012c).

A wide range of qualitative research also exists to challenge the 'record' levels of confidence in the PSNI set forth annually by the NIPB – as a key metric of community practices (NIPB 2014). Across many Loyalist and Republican communities – and especially in socio-economically deprived areas – the reality of policing is that a sizeable portion of the population are disengaged, dissatisfied and lack confidence in the PSNI as part of delivering this 'everyday' service (Ellison *et al.* 2013; Topping 2008a, 2008b, 2009; Ellison and O'Rawe 2010; Byrne and Monaghan 2008; Topping and Byrne 2012a). Yet it is precisely this tranche of society whose voices have been silenced in the official accountability discourse due to the limitations of current measures employed to capture community satisfaction with the PSNI (cf. Topping 2012). In this regard, the political imperative of policing being seen 'to be gotten right' may be observed as part of its centrality to the wider peace process in the country (O'Rawe 2003; Ellison 2007).

Finally, in regard to community policing as a metric of the performance accountability of the PSNI, it is important to return specifically to Brogden (1999) as part of considering internal, organisational issues in addition to the structural points already raised. As detailed by Fielding and Innes (2006: 129), 'the broad appeal of community policing relates more to its iconic status and homely name tag than to its conceptual clarity of concept or unambiguously demonstrable effects'. And no less for the PSNI, community policing within the rank and file of the organisation remains, at best, ill-defined. With no formal training within the PSNI for community policing, it is perhaps the 'catch-all' use of discretion which has become the public face of 'doing policing the community way' (*Newsletter* 2009). Yet far from feeding into the community relations and engagement, current data suggest that PSNI officers have often (mis)used and abused their discretion to dispose of offences for which it was arguably never intended, such as sexual assaults, possession of firearms, endangering aircraft and even hoax bomb alerts (*The Detail TV* 2013).

Similarly, the accountability of the PSNI for the delivery of community policing has also become skewed as part of the pervasive 'target culture' which also dominates the organisation – contrary to the principles of 'common sense' policing in the first place (Loveday 2006; Topping 2009). While current space precludes a more detailed analysis of the issue within PSNI, it is an indicative quotation by a community police officer who stated in relation to accountability, measurement and community policing:

> put it like this, for example last year, we said we'd increase our youth diversion referrals for the year ... that target might be five a month – you can get those in one night and that's it done for the month, so the rest of the month you needn't bother. It's the same for other targets you know.
>
> (Topping 2009: 177)

## Shadow policing: accounts of policing outside the PSNI

The final strand to consider as part of the complex picture of police accountability in Northern Ireland relates to policing delivered *outside* the state. However, it is not the intention here to consider policing from the perspective of well-rehearsed, paramilitary 'justice' as a form of policing during the conflict and post-conflict phases of transition (Morrissey and Pease 1982; Hillyard 1985; Brewer *et al.* 1998; Silke 1999; Knox 2002; Monaghan 2008; Topping and Byrne 2012b). Rather, a perhaps more interesting course of inquiry relates to the body of *legitimate*, non-state voluntary and community actors who engage in broad practices of *policing* – itself contributing to the low crime rates to which the country has become accustomed (Topping and Byrne 2012c).

With attention on policing and its reform so focused upon PSNI and its role per se, there exists an unchallenged, criminological presumption of PSNI 'ownership' in terms of dealing with crime and criminality within the jurisdiction. This has been further perpetuated by the fact Northern Ireland continues to act as Europe's low-crime capital, in spite of the recent internal armed conflict (Ellison and Mulcahy 2001; Van Dijk *et al.* 1990; Lyness *et al.* 2004; PSNI 2012). It may therefore be observed that 'a significant gap in academic or policy debate has been a sufficient interrogation of the dynamics underpinning the production of security generally, and policing specifically, with the presumption of causal security relations having remained firmly with PSNI' (Topping and Byrne forthcoming). On the one hand, it can be observed that substantive capital has been generated from the position the PSNI occupies as being widely regarded one of the most accountable, overseen police services anywhere in the world – with police-centric, bureaucratic accountability as *the* definition of police 'work' by PSNI (Bayley 2008; Ellison 2007). Yet on the other hand, this has reduced the space in which alternative policing discourses have been allowed to challenge the PSNI's 'expertise' and centrality over policing matters (Johnston and Shearing 2003; Topping and Byrne 2012a). And in spite of the fact that 'there is no monopoly on knowledge, or even no single vantage point from which the whole can be observed' (Black 2000: 599), it can be argued that the 'policing accountability vocabulary' in the country does not sufficiently recognise nor represent the diverse ways in which policing is exercised (Rose and Miller 1992). Indeed, research would point to the fact that communities have in fact been bypassing the state policing apparatus on crime issues, therein raising the need for dominant narratives of accountability for PSNI in the provision of policing to be re-examined (Baker 2002; Topping and Byrne forthcoming).

While empirically difficult to quantify within standard frameworks of police accountability and action, the issue of non-state community contributions to the policing landscape is by no means new. At least anecdotally, local and international academics have argued that a tradition of 'sorting things out' has long been a strength of the country's civil society networks stemming from the conflict (Jarman 2002, 2006; McEvoy *et al.* 2002; CJINI 2006). Even the OOC made a significant note on the capabilities of the community sector in Northern

Ireland, stating 'the Policing Board, the Police Service and the Northern Ireland Office need to be alert to the effects the well intentioned … community groups and their overlapping mandates can have on community engagement' (2007:16). The only recent attempts to quantify more fully these amorphous collectives of civil society organising around policing matters may be observed in the research of Topping and Byrne (2012c, 2014, forthcoming). Defining these policing contributions across six key categories of community advocacy, education and intervention, emergency response partnerships, crime prevention, and restorative justice/mediation, much of this policing activity tends to be concentrated in socio-economically deprived Loyalist and Republican areas of Northern Ireland – precisely where police interventions, legitimacy, trust and effectiveness are most vehemently challenged (Topping and Byrne 2014, forthcoming).

However, the intention here is not to detail nor quantify such non-state policing down to fine levels of granularity within the areas where it exists. Rather, it is the fact it *does exist* outside that of policing delivered by the PSNI which is of importance. In this regard, such 'shadow policing' may be seen to expose further the limited nature and rigidity of current police operational accountability metrics within what is a fluid and contested policing environment. Because accepting even to a minimal extent the existence of 'shadow policing', the PSNI cannot lay claim to sole responsibility for the control of *all* crime in the country – rendering their accountability metrics in terms of confidence, levels of recorded crime and victim satisfaction as only a partial account of their action (NIPB 2014). This argument may be further extended insofar as the existence and persistence of 'shadow policing' in the country points to the fact that metrics of PSNI performance are defined exclusively by police organisational *outputs* – devoid of accounts related to community-level *inputs* as defined through the 'shadow policing' reality (O'Mahony *et al.* 2000).

The genesis of this dichotomy may thus be drawn back to the centrality of 'getting policing right' to wider transition in the country, as the final piece of the peace process 'jigsaw' (O'Rawe 2003). Beyond the imperatives of structural change and reform of the PSNI, accountability for PSNI action thus acquires additional layers of meaning. On the one hand 'officially' accepting that such non-state policing exists may be viewed as an opportunity to enhance policing and develop accountability at a local, operational level. But on the other hand, it may also be seen to constitute a threat to the PSNI and all that it and the wider systems of accountability have come to stand for as part of attempts to build a new, inclusive and permanently acceptable policing 'system' for all sections of society (Topping 2008a).

## Conclusion

In overview of police accountability in Northern Ireland, aside from the broad lack of academic attention paid to the issue, it may be observed that developments in the country have implications for understandings of police accountability beyond the simple 'measurement' of what police organisations 'do'– and not just for societies emerging from conflict, but also for any countries under-pinned by Western policing traditions (Bayley 1994).

With police accountability in the country having attracted global attention because of its stringency and structure, questions of 'where to next?' remain. With little more to be achieved (at least structurally) as part of either the ICP or holding the PSNI to account for their actions, current regimes of austerity perhaps pose a threat to the high standards to which Northern Irish society has become accus-tomed on social, political and operational plains (McAleese 2013). The implication being that if the PSNI is at the top of the 'accountability tree', and to which other jurisdictions aspire, then can or should such levels be sustained indefinitely where the delivery of policing remains conflicted? And how long is enough?

As can be observed, police accountability also remains a significant strand of the wider political discourse in the country as a means of promoting legitimacy, social cohesion and post-conflict narrative. Yet at the same time, accountability precisely relies on these qualities to be effective in the first place as part of 'shared' understandings of policing. But as the evidence would suggest, the robust legal and structural police accountability measures in place appear to be a necessary feature of the policing landscape, as the nucleus from which com-munity and political trust in the police can grow.

Even if the 'new', post-ICP era of police accountability were to be trans-planted elsewhere, policing will remain an inherently unenviable task insofar as:

> the wholesome notions of community ... tends to elide the adversarial aspect of policing by implying whatever is done is done in the interest, and with the consent, of the people ... the fact that policing is usually done to someone, as well as on someone's behalf, is conveniently forgotten.
>
> (Dixon 2004: 252)

In this regard, the evidence points to the fact that – whether set against sectari-anism, race or class – what is fair in terms of policing for one section of society will remain unfair for another (Brogden 2005). Therefore, police accountability cannot be divorced from the wider societal conditions in which it is situated. And while far-reaching accountability mechanisms can be welcomed on prin-cipled grounds, as Northern Ireland has demonstrated, their presence can addi-tionally act as an expression of community distrust and lack of legitimacy in the police. Such policy dilemmas are reflective of deep-rooted social and political problems not readily resolved through structural change of police institutions alone. With the country still under a severe terrorist threat, there remains tension between holding the PSNI to account for 'everyday' policing and the (necessary) need for the organisation to retain its counterterrorist capability. Indeed, this paradox does not sit readily with the either the ICP's core aspiration of PSNI as a community-oriented service or the dominant community policing 'mode' of police accountability as effected through the policing institutions.

Finally, it is also clear that police accountability, as part of the country's transition, is a partisan term weighted to capturing the 'positive' realities of police activity. In turn, the harsh realities of the country as a post-conflict society have been conveniently 'ushered' to the side, as an aberration of that which is politically necessary to account for on policing matters. Similarly, alternative narratives of policing, such as those associated with non-state 'shadow policing', have been bureaucratically 'squeezed' out of police accountability discourse. As an informal (and sometimes competing) form of policing, it does not marry with PSNI's community policing performance and measures thereof. It is thus clear that police accountability, as set within the post-conflict landscape of Northern Ireland, is itself a site of empirical, policy and political contest and cannot be analysed nor understood through the lens of standard police metrics alone.

As Bayley (2008) contends, if this is what it has taken to fix Northern Irish policing in terms of international attention and expertise, finance and *the* grandest experiment in police reform ever attempted in the world, then the prospects for other societies are bleak. In this respect, *changes* to police accountability regimes should only ever be viewed as a means to an end where it is necessary to alter relations between the police and the public. However, it is the *maintenance* of accountability which should remain a negotiated and dynamic process, as both a mirror of societal relations (or lack of) with the state police, and a motor to empower those for whom policing is only something controlled by the police.

## References

Altebeker, A. (2005) *The Dirty Work of Democracy*, Johannesburg: Jonathon Bell.

Baker, B. (2002) 'Living with Non-State Policing in South Africa: The Issues and Dilemmas', *Journal of Modern African Studies*, 40(1): 29–53.

Bayley, D.H. (1994) *Patterns of Policing: A Comparative International Analysis*, New Brunswick, NJ: Rutgers University Press.

Bayley, D.H. (2008) 'Post-conflict Police Reform: Is Northern Ireland a Model?', *Policing*, 2(2): 233–40.

Belfast City Council (2014) *Belfast Policing and Community Safety Partnership Survey* (unpublished).

*Belfast Telegraph* (2008a) 'Civilians Targeted by Dissident Republicans', 27 October.

*Belfast Telegraph* (2008b) 'Dissident Republicans Blamed for Gun Attack on Police', 27 August.

*Belfast Telegraph* (2008c) 'Dissident Vowed to Kill Catholic Officer After McGuinness Visit', 26 November.

*Belfast Telegraph* (2010) 'Dissident Threat Severe After MI5 Attack', 13 April.

Bennett, J. (1979) *Report of the Committee of Inquiry into Police Interrogation Procedures in Northern Ireland Cmd.7497*. London: HMSO.

Black, J. (2000) 'Proceduralizing Regulation: Part I', *Oxford Journal of Legal Studies*, 20(4): 597–614.

Brewer, J. (2001) 'The Growth, Extent and Causes of Crime: Northern Ireland', in M. Shaw (ed.) *Crime and Policing in Transitional Societies Seminar Report*, Johannesburg: KAS.

Brogden, M. (1999) 'Community Policing as Cherry Pie', in R. Mawby (ed.) *Policing Across the World: Issues for the Twenty-First Century*, London: UCL Press Limited.

Brogden, M. (2000) 'Burning Churches and Victim Surveys: The Myth of Northern Ireland as Low-Crime Society', *Irish Journal of Sociology*, 10: 27–48.

Brogden, M. (2005) '"Horses for Courses" and "Thin Blue Lines": Community Policing in Transitional Societies', *Police Quarterly*, 8(1), 64–98.

Brogden, M. (2006) 'What's the Point of Community Policing', *Safer Society*, 28: 14–15.

Brewer, J., Lockhart, B. and Rodgers, P. (1998) Informal Social Controls and Crime Management in Belfast, *British Journal of Sociology*, 49(4): 570–85.

Bryan, D. (2000) *Orange Parades: The Politics of Ritual Tradition and Control*, London: Pluto Press.

Buckland, P. (1979) *The Factory of Grievances*, Dublin: Gill and MacMillan.

Byrne, J. and Monaghan, L. (2008) *Policing Loyalist and Republican Communities*, Belfast: Institute for Conflict Research.

Byrne, J., Jarman, N. and Topping, J.R. (2013) *Community Perspectives on Public Order Policing in Northern Ireland* (unpublished research report), Police Service of Northern Ireland.

Byrne, J., Topping, J.R. and Martin, R. (2014) *The Key Drivers of Public Confidence in Northern Ireland*, Belfast: NIPB.

Cameron, L. (1969) *Disturbances in Northern Ireland: Report of the Commission Appointed by the Governor of Northern Ireland Cmd. 532*, Belfast: HMSO.

Clarke, L. (2014) 'PSNI Chief Matt Baggott Hails Colleague in Eye of Storm Over Gerry Adams Arrest as they Brief MPs at Westminster', *Belfast Telegraph*, 8 May.

Committee on the Administration of Justice (CAJ) (1996) *The Misrule of Law: A Report on the Policing of Events During the Summer of 1996 in Northern Ireland*, Belfast: CAJ.

Committee on the Administration of Justice (CAJ) (1997) *Policing the Police: A Report on the Policing of Events During the Summer of 1997 in Northern Ireland*, Belfast: CAJ.

Committee on the Administration of Justice (CAJ) (2005) *Commentary on District Policing Partnerships*, Belfast: CAJ.

Criminal Justice Inspection Northern Ireland (CJINI) (2006) *Added Value? A Review of the Voluntary and Community Sectors' Contribution to the Northern Ireland Criminal Justice System*, Belfast: Criminal Justice Inspection Northern Ireland.

Dixon, B. (2004) 'Community Policing: "Cherry Pie" or Melktert?', *Society in Transition*, 35(2): 251–72.

Eide, E. and Holm, T. (eds.) (2000) *Peacebuilding and Police Reform*, London: Frank Cass Publishers.

Ellison, G. (2000) '"Reflecting all Shades of Opinion": Public Attitudinal Surveys and the Construction of Police Legitimacy in Northern Ireland', *British Journal of Criminology*, 40(1): 88–111.

Ellison, G. (2007) 'A Blueprint for Democratic Policing Anywhere in the World: Police Reform, Political Transition, and Conflict Resolution in Northern Ireland', *Police Quarterly*, 10(3): 243–69.

Ellison, G. and Mulcahy, A. (2001) 'Policing and Social Conflict in Northern Ireland', *Policing and Society*, 11: 243–58.

Ellison, G. and O'Rawe, M. (2010) 'Security Governance in Transition: The Compartmentalising, Crowding Out and Corralling of Policing and Security in Northern Ireland', *Theoretical Criminology*, 14(1): 31–57.

Ellison, G. and Smyth, J. (2000) *The Crowned Harp: Policing Northern Ireland*, London: Pluto Press.

Ellison, G., Pino, N. and Shirlow, P. (2013) 'Assessing the Determinants of Public Confidence in the Police: A Case Study of a Post-conflict Community in Northern Ireland', *Criminology and Criminal Justice*, 13(5): 552–76.

Fielding, N. and Innes, M. (2006) 'Reassurance Policing, Community Policing and Measuring Performance', *Policing and Society*, 16(2): 127–45.

Hayes, B. and McAllister, I. (2005) 'Public Support for Political Violence and Paramilitarism in Northern Ireland and the Republic of Ireland', *Terrorism and Political Violence*, 17: 599–617.

Her Majesty's Inspectorate of Constabulary (HMIC) (2007) *Baseline Assessment Police Service of Northern Ireland, October 2006*, London: HMIC.

Her Majesty's Inspectorate of Constabulary (HMIC) (2011) *Police Service of Northern Ireland, Inspection Findings*, London: HMIC.

Hillyard, P. (1985) 'Popular Justice in Northern Ireland: Continuities and Change', *Research in Law, Deviance and Social Control*, 7: 247–67.

Hillyard, P. (1988) 'Political and Social Dimensions of Emergency Law in Northern Ireland', in A. Jennings (ed.) *Justice Under Fire: The Abuse of Civil Liberties in Northern Ireland*, London: Pluto Press.

Hillyard, P. (1994) 'Irish People and the British Justice System', *Journal of Law and Society*, 21: 39–56

Hunt, B. (1969) *Report of the Advisory Committee on Police in Northern Ireland Cmd. 535*, Belfast: HMSO (The Hunt Report).

Independent Commission on Policing (ICP) (1999) *A New Beginning: Policing in Northern Ireland*, Belfast: The Stationery Office.

Independent Monitoring Commission (2010) *Twenty-third Report of the Independent Monitoring Commission*, London: The Stationery Office.

Innes, M. (2005) 'Why "Soft" Policing is Hard: On the Curious Development of Reassurance Policing, How It Became Neighbourhood Policing and What this Signifies About the Politics of Police Reform', *Journal of Community and Applied Social Psychology*, 15: 156–69.

*Irish News* (2008) 'Bombers Trying To Kill Officers: Detective, 11 September, p. 11.

*Irish News* (2009) 'Real IRA Determined to Murder PSNI Officers', 5 January, p. 8.

Jarman, N. (2002) *Managing Disorder: Responding to Interface Violence in North Belfast*, Belfast: Community Development Centre/Office of the First and Deputy First Minister.

Jarman, N. (2006) 'Peacebuilding and Policing – The Role of Community Based Initiatives', *Shared Space: A Research Journal on Peace, Conflict and Community Relations in Northern Ireland*, 3: 31–44.

Jesilow, P. and Parsons, D. (2000) 'Community Policing as Peacemaking', *Policing and Society*, 10(2): 163–82.

Johnston, L. and Shearing, C. (2003) *Governing Security: Explorations in Policing and Justice*, London: Routledge.

Kappeler, V.E. and Kraska, P.B. (1998) 'A Textual Critique of Community Policing: Police Adaptation to High Modernity', *Policing: An International Journal of Police Strategies and Management*, 21(2): 293–313.

Kearney, V. (2010) 'Dissident Threat Level Increases', available at http://news.bbc.co.uk/1/hi/northern_ireland/8638255.stm?ad=1 (last accessed 12 May 2010).

Knox, C. (2002) ' "See No Evil, Hear no Evil": Insidious Paramilitary Violence in Northern Ireland, *British Journal of Criminology*, 42(1): 64–185.

Loader, I. (2000) 'Plural Policing and Democratic Governance', *Social and Legal Studies*, 9(3): 323–45.

Loveday, B. (2006) 'Policing Performance: The Impact of Performance Targets on Police Forces', *International Journal of Police Science and Management*, 8: 282–92.

Lundy, P. (2011). 'Paradoxes and Challenges of Transitional Justice at the "Local" Level: Historical Enquiries in Northern Ireland', *Contemporary Social Science*, 6(1): 89–106.

Lyness, D., McEnarney, R. and Carmichael, M. (2004) *Digest of Information On the Northern Ireland Criminal Justice System*, Belfast: NIO.

McAleese, D. (2013) 'We Need 300 More Officers to Hold the Line, Says PSNI Chief Constable Matt Baggott', *Belfast Telegraph*, 31 January.

McDonald, H. (2011a) 'Northern Ireland Terror Threat At "Severe" Level', *Guardian*, 4 February.

McDonald, H. (2011b) 'The Truth About Belfast's Riots', *Guardian*, 27 June.

McDonald, H. (2012) 'Police Say 1200 Officers Have Been Hurt in Northern Ireland Riots in Seven Year', *Guardian*, 4 September.

McDonald, H. and Townsend, M. (2011) 'For Ireland's Hardcore Dissidents "The Queen is a Legitimate Target"', *Observer*, 24 April.

McEvoy, K., Gormally, B. and Mika, H. (2002) 'Conflict, Crime Control and the "Re"-Constitution of State-Community Relations in Northern Ireland', in G. Hughes, E. McLauglin and J. Muncie (eds) *Crime Prevention and Community Safety: New Directions*, London: Sage Publications.

McGloin, J. (2003) 'Shifting Paradigms: Policing in Northern Ireland', *Policing: An International Journal of Police Strategy and Management*, 26(1): 118–43.

Monaghan, R. (2008) 'Community-based Justice in Northern Ireland and South Africa', *International Criminal Justice Review*, 18: 83–105.

Moran, J. (2008) *Policing the Peace in Northern Ireland: Politics, Crime and Security After the Belfast Agreement*, Manchester: Manchester University Press.

Morrissey, M. and Pease, K. (1982) The Black Criminal Justice System in West Belfast, *The Howard Journal*, 2: 159–66.

Mulcahy, A. (1999) 'Visions of Normality: Peace and the Reconstruction of Policing in Northern Ireland', *Social and Legal Studies*, 8(2): 277–95.

Mulcahy, A. (2000) 'Policing History and the Official Discourse and Organisational Memory of the Royal Ulster Constabulary', *British Journal of Criminology*, 40: 68–87.

Mulcahy, A. (2006) *Policing in Northern Ireland: Conflict, Legitimacy and Reform*, Cullompton, Devon: Willan.

Mulgrew, J. and Erwin, A. (2014) 'Loyalist Flag Protests: PSNI Chief Matt Baggott will Appeal Judgement That Force Was Wrong to Allow Illegal Violent Protest Marches', *Belfast Telegraph*, 28 April.

*Newsletter* (2009) 'PSNI Has Lost Touch – Report', 27 August.

Ni Aolain, F. (2000) *The Politics of Force: Conflict Management and State Violence in Northern Ireland*, Belfast: Blackstaff Press.

Northern Ireland Audit Office (NIAO) (2013) *Continuous Improvement Arrangements in Policing*, Belfast: NIAO.

Northern Ireland Audit Office (NIAO) (2014) *Continuous Improvement Arrangements in Policing*, Belfast: NIAO.

Northern Ireland Policing Board (NIPB) (2007) *Research into Recent Crime Trends in Northern Ireland*, Belfast: Ipsos MORI.

Northern Ireland Policing Board (NIPB) (2013) *Annual Report and Accounts*, Belfast: NIPB.

Northern Ireland Policing Board (NIPB) (2014) *Perceptions of the Police, PCSPs and the Northern Ireland Policing Board*, Belfast: NIPB.

O'Hara, S. (1996) *Community Policing – Notion or Reality?*, MA thesis, University of Ulster.

O'Leary, B. and McGarry, J. (1996) *The Politics of Antagonism: Understanding Northern Ireland* (2nd edn), London: Athlone Press.

O'Mahony, D., Geary, R., McEvoy, K. and Morison, J. (2000) *Crime, Community and Locale: The Northern Ireland Communities Crime Survey*, Aldershot, Ashgate Publishing Company.

O'Rawe, M. (2003) 'Transitional Policing Arrangements in Northern Ireland: The Can't and Won't of Change Dialect', *Fordham International Law Journal*, 22: 1015–73.

Office of the Oversight Commissioner (OOC) (2007) *Overseeing the Proposed Revisions for the Policing Services of Northern Ireland Report 19*, Belfast: Office of the Oversight Commissioner.

Office of the Police Ombudsman for Northern Ireland (2010) *Ten Year Statistical Bulletin for the Office of the Police Ombudsman for Northern Ireland, 2000/1–2009/10*, Belfast: OPONI.

Office of the Police Ombudsman for Northern Ireland (2011) *Annual Statistical Bulletin for the Police Ombudsman for Northern Ireland 2011/12*, Belfast: OPONI

Office of the Police Ombudsman for Northern Ireland (2012) *Analysis of Oppressive Behaviour Allegations Received by the Office of the Police Ombudsman for Northern Ireland 2000–2012*, Belfast: OPONI.

Office of the Police Ombudsman for Northern Ireland (2013) *Annual Report and Accounts*, Belfast: OPONI.

Owen, J. and Dutta, K. (2011) 'More People Go Armed as Ulster Dissident Threat Grows', *The Independent*, 5 June.

Parades Commission (2012) *Annual Report and Financial Statement for the Year Ending 31st March 2011*, Belfast: Parades Commission.

Police Service of Northern Ireland (PSNI) (2012) *Policing with the Community 2020 Strategy*, Belfast: PSNI.

Police Service of Northern Ireland (PSNI) (2014) *Strength of Service Statistics*, available at www.psni.police.uk/index/updates/updates_statistics/updates_strength_of_police_service_statistics.htm (last accessed 7 June 2014).

Raine, J.W. and Keasey, P. (2012) 'From Police Authorities to Police and Crime Commissioners: Might Policing Become More Publicly Accountable?', *International Journal of Emergency Services*, 1(2): 122–34.

Rose, N. and Miller, P. (1992) 'Political Power Beyond the State: Problematics of Government', *British Journal of Sociology*, 43(2): 173–205.

Ryder, C. (2004) *The Fateful Split: Catholics and the Royal Ulster Constabulary*, London: Methuen Publishing Ltd.

Scarman, J. (1972) *Government of Northern Ireland: Violence and Civil Disturbances in Northern Ireland Report of Tribunal of Inquiry Cmd. 566*, Belfast: HMSO.

Scorer, C. and Hewitt, P. (1981) *The Prevention of Terrorism Act: The Case of Repeal*, London: National Council for Civil Liberties.

Shaw, M. and Shearing, C. (1998) 'Reshaping Security: An Examination of the Governance of Security in South Africa', *African Security Review*, 7(3): 3–12.

Shirlow, P. and Murtagh, B. (2006) *Belfast: Segregation, Violence and the City*, London: Pluto Press.

Silke, A. (1999) 'Ragged Justice: Loyalist Vigilantism in Northern Ireland', *Terrorism and Political Violence*, 11(3): 1–31.

*Telegraph* (2013) 'Fresh Violence in Belfast Flag Protests', 12 January.

*The Detail TV* (2013) 'How Discretion Has Been Used For Crime Here', 7 February, available at www.thedetail.tv/issues/163/speedy-justice/how-discretion-has-been-used-for-crime-here (last accessed 13 March 2013).

Toner, S. and Freel, R. (2010) *Experience of Crime: Findings from the 2009/10 Northern Ireland Crime Survey*, Belfast: Department of Justice Northern Ireland.

Topping, J.R. (2008a) 'Community Policing in Northern Ireland: A Resistance Narrative', *Policing and Society*, 18(4): 377–98.

Topping, J.R. (2008b) 'Diversifying from Within: Community Policing and the Governance of Security in Northern Ireland', *British Journal of Criminology*, 48(6): 778–97.

Topping, J.R. (2009) *Beyond the Patten Report: The Governance of Security in Policing with the Community*. PhD Thesis: University of Ulster.

Topping, J.R. (2012) 'Policing and the Process of Confidence In Northern Ireland: More Than Community Metrics', Invited Speaker at Northern Ireland Policing Board, 27 February, available at www.nipolicingboard.org.uk/policing_and_the_process_of_confidence_in_ni.pdf (last accessed 28 April 2015).

Topping, J.R. and Byrne, J. (2012a) *Community Safety: A Decade of Development, Delivery, Challenge and Change in Northern Ireland*, Belfast: Belfast Conflict Resolution Consortium.

Topping, J.R. and Byrne, J. (2012b) 'Paramilitary Punishments in Belfast: Policing Beneath the Peace', *Behavioral Sciences of Terrorism and Political Aggression*, 4(1): 41–59.

Topping, J.R. and Byrne, J. (2012c) 'Policing, Terrorism and The Conundrum of "Community": A Northern Ireland Perspective', in B. Spalek (ed.) *Counter-Terrorism: Community-based Approaches to Preventing Terror Crime*, Basingstoke: Palgrave Macmillan.

Topping, J.R. and Byrne, J. (2014) 'Shadow Policing: The Boundaries of Community Based "Policing" in Northern Ireland', *Policing and Society*, Online Advanced Access.

Van Dijk, J.J.M., Mayhew, P. and Killias, M. (1990) *Experiences of Crime Across the World: Key Findings from the 1989 International Crime Survey*, Deventer, the Netherlands: Kluwer Law and Taxation.

Weitzer, R. (1999) 'Policing and Security', in P. Mitchell and R. Wilford (eds) *Politics in Northern Ireland*, Boulder, CO: Westview Press, 170–94.

Widgery, L. (1972) *Report of the Tribunal of Inquiry Appointed to Inquire Into the Events of Sunday 30th January 1972, Which Led to Loss of Life in Connection with the Procession in Londonderry on that Day H.L.101, H.C.220*, London: HMSO.

# 9 Private security and the politics of accountability

*Adam White*[1]

The private security industry occupies a paradoxical position in liberal democratic politics. On one side, liberal thought is founded upon the idea that individuals ought to be given the freedom to engage in private enterprise so long as it does not bring harm upon others. This freedom is not only regarded as an intrinsic right, but also the means to a wealthy and progressive society, for it is through the aggregated efforts of individual private enterprise that goods and services are most effectively produced and distributed. On the other side, liberal thought holds that the task of maintaining law and order in civil society ought to be carried out exclusively by a constitutionally bound state, for only this collective public institution is capable of ensuring that the freedoms of all individuals are realised in an equal and fair manner. Within these governance arrangements – which are recognisable in different permutations and to varying degrees throughout the liberal democratic world – private security is paradoxically cast as *both* an extension of private enterprise *and* a usurper of the state's law and order functions. The chapter argues that this paradox serves as a valuable lens through which to analyse the mechanisms used to hold private security to account in today's liberal democracies. Not only does it illustrate how these mechanisms fall into two broad categories: those which regard private security as an ordinary private enterprise, such as criminal law, civil law and market self-regulation; and those which regard private security as a usurper of the state-guaranteed liberal democratic order, such as critical public discourse and statutory regulation specifically targeting this 'tainted trade'.[2] But it also demonstrates that while these mechanisms hold private security accountable to sound principles and impose a range of sanctions for non-compliance, they also run against each other in key respects, simultaneously enabling and limiting the industry's operations.

The chapter is divided into four sections. The first section situates the analysis within the broader academic literature on the accountability of private security. It contends that most of this literature is 'formal-legal' in character and focuses almost entirely on just one accountability mechanism: statutory regulation. It contrasts this with the more far-reaching 'political' approach taken in this chapter, which is concerned with how a wide variety of accountability mechanisms fit into the changing power relations between state, economy and society under the conditions of contemporary liberal democracy. Drawing primarily on the British case, the subsequent two sections then survey the key accountability mechanisms on either side of the liberal democratic paradox, looking first at those which regard private security as an ordinary private enterprise, before moving on to those which regard private security as a usurper of an inherently sovereign function. The final section explores the contradictions which run through these different accountability mechanisms, thereby undermining the notion that they represent rational 'solutions' to the 'problems' associated with private security provision.

## From the formal-legal to the political

There are three main strands to the literature on private security. The first is concerned with the industry's growth trajectories in the post-war era, which are variously attributed to shifting modes of capitalist accumulation (Spitzer and Scull 1977; Spitzer 1993), the emergence of 'mass private property' (Shearing and Stenning 1981, 1983), the rise of neo-liberal governing mentalities and consumption patterns (Reiner 1992; Garland 1996, 2000; Johnston 2000), the 'formalisation of social control' (Jones and Newburn 1999, 2002), an intensified fear of crime (Zedner 2003) and changing contours of legitimacy in the contemporary security sector (White 2010, 2012; Thumala *et al.* 2011), alongside a range of other geographically specific explanations. The second is concerned with the macro-level theoretical implications of these growth trajectories, exploring how the industry fits into twenty-first-century social relations (Loader and Walker 2007; Wood and Shearing 2007). The third is concerned with the everyday, street-level practices of private security actors, especially in their engagements with each other, individual citizens, police officers and other members of the widening 'crime fighting family' (Jones and Newburn 1998; Rigakos 2002; Hobbs *et al.* 2003; Wakefield 2003; Crawford and Lister 2004; Button 2007a; Noaks 2008; van Steden and Nalla 2010; White and Gill 2013; Rowland and Coupe 2013). While discussions of accountability do regularly appear in these strands, this is usually only as a background issue.

The literature which does explicitly bring questions of accountability into the foreground is rather limited by comparison (Johnston 1992; George and Button 1997; Sarre 1998; Prenzler and Sarre 1999, 2008; Stenning 2000; Lister *et al.* 2001; Button and George 2006; Button 2007b, 2012; White 2013). On surveying this literature two features immediately stand out. The first is a preoccupation with statutory regulation, most often the licensing or registration of private security officers and/or companies. This is unsurprising given that statutory regulation is probably the most visible and focused accountability mechanism. Yet it represents just one dimension of the overall accountability architecture in most contemporary liberal democracies. Only Sarre (1998) and Stenning (2000) offer an extended and systematic analysis of additional accountability mechanisms, focusing primarily on relevant aspects of criminal law and civil law. The second is a default orientation towards the elitist 'formal-legal' approach when interpreting the character of these accountability mechanisms. This approach sees 'legal rules and procedures as the basic independent variable, and the functioning and fate of democracies as the dependent variable' (Rhodes 1997: 67). As such, the literature tends to generate a narrative in which: (1) a 'problem' is identified (most commonly in the contract manned security sector); (2) a corresponding legal 'solution' is formulated (most frequently statutory regulation); and (3) the legal 'solution' resolves the 'problem' – or if not the recourse is to simply add more legal solutions to the equation until the problem is finally resolved.

It is of course important to explore the mechanisms used to hold private security to account in formal-legal terms – not least because this form of legal positivism is how most legislators tend to think – and it makes sense to concentrate on the most visible and focused mechanism: statutory regulation. At the same time, however, this approach tends to lack an appreciation of how the broader accountability architecture is shaped by – and indeed gives shape to – the complex and often contradictory power relations between state, economy and society under the conditions of contemporary liberal democracy. It is a truism that over recent decades the liberal democratic state has to varying degrees been 'hollowed out' upwards, downwards and sideways (Rhodes 1996; Pierre and Peters 2000). This has not only created highly nebulous governance arrangements which stretch unevenly across the globe – the increasingly pluralised nature of domestic security being one of the key examples – but also means that economic and societal actors are no longer 'dependent variables' who simply bend to the will of public law in a predictable manner (if indeed they ever were). Hierarchy has increasingly given way to heterarchy, positional power relations to relational power relations, government to governance.

With this in mind, the chapter builds upon the few studies which have already started the process of interpreting the mechanisms which hold private security to account in these more 'political' terms (O'Connor *et al.* 2008; White 2010; Smith and White 2013). In doing so, it focuses on a range of (often less obvious) accountability mechanisms situated on the shifting sands between state, economy and society under the conditions of contemporary liberal democracy. To bring order to this exercise, these mechanisms are organised in line with the liberal democratic paradox in which private security is at once cast as an ordinary private enterprise *and* a usurper of core state functions – a paradox which lies at the heart of these shifting sands. Before turning to these mechanisms, however, two brief caveats are necessary. First, this exercise does not mean eschewing the research which has already been undertaken within the formal-legal approach, but rather reframing key elements of this research within a more political framework. Second, while this analysis is wide in scope, it is by no means comprehensive. In particular, it focuses primarily on national-level accountability mechanisms as opposed to supranational ones, and it concentrates almost entirely on external accountability mechanisms to the exclusion of internal ones such as corporate governance.

## Private security as private enterprise

Private enterprise refers to the range of activities carried out by individuals and organisations across economy and society whether for profit, altruism or pleasure. In liberal democracies, private enterprise is for the most part limited only by one overarching principle: that it does not bring harm upon others (where harm is defined through democratic dialogue). Any individual or organisation whose activities do bring harm upon others will – in theory at least – be held to account within a state-administered system of law and order. Traditionally speaking, security provision has not been regarded as an ordinary private enterprise, other than in the limited circumstances of self defence, primarily because of its obvious capacity to arbitrarily bring harm upon others on a regular basis and therefore erode the social order as a whole. Instead, security provision has been regarded as an intrinsic part of the law and order functions of the state, for only this collective and democratically mandated institution has the theoretical capability to exercise security powers in a manner which ensures the freedoms of all individuals are realised in an equal and fair manner (even though in reality the state often falls short of this promise as widespread accounts of heavy-handed and iniquitous police behaviour attest). For reasons briefly mentioned above, however, security provision has in recent decades grown as a private enterprise, carried out for profit by individuals and companies operating under contractual (outsourcing) and in-house (insourcing) arrangements in a variety of roles (e.g. mobile patrol, static guarding, close protection and surveillance) (for overviews of private security growth drivers and patterns see Kempa *et al.* 1999; van Steden 2007; White 2012). Through this process, the industry has automatically become subject to the exact same accountability mechanisms as any other private enterprise. The list of such mechanisms is of course extensive. As such, this section surveys only some of the most relevant mechanisms within broad two categories: criminal law and civil law where the industry is held accountable to some external principle or actor; and market self-regulation where the industry holds itself to account.

### *Criminal law and civil law*

As with any other private enterprise, the activities of private security officers in any subsector of the industry are held to account through criminal law, which is in principle designed to serve the public interest as a whole. In the immediate post-war era, the relationship between criminal law and private security in Britain was for the most part taken for granted and left unexamined by academics and legal practitioners. It was not until 1979 that the Home Office, responding to a range of pressures for enhanced public accountability within the industry (see White 2010: 80–101), outlined for the first time the key sections of criminal law which, in its view, had particular relevance for private security officers. It focused on four limited or prohibited activities: stopping, searching and/or arresting members of the public; carrying or using offensive weapons;

wearing police-like uniforms in a calculated effort to deceive; and controlling, managing and training any association with the intention of usurping the functions of the police or armed forces (Home Office 1979: 8–9). The Home Office could have enumerated any criminal offence in this list as they all apply equally, so its choices are in themselves interesting. They demonstrate how, from an official perspective, private security officers were seen to be engaging in activities which directly mirror those of the police. But whereas police officers have, to use the Home Office's (1979: 8) terms, 'special legal obligations' and 'special legal privileges' (warranted powers) to carry out such activities – in line with their own strict accountability structures – private security officers do not. As such, the Home Office emphasised that any private security officer found to be engaging in these activities in a manner which goes beyond the ordinary powers given all private citizens (such as universal arrest) was – and still is – subject to criminal prosecution (see Stenning 2000: 341).

Unfortunately, due to problems of data collection, detailed evidence on the scale and type of criminal offences committed by private security officers is difficult to come by. One valuable source is the House of Commons Home Affairs Committee's 1995 enquiry into the activities of the private security industry in Britain (HC 17-I [1994–5]; HC 17-II [1994–5]) – the only enquiry of its kind ever to be undertaken in the country. The Association of Chief Police Officers (ACPO) written submission to the enquiry included a breakdown of criminal offences committed by private security officers within Lancashire Constabulary: 'in a local industry of 4,500 people, during 1993 and up to September 1994, 130 private security employees committed 249 criminal offences' (HC 17-II [1994–5]: 103). From these base statistics, the ACPO submission goes on to explain that, first, this is an offending rate 21 times greater than in the police force and six times greater than the postal service and, second, when scaled up this indicates a national offending rate of roughly 2,600 offences per annum within the industry (HC 17-II [1994–5]: 103). ACPO supplemented these statistics with typical examples of the offences committed drawn from around the country: murder, assault, theft, perjury, perverting the course of justice and wasting police time (HC 17-II [1994–5]: 103–5). Notwithstanding the fact that these statistics are two decades old, they do nevertheless illustrate that private security officers are held to account through the criminal law – though clearly not just by those laws enacted against private citizens carrying out police-like activities without a warrant.

Likewise, the industry is also held to account through different parts of civil law, in particular tort law and contract law (both of which serve the interests of individuals and organisations directly rather than the public interest as a whole). It is useful to begin by noting that the application of civil law may accompany a criminal conviction. For instance, a private security officer who is found guilty of assault while denying someone access to some form of mass private property (an industrial complex, leisure park, shopping mall or similar) may also be sued by the victim for damages under tort law (e.g. for medical expenses and loss of earnings) and at the same time have their terms of employment severed under contract law (see Heiss 2008: 97–100). Of course, tort law and contract law can be administered without an accompanying criminal conviction, though civil actions are more likely to succeed if there is criminal conviction due to the higher standard of proof required in a criminal court. It is difficult to assess the scope and frequency of such actions in Britain because there have been no efforts to systematically collect data on cases brought against private security officers and companies under tort law and contract law. That said, significant cases do regularly appear in the national media, with the civil action against G4S for the unlawful death of Jimmy Mubenga during a deportation escort attracting the headlines in recent years (*Guardian* 2013a).

Finally, it is also important to emphasise that some parts of civil law apply to certain subsectors of the private security industry more than others. A notable case in point is the contract security sector where contract law unsurprisingly takes on much greater significance as an accountability mechanism, especially at the organisational level. During the post-war era, contract security has transformed into big business, with the British market dominated by huge multinationals (e.g. G4S, Securitas and Mitie) offering an array of security services. This means that while 50 years ago contracts were by and large relatively simple documents setting out basic guarding services, today they are often multi-volume tomes with clauses, subclauses and spreadsheets relating to multiple and concurrent services running to thousands of pages. This is especially the case in large public sector outsourcing contracts – such as Lincolnshire Police's £200 million contract with G4S to deliver 18 services areas including frontline operations over a ten-year period – where complex public services are distilled into contractual stipulations.

Embedded throughout these contracts are accountability mechanisms known as key performance indicators (KPIs): quantifiable criteria agreed by the principal and agent before the contract is signed for the purpose of measuring the successful delivery of any given service function. Failure on the part of the contractor to meet a KPI may result in some form of penalty, ranging from a fine to the severing of the contract. By far the most high-profile example of this mechanism in action has been G4S's failure to meet the criteria of its £284 million contract to deliver security functions at the London 2012 Olympic Games. As the House of Commons Home Affairs Committee's review of the episode emphasises:

> The contract provides for various penalties and remedies in the event of G4S's failure – LOCOG [London Organising Committee of the Olympic and Paralympic Games] only pays for hours delivered, it has the right to retain a proportion of the management fee if G4S fails to achieve a specified proportion of the scheduled hours, and G4S must meet the costs incurred in bringing in alternative providers, such as the armed forces.
>
> (HC 531-I [2012–13]: 3)

After various contractual negotiations, G4S eventually conceded a £70 million payout to LOCOG for its failure to supply an adequate number of private security officers on schedule (*Guardian* 2013b) – and because this contract impacted so acutely upon the public interest this was not the only accountability mechanism in play, as the chapter illustrates later on.

### Market self-regulation

While criminal law and contract law hold the private security industry accountable to some external principle or actor just like any other private enterprise, the industry also holds itself to account within the marketplace in a manner similar to other ordinary market-based private enterprises. This internal accountability mechanism is known as market self-regulation. As Lodge and Wegrich (2012: 102–5) observe, this mechanism commonly comes in two forms: 'professional' self-regulation, in which a market-based association holds individuals working in a given sector accountable to an agreed set of standards and behaviours, for example the Royal Charter of Accountants or Engineers; and 'industry' self-regulation, in which a market-based association holds companies operating in a given sector accountable to an agreed set of standards and behaviours, for instance the Press Complaints Commission or the Chemical Industries Association.

In operational terms, both forms of market self-regulation can usually be broken down in accordance with the following scenario: a group of industry leaders band together within and fund the administration costs of a market-based association (sometimes with government backing, a process also known as 'co-regulation'); membership of the association is dependent upon satisfying an agreed set of standards and behaviours relating to a combination of training qualifications, codes of conduct and best practice (which frequently have significant overlap with criminal law); failure to satisfy these standards and behaviours results in either non-admission for potential members or punishment for admitted members (such as a fine or exclusion), which theoretically constrains their ability to trade in the sector. The success of these processes rests on a circular relationship between accountability and market value: self-regulation in principle results in higher levels of discipline and accountability; once proven, these virtues begin to take on market value, for consumers use membership as an indicator of quality and reliability; and the more consumers seek this assurance, the more both potential and admitted members are motivated to adhere to the association's standards and behaviours and fear its accountability mechanisms; conversely, if consumers regard these accountability mechanisms as ineffective, then there is little motivation to pursue association membership, thereby undermining the self-regulatory regime.

To varying degrees, the private security industry has constructed both types of regime in post-war Britain. Regarding professional self-regulation, a number of notable mechanisms have emerged of late, in particular the issuing of a Royal Charter to the Worshipful Company of Security Professionals in 2010 and the now common stipulation in many companies that a Bachelor's degree in Security and Risk Management (or similar) is required to progress into the higher echelons of management. But while there is momentum, this does not yet add up to a coherent regime of professional self-regulation, as Wakefield and Button (2013: 264) note: 'Private security's professional project has been hindered by a lack of overall co-ordination and common purpose, and has a long way still to go'. By contrast, over the past 50 years or so, industry leaders have put together a fairly well-evolved system of industry self-regulation, especially in the contract security sector. Broadly speaking, this system has gone through three distinct stages of development, each of which fits into the overall accountability architecture in different ways.

The first stage, lasting from the mid-1950s to the early 1980s, was characterised by relatively informal self-regulatory arrangements administered by two trade associations: the International Professional Security Association (IPSA), founded in 1958 to represent smaller contract security companies and in-house security providers; and the British Security Industry Association (BSIA), founded in 1966 to represent larger contract security companies (White 2010). During this time, the operating logic of these associations was modelled on a simple arrangement in which potential members were required to satisfy a range of criteria relating to sound management, insurance, employee screening and training, and admitted members were then monitored by the association. Accountability mechanisms in these associations were generally applied on a forgiving basis, as illustrated by John Wheeler, Director General of the BSIA, speaking in the mid-1970s:

> The attitude of the BSIA is that if the slip-up [by a member company] is merely due to incompetence and carelessness then no action will be taken. If the slip-up was wilful then the member will be pulled up in front of the Council and if the company does not intend to remedy the fault it will be thrown out of the Association.
>
> (quoted in Draper 1978: 130)

There is no available data on how many BSIA members were 'thrown out' during this period, but judging by the easy-going operating principles evident in this quote, it is unlikely to be many.

The second stage, running from the early 1980s to the mid-2000s, can be seen as a direct reaction to this informality and is characterised by the formalisation of accountability structures, especially in the increasingly prominent BSIA whose members (such as the pre-merged Group 4 and Securicor) were winning more and more business in the market-friendly neo-liberal climate. While processes of institutionalisation, codification and juridification were taking place throughout Britain's self-regulatory regimes at the time (see Moran 2003: 67–94), the pressure to do so in the private security industry came specifically from the Home Office's 1979 review of the sector, which responded to calls for greater accountability by helping the BSIA in particular (with which it had a historical relationship, see White 2010: 70–6) to strengthen its accountability mechanisms. This process resulted in the National Inspectorate of Security

Guard, Patrol and Transport Services: a new market-based body specifically designed to hold BSIA members accountable to a more stringent set of criteria (for an anatomy of this Inspectorate see HC 397-II [1983–4]: 238–41). Available data show that expulsions were still rare, though less severe disciplinary cases did occur on a more regular basis. For example, in 1990 disciplinary cases were pursued against five BSIA members resulting in two £5,000 fines plus costs (Johnston 1992: 6). This was still not seen to be sufficient, however. Following further pressures for greater accountability in the late 1980s and early 1990s, as well as a second Home Office review (1991), this regime was subjected to another round of government-backed formalisation leading to the establishment of the Inspectorate of the Security Industry (ISI), which administered a certification scheme centred upon British Standards 5750 (Quality Management Systems) and 7499 (Manned Security Services). According to its written submission to the House of Commons Home Affairs Committee in 1995, the ISI functioned primarily on the basis of non-admittance of those who failed to meet these standards rather than punishment of existing members, though statistics are rather sketchy (HC 17-II [1994–5]: 137–9).

The third stage, from the early 2000s to the present day, is characterised by the eclipse of industry self-regulation by statutory regulation, which was introduced in 2001 as a result of increasingly prominent calls for greater public as opposed to market accountability (and is examined in the next section). With a new compulsory system in place, consumers of private security services became less and less interested in self-regulation as a measure of reliance and quality. Yet it is important to stress that this eclipse was only partial, for there was (and still is) demand for industry self-regulation as a means of differentiation in a competitive marketplace. All companies essentially look the same through the lens of statutory regulation – they are all given the exact same government stamp of approval – so being in a position to advertise compliance with additional (and often higher) standards and behaviours within a system industry self-regulation is a selling point. As a consequence, a variety of regimes remain in operation, with the BSIA and the ISI's successor the National Security Inspectorate at the forefront of the sector.

Market self-regulation, like criminal law and civil law, therefore holds the private security industry to account in the same manner as any other private enterprise. However, it is important to round off this discussion by emphasising that these accountability mechanisms are nevertheless very different in scope and rigour. All private security officers – without exception – are accountable in front of the law and punishments are meted out in accordance with the principles of impartiality and consistency. By contrast, market self-regulation only holds to account those individuals and companies who sign up to it and punishments are dependent upon the ethos and capacity of the association responsible for its administration. At various times, for instance, it has been estimated that BSIA membership has equated to around 70–90 percent of the contract security sector in terms of turnover (see Home Office 1979: 4; BSIA 2013) and the BSIA has administered a range of punishment regimes in relation to its membership – a lack of coverage and consistency which has been the subject of much criticism (Draper 1978; South 1988; Johnston 1992). Despite these differences, however, for present purposes the overriding message is that criminal law, civil law and market self-regulation are nonetheless joined together by a key commonality: they all hold private security to account as an ordinary private enterprise. This is an important message because the accountability mechanisms examined in the next section have emerged from the observation that the industry is anything but ordinary.

## Private security as usurper of state functions

While liberal thought holds that all individuals in economy and society are free to engage in private enterprise so long as it does not bring harm upon others, this privilege does not in principle extend to security provision (other than in the limited circumstances of self-defence). This 'primary' good is instead seen to be the exclusive preserve of the state. The reasoning behind this proposition is three-fold. First, to properly engage in and reap the benefits of private enterprise, individuals need to live in a stable and predictable social order in which their freedoms are realised in an equal and fair manner – they need security. Second, a good of this nature cannot be delivered as a private enterprise because this will inevitably lead to an iniquitous social order in which the freedoms of some individuals (the rich) are realised at the expense of others (the poor). Third, the responsibility for delivering this good should therefore be consensually transferred to a constitution-ally bound collective institution which has the theoretical capability to protect the freedoms of all individuals in an equal and fair manner – the modern state. This distinctly liberal governance arrangement was a cornerstone of modern political thought (see Thomas Hobbes's *Leviathan* or John Locke's *Second Treatise of Government*) and deeply informed the state-building process taking place across Europe and its colonies during the eighteenth and nineteenth centuries, giving rise to the first modern police forces (see Emsley 1999). By the middle of the twentieth century, police forces had become ubiquitous, dominating domestic security provision across the liberal democratic world. Consequently, as the private security industry has expanded throughout the post-war era, it has been seen by many to be entering into the special and exclusive domain of the police. This concern has in turn prompted the emergence of a further set of accountability mechanisms which regard the industry not as an ordinary private enterprise but as a usurper of core state functions. This section focuses on two of these mechanisms: critical public discourse and statutory regulation.

### Critical public discourse

The process of establishing police forces was not without controversy. While these public bodies are never going to perfectly resemble the benevolent institu-tions depicted in liberal thought, in their early history they often operated at a great distance from this ideal type, at various times becoming instruments of authoritarian, fascist and bourgeois repression, usually against the propertyless classes (see Spitzer 1993). However, as police forces became more professional in their practices and more accountable through the extension of the franchise, they gradually won acceptance from the majority of citizens in most liberal democracies. Indeed, more than this, by the mid-twentieth century many police forces had come to be seen as an intrinsic part of the social order – what Reiner (2010: 3) terms 'police fetishism'. This was certainly the case in Britain where 'by the 1950s the police had become not merely accepted but lionized by the broad spectrum of opinion' (Reiner 2010: 48). To be sure, this 'golden age' faded somewhat in subsequent decades as the police were dragged through a series scandals and crises, yet there has remained, in Loader's words (1997: 11), 'an underlying reservoir of support upon which the police can rely'.

Against this backdrop, the expansion of the private security industry – an industry which profits from a good which in many people's eyes ought to be delivered exclusively by the police – has been met with notable scepticism among British citizens. Repeated studies have shown, for instance, that members of the public tend to experience much greater levels of reassurance from police officers when compared with private security officers (see Audit Commission 1996; Crawford *et al.* 2005; Rowland and Coupe 2013). This is not to say that British citizens actively reject the private security industry per se – indeed, as consumers they are responsible for much of its growth – but that the industry has to date remained second best to the police: a 'grudge' purchase. Significantly, this scepticism has generated a long-running (if uneven) critical public discourse specifically targeted at the industry. To paraphrase Loader, it can be said that there is an underlying reservoir of criticism upon which the private security industry can rely.

The primary voice box for this criticism has been the national press media. In their review of how the industry is portrayed in the major British newspapers, Livingstone and Hart (2003) observe three stereotypes which come to the fore during newsworthy scandals and crises: the 'watchman', a figure of incompetence who was particularly prominent during the Group 4 prison escort escapes in the mid-1990s; the 'gangster', a cheating and villainous character who frequently appears in stories related to drug dealing and organised crime; and the 'hired gun', a paid enforcer with few morals who plays a lead role in breaking up protests, for example during environmental lobby group opposition to the Newbury bypass development during the mid-1990s. These stereotypes serve as a ready-made discursive stick with which to beat the industry whenever something goes wrong and as a consequence they represent an important mechanism for holding the industry to account. Of course, many controversial industries are subject to such discursive stick-beating, with pharmaceutical and energy companies perhaps being the obvious examples. Yet because for many citizens the private security industry burrows into and challenges a particularly deep and reactive set of emotions – that is, their 'profound hopes, fears, fantasies and anxieties about matters such as life/death, order/chaos and protection/vulnerability' (Loader and Walker 2001: 20) – they are confronted with an especially big stick and live in fear of it.

Interestingly, the most recent high-profile example of such discursive stick-beating in the national press media – the aftermath of G4S's last-minute failure to provide enough private security officers to satisfy the conditions of its London 2012 Olympics contract (see, for example, *Guardian* 2012) – brought with it an additional voice box: Parliament. To be sure, Parliament has projected a great deal of critical public discourse towards the industry during moments of scandal and crisis (see White 2010), but the House of Commons Home Affairs Committee's 'Olympic Security' enquiry took this to another level – in part a reflection of the growing prominence of parliamentary committees in British politics. The ostensible rationale for holding this enquiry was twofold: to comment on and influence the negotiations over G4S's financial penalty under the terms of its LOCOG contract and to draw lessons for contracting with private security companies both in future mega-events and the criminal justice system in general (HC 531-I [2012–13]: 3). The language and pitch of the enquiry, however, reveals a further unstated but barely hidden purpose: to condemn G4S on the public stage. The narrative of this condemnation is, broadly speaking, divided into two focal points: what went wrong and how to make amends.

In terms of what went wrong, the Committee's Report stresses that there were many early warnings that G4S might not meet its contractual obligations:

> Reports commissioned by LOCOG [before] the Games indicated clearly that there were problems with G4S's recruitment, training and communications. They also found that the management information presented to LOCOG by G4S were fundamentally unreliable. G4S, meanwhile, continued to insist that it was in a position to deliver its contract.
>
> (HC 531-I [2012–13]: 6)

But despite these early warnings, it was not until just over three weeks before the opening ceremony that, in the Report's patronising phraseology, the 'penny finally dropped' among G4S board members that the company would not meet its recruitment targets (ibid.: 9). When this reality struck, the Report notes, Nick Buckles (G4S Chief Executive Officer [CEO]) had to be disturbed on holiday – an incidental fact mentioned no less than three times (ibid.: 9, 16 and 23), presumably to emphasise that in the run-up to the biggest event in the company's history the G4S CEO had taken time out to relax. What made matters worse, in the Report's view, was that Buckles then kept this information hidden from the Home Secretary for a full week, during which time Ian Horseman-Sewell (Director of Major Event) was found 'boasting recklessly in the press that G4S would have been more than capable of simultaneously delivering multiple Olympics security projects around the world' – another incidental fact mentioned three times (ibid.: 9, 13 and 16), seemingly in an effort to highlight the company's arrogance and conceit. These small but salient details, which define the tone of the Report throughout, illustrate that this account of what went wrong was very specifically designed to shame G4S in front of the public.

In discussing how G4S can make amends for what went wrong, the Report focuses on three groups. First, the troops and police officers who stepped in at late notice as part of the contingency plan. To emphasise the scale of the debt owed to the armed forces in particular, the Report includes the following quotation from Lord Coe (Chair of LOCOG): 'I am acutely aware that I displaced family plans, the military came to the table, some of them had been on active duty until relatively recently, some were expecting to see more of their families during the summer months' (ibid.: 9). This emotive language is used to show that G4S owed not simply a debt to 3,500 'troops' as an abstract entity, but to weary soldiers and their families who would have been able to enjoy more time with each other had the company not failed to meet its contractual obligations. G4S eventually pledged £2.5 million to armed force charities in addition to their £70 million payout to LOCOG (*Guardian* 2013b). Second, the individuals who entered into the training process to become a G4S security officer at the Games but as a result of 'poor management' were never deployed. To indicate the scale of debt owed to this group, the Report notes that 'many people undertook training and made themselves available not just because work was being offered, but because they believed that they would be helping in a *national initiative*' (HC 531-I [2012–13]: 11, emphasis added). Because G4S caused these individuals not only financial difficulties but also emotional distress by undermining a broader nationalist spirit, the Report concludes that 'G4S is under a *moral obligation* to immediately make generous *ex gratia* payments by way of apology' (ibid.: 11, emphasis added). Third, the British taxpayers who, according to the Report, are also owed a significant debt:

> We believe that the company should look to the bigger picture, and its long-standing relationship with its biggest client in the UK: the taxpayer. By waiving the £57 million management fee in its entirety, a small fraction of the £759 million that it receives from the British taxpayer every year, G4S would send a strong signal to the public that it is serious about offering fair and reasonable redress when things go badly wrong.
>
> (Ibid.: 13)

The Report concedes that the waiving of this fee is in reality a legal matter, but the 'bigger picture' rhetoric is employed to emphasise that G4S broke not just a legal contract but a kind of social contract with the British public.

In its discussion of what went wrong and how to make amends, the Home Affairs Committee thus rejects a dispassionate black and white analysis in favour of a broader critical discourse in which G4S are given a kind of 'public hanging'. As with the negative media stereotypes, the severity of this hanging is a reflection of the fact G4S are operating in an emotionally charged sector which many regard as the exclusive domain of the state, and so any failure can quickly become amplified beyond ordinary proportions. As such, critical public discourse of this nature serves as a potent accountability mechanism, for the industry fears it. The G4S brand has suffered significantly as a consequence of the post-Olympic public hanging, with the company immediately announcing that it would not compete for the lucrative Rio 2016 Olympics security contract – a decision endorsed by the Report (ibid.: 13) – and soon after suffering the resignation of its long-standing CEO.

## Statutory regulation

As this kind of critical public discourse gathers momentum it frequently leads to the emergence of a further accountability mechanism specifically targeted at the industry: statutory (or state) regulation. History suggests that this process takes shape along three distinct axes: society, state and economy. On the society axis, as negative media coverage builds commentators begin to announce that 'something must be done', and look specifically in the direction of the state which is regarded as the 'fixer' of all security matters due to its historical dominance in this sector. On the state axis, public officials accordingly seek to regulate the industry either in response to or in anticipation of this announcement. On the economy axis, (sections of) the industry may also lobby for the introduction of statutory regulation in an effort to legitimate their 'tainted' operations in the eyes of sceptical citizens – though it is important to add that the industry may also pursue statutory regulation in order to manipulate the market through regulatory capture, a process which particularly applies to large companies seeking to push smaller companies out of the market by raising entry costs (see Stigler 1971).

Yet while in broad terms momentum towards statutory regulation builds along these three axes, the pressures within each axis and the balance between them inevitably varies from country to country, thereby resulting in different types of statutory regulation. This can be illustrated with ideal-types scenarios at either end of this spectrum. Where critical public discourse is especially intense, the state is more likely to respond with strong regulation which holds the industry to account in a comprehensive and rigorous manner, and the industry is more likely to support this response in anticipation that the resulting regime will enhance the legitimacy of its tainted operations. Conversely, where critical public discourse is weak and piecemeal, the state is more likely to respond with weak regulation which holds the industry to account in a relatively light touch manner, and the industry may either support this response or perhaps resist the introduction of statutory regulation altogether. Furthermore, regimes of statutory regulation may move between these extremes over time in accordance with changing contextual conditions. The British case highlights this ebb and flow to great effect.

The history of statutory regulation in post-war Britain is a long and complex one (see White 2010, 2013, forthcoming; Smith and White 2013). To illustrate its direction of travel along the above spectrum, however, it is sufficient to divide this history into three stages: pre-regulation, regulation and deregulation. In the pre-regulation stage, running from the 1950s to the mid-1990s, the society axis remained on a relatively constant trajectory, generating a more or less consistent stream of critical public discourse, especially during moments of scandal and crisis. As Clayton (1967: 12) observes, in the immediate post-war era the '[p]ress, public and police were uniformly hostile to the idea of private night watchmen'. While this hostility did not always translate into explicit calls for statutory regulation, the preconditions for such calls were certainly being laid. The economy axis also maintained a comparatively constant course, with prominent industry representatives – especially in the contract manned security sector – lobbying in favour of statutory regulation in order to placate this public scepticism. Interestingly, the BSIA was a key player in this movement, thus giving it a rather Janus-faced character, in one direction enabling industry self-regulation and in the other promoting statutory regulation (White 2010, forthcoming). However, the state axis was less predictable. In the 1960s and 1970s, the Home Office objected to statutory regulation on the basis that such a legally grounded connection with the state would serve to empower rather than constrain the industry. Then in the 1980s the Home Office increasingly came to dismiss statutory regulation on the neo-liberal grounds that an unfettered industry was best placed to serve the public (a position which many in the industry understandably bought into at the time) (White 2010, forthcoming).

In the regulation stage, lasting from the mid-1990s to the mid-2000s, the society and economy axes pursued the same pro-regulatory course with ever greater focus, with the state axis finally following suit. Two contextual shifts brought about this realignment. The first was the rising number of scandals surrounding industry, the best known examples being Reliance Security's failure to protect the Royal Marines barracks at Deal from an Irish Republican Army bomb in 1989 and Group 4's loss of prisoners during escort in 1993. These and other incidents – many of them documented in the House of Commons Home Affairs Committee's 1995 enquiry into the industry – served to intensify both the critical public discourse within the national media resulting in repeated calls that 'something must be done' and the desire of industry representatives and public officials to respond to these calls through statutory regulation (White 2010). The second was the fact that the industry was taking on more and more police-like functions at this time, prompting many commentators in state, economy and society to argue that the industry accordingly needed to be subject to higher standards of public accountability – a discourse again evident throughout the Home Affairs Committee's 1995 enquiry. After a long period of consultations and a change in government, statutory regulation was finally introduced in the form of the Private Security Industry Act 2001.

This legislation provided for the establishment of the Security Industry Authority, a non-departmental public body accountable to the Home Office and responsible for regulating seven subsectors of the industry in England and Wales (and later Scotland and Northern Ireland): security guarding (contract); door supervision (contract and in-house); cash and valuables in transit (contract); close protection (contract); public space surveillance (CCTV) (contract); the immobilisation, restriction and removal of vehicles (contract and in-house); and key holding (contract). The SIA is empowered to licence individuals in line with 'fit and proper' person criteria and training requirements. If an individual is found working in one of these licensable roles without a valid licence both the individual and their employer may be subject to a range of punishments set out in criminal law. The SIA is also empowered to accredit companies which voluntarily meet certain standards of delivery (for a more detailed breakdown and analysis of these regulatory functions see White 2013). By 2006, when this regime had become fully operational, the industry was therefore subject to a more focused accountability mechanism than ever before. This does not mean, however, that the SIA was comprehensive and rigorous in its regulatory activities. At this time, Mark Button (2007b) ranked statutory regulation in 15 European countries in accordance with measures of coverage and training and positioned the SIA's regime second to last. White (2013) also found that there were persistent problems relating to enforcement from the outset. As such, despite strong critical public discourse in the lead-up to statutory regulation, the resulting regime did not necessarily achieve a high level of public accountability.

In the deregulation stage, which began in the mid-2000s and continues today, the rigour of this accountability mechanism has been further chipped away. This process began in 2007 when the Labour Government sought to reduce the burden of regulatory compliance across the private sector in order to stimulate economic growth. This meant that the SIA became more shackled in its ability to enforce compliance than was previously the case (Smith and White 2013). Then in 2010 the Coalition Government announced a 'bonfire of quangos' in an effort to reduce public spending and stimulate economic growth. The SIA was earmarked for the bonfire, but was soon saved by a pro-regulation industry lobby group known as the Security Alliance, which calculated that with more and more public sector contracts going to the industry in the post-financial crisis politics of austerity, the legitimacy generated by statutory regulation was arguably more important than ever before (White, forthcoming). But while the Coalition Government may have performed a U-turn on the abolition of the SIA, it nevertheless stipulated that the burden of the SIA's regulatory regime must be further reduced, thereby weakening once again the ability of this regime to hold the industry to account (SIA 2012). These three stages illustrate, then, that while statutory regulation may be the most focused accountability mechanism, its purpose and effectiveness changes shape over time in line with contextual shifts such as changes in political economic climate and governmental regime.

While both statutory regulation and the critical public discourse from which it originates approach private security as a usurper of core state functions, it is important to emphasise that these accountability mechanisms are variable in their intensity. Critical public discourse can be a highly potent and far-reaching mechanism, yet it ebbs and flows considerably over time, reaching a fever pitch during times of scandal and crisis before simmering down during periods of relative calm. This means that isolated and low-profile instances of industry malpractice may well bypass this mechanism entirely, even if they are serious in nature. By contrast, once established statutory regulation is more consistent, holding all private security officers and companies within its purview to account through a specially configured part of the legal system – though of course this apparent consistency is still vulnerable to the logic of the prevailing political economic climate. Despite these notable differences in intensity, however, for present purposes the central message is that critical public discourse and statutory regulation are united by a key commonality: they both hold private security to account as a usurper of core state functions.

## Conclusion

This chapter has now surveyed four key mechanisms for holding private security to account: criminal law and civil law, market self-regulation, critical public discourse and statutory regulation. While they all to varying degrees exercise a positive influence over the industry, holding private security officers and companies accountable to the public interest, individual victims and a variety of professional standards, it is important to emphasise that they do not neatly tessellate in a rational and parsimonious manner. They are structured by a liberal paradox in which criminal law, civil law and market self-regulation approach the industry as an ordinary private enterprise, and critical public discourse and statutory regulation approach the industry as a usurper of state functions. When viewed through this paradox, it quickly becomes apparent these accountability mechanisms actually run against each other in certain respects. By normalising private security, criminal law, civil law and market self-regulation in effect serve to empower the industry by facilitating its expansion into the heart of the contemporary security sector where it is able to quietly assume responsibility for operations formerly monopolised by the police. Conversely, critical public discourse and statutory regulation have the opposite effect, emphasising that the industry is straying into what is commonly regarded as sovereign territory and thus needs to be constrained with additional checks and balances – though of course statutory regulation is also in constant danger of being appropriated as a tool of legitimation which further enables the industry's expansion. In sum, there is a paradoxical politics at the heart of these accountability mechanisms. They do not represent clearly defined 'solutions' to the 'problems' commonly associated with private security. They are piecemeal and imperfect: a reflection of the complex relations between state, economy and society under the conditions of contemporary liberal democracy.

## Notes

1  I would like to thank Alexandra Bohm, Stuart Lister, Ian Loader and Mike Rowe for their helpful comments on this chapter – all errors remain my own.
2  The description of private security operations as 'tainted' comes from Thumala *et al.* 2011.

## References

Audit Commission (1996) *Streetwise: Effective Street Patrol*, London: HMSO.
BSIA (2013) 'About Us', available at www.bsia.co.uk/about-us.aspx (last accessed 28 April 2015).

Button, M. (2007a) *Security Officers and Policing: Powers, Culture and Control in the Governance of Private Space*, Aldershot: Ashgate.

Button, M. (2007b) 'Assessing the Regulation of Private Security Across Europe', *European Journal of Criminology*, 4: 109–28.

Button, M. (2012) 'Optimising Security through Effective Regulation: Lessons from around the Globe', in T. Prenzler (ed.) *Policing and Security in Practice: Challenges and Achievements*, New York: Palgrave Macmillan, 204–20.

Button, M. and George, B. (2006) 'Regulation of Private Security: Models for Analysis', in M. Gill (ed.) *The Handbook of Security*, Basingstoke: Palgrave Macmillan, 563–85.

Clayton, T. (1967) *The Protectors: The Inside Story of Britain's Private Security Forces*, London: Osbourne.

Crawford, A. and Lister, S. (2004) *The Extended Police Family*, York: York Publishing.

Crawford, A., Lister, S., Blackburn, S. and Burnett, J. (2005) *Plural Policing: the Mixed Economy of Visible Patrols in England and Wales*, Bristol: Policy Press.

Draper, H. (1978) *Private Police*, Sussex: Harvester Press.

Emsley, C. (1999) 'The Origins of the Modern Police', *History Today*, 49(4): 8–14.

Garland, D. (1996) 'The Limits of the Sovereign State: Strategies of Crime Control in Contemporary Society', *British Journal of Criminology*, 36(4): 445–70.

Garland, D. (2000) 'The Culture of High Crime Societies: Some Preconditions of Recent "Law and Order" Policies', *British Journal of Criminology*, 40: 347–75.

George, B. and Button, M. (1997) 'Private Security Industry Regulation: Lessons From Abroad for the United Kingdom', *International Journal of Risk, Security and Crime Prevention*, 2(3): 187–200.

*Guardian* (2012) 'Olympic Security Chaos: Depth of G4S Security Crisis Revealed', 13 July.

*Guardian* (2013a) 'G4S Faces Damages Claim Over Killing of Jimmy Mbenga', 9 July.

*Guardian* (2013b) 'G4S Olympic Security Contract Losses Increase to £88m', 12 February.

HC 397-II (1983–4) *Second Report from the House of Commons Defence Committee: The Physical Security of Military Installations in the United Kingdom*, London: HMSO.

HC 17-I (1994–5) *First Report from the House of Commons Home Affairs Committee: The Private Security Industry*, London: HMSO.

HC 17-II (1994–5) *First Report of the House of Commons Home Affairs Committee: The Private Security Industry*, London: HMSO.

HC 531-I (2012–13) *Olympics Security*, London: TSO.

Hobbs, D., Hadfield, P. Lister, S. and Winlow, S. (2003) *Bouncers: Violence and Governance in the Night-Time Economy*, Oxford: Oxford University Press.

Home Office (1979) *The Private Security Industry: A Discussion Paper*, London: HMSO.

Home Office (1991) *The Private Security Industry Background Paper*, unpublished.

Johnston, L. (1992) 'Regulating Private Security', *International Journal of the Sociology of Law*, 20(1): 1–16.

Johnston, L. (2000) *Policing Britain*, Harlow: Longman.

Jones, T. and Newburn, T. (1998) *Private Security and Public Policing*, Oxford: Clarendon Press.

Jones, T. and Newburn, T. (1999) 'Urban Change and Policing: Mass Private Property Re-Considered', *European Journal on Criminal Policy and Research*, 7: 225–44.

Jones, T. and Newburn, T. (2002) 'The Transformation of Policing? Understanding Current Trends in Policing Systems', *British Journal of Criminology*, 42(1): 129–46.

Kempa, M., Stenning, P. and Wood, J. (2004) 'Policing Communal Spaces: A Reconfiguration of the "Mass Private Property" Hypothesis', *British Journal of Criminology*, 44: 562–81.

Lister, S., Hadfield, P., Hobbs, D. and Winlow, S. (2001) 'Accounting for Bouncers: Occupational Licensing as a Mechanism for Regulation', *Criminology and Criminal Justice*, 1(4): 363–84.

Livingstone, K. and Hart, J. (2003) 'The Wrong Arm of the Law? Public Images of Private Security', *Policing and Society*, 13(2): 159–70.

Loader, I. (1997) 'Policing and the Social: Questions of Symbolic Power', *The British Journal of Sociology*, 48(1): 1–18.

Loader, I. and Walker, N. (2001) 'Policing as a Public Good: Reconstituting the Connections Between Policing and the State', *Theoretical Criminology*, 5(1): 9–35.

Loader, I. and Walker, N. (2007) *Civilizing Security*, Cambridge: Cambridge University Press.

Lodge, M. and Wegrich, K. (2012) *Managing Regulation: Regulatory Analysis, Politics and Policy*, Basingstoke: Palgrave Macmillan.

Moran, M. (2003) *The British Regulatory State: High Modernism and Hyper-Innovation*, Oxford: Oxford University Press.

Noaks, L. (2008) 'Private and Public Policing in the UK: A Citizen Perspective on Partnership', *Policing and Society*, 18(2): 156–68.

O'Connor, D., Lippert, R., Spencer, D. and Smylie, L. (2008) 'See Private Security Like a State', *Criminology and Criminal Justice*, 8(2): 203–26.

Prenzler, T. and Sarre, R. (1999) 'A Survey of Security Legislation and Regulatory Strategies in Australia', *Security Journal*, 12(3): 7–17.

Prenzler, T. and Sarre, R. (2008) 'Developing a Risk Profile and Model Regulatory System for the Security Industry', *Security Journal*, 21(4): 264–77.

Pierre, J. and Peters, B.G. (2000) *Governance, Politics and the State*, Basingstoke: Palgrave Macmillan.

Reiner, R. (1992) 'Policing a Postmodern Society', *Modern Law Review*, 55(6): 761–81.

Reiner, R. (2010) *The Politics of the Police* (4th edn), Oxford: Oxford University Press.

Rhodes, R.A.W. (1996) 'The New Governance: Governing Without Government', *Political Studies*, 44(4): 652–67.

Rhodes, R.A.W. (1997) *Understanding Governance: Policy Networks, Governance, Reflexivity and Accountability*, Maidenhead: Open University Press.

Rigakos, G. (2002) *The New Parapolice: Risk Markets and Commodified Social Control*, Toronto: University of Toronto Press.

Rowland, R. and Coupe, T. (2013) 'Patrol Officers and Public Reassurance: A Comparative Evaluation of Police Officers, PSCOs, ACSOs and Private Security Guards', *Policing and Society*, DOI: 10.1080/10439463.2013.784300.

Sarre, R. (1998) 'Accountability and the Private Sector: Putting Accountability of Private Security Under the Spotlight', *Security Journal*, 10(2): 97–102.

Security Industry Authority (SIA) (2012) *SIA Conference 2012*, London: SIA.

Shearing, C. and Stenning, P. (1981) 'Modern Private Security: Its Growth and Implications', *Crime and Justice*, 3: 193–245.

Shearing, C. and Stenning, P. (1983) 'Private Security – Implications for Social Control', *Social Problems*, 30(5): 493–506.

Smith, M.J. and White, A. (2013) 'The Paradox of Security Regulation: Public Protection Versus Normative Legitimation', *Policy and Politics*, DOI: 10.1332/030557312 X655495.

South, N. (1988) *Policing For Profit: The Private Security Sector*, London: Sage.

Spitzer, S. (1993) 'The Political Economy of Policing', in D.F. Greenberg (ed.) *Crime and Capitalism: Readings in Marxist Criminology*, Philadelphia: Temple University Press, 568–95.

Spitzer, S. and Scull, A. (1977) 'Privatization and Capitalist Development: The Case of the Private Police', *Social Problems*, 25(1): 18–29.

Stenning, P. (2000) 'Powers and Accountability of Private Police', *European Journal on Criminal Policy and Research*, 8(3): 325–52.

Stigler, G.J. (1971) 'The Theory of Economic Regulation', *The Bell Journal of Economics and Management Science*, 2(1): 3–21.

Thumala, A., Goold, B. and Loader, I. (2011) 'A Tainted Trade? Moral Ambivalence and Legitimation Work in the Private Security Industry', *British Journal of Sociology*, 62(2): 283–303.

van Steden, R. (2007) *Privatizing Policing: Describing and Explaining the Growth of Private Security*, Amsterdam: BJU.

van Steden, R. and Nalla, M. (2010) 'Citizen Satisfaction with Private Security Guards in the Netherlands: Perceptions of an Ambiguous Occupation', *European Journal of Criminology*, 7(3): 214–34.

Wakefield, A. (2003) *Selling Security: The Private Policing of Public Space*, Cullompton, Devon: Willan.

Wakefield, A. and Button, M. (2013) 'New Perspectives on Police Education and Training: Lessons from the Private Security Sector', in P. Stanislas (ed.) *International Perspectives on Police Education and Training*, London: Routledge, 254–73.

White, A. (2010) *The Politics of Private Security: Regulation, Reform and Re-Legitimation*, Basingstoke: Palgrave Macmillan.

White, A. (2012) 'The New Political Economy of Private Security', *Theoretical Criminology*, 16(1): 85–101.

White, A. (2013) 'The Impact of the Private Security Industry Act 2001', *Security Journal*. DOI: 10.1057/sj.2012.53.

White, A. (forthcoming) 'Just Another Industry? (De)Regulation, Public Expectations and Private Security', in A. Hucklesby and S. Lister (eds) *Private Sector Involvement in Criminal Justice*, Basingstoke: Palgrave Macmillan.

White, A. and Gill, M. (2013) 'The Transformation of Policing: From Ratios to Rationalities', *British Journal of Criminology*, 53(1): 74–93.

Wood, J. and Shearing, C. (2007) *Imagining Security*, Cullompton, Devon: Willan.

Zedner, L. (2003) 'Too Much Security?', *International Journal of the Sociology of Law*, 31: 155–84.

# 10 Plural policing and the challenge of democratic accountability

*Stuart Lister and Trevor Jones*[1]

Democratic accountability is a key concept in thinking and writing about Western political systems. The normative prescription that those in positions of power should be obliged to justify their use of power within a political forum that may lead to sanction is widely seen to be an intrinsic characteristic of 'democratic governance' (Bovens 2005). As policing concerns the institutionalised use of authority in the task of 'governing security' (Johnston and Shearing 2003), so – in turn – it requires governing in ways that hold those responsible accountable to democratic bodies. Accordingly, a key focus of policing debates has been on the institutional arrangements established for ensuring its structures of governance are democratically accountable. To date, however, research on the 'democratic' or 'political' accountability of policing has focused almost exclusively upon public police organisations (see, for example, Lustgarten 1986; Reiner 1993, 1995; Jones and Newburn 1997; Walker 2000). Relatively few authors have discussed private and other plural forms of 'policing beyond the state' when reviewing options for establishing democratically accountable policing (though see Loader 2000; Crawford *et al.* 2005; Sarre and Prenzler 2005; Stenning 2009). This tendency to restrict discussions to state-centric analyses of the nature of power and authority reflects a broader 'myopia' in policing scholarship (Shearing 2006; Stenning 2009). It appears, for instance, to be increasingly anomalous in light of recent empirical studies tracing the growing role of non-governmental, frequently commercial (or so-called for-profit), agencies in the authorisation and provision of policing (see, for example, Jones and Newburn 1998; Noaks 2000; Wakefield 2003; Crawford *et al.* 2005).

In the light of this 'myopia', this chapter seeks to substantially broaden debates about accountability and policing. It does so by analysing the extent to which the mixed economy of public and private policing can be governed according to, and accommodated within, democratic principles (cf. Stenning 2009). These principles, we suggest, offer a set of criteria for thinking about the challenges of governing plural policing networks in ways that are democratically accountable, and which, in turn, promote the idea of policing as a public good. This, we assert, is crucial because policing is a normative enterprise that holds significant implications not only for principles of human rights, due process and fair treatment (Crawford 2007), but also for utilitarian objectives of ensuring that citizens live in just and safe societies. A key challenge, however, is presented by the role of the market in determining the extent to which policing is distributed and delivered equitably and effectively. In pursuing our argument, we query the extent to which market forces and free competition, even when seemingly functioning well, will serve to govern policing in ways that ensures its allocation and delivery accord with democratic values (cf. Trebilcock and Iacobucci 2003).

Our line of enquiry focuses on 'local security networks' (Dupont 2004) in England and Wales, the remit of which usually extends both to crime and disorder reduction, inclusive of the protection of public and private assets. These multi-organisational networks are constitutive of broader shifts in how power and authority are contemporaneously arranged, exercised and governed in late-modern societies. The statist, 'command and control' model of 'government' is said to have given way to a more 'networked governance' model, in which authority is not dominated by a single locus but exercised through dispersed, less hierarchical and a more pluralistic or 'nodal' set of institutional formations (Rose and Miller 1992; Rhodes 1997; Rose 2000; Moran 2001). In this context, governmentality theorists have highlighted how neo-liberal governmental reforms have separated the 'steering' functions of governance from the 'rowing' functions, transforming the role of the state to that of a regulator or facilitator of the governing activities of others (Osborne and Gaebler 1992). In turn, governance and accountability relations have themselves become increasingly diversified and pluralistic (Mulgan 1997; Baberis 1998). As a consequence, the act of governing is no longer contingent on vertical chains of accountability that link providers of public services with institutional structures of the democratic polity. The rise of security networks comprising state, civil society and market actors, whose governance and accountability structures frequently stand outside of extant political structures, raises specific challenges if they are to be governed not only effectively but also democratically.

The chapter is divided into the following sections. The first outlines the recent growth of plural policing, identifying the conceptual implications that arise from this empirical development. The second contextualises the regulatory challenge of plural policing, before critiquing recent legal and policy responses. The third assesses plural policing against a set of democratic criteria, drawing attention to the governance and accountability challenges of prioritising these democratic credentials. The fourth emphasises the need for a holistic approach to the governance of plural policing networks, and considers how this might be secured in ways that are democratically accountable.

## The re-emergence of plural policing

Over the last four decades there has been a substantial growth of scholarly interest in the pluralisation of policing. A widespread process of restructuring has seen policing become increasingly fragmented, multi-tiered and dispersed, resulting in the proliferation of forms of policing both 'within' and 'beyond' government (Bayley and Shearing 1996, 2001). Indeed, the very idea of the police as monopolistic guardians of law and order has dissolved in the face of neo-liberal traits of governing that have stimulated twin processes of pluralisation and marketisation of policing (Johnston 2007). Much of the academic interest has focused on the so-called rebirth of 'private policing' within the late-modern era (Johnston 1992; Button 2002; van Steden 2007), and particularly the commercial activities of the private security industry. The rise, for example, of private security guards has attracted much attention (see Rigakos 2002; Wakefield 2003; Button 2007), generating debates inter alia of the similarities and differences between 'public police' and 'private security', particularly with regard to the interests each serves, their organisational forms as well as their mentalities, techniques and practices (Shearing and Stenning 1983; Johnston and Shearing 2003; Wood and Shearing 2007).

The post-war development of the private security industry has been famously described by Stenning and Shearing (1980) as a 'quiet revolution' in policing. Research has revealed how a burgeoning global private security industry undertakes a wide array of policing activities (Stenning 2000; Johnston 2007; van Steden 2007), including the core police functions of law enforcement, order maintenance and crime investigation. Although problems of estimation mean that all figures have to be treated with caution, there is a consensus that the private security industry in England and Wales has expanded considerably in recent years and now employs significantly more people than the state's public police forces (Jones and Lister 2015). The growth of the industry has been fuelled by increasing demands for protective services across a range of economic and social contexts. Although much of the initial discussion about private security linked its expansion to the growth of 'mass private property' (Shearing and Stenning 1981, 1983), such as shopping centres, holiday complexes, retail parks, educational campuses and leisure parks, its presence is now increasing in more openly accessible, public places, such as residential areas and town centres (Crawford 2011). Accordingly, the orthodoxy that private security should be considered the 'junior partner' to the public police has become increasingly challenged. Many citizens therefore now live, work, shop and spend their leisure time in places where they are more likely to encounter private security guards rather than public police officers. As a consequence, the nature of the social order that private actors are tasked with constructing, and the styles of policing they subsequently deliver, bears significant implications for notions of citizenship (Shearing and Stenning 1981).

The growth of private security, however, is but one focus of the broadening analytical lens through which developments in local policing must be viewed. Over the last two decades we have seen diversification and pluralisation across a range of state and non-state actors delivering visible and organised forms of security-orientated patrols. The emergence of this mixed economy has been stimulated not only by citizens' demands for order and security, but also by a series of governmental initiatives that have encouraged local authorities, social housing providers, private businesses, voluntary sector and residents' groups to take greater responsibility for their own policing needs (Lister 2007). The inter-linked 'community safety' and 'antisocial behaviour' agendas in the latter part of the 1990s, for example, fuelled the growth of 'municipal patrols' such as 'neigh-bourhood wardens', 'street wardens' and 'city centre ambassadors' (Crawford *et al.* 2005). Broadly aimed at improving the social and economic well-being of public spaces, these new public auxiliaries were designed to contribute to local systems of social control by introducing an additional layer of intermediary per-sonnel within civil society (Crawford and Lister 2004). By 2003 it was estimated that almost 500 warden schemes were in operation in England and Wales (NACRO 2003), although the number has subsequently declined as a result of the loss of ring-fenced central government funding and the arrival of a new police patrol auxiliary in the form of 'police community support officers' (PCSOs).

Established by the Police Reform Act of 2002, PCSOs provide a uniformed presence on the streets and represent a further degree of pluralisation of 'polic-ing by government' (Loader 2000). PCSOs are 'civilian' officers directed and controlled by the Chief Constable, but undergo less training and have fewer legal powers than professional police officers. With a core remit to reassure the public and reduce antisocial behaviour, PCSOs represent the visible face of the com-munity safety agenda. There are now just over 13,500 PCSOs in England and Wales undertaking a wide range of frontline policing duties. As they are cheaper to recruit and deploy then police officers and lend themselves to more stable assignments, PCSOs have enabled the police to assert a degree of control over the patrol function by competing more effectively with other (non-police) pro-viders in local markets for patrol (see Blair 2003). Local authorities, along with other social housing providers and private businesses, have increasingly entered into contractual agreements with police forces to fund the localised provision of PCSOs. Consequently the introduction of PCSOs has been interpreted not only as a governmental attempt to ensure the police retained greater control over the patrol function, but also as a 'monopolistic' state approach to integrating the activities of plural policing within the police organisation (Crawford 2008).

Over the same period we have also seen further 'pluralisation below the state' in the form of order-definition and maintenance, rule-making and regulation exercised by non-commercial, community and voluntary organisations (Lea and Stenson 2007). Part of this has arisen from new developments in the 'responsibi-lisation' of non-state organisations to take control of their own security, and the spreading language of partnership, co-production and community self-governance (Garland 2001; Wood and Shearing 2007). Although it is difficult to assess claims about changes in policing 'from below' in the absence of reliable longitudinal data, Bayley and Shearing (1996) have suggested that 'citizen-led' policing expanded in many countries in the latter part of the twentieth century. Indeed, although in England and Wales 'citizen-led' patrols, such as organised residents' groups, crime prevention associations and faith-based organisations, have not been extensively researched, they do appear to have increased recently both in diversity, scale and degree of organisation (Crawford 2008; Jones and Lister 2015). Suffice to say, the activities of these 'citizen-led' and 'third sector' groups add further complexity to the localised division of labour between public, private and hybrid policing actors (Johnston 1992).

These developments signify that it has become increasingly acceptable for organisations other than central government to assert a degree of control over their own security needs, often by purchasing policing services on the open market. Policing has become not only pluralised but also increasingly marketised, commercially arranged and governed by market-based and privately contracted forms of accountability. The separation of those authorising from those delivering policing reflects the growth of purchaser/provider splits in its arrangement and provision (Bayley and Shearing 1996). Subsequently, public bodies have become major purchasers of policing services from both the public and private sectors; equally, private sector, commercial organisations routinely purchase policing services from the state's public police forces. The complexity of these decentralised and multilateral arrangements demonstrates their 'hybrid' character, in which conceptually and empirically they straddle the traditional public/private divide (Bayley and Shearing 1996; Dupont 2004). There is no neat compartmentalisation of public and private policing resources deployed to 'public' or 'private' spaces, for instance (Stenning 2009). Rather, the mounting spatial complexity of urban life is stimulating increasingly complex policing arrangements. Privately funded policing, though predominantly found on private property or land, is not restricted in this way. The growth of commercial areas leased to and managed by private sector landlords in many British towns and cities, for instance, has seen an increase in private security guards patrolling public spaces (Crawford 2011; Jones and Lister 2015). Likewise, privately purchased 'public' police officers can also be found operating within spaces owned or temporarily managed by private corporations, such as leisure festival venues or sports stadia. As a consequence, the nature of what is 'public' and what is 'private' has itself become increasingly conceptually contested.

Such conceptual and empirical developments have significant implications for how we might understand the character of contemporary policing, as well as how it might be democratically governed. As alluded to above, the growing diversity and heterogeneity of policing providers has rendered the idea of hierarchical formulations of power increasingly redundant such that the state is but one (albeit important) node within a broader network of policing or 'security governance', more broadly defined (Johnston and Shearing 2003). Rhetorically referred to within policy discourses as the 'extended policing family' (Home Office 2001), the emergence of these multi-organisational security networks raises acute questions of coordination, oversight and effectiveness. Harnessing the diverse efforts of the assemblage of local providers has foregrounded 'partnership' approaches to policing and community safety, which seek to integrate the breadth of activities and increase the functionality and effectiveness of the network as a whole. Whilst of itself this ambition raises considerable challenges, these arguably pale in comparison to the challenges of subjecting networked or 'nodal policing' to democratic governance. It is in consideration of this regulatory challenge to which the remainder of this chapter now turns.

## Regulating plural policing

Given the prevalence of plural orders of policing in contemporary systems of social control, it is important to develop ways of connecting them to democratic structures of governance. As Loader (2000: 324) suggests, 'the questions ... that have long vexed discussions of police policy and (mal)practice in liberal democratic societies press themselves with renewed force under the altered conditions of plural policing'. Yet, if the contested nature of *police* 'governance' and 'accountability' relations gives rise to complex and daunting challenges, they become even more so when considering the complex 'policing web' (Brodeur 2010) of public *and* private agencies and actors. Where police – at both the individual and institutional level – in England and Wales are rendered accountable through a series of principal-agent relationship chains that link them to elected political structures, offering a symbolic as well as a functional element of democratic responsibility for, and control over, local policing, there is no equivalent apex of authority governing plural policing networks. Rather, the emergence of a pluralised and marketised landscape of policing has given rise to a more diversified set of horizontal accountability relations, undermining reliance on vertical chains of political accountability that have traditionally characterised accountability relations within more monopolistic, state-based formations of policing (Bovens 2005).

The shift towards market-based allocations of policing, therefore, raises acute regulatory challenges if the activities of autonomous private providers are to be aligned with public values and democratic principles (Greve 2008). The form of contractual governance within market arrangements is highly individualised and distinct from the wider modes of responsiveness to democratic bodies envisaged in idealised notions of local police accountability. It tends to be a narrow style of managerial accountability, related to costs and outputs, rather than deeper questions of resource allocation, priorities and policing styles. Moreover, as Shearing and Stenning (1983) famously asserted, commercially arranged policing has a 'client-defined' mandate. It is overwhelmingly instrumental in purpose, designed to serve the exclusive, and often elitist, interests of those who pay for its provision. It therefore risks sidelining the interests of non-paying parties, who may experience malign effects from such arrangements but have no forum to give voice to their concerns (Reiner 2010). Rendering market-based policing responsive to and considerate of the wider public interest thus presents a significant policy challenge, particularly if both the authoriser and the provider are private sector bodies.

This is not to say, however, that there have been no attempts to bring public accountability to plural forms of policing. Whilst the institutional mechanisms of police accountability pay little attention to non-state policing providers, recent legal and policy developments in England and Wales have attempted to address this gap. The main mechanism of external accountability introduced has been in the form of systems of regulation of the private security industry. The Private Security Industry Act 2001 established the Security Industry Authority (SIA) to license those working in particular sectors of the industry, including static guards, door supervisors, wheel-clampers, bodyguards, private investigators and security consultants. Employment in these sectors requires a licence, which is contingent on both training and criminal records vetting. The Act makes it an offence to work without a licence or to employ someone without a licence. Breaching various conditions, including gaining a conviction prescribed as relevant, can lead to licence revocation. Although the Act did not introduce mandatory licensing for security companies, it did establish a voluntary scheme to which they can submit themselves.

The licensing regime has, however, attracted a significant amount of criticism. For some its scope is too narrow, excluding significant sectors of the security industry such as security systems installers and in-house guards (White 2010). Others have argued that the voluntary licensing of companies amounts to little more than an ineffective self-regulatory model (Button 2002). Moreover, the narrow scope of the regulation signifies its failure to recognise the role of multilateral networks in policing, and – perhaps as a consequence – it has largely failed to improve relations between public police and private security firms, which remain widely plagued by mutual distrust trust and antipathy (White and Smith 2009). According to plans of the Coalition Government, however, the regulation of private security is set to change to a more self-regulatory 'business licensing' regime in which the focus of control will shift from licensing individuals to the licensing of private security firms. Under the proposed reforms, the state will adopt a more 'arm's-length' approach with companies handed responsibility for ensuring that required checks on individual employees are carried out. Although it remains to be seen what impact these changes will have on the private security industry (see White, this collection), it seems apparent that the regulation will continue to focus primarily on protecting members of the public rather than safeguarding broader notions of the public good (Stenning 2009).

The narrow focus of the SIA licensing regime can be contrasted with 'Community Safety Accreditation Schemes', which were introduced by the Police Reform Act 2002. The Act gives Chief Constables authority to accredit neighbourhood wardens, private security guards and other 'non-police' actors who meet a prescribed standard of professionalism, for example, in training and vetting arrangements. In so doing, accreditation schemes aspire to foster techniques of 'arm's-length' governance, offering the police a potential means for harnessing and steering the community safety efforts of those deemed to be 'police compliant' (Blair 2003). Furthermore, in choosing who and who not to bestow accreditation upon, the police may be able to influence market demand for specific security providers. This, however, raises the spectre of the police – in effect – regulating those they compete with in the market place (Loader 2000; Crawford *et al.* 2005). In practice, however, accreditation has not gained widespread support from either the police or the private security sector. As Crawford (2013) notes, the market benefits to be accrued from gaining accreditation status do not appear to outweigh the costs of securing this status. By the end of 2010, across 26 participating forces, there were 2,219 accredited persons (ACPO 2011), most of whom were local authority employed wardens and antisocial behaviour enforcement officers. Consequently attempts to establish holistic oversight mechanisms over plural policing networks have been few and entirely limited to highly localised, short-lived efforts by police and community safety partners.

Despite the introduction of these legal and policy responses to the growth of plural policing in England and Wales, their impact on the function and orientation of local policing systems is narrow and appears, at best, to be limited. In the following section we offer a set of democratic principles, which serve as a means for thinking about the challenges of governing plural policing networks in ways that ensure their arrangement and provision advance democratic values. In so doing, we draw on a range of debates to identify the normative prospects and governance challenges of aligning plural policing to these democratic criteria.

## Plural policing and democratic values

Previous work involving one of the authors identified a number of 'democratic criteria' against which governance and accountability mechanisms for policing can be assessed (Jones *et al.* 1996). This work suggested that a combination of themes or values can be associated with democratic arrangements, and that distinct policing systems place a different order of priority on these. The criteria identified were: equity, delivery of service, responsiveness, distribution of power, information, redress, and participation.

### *Equity*

Perhaps the greatest democratic challenge for plural policing concerns equity, the idea that resources should be distributed fairly between groups and individuals such that the benefits (or harms) to be derived are spread equitably. Debates here must be seen in the context of pluralisation under market auspices, as described above. As problems of crime and disorder tend to cluster in places that are socially and economically marginalised, free market allocations of policing are likely to skew resources towards those communities of least need. The burden of harm on disadvantaged areas will be further increased if territorially defined policing merely displaces rather than prevents local problems. Although the benefits of policing may bleed into neighbouring areas, commercialised policing, by definition, privileges the narrow and partisan interests of its paymasters (Crawford and Lister 2006). As such, accountability to market-based contracts promotes exclusion and social selectivity. Furthermore, if those turning to commercial policing refuse to pay twice, through both taxation and fee-based arrangements, and withdraw their financial and political support for state policing, then those unable to turn to the market may experience a qualitative and quantitative poorer service (Bayley and Shearing 1996).

On this view, then, much pluralised provision threatens to exacerbate unequal provision of policing services, in terms of both over-coercion and under-protection of disadvantaged groups. The increasingly fragmented policing landscape has clear exclusionary and polarising tendencies. Whilst the rich are increasingly protected within commercially governed and safe 'private' spaces, the have-nots are left to fend for themselves in increasingly dangerous 'public' spaces, policed by an increasingly adversarial public police force (Minton 2012). This is not to deny, however, that state policing in Britain also has a problematic history in terms of equity. Even in those spaces that remain unconditionally 'public' and open access, security and policing provision is increasingly following the exclusionary and risk-based policies privileged by private forms of government. The spread of crime prevention by environmental design, as well as the exclusionary use of 'antisocial behaviour orders' and other such anticipatory interventions (e.g. dispersal orders, youth curfews) are serving to privatise public space by public means (Crawford 2011; Minton 2012). 'Banishment', as Van Swaaningen (2005: 303) notes, 'is the new metaphor of this politics of public safety and the fears of law-abiding citizens are the driving force behind it'. On the other hand, it has been argued that, in any case, the public police organisation is predicated upon universalist egalitarian principles, even if they have repeatedly failed to live up to such principles (Zedner 2006). Above all, the public police are supposed to deliver equal policing services to all citizens, 'without fear or favour'.

Whilst this normative conception of public policing draws sharp contrast with private government, it has been nonetheless argued that the pluralisation and marketisation of policing may offer groundbreaking possibilities for a more democratic and just distribution of security services. Almost two decades ago, Bayley and Shearing (1996) argued that publicly funded 'voucher schemes' or 'block grants' could enable especially underprivileged communities to participate in security markets. Enhancing access to security in this way, the argument runs, would address the distributional inequalities raised by the growth of commercial policing, but also serve the interests of these communities more directly than has been the case under state-organised policing arrangements. This example of local governance can be seen as an experiment in which allowing citizens to self-organise their policing may lead to a more equitable and fairer deliverance of security (Wood and Shearing 2007). Whilst this argument offers a potential means for addressing a key democratic challenge of policing under pluralised conditions, greater engagement with, and the subsequent expansion of, the market may have far-reaching consequences. Security goods have a self-fulfilling and expansionist logic, as the more they are actively pursued, the more they may not only fuel further public anxieties but also heighten unrealistic public expectations about the extent to which 'policing' alone can deliver harmonious forms of social order (Crawford and Lister 2006; Jones 2012; Zedner 2009). If security begets security, then broader and deeper engagement with market forces raises pressing and interlinked questions of sustainability and desirability.

## *Service delivery*

Several authors have argued that plural policing heralds the possibility of improvements in the efficiency and effectiveness of service delivery. For example, Bayley and Shearing (1996, 2001) have suggested that the numerical expansion of policing agents due to the proliferation of providers would enhance aggregate levels of security in society. In addition, the distinctive nature of private policing – in terms of its innovative, embedded, consensual and risk-oriented preventive approaches – has been contrasted favourably with the slow-moving, bureaucratic and punishment-oriented approach of the public police (Johnston and Shearing 2003; Wood and Shearing 2007). The assumption posited here is that the privileging of 'security' within the mentalities of private security lends itself to problem-focused approaches, which in turn provide greater levels of safety for local communities (Bayley and Shearing 1996). In a related argument, it might be suggested that the competitive dynamic engendered by plural policing, in which providers compete in the market, helps to encourage value for money, innovation and efficiency. An exemplar of this argument is the aforementioned 'police community support officer' (PCSO), the introduction of which led to substantive increases in police visibility within local neighbour-hoods (see Crawford *et al.* 2005).

Against this, however, the fragmentation and multiplication of policing provid-ers can generate inefficiencies. As policing is increasingly market-arranged, attempts to coordinate activities and construct mutually beneficial alliances between different providers may be undermined by the pursuit of market advantage (Jones and Newburn 1998; Noaks 2000). The research of Crawford *et al.* (2005) in northern England, for instance, found strong evidence of 'market failure' in the provision of local patrol services. Local efforts to tackle crime and disorder were undermined by a lack of cooperation and information-sharing between policing agencies. Furthermore, these researchers reported that well-developed, joined-up working practices between different providers were relatively rare and relations between them were often highly varied. Where local police did seek to establish partnership relations, their efforts were at times hampered by the sheer number and diversity of local providers. They also found that partnership relations were stymied by different working cultures, mentalities and practices, as well as by deep-rooted structural obstacles, both at operational and strategic levels. Municipal policing actors, for example, reported being fearful of jeopardising their good rela-tions with local residents if they were perceived to be working too closely with the police. The resulting coordination deficits hampered attempts to ensure an effective response to local problems of security and order.

A further way in which plural policing may reduce effective service delivery arises from its concentration in local neighbourhoods at the relatively 'soft' end of policing functions (e.g. 'reassurance', 'community work' and 'social service' activities). Given this focus, an effect of pluralisation may be to free up police officers to focus on more serious incidents of crime and disorder. In so doing, however, it may reduce the amount of 'non-adversarial' contact that police offic-ers have with the wider public (Crawford and Lister 2006). If 'community polic-ing' is entirely devolved to state and non-state policing auxiliaries, then the police risk becoming a 'residualised' service focused mostly upon law enforce-ment and aggressive intervention in situations of conflict. The possible negative implications for notions of 'policing by consent' could have serious ramifications for the effectiveness of the organisation along a range of performance dimensions. If the police lack legitimacy in the eyes of the public, then citizens are less likely to pass on crime and disorder related information, cooperate as witnesses, respond positively to requests for assistance from police officers, and comply with police directives. On this view, 'democratically accountable' policing is not just morally desirable, but is instrumentally superior to 'unaccountable' policing.

### Responsiveness

The extent to which policing is responsive to local publics has become viewed, at a policy level at least, as increasingly important, reinforcing the idea that democratic policing ought to reflect the wishes of the people it serves (Manning 2011). To this end, successive recent governments have attempted to increase police engagement and consultation with local communities, as demonstrated by the advent of the mutually reinforcing 'citizen-focused' and 'neighbourhood' policing agendas (Home Office 2010). The difficulties of ensuring that police engage in dialogue with and respond meaningfully to the wants and needs of local communities are, however, historical and arguably deeply entrenched (Keith 1988; Jones and Newburn 2001). As police governance in England and Wales became more and more centralised, particularly over the last three decades, so police forces became increasingly responsive to the bureaucratic and political imperatives of the Home Office, at the expense of local communities (McLaughlin 2005). Although the recent introduction of elected Police and Crime Commissioners (PCCs), designed to be democratic advocates for local communities, aimed to reverse this trend by ensuring the police do respond to community concerns, there remain significant structural and cultural obstacles to overcome if this is to be achieved in a fair and meaningfully way (see Reiner, Raine, this collection).

Against this, local private and community-organised forms of security provision may not only be more responsive to community concerns, but also able to draw more effectively upon local capacities and knowledge when compared to the top-down hierarchical bureaucracies that have traditionally characterised public policing (Bayley and Shearing 1996). The legal role of contracts within accountability arrangements governing commercial policing gives opportunity for those paying to articulate and specify a clear set of 'service expectations' to which providers must attend. Where policing is purchased from a private security firm by a public body (e.g. the local authority) on behalf of its constituents, again market logics suggest the provider will make some attempt to demonstrate value for money by responding to the needs of beneficiaries. Critics, however, stress that local and multiple publics seldom speak with a consensus and, moreover, it is open for debate whether what 'the public' wants of local policing is always desirable (Johnston 1992). Although security is often promoted as a universal and democratic good for the benefit of all, in fact its pursuit runs the risk of fostering intolerance and aggravating social exclusion if a community wishes to seek isolation and seclusion (Zedner 2009). It would be very undemocratic for police and policing professionals to adopt such a segregating, and perhaps discriminatory, policy.

## *Power distribution*

According to this democratic ideal, power to influence and review policing policy should not be concentrated in too few hands, but should be distributed across a number of institutions and agencies. The intention here is to negate conflicts between different constituents within any given social formation, and ensure stable compromises such that scarce policing resources can be allocated in ways that serve the interests of all constituents (Jones *et al.* 1996). Plural policing arguably scores highly on this democratic criterion. Rather than concentrating power in the hands of a single, centralised state bureaucracy, by definition it involves a range of alternative providers and authorisers. As suggested above, local authorities that are dissatisfied with public policing provision in their area of jurisdiction, for example, can organise and direct their own municipal auxiliary patrols, either by employing community warden-type providers, or by contracting out the service to commercial security companies. Markets imply choice, and efficient markets presuppose the presence of suitable, alternative providers.

Against this, however, we should not ignore the structuring tendencies of security markets to accumulate power and market share within the auspices of a handful of institutions. The corporate takeovers and mergers that characterise the development of the domestic and global private security industry have resulted in market domination by a few very large companies (Johnston 2007; White 2010). If the oligopoly conditions found within the private sector provision of criminal justice services are repeated in the domain of security and policing, then the resulting concentration of power is likely to be to the detriment of democratic accountability. Moreover, despite the appearance that power may be distributed more locally, unregulated cooperation and information-sharing by plural policing bodies may result in 'policing beyond the police' ultimately forming a formidable and sinister 'reserve arsenal' of social control for the state (Cohen 1985). Although – as described above – the empirical evidence suggests that disorganisation and lack of coordination are, in fact, the norm in pluralised security networks (Crawford *et al.* 2005; Terpstra *et al.* 2013), from a democratic viewpoint, it is vital to recognise the potential for abuse. Simultaneously, where plural forms of policing are arranged and delivered wholly under private auspices then the distribution of power is highly skewed towards serving the specific and parochial interests of those paying for its provision.

## *Information*

The provision of a good level of information is a requirement for democratic accountability, enabling the authorities and the public to be informed about local policing. Securing this objective is potentially problematic in diversified policing networks, not least because fundamental information, such as who is authorising policing and who is providing it, may be unclear. In this, the multifaceted structures of relationships between public and private policing bodies blur the boundaries of responsibilities between them, which, in turn, can hamper the transparency of arrangements (Mashaw 2006). Such amorphous, hybrid arrangements can also generate accountability deficits by obscuring not only 'who is responsible to whom and for what' (Rhodes 1997), but also how a specific policing arrangement is organised and whose interests it serves. In this context, the average citizen in any British urban area might find themselves moving through areas that are policed by an array of public and private actors wearing a range of official police-type uniforms, but have little sense of the different interest groups represented. In their study of plural policing patrols, Crawford *et al.* (2005) highlight how, within this context, the blurring of roles, responsibilities, powers and identities, both of and between plural policing personnel, can foster public confusion and create uncertainties over what the public might expect of different providers. Such concerns are by no means baseless. The activities of the public police have traditionally been primarily focused upon unambiguously public spaces. Hence residential streets, public parks and open spaces, public roads and motorways, etc. have formed their primary spatial locus. But, as mentioned above, sizeable tracts of commercially developed land, traditionally seen as 'public' spaces and therefore subject to public forms of authority, are now increasingly leased to and controlled by private, corporate interests (Crawford 2011). It would be unsurprising if such developments did not generate uncertainty among some citizens, unsure of the legitimate authority of those private guards policing such areas. If this holds true, then the growing spatial complexity of land patterns, and the knowledge deficits that may arise, are likely to harbour problematic implications for democratic notions of policing.

### Redress

How the malpractice of individual policing agents is dealt with is a key question in any system of accountability. Where an individual has been wronged then there should be access to a formal and external procedure to ensure that grievance is investigated and acted on accordingly. The importance of this principle is reflected, both at rhetorical and practical levels, by police officers being held accountable to the criminal law for their actions when on duty. Whilst formal complaints mechanisms are now an established part of the police accountability framework in England and Wales, these have yet to develop comprehensively in the field of plural policing. For example, there are no such procedures of redress for private and volunteer-based forms of plural policing, raising concerns of unaccountable vigilante groups (Johnston 1992). Although the licensing procedures discussed above, introduced for contracted private security actors, do offer a means for redress where required standards of conduct have been breached, their effectiveness, for instance, to remove rogue elements from the industry by refusing or revoking licences is limited (White and Smith 2009). Indeed, there is some evidence to show that citizens do not readily complain to external bodies about the conduct of private security actors when the circumstances indicate they have strong grounds to do so (Lister *et al.* 2000). Furthermore, the types of surveillance and order-maintenance that have arisen within many of the quasi-public spaces policed by private actors may herald a more invasive approach to citizen privacy than traditionally apply in other spatial contexts. Contracted private security guards derive considerable de facto legal powers from property law, which allows them to exclude people or subject visitors to random searches of their possessions before entering premises such as football stadia, nightclubs and airport terminals. A key concern of critics here is the absence of formal restrictions on the exercise of this private authority coupled with the limited nature of the external accountability relations that govern its use (Reiner 2010). Institutional mechanisms of democratic accountability have not kept pace with these trends, leading to debates about exacerbating 'democratic deficits'.

Whilst these observations suggest the public police meet this criteria more than other sectors of policing, significantly the police complaints system has been dogged by perceptions of inefficiency and ineffectiveness, resulting in a succession of 'failed' watchdog bodies (Smith 2006). Further, notwithstanding the recent infusion of private sector management principles within the public police, in all but fairly serious incidents of misconduct it remains bureaucratically and legally complex to remove or dismiss a police officer for wrongdoing. By contrast, it can be argued that market disciplines pressurise commercial policing bodies to be more responsive in this regard than existing state arrangements. For example, an inefficient or ineffective security company can expect to lose its contract with the purchaser, and individual security officers who underperform or misbehave can expect to be sacked. In this respect lay narratives of policing, which commonly draw a sharp distinction between 'accountable' public police officers and 'unaccountable' private security guards, tend to be overstated.

## *Participation*

Various authors have argued that plural policing can provide great opportunity for community participation in the organisation and delivery of security. In particular, Shearing and colleagues have described innovative forms of community self-governance in less advantaged communities such as the 'peace committees' of Zwelethemba in South Africa (Wood and Shearing 2007). A fundamental advantage claimed for such arrangements is that they closely reflect the requirements of local people, and involve them in deliberative decision-making about potential solutions to security (and other) problems. This argument stems from the recognition that contractually governed forms of policing have a 'client-defined' mandate: they purposefully serve first, foremost and arguably exclusively, the interests of the paying customer. This, however, is something of a double-edged sword. Whilst it may enable 'consumers' of policing to have their voices heard, equally it risks the likelihood of an accountability deficit for those non-participants who may nonetheless experience negative consequences of the arrangement. Crawford and Lister (2006) found such evidence in their study of a privately paid, public policing initiative in northern England. They reported how residents in an adjacent area to this initiative felt that they had suffered a loss of policing as a result of the police being contractually bound to provide an additional level of resources to the area covered by the contract. Furthermore, these 'non-participating' residents also perceived that crime and disorder had been displaced into their village as a result of the greater policing presence in their neighbours' area. As such, beneficiaries of commercial policing tend to be a narrowly constructed group, which may generate tensions with those who are excluded (Loader 2000; Zedner 2009).

## Responding to the democratic governance challenge of plural policing

The pluralised nature of contemporary policing brings both challenges and opportunities for democratic governance. From the above discussion, it offers some potential opportunities for enhancing the democratic content of security governance. For example, community forms of security governance 'from below' may extend participation in the organisation of local policing and render its impacts more equitable; market choice may provide real alternatives in cases of ineffective or unjust policing; and contractual forms of market regulation may offer a much more direct form of accountability than traditional institutional mechanisms are able to deliver. However, at the same time pluralisation raises particular concerns of inequitable distribution of policing, potential confusion about the functions and legal powers of different policing bodies, and threats to effective service delivery due to lack of coordination and duplication of functions. The central challenge, however, concerns the fact that there are no institutional mechanisms for rendering local patchworks of security governance responsive to democratic direction and oversight.

Structures of governance and accountability within the web of policing – mirroring formations of policing – are dispersed, fragmented and splintered. Hence, institutionalised practices of account giving are mostly compartmentalised, segmented and bureaucratically aligned (Crawford and Lister 2006).[2] Moreover, many of the accountability relations within these networks are not 'public' in that they are neither transparent to the public, nor involve 'public' sector bodies. Indeed, the contracts governing commercially arranged policing initiatives are frequently subject to commercial confidentiality clauses, shrouding normative assessments of their compatibility with the public interest. It is therefore important to underline the need to establish holistic mechanisms of oversight and accountability, which connect policing networks with democratic structures. Democratically accountable policing should be 'congruent with the values of the community in which it works and responsive to the discrepancies when they are pointed out' (Bayley 1983: 146). Not only must we develop ways of subjecting policing authorisers and providers other than the state and public police to regulation and control, but in addition 'plural policing has to be assessed as a whole, in terms of its complexly interconnected practice and impact' (Walker 2000: 280). Yet, as different providers within policing networks tend to be subject to different regulatory regimes, there is no single point of governance of the networks' various nodes. As a consequence, there is no oversight mechanism for the totality of 'nodal policing' in any given locale. This is not to argue that plural policing networks are completely unaccountable and unregulated: elements of such networks clearly do operate with varying degrees of accountability to different audiences. It remains the case, however, that under current institutional arrangements in England and Wales there are no formal mechanisms for rendering plural policing networks as a whole accountable to democratic values.

One possible way forward, and one that acknowledges the changed landscape of contemporary security governance whilst reasserting the notion of security as a public good, has been put forward by Loader (2000). He suggests the establishment of significant new accountability institutions – Policing Commissions – to take responsibility for coordinating and monitoring the range of bodies involved in policing and security provision at the local, regional and national levels. Such Commissions would be democratically driven and inclusive, with part of the membership being directly elected, but the other part appointed to ensure adequate representation from a range of social groups. The proposed Policing Commissions would have a formidable range of powers and functions, including the role formulating and coordinating policy, licensing security providers, subsidising extra provision in under-serviced areas, and the monitoring and evaluation of standards. They would have a statutory responsibility to ensure that all citizens receive a 'fair' share of policing services, which would require attention both to over-policing and under-protection of particular social groups.

These proposals appear to offer an imaginative way forward for promoting the effective involvement of local community knowledge and capacities in security governance. They also offer the possibility of public, democratic fora that can provide more effective coordination of the complex networks of security governance. In so doing, they could promote more equitable provision that balances the demands of security against those of other valued social goods. The proposals have been supported by Crawford *et al.* (2005) following their empirical study of plural policing in various parts of England and Wales. They argue it is at the regional level that such Commissions might have most impact. Operating at this scale, Commissions could not only balance the competing pressures of local and national interests so evident in the push and pull of policing policy, but also provide oversight of the diverse range of policing and community safety agencies operating across local authority and current police force boundaries. In addition, it would align better with any shift towards regional police forces, whilst closely mapping the jurisdiction of Commissions to the regional bases of the corporate private security industry.

Alternatively, and in the absence of any new institutional architecture, such as policing commissions described above, it might be plausible to hand responsibility for regulating local plural policing networks to elected Police and Crime Commissioners (PCCs) (Crawford 2013), a powerful democratic institution operating at local and regional levels. There is a logic to this suggestion, not least as PCCs already have responsibility for the oversight and accountability of 'policing by the police', and moreover are required by law to work with local community safety partners to produce holistic and coordinated responses to crime and disorder. This option, however, raises both normative and practical concerns.

First, serious doubts remain about the design of this model of governance (Jones *et al.* 2012). By definition PCCs are 'Police' commissioners, not 'Policing' commissioners (Loader 2013; Crawford 2013), suggesting a narrow focus to the role that is reinforced by the relevant legislation defining the 'totality' of local policing for which they have responsibility solely in terms of those resources controlled by the Chief Constable (Lister and Rowe 2014). Whilst legislative reform could address this conceptual shortcoming, the wind of political pressure to expand the role of PCCs is blowing forcefully towards it subsuming responsibility for other criminal justice institutions and emergency services rather than regulating non-police providers of policing (Home Office, 2010; May 2013). Second, there remains a broader concern that PCCs stand outside the established local system of public service administration. This is likely to restrict the capacity of PCCs to engage and influence the range of public policy domains (e.g. housing, education, youth services, health, etc.) under the auspices of which plural policing initiatives are arranged and delivered. As a consequence, to be effective, PCCs would need to overcome significant administrative and organisational barriers were they to gain this responsibility. Third, as PCCS are 'commissioners' of *policing* services it follows that they ought not to be tasked with regulating the market within which they are significant participants. Just as Loader (2000) suggests the police – as providers of policing services – should not be given responsibility for rendering accountable other providers within the network, so it is normatively unsustainable for a purchaser within the marketplace to have this overarching responsibility. Indeed, as we have stressed throughout this chapter, purchaser/provider accountability arrangements tend to be narrow, insular and structured to serve parochial interests less so commonplace, public interests. As such, in our view, any new institutional architecture designed to regulate marketised networks of policing ought to have administrative separation from the market and its participants. Fourth, such an option would reflect a wholly state-centric model of regulation, which acting alone may be unable to address the fundamental problem of asserting democratic leverage over 'private government'. As open 'public spaces' are increasingly located within privately owned or managed land, and legal rulings during the past decade or so have confirmed the power of corporations to organise and undertake security provision themselves, then making them responsive to or compliant with democratic principles may be an uphill struggle. In short, PCCs have no more legal authority over the operation of private policing in mass private property than did local police authorities and chief constables under the former system of police governance. For this reason, and following Stenning

(2009), it seems logical to suggest that any regulatory framework for policing ought to comprise a plurality of organisational modes. Bringing together multi-lateral representation from different sectors would also address the age-old concern that the governance of policing should not be rendered accountable to, and thus risk being 'captured' by, any one single locus of democratic, political authority (Lustgarten 1986).

Despite the challenges and opportunities brought by the pluralisation and marketisation of policing, concerns over the absence of any external regulator of market-led policing networks remain largely confined to the academy. Yet the need for such institutional innovation is likely to become more pressing with the continued impact of austerity policies on the further fragmentation of policing. Sizeable cuts to police budgets have already led to substantial reductions in the numbers of police officers and PCSOs, and government ministers have indicated that further expenditure reductions will be imposed on public police forces over the period of the current parliament. At the same time, austerity policies have reduced the capacity of the local state to fund the purchase of commercial and municipal forms of visible patrol. Partly as a result of these developments, polic-ing forms 'below government' (in the form of provision by voluntary, com-munity and faith-based groups) appear to have been increasing both in scale and diversity (Jones and Lister 2015). The accountability challenges raised by plu-ralisation are thus likely to become more rather than less daunting in future years.

## Conclusions

The growth of multilateral, local security networks reflects the shifting nature of responsibility for policing and community safety between the market, civil society and the state. Their proliferation raises a number of conceptual, empiri-cal and normative questions that have far-reaching implications for security gov-ernance. As we have suggested, they give rise to a series of what we might term 'constitutional issues' over how we can govern these networks in ways that ensure they function in ways that accord with democratic principles. To this end, our primary aim in this chapter has been to steer debates towards the challenges of aligning the order of plural policing to a set of democratic criteria. In so doing, we have drawn caution to the role of the market in ordering the patterns and practices of plural policing. This is not to argue that plural policing cannot deliver socially desirable goals, such as improved security for local neighbour-hoods, but, rather, we suggest an unregulated market for policing services may be counterproductive to securing social justice. As we have described, this is an area within policing scholarship which is beginning to emerge from the long shadow cast by the state provision of policing and security; it is also one that has given rise to rich theoretical and practical debate. On one view, for example, the growth of plural policing networks provides the possibilities for a more just and accountable provision of security (Johnston and Shearing 2003; Wood and Shearing 2007). On the other hand, the proliferation of policing authorisers and providers raises concerns amongst other authors, not least in terms of the potential for exacerbating social exclusion and polarisation (Crawford and Lister 2006; Reiner 2010; Jones 2012). Within these debates, however, there is consensus for plural policing networks to be subjected to democratic processes of regulation in order to ensure their arrangement and provision attends to the public good. As Stenning has argued, how this is to be achieved in terms of designing suitable institutional architecture will require not only sophisticated theoretical modelling, but also persuasive and impactful arguments that are able to mobilise the necessary political resources behind the cause.

## Notes

1 The authors wish to acknowledge that this chapter has benefitted significantly from discussions with Ronald van Steden.
2 An important recent exception to this has been introduced by the Anti-social Behaviour, Crime and Policing Act 2014. Section 135 of the Act extends the remit of the Independent Police Complaints Commission to private sector actors who are contracted by the police to provide services (e.g. detention officers).

## References

Association of Chief Police Officers (ACPO) (2011) *A Survey of Employers Involved in the Community Safety Accreditation Scheme*, London: ACPO.

Baberis, P. (1998) 'The New Public Management and a New Accountability', *Public Administration*, 76: 451–70.

Bayley, D. (1983) 'Accountability and Control of the Police: Lessons from Britain', in T. Bennett (ed.) *The Future of Policing*, Cambridge: Cambridge University Press.

Bayley, D. and Shearing, C. (1996) 'The Future of Policing', *Law and Society Review*, 20(3): 585–606.

Bayley, D. and Shearing, C. (2001) *The New Structure of Policing*, Washington, DC: National Institute of Justice.

Blair, I. (2003) *Leading Towards the Future*, speech to 'The Future of Policing Conference', 10 October, London School of Economics.

Bovens, M. (2005) 'Public Accountability', in E. Ferlie, L.E. Lynn and C. Pollitt (eds) *The Oxford Handbook of Public Management*, Oxford: Oxford University Press, 182–208.

Brodeur, J.-P. (2010) *The Policing Web*, Oxford: Oxford University Press.

Button, M. (2002) *Private Policing*, Cullompton, Devon: Willan Publishing.

Button, M. (2007) *Security Officers and Policing*, Aldershot: Ashgate.

Cohen, S. (1985) *Visions of Social Control*, Cambridge: Polity Press.

Crawford, A. (2007) 'Reassurance Policing: Feeling is Believing', in A. Henry and D.J. Smith (eds) *Transformations of Policing*, Aldershot: Ashgate, 143–68.

Crawford, A. (2008) 'The Pattern of Policing in the UK: Policing beyond the Police', in T. Newburn (ed.) *The Handbook of Policing* (2nd edn), Cullompton, Devon: Willan, 136–68.

Crawford, A. (2011) 'From the Shopping Mall to the Street Corner: Dynamics of Exclusion in the Governance of Public Space', in A. Crawford (ed.) *International and Comparative Criminal Justice and Urban Governance*, Cambridge: Cambridge University Press, 483–518.

Crawford, A. (2013) 'The Police, Policing and the Future of the "Extended Police Family"', in J. Brown (ed.) *The Future of Policing*, London: Routledge, 173–190.

Crawford, A. and Lister, S. (2004) *The Extended Policing Family: Visible Patrols in Residential Areas*, York: Joseph Rowntree Foundation.

Crawford, A. and Lister, S. (2006) 'Additional Security Patrols in Residential Areas: Notes from the Marketplace', *Policing and Society*, 16(2): 164–88.

Crawford, A., Lister, S., Blackburn, S. and Burnett, J. (2005) *Plural Policing: The Mixed Economy of Visible Security Patrols*, Bristol: Policy Press.

Dupont, B. (2004) 'Security in the Age of Networks', *Policing and Society*, 14(1): 76–91.

Garland, D. (2001) *The Culture of Control*, Oxford: Oxford University Press.

Greve, C. (2008) *Contracting for Public Services*, London: Routledge.

Home Office (2001) *Policing a New Century: A Blueprint for Reform*, London: Home Office.

Home Office (2010) *Policing in the 21st Century: Reconnecting Police and the People*, London: Home Office.

Johnston, L. (1992) *The Rebirth of Private Policing*, London: Routledge.

Johnston, L. (2007) 'Transnational Security Governance', in J. Wood and B. Dupont (eds) *Democracy, Society and the Governance of Security*, Cambridge: Cambridge University Press, 33–51.

Johnston, L. and Shearing, C. (2003) *Governing Security*, London: Routledge.

Jones, T. (2012) 'Governing Security: Pluralization, Privatization, and Polarization in Crime Control and Policing', in M. Maguire, R. Morgan and R. Reiner (eds) *The Oxford Handbook of Criminology* (5th edn), Oxford: Oxford University Press, 743–68.

Jones, T. and Lister, S. (2015) 'The Policing of Public Space: Recent Developments in Plural Policing in England and Wales', *European Journal of Policing Studies*, 2(3): 245–66.

Jones, T. and Newburn, T. (1997) *Policing After the Act: Police Governance after the Police and Magistrates' Courts Act 1994*, London: Policy Studies Institute.

Jones, T. and Newburn, T. (1998) *Private Security and Public Policing*, Oxford: Clarendon Press.

Jones, T. and Newburn, T. (2001) *Widening Access: Improving Police Relations with Hard to Reach Groups*, Police Research Series Paper 138, London: Home Office.

Jones, T., Newburn, T. and Smith, D.J. (1996) 'Policing and the Idea of Democracy', *British Journal of Criminology*, 36(2): 182–98.

Jones, T., Newburn, T. and Smith, D (2012) 'Democracy and Police and Crime Commissioners', in T. Newburn and J. Peay (eds) *Policing: Politics, Culture and Control*, Oxford: Hart, 219–44.

Keith, M. (1988) 'Squaring the circles? Consultation and Inner-city Policing', *New Community*, 15(1): 63–77.

Lea, J. and Stenson, K. (2007) 'Security, Sovereignty, and Non-State Governance "From Below"', *Canadian Journal of Law and Society*, 22(2): 9–27.

Lister, S. (2007) 'Plural Policing, Local Communities and the Market in Visible Patrols', in A. Dearling T. Newburn and P. Somerville (eds) *Supporting Safe Communities: Housing, crime and communities*, London: Chartered Institute of Housing, 95–113.

Lister, S. and Rowe, M. (2014) 'Electing Police and Crime Commissioners in England and Wales: Prospecting for the Democratisation of Policing', *Policing and Society*, online access.

Lister, S., Hobbs, D., Hall, S. and Winlow, S. (2000) 'Violence in the Night-Time Economy; Bouncers: The Reporting, Recording and Prosecution of Assaults', *Policing and Society*, 10(4): 383–402.

Loader, I. (2000) 'Plural Policing and Democratic Governance', *Social and Legal Studies*, 9: 323–45.

Loader, I. (2013) 'Why do the Police Matter? Beyond the Myth of Crime-fighting', in J. Brown (ed.) *The Future of Policing*, London: Routledge, 40–51.

Lustgarten, L. (1986) *The Governance of the Police*, London: Sweet & Maxwell.

McLaughlin, E. (2005) 'Forcing the Issue: New Labour, New Localism and the Democratic Renewal of Police Accountability', *The Howard Journal*, 44(5): 473–89.

Manning, P. (2011) *Democratic Policing in a Changing World*, Boulder, CO: Paradigm.

Mashaw, J.L. (2006) 'Accountability and Institutional Design: Some Thoughts on the Grammar of Governance', in M.W. Dowdle (ed.) *Public Accountability: Designs, Dilemmas and Experiences*, Cambridge: Cambridge University Press, 115–57.

May, T. (2013) *Police and Crime Commissioners, One Year on: Warts and All*, speech to Policy Exchange, 7 November 2013, available at www.gov.uk/government/speeches/police-and-crime-commissioners-one-year-on-warts-and-all (last accessed 13 January 2015).

Minton, A. (2012) *Ground Control: Fear and Happiness in the Twenty-first Century City* (2nd edn), London: Penguin.

Moran, M. (2001) 'The Rise of the Regulatory State in Britain', *Parliamentary Affairs*, 54(1): 19–34.

Mulgan, R. (1997) 'The Process of Public Accountability', *Australian Journal of Public Administration*, 56(1): 25–36.

NACRO (2003) *Eyes and Ears: The Role of Neighbourhood Wardens*, London: National Association for the Care and Resettlement of Offenders.

Noaks, L. (2000) 'Private Cops on the Block: A Review of the Role of Private Security in Residential Communities', *Policing and Society*, 10(2): 143–61.

Osborne, D. and Gaebler, T. (1992) *Reinventing Government: How the Entrepreneurial Spirit is Transforming the Public Sector*, Reading, MA: Addison-Wesley.

Reiner, R. (1993) 'Police Accountability: Principles, Patterns and Practices', in R. Reiner and S. Spencer (eds) *Accountable Policing: Effectiveness, Empowerment and Equality*, London: Institute for Public Policy Research, 1–23.

Reiner, R. (1995) 'Counting the Coppers: Accountability in Policing', in P. Stenning *Accountability for Criminal Justice*, Toronto: University of Toronto Press, 74–92.

Reiner, R. (2010) *The Politics of the Police* (4th edn), Oxford: Oxford University Press.

Rhodes, R.A.W. (1997) *Understanding Governance: Policy Networks, Governance, Reflexivity, and Accountability*, Milton Keynes: Open University Press.

Rigakos, G. (2002) *The New Parapolice: Risk Markets and Commodified Social Control*, Toronto: University of Toronto Press.

Rose, N. (2000) 'Government and Control', *British Journal of Criminology*, 40(2): 321–39.

Rose, N. and Miller, P. (1992) 'Political Power Beyond the State: Problematics of Government', *British Journal of Sociology*, 43(2): 173–205.

Sarre, R. and Prenzler, T. (2005) *The Law of Private Security in Australia*, Sydney: Lawbook.

Shearing, C. (2006) 'Reflections on the Refusal to Acknowledge Private Governments', in J. Wood and B. Dupont (eds) *Democracy, Society and the Governance of Security*, Cambridge: Cambridge University Press, 11–32.

Shearing, C. and Stenning, P. (1981) 'Modern Private Security: Its Growth and Implications', *Crime and Justice: An Annual Review of Research*, 3: 193–245.

Shearing, C. and Stenning, P. (1983) 'Private Security: Implications for Social Control', *Social Problems*, 30(5): 493–505.

Smith, G. (2006) 'A Most Enduring Problem: Police Complaints Reform in England and Wales, *Journal of Social Policy*, 35(1): 121–41.

Stenning, P. (2000) 'Powers and Accountability of Private Police', *European Journal on Criminal Policy and Research*, 8(3): 325–52.

Stenning, P. (2009) 'Governance and Accountability in a Plural Policing Environment – the Story So Far', *Policing: A Journal of Policy and Practice*, 3(1): 22–33.

Stenning, P. and Shearing, C. (1980) 'The Quiet Revolution: The Nature, Development and General Legal Implications of Private Policing in Canada', *Criminal Law Quarterly*, 22: 220–48.

Terpstra, J., van Stokkom, B. and Spreeuwers, R. (2013) *Who Patrols the Streets?*, The Hague: Eleven International Publishing.

Trebilcock, M.J. and Iacobucci, E.M. (2003) 'Privatisation and Accountability', *Harvard Law Review*, 116: 1422–53.

van Steden, R. (2007) *Privatizing Policing: Describing and Explaining the Growth of Private Security*, Amsterdam: BJU Publishers.

Van Swaaningen, R. (2005) 'Public Safety and the Management of Fear', *Theoretical Criminology*, 9(3): 289–305.

Wakefield, A. (2003) *Selling Security: The Private Policing of Public Space*, Cullompton, Devon: Willan.

Walker, N. (2000) *Policing in a Changing Constitutional Order*, London: Sweet & Maxwell.

White, A. (2010) *The Politics of Private Security: Regulation, Reform and Re-Legitimation*, Basingstoke: Palgrave Macmillan.

White, A. and Smith, M. (2009) *The Security Industry Authority: A Baseline Review*, Sheffield: University of Sheffield, available at www.sia.homeoffice.gov.uk/Documents/research/sia_baseline_review.pdf (last accessed 14 August 2014).

Wood, J. and Shearing, C. (2007) *Imagining Security*, Cullompton, Devon: Willan.

Zedner, L. (2006) 'Policing Before and After the Police: The Historical Antecedents of Contemporary Crime Control', *British Journal of Criminology*, 46(1): 78–96.

Zedner, L. (2009) *Security*, London: Routledge.

# 11  Reflections on legal and political accountability for global policing

*Ben Bowling and James Sheptycki*

Academics in all domains are currently under pressure to demonstrate the 'impact' of their scholarly endeavours – beyond such things as number of publications, citations and the like – which gives rise to perplexity in some areas as to how 'impact' may be measured. Under such conditions, it is well to maintain a stoic outlook. Indeed because of the inherent absurdity of the situation, where academic institutions manage knowledge production in the same manner and with the same enthusiasm as the experimentalists at the Hawthorne Electric Plant once did, an existentialist outlook is an even stronger philosophical foundation. We therefore begin here by recalling the words of Albert Camus, at the end of *The Myth of Sisyphus*, to wit:

> The gods had condemned Sisyphus to ceaselessly rolling a rock to the top of a mountain, whence the stone would fall back of its own weight. They had thought with some reason that there is no more dreadful punishment than futile and hopeless labour.... I leave Sisyphus at the foot of the mountain! One always finds one's burden again. But Sisyphus teaches the higher fidelity that negates the gods and raises rocks. He too concludes that all is well. This universe henceforth without a master seems to him neither sterile nor futile. Each atom of that stone, each mineral flake of that night filled mountain, in itself forms a world. The struggle itself toward the heights is enough to fill a man's heart. One must imagine Sisyphus happy.
>
> (Albert Camus 1942, *The Myth of Sisyphus*)

We began our book *Global Policing* (2012) with a story about the travails of a man named Derek Bond. Mr Bond was the unfortunate victim of mistaken identity who ended up spending three weeks incarcerated in Durban, South Africa, trapped in the Kafkaesque world of transnational policing. During his penal holiday, he had no way of appealing or inquiring as to the reasons and evidence underlying his condition. He and his hapless family were lost in a welter of transnational police communications between the FBI, Interpol, the South African Police Service and others. In the end he had no effective means of redress, nor was it clear who was to blame. A local police agency in Las Vegas or Texas? The FBI? Interpol? The South African Police Service? We used the case of Mr Bond to make the point that anybody could become the subject of transnational policing and emphasised that, more often, it is people suffering 'structural disadvantage' who do so in their legions.

Our theory of global policing went on to suggest that it is legitimated, by and large, through a discourse about suitable enemies; an array of folk devils who constitute reasons for allowing policing power to extend, largely unfettered, across the globe. We argued that there is a theoretical object that we call the transnational subculture of policing. While acknowledging that there are important differences in policing culture in Mumbai and Montreal, Tbilisi and Toronto, Cape Town and Calgary we also suggest that there is an important 'family resemblance' between policing agents everywhere. Police agents have an almost tribal affinity behind the 'thin blue line'. This is attested to in the police custom of 'patching'. When police officers go abroad on vacation, they sometimes bring with them the patches or emblems of their own organisation which they exchange with brethren in the countries they are visiting. Visit any police headquarters and one will usually find on display symbolic paraphernalia from other agencies around the world, displayed with pride – perhaps in the corridor just outside the Chief Officer's office or in the reception area where more visitor traffic ensures a greater audience of appreciation.

There is also a subculture of transnational policing. Here we refer to what Robert Reiner (2010: 7) (evidently inspired by Rosa Luxemburg) called the 'new internationale of technocratic police experts' who patrol the globe disseminating the fads and fashions necessary for a constantly innovating police professionalism. These are numerous and constantly changing: 'community policing', 'zero tolerance policing', 'intelligence-led policing', 'reassurance policing', 'pulling levers policing', and 'pushing buttons policing'. We made the last one up, but the others are in circulation among the personnel who make up the subculture of transnational policing. One can read all about them in the literature. These transnational technocratic police experts have important effects on policing at the local level, and that is why the transnational subculture of policing is becoming more homogenous, despite the residual variation. This interactive process between the transnational subculture of policing and the subculture of transnational policing contributes to and 'makes up' Global Policing.

The values and norms of police subculture are significantly shaped by a 'law enforcement' and 'crime control' discourse which projects, as we have already said, images of suitable enemies. We do not deny that, under conditions of globalisation, there are a great many people who seek to profit from other people's misery and by the misuse of power. The capacity to muster coercion to the detriment of human rights is an undeniable feature of the global social order. However, we also suggest that the conventional pantheon of folk devils used to justify and legitimate the emergent patterns of global policing are an inadequate description of the ailments plaguing the global system. There certainly are problems worthy of a global policing response, but talk of narco-terrorists and the 'Mr Bigs' of transnational organised crime should be regarded for what it is: a highly rhetorical discourse of legitimation. Criticism of this rhetoric is an important step in bringing global policing to account.

In this essay we would like to move beyond the critique of global policing rhetoric and reflect upon the way in which global policing is politically and legally accountable and to try to advance thinking a bit further by considering how it ought to be. This is a task for Sisyphus. For one thing, regulating global policing in order to ensure that it is broadly responsive to the world commonwealth is extremely difficult because our standard model for structuring police accountability is so ill-fitting.

## Accountability and the architecture of transnational policing

In *Global Policing* (2012) we developed the metaphor of an 'architecture of transnational policing'. Observing that there is no headquarters for the global police and that global policing was, in actuality, a complex concatenation of institutions, it is very difficult to outline a system for its political and legal accountability (see also Loader 2002; Sheptycki 2002). First of all, and following the important scholarship of people like Johnston and Shearing (2003) and Bayley and Shearing (1996), we noted that policing is undertaken by a variety of institutions which work under either private or state-based auspices or sometimes a hybrid of the two. Second, and following Jean-Paul Brodeur (1983) we noted that 'high policing' is often undertaken on behalf of political interests characterised using the terms of state sovereignty, and (to add to the confusion) that 'high policing' may also serve the private interests of particular economic elites. Then we noted the peculiar 'glocal' nature of policing; that even when it pertains to practices at the local level, it often entails transnational or global influences (not least those brought to bear by international police liaison officers or through transnational communications linkages of one kind or another). The architecture of transnational policing is sometimes presented in terms of a rational hierarchy, a rank-structured bureaucracy, but as Mathiew Deflem (2000, 2002) correctly points out, transnational police agencies, and even police agencies firmly embedded within sovereign states, have a significant degree of bureaucratic semi-autonomy. When this complex concatenation of global policing is looked at in its entirety, the architecture does not resemble a rank-structured bureaucracy of the Weberian kind at all. To use a fashionable term from postmodern cultural theory, the structure is *rhizomic* (Deleuze and Guattari 1993). That is why the 'standard model' for policing accountability, which rests on notions of local democratic control, the separation of powers, rule of law, etc. seems so ill-fitting.

The trouble is that our conventional models for structuring the political and legal accountability of policing are modern ones. They are precisely predicated on the assumption that Max Weber made about the nature of the sovereign state: that it is a monopoly provider of institutional social ordering over a given territory. This basic assumption underlies traditional thinking about the relationship between law and the state and is why the American legal theorist John Austin could scoff at the very notion of 'international law' because to him (and in common with much Hobbesian thinking about the nature of the world system) law is the 'command of the sovereign'. Given that, the global system is a poly-centric power grid where there is no single sovereign to command, where a variety of competing power players vie for their own interests, our traditional modernist assumption about political and legal accountability – that 'the buck' needs to stop somewhere – simply does not apply.

## Global policing as a synecdoche of the global system

In *Global Policing* (2012) we argued that the object of our study was far more interesting than what is conventionally described by criminologists. We suggested that global policing was, in fact, a synecdoche of the global system. That is to say, transnational policing is the precondition for the world system as we know it. Transnational policing practice offers particular examples of global governance generally. It is a part of the global system without which the systemic whole could not exist. In general, it prescribes all the particular features of global governance that hold together the global system *as a system*. As such, the study of global policing is interesting to political sociologists, social theorists, human geographers and so on, as much as it is to criminologists narrowly defined. It follows that global policing must be a central feature of any socio-legal theory pertaining to globalisation and that inevitably brings us to the topic that concerns us here, namely its political and legal accountability.

The difficulty is that the details of the institutional matrix of global policing (including such supranational institutions as Interpol and Europol, national police agencies, private security companies and so forth) and their relationship with other institutions of governance (including, among others, the United Nations and the European Union) and institutions of legal decision-making (including, at the supranational level, the International Criminal Court and the International Court of Justice – with their limited functional and jurisdictional remits – and, at the domestic level, the courts systems embedded within sovereign states) tends to discourage all but the most resolute. It is easy to get lost in the detail.

Many aspects of the global system that evolved during the modern period did so radically towards the end of the twentieth century. International law and political organisation were far from being the only drivers of this transformation. As several visionaries of the nineteenth and twentieth centuries foresaw, technological progress leads to cultural, economic and social-structural change. The result was, in Marshall McLuhan's term of art, a 'global village'. The trouble has been that the village consists of quite a number of dysfunctional 'families' (i.e. nation states), some of whom are not on speaking terms with each other, if not openly hostile. This dysfunctional hostility affects both people who reside within the household confines of sovereign state territories and neighbouring peoples. Hence the call for global policing, but the problem of its political and legal accountability is acutely felt because police agents are either a part of the problem or part of the solution to 'situations that ought not to be happening and about which someone had better do something now' (Bittner, quoted in Brodeur 2007). Consequently, a practical problem, as well as a theoretical one, is how to make global policing accountable for the sake of the global commonwealth.

## Some possible ways of bringing global policing to account

So how can global policing be made accountable? Here we draw inspiration from den Boer *et al.* (2008) who look at the sources of democratic, legal and social legitimacy of security actors in relation to various forms of accountability. Democratic legitimacy is indicated by the scrutiny of governmental legislators, for example parliaments, who seek control of such matters as appointments, policy plans and budgets. Legal legitimacy derives from binding legal instruments that clarify inter alia, the jurisdiction, mandate, means, procedures, procedural safeguards and complaint mechanisms. Finally, social legitimacy is indicated by transparency through public reporting, independent monitoring and citizen consultation.

Perhaps political accountability could be achieved under the auspices of the United Nations. With its broad membership of states (currently 193), it is the most inclusive intergovernmental 'club' and it might be hoped that it could begin to show the way in upholding human rights. However, while the UN General Assembly approved the Universal Declaration of Human Rights in 1948, it is not technically a binding international treaty even though it has the sanctity of being part of the UN Charter. True, in 1966 two formal treaties concerning human rights were adopted – one of economic, social and cultural rights and the other on civil and political rights – but their negotiation was far from easy. There remain many instances of hypocrisy where some state parties are quick to criticise their adversaries and eager to hide their own malpractice. The United States, for example, will not allow international NGOs into the US prisons to observe if the regime conforms to human rights norms and continues to practise the death penalty (even, in some notorious cases, when it involves individuals who demonstratively do not have the capacity for adult reasoning). At the same time US officials are quick to lecture other countries, for example Iran, for their abuse of human rights. In the end, it is no surprise that the formal powers of the 'international community' (as it is embodied in the institutions of the United Nations) to bring global policing issues to account have proved to be limited.

This can be regarded as a particular disappointment, since the United Nations has a policing capacity of its own. UNPOL, the UN Police, are typically deployed alongside military personnel in 'peacekeeping' operations and sometimes operate as special advisors in UN political missions. UNPOL has been put in a position where it may back up domestic police and they are supposed to help promote peace, public safety and the rule of law. In the early years of the twenty-first century it has been expanded rapidly and the roles expected of it are multi-dimensional (reflecting the multifunctional nature of policing generally). Here the record is mixed at best. The United Nations has used its institutional capacity to undertake many peacekeeping missions and perhaps the majority of these efforts have had some measure of success. On the other hand, there are widespread examples of malpractice and incompetence. UN Peacekeepers have been accused of war crimes, child rape and sexual abuse, as well as mission failure.

This mixed record is partly a failure of models and practices of police professionalism and partly a failure of the systems for legal and political accountability (Goldsmith and Sheptycki 2007). In terms of the political, legal and social accountability framework of analysis set out by den Boer *et al.* (2008), the United Nations and the UNPOL can be considered, at best, a qualified failure. In political accountability terms, these efforts have foundered on the rock of the principle of national sovereignty. Legal accountability is left swirling in the whirlpool of legal-pluralistic relativism seemingly bereft of commonly agreed upon norms, values and principles. Social legitimacy, meanwhile, is sunk in an awareness of the palpable failures of UN peacekeeping and police missions rather than being buoyed up by any evidence of positive achievement (Dobbins *et al.* 2005).

Perhaps global policing could be made accountable by being brought under the umbrella of 'Brand Interpol' (Sheptycki forthcoming). However, Interpol has a high degree of institutional autonomy, even while its operational powers are limited (Sheptycki 2004). Constitutionally, it is not founded on a legal treaty or any other analogous kind of legal instrument. It is in effect a police 'club', not a compact between nation states. Paradoxically it has attained the status of an International Governmental Organisation (IGO). Interpol is governed by a General Assembly and Executive Committee, and effectively funded by taxpayers, but voting members and members of its executive are unelected police bureaucrats who are not answerable to the 'general public' however one might construe the notion. Its senior officials cannot be fired, cannot be sued for acts undertaken under the agency's banner and have full diplomatic immunity (even in retirement). Currently there are moves to create an 'Interpol Passport' for liaison officers working in foreign jurisdictions, which would bring global diplomatic immunity to these particular transnational police agents. The organisation enjoys a high level of public awareness (albeit one based more on myth than fact), and its website offers a wide range of information, lending it an appreciable degree of social legitimacy. Nonetheless, of the ten IGOs surveyed in *Global Accountability Report* for 2007, Interpol came bottom of the league table in terms of overall accountability (Lloyd *et al.* 2007). That report commented on Interpol's transparency, noting that the organisation is involved in crime control, a 'generally closed and secretive [activity] traditionally dominated by states and not open to civil society involvement'. In sum, any social legitimacy the organisation may claim belies its substantive lack of political and legal accountability.

Interpol's lack of formal legal and political accountability, together with its apparently high degree of social legitimacy, combined with the evident weaknesses of the United Nations as the basis for democratic global governance is especially troubling given that, in October 2009, the *New York Times* reported that 'Interpol and the United Nations are poised to become partners in fighting crime by jointly grooming a global police force' (Carvajal 2009). This global police force 'would be deployed as peacekeepers among rogue nations riven by war and organized crime'. After a meeting of justice and foreign ministers from 60 countries, including the USA and China, jointly hosted by Interpol and the UN Police division 'the first step toward creating a "global policing doctrine"' was announced. Ronald K. Noble, secretary general of Interpol, said 'We have a visionary model ... police will be trained and equipped differently with resources. When they stop someone, they will be consulting global databases to determine who they are stopping'. Given that a global policing doctrine seems to be increasingly likely, perhaps the requisite legal accountability should be anchored to the International Criminal Court.

The International Criminal Court (ICC) was established on 1 July 2002 after a protracted and difficult set of international negotiations led in significant respects by US-based legal scholars and practitioners. Its establishment followed two ad hoc tribunals in the 1990s which prosecuted war crimes in Rwanda and the former Yugoslavia. The Court's membership includes a total of 108 states, with notable exceptions being China, India, Russia and – ironically – the United States. Both the US and Russia are permanent members of the UN Security Council. The ICC's territorial jurisdiction is nominally universal, but its functional jurisdiction is strictly limited to genocide, crimes against humanity and war crimes. Thus the advancing 'global police doctrine' (concerning, inter alia, drugs, weapons or human trafficking, crimes against the environment, economic or financial crimes, etc.) is not actually covered in the ICC statute. Arguments to widen the Court's functional jurisdiction have been ongoing since its inception, but have yet to lead to concrete developments and seem unlikely to do so.[1]

The principle of complementarity presents a fundamental limitation to the Court's jurisdiction; it can only act where national authorities are 'unable or unwilling' to prosecute. So, while the ICC's prosecution division has the power to collect and examine evidence, interview witnesses and so forth (but only with regard to its strictly limited areas of competence, e.g. war crimes) it ultimately lacks the power of arrest. The ICC can issue arrest warrants but must rely on states to execute them. The rule of law principle that ultimately could give the ICC legitimacy standing at the apex of a system of global legal accountability conflicts with the bedrock political principle of global governance which is based on the notion of state sovereignty.

The ICC has many virtues. It has a treaty basis in the Rome Statute and is developing procedural law. The social legitimacy of the ICC is also reasonably strong; war crimes and crimes against humanity are, from the point of view of most people, universally abhorrent. The workings of the Court are transparent and open; televised proceedings are streamed live from its two courtrooms. However, despite this degree of legitimacy, the continued opposition of seigneurial states like China, India, Russia and the United States to its existence and functioning makes it unlikely that the Court could act as the legal arbiter of global policing any time in the foreseeable future.

# From 'is' to 'ought'? Some further thoughts on making global policing accountable

We argue intensely and incessantly. We agree that it is uselessly utopian to believe that the world system can be without some form of policing. All social orders are policed, and this has been the case since premodern times, although it is true that the institutions we commonly name 'the police' are thoroughly modern. The question is not 'should the global system be policed?', but rather, 'what kind of global policing ought we to have?' The present is marked by one seemingly irresistible force dominating people's lives, hopes and fears; we call it globalisation. Globalisation – where the entire world of humans is linked through an instantaneous and permanent 'butterfly effect' – is not just an ecological, technological, cultural, economic or sociological idea. Information, knowledge and risk communications provides its material basis. The moment something becomes knowable it becomes 'news'. The death of a statesman, the price of stocks and bonds, the patenting of a new drug, any 'fact' entered into a computer in Dublin, Denver or Durban is instantly knowable around the world.

The transnational condition is due to more than the instantaneity of communication. The *One World* (Singer 2004) is marked by an array of cleavages and divisions, and yet still holds the promise of a possible overarching meta-ethic. Social structural disadvantage, the pronounced symptom of global economic integration, systematically destroys the basis of human solidarity and well-being (Wilkinson and Pickett 2009). New divisions emerge and new lines of conflict are drawn as the transnational 'networked society' creates boundaries of exclusion in the brave new world of globalisation (Castells 1998). There are many who are left out, or feel themselves to be, and their stories of anomie and alienation bear witness to the social disintegration concomitant with the absence of any binding norms besides those of the marketplace. The transnational capitalist class enjoys the bounties of globalisation (Sklair 2009), but simultaneously there is an underclass of the truly disadvantaged who enjoy destitution and early death (Bauman 1998). Global policing turns out to be the front-end loader of a global 'prison industrial complex' (Christie 2013). Disasters like that which took place at the Fukushima Power Plant in 2011, or the Deepwater Horizon oil rig in 2010, or in the aftermath of the earthquake in Haiti in the same year are projected instantly as discrete incidents of calamity instead of being analysed as ticking time bombs established by human agency (Klein 2010).

Ordinary people are mesmerised by the continuous projection of conflict, calamity, wars and natural disaster. Like the authors of a chapter about the accountability of global policing in a book about police accountability, they swing between caring too much and despairing of what to do. Palpably, global economic and political elites manifest incapacity for caring whist at the same time (and without a sense of irony) parading the promise that the great and the good can fix the situation. If we assume for the moment that the policing of the global system is part of the solution to our difficulties, what should we expect and how can we ensure that these expectations are met?

We follow an essentially Bittnerian view of policing. Egon Bittner (1974) succinctly defined policing as an activity which is the response to a situation that ought not to be happening and about which something had better be done, now! He argued that policing agents are to perform a bewildering array of tasks, from traffic control to counterterrorism. The common feature of the tasks that involve police work is not any specific social function such as crime control, order maintenance, law enforcement or political repression. Rather, legitimate policing activities arise out of emergencies of all sorts, usually where there is an element (or at least the potential) for social conflict. In such situations, policing agents rely on the ability to invoke customary legal capacities to employ force in order to handle the situation, but most often are expected to be able to keep this power in reserve – only using it as a means of last resort. We say customary legal capacity in order to emphasise that the legitimacy of policing rests upon the consent of a public which both understands and endorses the police mission to ensure social peace and good order. The letter of the law may allow for use of force but if, in a given instance, the use of force contradicts commonly held norms, whether formally legal or not, it will be judged by onlookers to be illegitimate. Underlying policing tactics for consensual peacekeeping is a 'bottom line' power to wield coercive sanctions and constraints, but the expectation is that other means of resolving the conflict or emergency situation will be attempted first. The art of good policing customarily rests on the minimal use of force.

The Peelian principles of democratic policing begin with the supposition that police agents are 'citizens in uniform'. We would argue that this supposition is, *mutatis mutandis*, applicable under conditions of transnationalisation, but there are a lot of details to consider. In the global system, plural policing has replaced the presumption of the state's monopoly of policing power. Globalisation means that citizenship and identity are blurred and not easily bound by allegiances to this or that nation state. Nevertheless, we are all, police agents included, equally human and if some people are granted the responsibilities to respond to situational exigencies of the kind that Bittner assigns to the policing office, it is all the more certain that the legitimacy of that office rests upon consent which, we believe, can only be based on common humanity. Having said that, when it comes down to it, there is always someone who is policed against. Can we really depend on the goodwill and the high principles of police as mere 'citizens in uniform' to ensure that things do not get out of hand?

The leitmotif of policing is essentially tragic. It is also caught up in games of power. The will to power is often present in modes of human organisation and this impinges on policing. The classic social theorist Robert Michels (1962 [1911]) summed up the problem as the 'iron law of oligarchy'. Even in the most resolutely democratic societies, he thought that social organisation gives rise to the dominion of the elected over the electors and the delegates over the delegators. Michels argued that oligarchy springs naturally from the imperatives of social organisation: competent authority and the division of labour eventually give rise to a caste of leaders who gain superior knowledge, skills and status which, combined with control of organisational resources such as communications or training, allow for oligarchic institutional domination.

Social power and social organisation are inseparable and it follows that global policing reinforces social hierarchy on a worldwide basis. The enforcement of inequality, for that is then what policing inevitably becomes, might be justified on Rawlsian grounds (cf. Manning 2010). In a *Theory of Justice* (1971), John Rawls argues for the 'difference principle' that inequality and social hierarchy are justifiable if they allow the least well-off to be more well off than they might otherwise be. There is a certain degree of ambiguity in this reasoning, and we are not sure how far to endorse this principle, but even granting that it could be right, it is not difficult to imagine that, over time, even those inequalities that make the least well-off better off (for example by allowing talented people to become doctors who minister to the sick and dying, even if it means that others are consigned to garbage duty) will be policed in such a way that inequality grows to the levels we presently have, which are difficult for us to legitimate.[2]

That is why systems of political, legal and social accountability matter. By these means policing practice has to be justified. By these means it ensures that somebody, other than the police, must authorise them in their mission. By these means, the proportionality of what police do may be rigorously assessed. By these means, the necessity of this or that police action may be assessed. The 'separation of powers' – conventionally between the legislature, the executive and the judiciary – is the 'standard model' by which legitimate authority is constituted in democratic forms of representative government. By separating the powers to make policy, to act on policy and to adjudicate the results and by making those who perform these functions accountable along different political, legal and social tracks some degree of democratic accountability is ensured. By these means (it is hoped) the tendencies summed up by the 'iron law of oligarchy' might be warded off.

The literature on the sociology of the global system makes clear that its constitution is lacking in significant respects (for a more detailed discussion see Held 2006). Our brief discussion of the UN, Interpol and the ICC is enough, or nearly enough, to conclude that the presently existing global system offers an inadequate way to assure accountability for global policing (see also Sheptycki 2011). The standard model of democratic accountability does not fit the global system or its machinery of policing. Moving from the situation that *is* (a global constitution of inequality) to a situation that *ought to be* (a global system that lives up to the principles of the Universal Declaration of Human Rights and frees the capacities of all people) is difficult to imagine. In order to move from 'is' to 'ought' and bring global policing to account we must venture outside that standard accountability model. The efforts of critical scholars and other non-governmental 'watchdogs' are crucial in this regard. They challenge the legitimacy of actually existing global policing by documenting its practices.

## Hopeful thoughts

We are here trying to provide some insight into the difficulties of holding global policing to account. Lest we appear altogether too pessimistic let us briefly mention some positive examples which show transnational actors in global civil society working to this end. Thankfully, we are not alone in studying policing on a global scale (see, for example, Baker 2009; Bayley 2006; Beare 2003; Edwards and Gill 2004; Ellison and Pino 2012; Gill *et al.* 2008; Grabosky 2009; Henry and Smith 2007; Hills 2009; Hughs *et al.* 2013; Larsen and Smandych 2007; Lemieux 2010; Lemain-Langlois 2012; Manning 2010; Nelken 2011). Scholarly scrutiny has established a catalogue of empirical accounts which contextualise the reality of global crime and policing rendering it visible as an object of critical appraisal. Read together, these academic studies help make the practices of transnational policing transparent and provide a basis upon which to gauge the political, legal and social accountability and legitimacy of global policing. A collegium of independent scholars may probe claims concerning emerging global policing 'doctrine'. This curia is not a choir that sings with one voice, nor should we expect it to be (cf. Sherman 2009). The value of free academic inquiry generally is its heterodox and pluralistic nature which allows ideas to be tested through vigorous and open debate. Especially when notions like 'policing doctrine' and 'police science' are advanced, Lysenkoism is a concern. One hopeful sign, therefore, is that the academic literature in this field employs a range of theoretical perspectives and methodological approaches which are productive of a variety of views on how to bridge the gap between the practical reality of actually existing policing and prescriptions for better policing.

Putting theory into practice is not easy. There is frequently a perceived gap between academic theory and what can be manifest in practical settings. Some scholars seek to directly address this through 'action research', 'practice-based research', 'practice-as-research' and the like. There are also a variety of 'watchdogs', international human rights NGOs, who also contribute to the monitoring and evaluation of police transformation, innovation and change. For example, since 1961 the Vera Institute of Justice has been engaged in ongoing work concerning the fairness and openness of criminal justice systems, holding these institutions to account and challenging the legitimacy of what they do. Originally funded by private philanthropists Louis Schwietzer and Herb Sturz, who worried that the bail system in New York city was unjust and served the interests of the wealthy to the detriment of those less well off than themselves, in time the Vera Institute gained funding from a number of different charitable foundations and trusts including the Ford Foundation, the Pew Trust, and the Open Society Institute. Historically its purview was restricted to criminal justice institutions in the United States, but since 1997 it has been engaged in international projects examining police accountability structures and public safety initiatives (Stone and Ward 2000). Stone and Ward argue that the prospects for achieving democratic and rights-based policing are good and that a number of innovations in policing and police accountability augment this process. They proceed to argue:

These innovations include such otherwise disparate developments as community policing, real-time analysis of crime statistics, victimisation surveys, civilian complaint review boards, civil rights and human rights prosecutions of police, integrity units within police agencies, exclusionary rules of evidence, laws mandating arrest in domestic violence cases and more.

(Ibid.: 13)

Projects undertaken by the Vera Institute in many different countries illustrate the importance of *local* knowledge and adapting *local* governmental capacities to the needs of *local* communities. Human Rights NGOs like Vera and also Human Rights Watch, Amnesty International, the Small Arms Survey and others perform a watchdog function and they also try to engineer the cooperation of senior policing administrators, government officials and local community members and stakeholders in policing initiatives. The incremental goal of such efforts is to improve the way policing agents, both public and privately contracted, treat people every day (Sheptycki 2000). Looking at the process of police reform in Northern Ireland, Maggie Beirne (2001) observed that human rights language often remains at a high level of generality and that its universality can render operationalisation in the policing context difficult and this is no less true in other locations. Faltering progress towards a democratically accountable system of global policing suggests that sustained and constant watchfulness by independent observers is essential if democratic policing norms are to ever take root.

Critical scrutiny by Human Rights watchdogs consistently identifies a cluster of issues which plague policing practice around the world. A partial list would include: police brutality and misconduct, corruption, failure to perform basic tasks, refusal to register complaints from the public, poor investigative skills, surveillance overreach, over-policing, under-policing and partisan politicisation. Each of these problems can be attributed to weak accountability or, very often, lack of accountability altogether. Policing is one of many issues pervading debates about the character of global governance and the concern to democratise policing globally is, we think, the most important political problem of the world system. Democratic control of policing has always been problematic, and it is even more so in the transnational era. Policing agents in all sectors of the policing field are significant transnational actors. At the same time, presumptions about the sovereignty of the state are made in the context of a complex polycentric system of global governance. It is difficult to explain the interplay of institutional power and vested interest that goes on under these conditions using a standard model of policing accountability (Sheptycki 2000; Bowling and Sheptycki 2012). The danger of the contemporary period is that policing has been decoupled from an overarching commitment to the general good. It has degenerated into an array of institutional capacities that selectively police the particular interests of specific power groups. Bolstering the ideals of democratic policing under transnational conditions is like rolling a rock up a hill and it requires the combined attentions of critical scholars, human rights watchdogs and policing leaders.

## Nagging doubts

A classic distinction is conventionally made in political theory, from the Ancient Greeks until today, between the polity and the *demos*. This distinction is very useful in thinking about political and legal order in the world system. It helps to explain why the standard model for thinking about police accountability, which rests on practical things like domestic arrangements for achieving police accountability, ill suits the global system. Accountability for global policing is difficult partly because of the diversity and complexity of the policing field. This is a difficulty inherent in the global system of which global policing is both a symptom and a part. The 'machinery of global governance', including the UN and (separately) the states that belong to it, the ICC, the World Bank, the IMF and the OECD and so on, makes up the *polity* of the global system. The companion term '*demos*' refers to 'the people', 'the commons' or 'the Volk'. Its attendant notion – democracy – denotes a political order (a polity) in which governmental authority is vested in the people as a whole. The polity is merely a political system. It is an institutional form of administration. Christendom in the Europe of the Middle Ages was a polity. Byzantium was a polity. But neither was a polity of the *demos*. Neither is the present age of the Global System a polity of the *demos*. Nor could it be. The 'global community' is an oxymoron. The global system is a complex array of groups, cultures, nations, societies, indeed perhaps even 'civilisations'. It also includes 'legal persons', that is, multinational corporations. The global polity is a complex polycentric power system. It has no counterpart which could rightly be called a *demos* which could hold it to account on behalf of a commonwealth.

The *demos* is a subjective social-psychological epiphenomenon rooted in objective social, political and economic conditions. Both the subjective and the objective dimensions can be observed empirically which leads us to the conclusion that there is no self-consciously global *demos*. Instead, the peoples of the world are divided by processes of economic exclusion, they are held in conditions of anomie through the politics of fear and anxiety, they are alienated from each other by patterns of inter- and intra-cultural conflict. Hence the continuing legitimation of global policing via discourses of suitable enemies and awesome folk devils. These discourses may appear to arise out of some deep emotional lava in which people are mired and unable to resist. But that is not the case. They result from the mobilisation of emotion by people occupying the commanding heights of the global system. The ceaseless projection of threat and danger justify power and authority and would cease to exist as risks to liberty and security were it not for those who exploit them in pursuit of their own interests. Making global policing democratically accountable entails the emergence of a global polity of the *demos* – a *demos* which, at present, remains divided and ruled through the politics of fear and insecurity.

## Conclusion

Joseph Conrad, reflecting on the Hague Peace Conferences which took place prior to the Great War and ushered in the twentieth century, remarked that those meetings constituted 'solemnly official recognition of the Earth as a House of Strife'. He went on to observe that 'to him whose indignation is qualified by a measure of hope and affection, the efforts of mankind to work its own salvation present a sight of alarming comicality' (Conrad 1905). Throughout the twentieth century, there has been an underlying tension between two logically incompatible sets of ideas: the sovereignty of states on the one hand, and the creations of a supranational order of international law and organisation on the other. Sovereignty implies the right of each state to have its own rules and institutions. International law and organisation implies a serious limitation of sovereignty. Global policing practice is mixed up with both tendencies. Thinking about accountability for global policing shows that the global social order is paradoxical because it is based on two logically incompatible sets of ideas, each of which needs the other in order to remedy its own inherent limitations. The troubling thing about global policing is that it simultaneously purports to contain systemic insecurity while being a contributor to that insecurity.

Hope and despair exist in equal measure. The problems and opportunities inherent in the global system are finely balanced. We argue that global policing is a synecdoche of the global system, a polycentric and oligarchic power system legitimated through the politics of fear. We believe that global policing ought to support the conditions that allow all people to make use of economic opportunities in the global marketplace whilst preserving (or perhaps creating) cohesive civil societies and achieving those aims by fostering open political institutions. Prosperity, civility, social trust and liberty all have to be policed. In a global context, that means fostering economic relations and respecting cultural difference. And, we are increasingly aware, it also means fostering respect for the ecology of the planet itself. The global commonwealth remains elusive and so actually existing global policing remains an object of vigorous criticism. The search for adequate legal and political means by which to bring global policing to account is a major task and it remains in front of us.

This essay began with a quotation from Albert Camus because bringing global policing to account is a punishing effort worthy of Sisyphus. For both Camus and Kafka, Sisyphus personified the absurd hero who struggled to reach the heights only to be thrown down again and again to the depths, destined to remain solitary and alone. Keeping in mind the story of Derek Bond, and of the many, many stories of people whose suffering is even greater, we draw this conclusion about the struggle to bring global policing (and, by extension, the global system) to account: we are all alone in this together.

## Notes

1 It is perhaps worth noting that the 1998 Rome Statute does make provision for crimes such as terrorism and drugs offences to be included at a later date. In Annex 1(E) of the Rome Conference Final Act:

> Recommends that a Review Conference pursuant to Article III of the Statute of the ICC consider the crimes of terrorism and drug crimes with a view to arriving

at an acceptable definition and their inclusion in the list of crimes within the jurisdiction of the court.

2 In his widely acclaimed book *Democratic Policing in a Changing World* (2010) Peter
Manning asks what the organisation of policing is good for and how can we evaluate it
to see if it is democratic. His answer draws significantly on Rawlsian theory. He argues
that police 'are an agency that distributes and redistributes social goods' that alter life
chances (ibid.: 248). He suggests that where policing practices increase social inequalities, they should be seen as failing, thus largely sidestepping the thorny issue contained
in the Rawlsian 'difference principle' that allows that the equal distribution of resources
is abridgeable if (and only if) it improves the lot of the least well-off. This allowance
of the Rawlsian difference principle, it seems to us, is the first step down the slippery
slope to oligarchy.

# References

Baker, B. (2009) 'Introduction: Policing Post-Conflict Societies; Helping out the State',
*Policing and Society, Special Issue on Policing Post-Conflict Societies*, 19(4): 329–32.
Bauman, Z. (1998) *Globalization: The Human Consequences*, New York: Columbia Uni-
versity Press.
Bayley, D. (2006) *Changing the Guard: Developing Democratic Policing Abroad*,
Oxford: Oxford University Press.
Bayley, D. and Shearing, C. (1996) 'The Future of Policing', *Law and Society Review*,
30(3): 586–606.
Beare, M. (2003) *Critical Reflections on Transnational Organized Crime, Money Laun-
dering and Corruption*, Toronto: Toronto University Press.
Beirne, M. (2001) 'Progress or Placebo? The Patten Report and the Future of Policing in
Northern Ireland', *Policing and Society*, 11(3–4), Special Issue on Policing in Northern
Ireland, 297–320.
Bittner, E. (1974) *The Functions of Police in Modern Society*, Chevy Chase, MD:
National Institute of Mental Health.
Bowling, B. and Sheptycki, J. (2012) *Global Policing*, London: Sage.
Brodeur, J.-P. (1983) 'High Policing and Low Policing: Remarks about the Policing of
Political Activities', *Social Problems*, 30(5): 507–20.
Brodeur, J.-P. (2007) 'An Encounter with Egon Bitter', *Crime, Law and Social Change*,
48: 105–32.
Carvajal, D. (2009) 'Interpol and UN Back "Global Policing Doctrine"', *New York
Times*, 11 October 2009, available at www.nytimes.com/2009/10/12/world/
europe/12iht-interpol.html?_r=0 (last accessed 6 September 2013).
Castells, M. (1998 [2nd edn 2000]) *End of the Millennium: The Information Age,
Economy, Society and Culture Vol. 3*, Oxford: Basil Blackwell.
Christie, N. (2013) *Crime Control as Industry: Towards Gulags, Western Style* (3rd
revised edn), London: Taylor and Francis.
Conrad, J. (1905) 'Autocracy and War', in J.H. Stape and A. Busza (eds.) *Notes of Life
and Letters*, Cambridge: Cambridge University Press, 71–93.
Den Boer, M., Hillebrand, C. and Nölke, A. (2008) 'Legitimacy under Pressure: The
European Web of Counter-Terrorism Networks', *Journal of Common Market Studies*,
46(1): 101–24. See in particular Table 1, at 109.
Deflem, M. (2000) 'Bureaucratization and Social Control: Historical Foundations of
International Police Cooperation', *Law and Society Review*, 34(3): 601–40.

Deflem, M. (2002) *Policing World Society: Historical Foundations of International Police Co-operation*, Oxford, Oxford University Press.

Deleuze, G. and Guattari, F. (1993) *A Thousand Plateaus: Capitalism and Schizophrenia*, Minneapolis: University of Minnesota Press.

Dobbins, J., Jones, S.G., Crane, K., Rathmell, A., Steele, B., Teltschik, R. and Timilsina, A. (2005) *The UN's Role in Nation Building: From the Congo to Iraq*, Santa Monica, CA: RAND Corp.

Edwards, A. and Gill, P. (2004) *Transnational Organised Crime: Perspectives on Global Security*, London: Routledge.

Ellison, G. and Pino, N. (2012) *Globalization, Police Reform and Development: Doing it the Western Way*, London: Palgrave.

Gill, P., Marrin, S. and Phythian, M. (2008) *Intelligence Theory: Key Questions and Debates*, London: Routledge.

Goldsmith, A. and Sheptycki, J. (2007) *Crafting Transnational Policing*, Oxford: Hart.

Grabosky, P. (2009) 'Police as International Peacekeepers', *Policing and Society Special Issue on Policing and Peace-Keeping*, 101–5.

Held, D. (2006) *Models of Democracy*, Stanford, CA: Stanford University Press.

Henry, A. and Smith, D.J. (2007) *Transformations in Policing*, Aldershot: Ashgate.

Hills, A. (2009) 'The possibility of transnational policing, *Policing and Society*, 19(3): 300–17.

Hughs, B., Hunt, C.T. and Curth-Bib, J. (2013) *Forging New Conventional Wisdom Beyond International Policing: Leaning from Complex Realities*, Leiden: Martinus Ninhoff.

Johnston, L. and Shearing, C. (2003) *Governing Security*, London: Routledge.

Klein, N. (2010) *The Shock Doctrine: The Rise of Disaster Capitalism*, New York: Henry Holt.

Larsen, N. and Smandych, R. (2007) *Global Criminology and Criminal Justice: Current Issues and Perspectives*, Toronto: University of Toronto Press.

Lemain-Langlois, S. (2012) *Technocrime: Policing and Surveillance* London: Taylor & Francis.

Lemieux, F. (2010) *International Police Co-operation: Emerging Issues, Theory and Practice*, Cullompton, Devon: Willan.

Lloyd, R., Oatham, J. and Hammer, M. (2007) *2007 Global Accountability Report*, London: One World Trust.

Loader, I. (2002) 'Governing European Policing: Some Problems and Prospects', *Policing and Society*, 12(4): 291–305.

Manning, P.K. (2010) *Democratic Policing in a Changing World*, Boulder, CO: Paradigm Publishers.

Michels, R. (1962 [1911]) *Political Parties: A Sociological Study of the Oligarchical Tendencies of Modern Democracy*, New York: Collier Books.

Nelken, D. (2011) *Comparative Criminal Justice and Globalization*, Aldershot: Ashgate.

Rawls, J. (1971) *A Theory of Justice*, Cambridge, MA: Harvard University Press.

Reiner, R. (2010) *The Politics of the Police* (4th edn), Oxford: Oxford University Press.

Sheptycki, J. (2000) 'Policing and Human Rights: An Introduction', *Policing and Society*, 10(1): 1–10.

Sheptycki, J. (2002) 'Accountability Across the Policing Field: Towards a General Cartography of Accountability for Post-Modern Policing', *Policing and Society*, 12(4): 323–38.

Sheptycki, J. (2004) 'The Accountability of Transnational Policing Institutions: The Strange Case of Interpol', *The Canadian Journal of Law and Society*, 19(1): 107–34.

Sheptycki, J. (2011) *Transnational Crime and Policing*, Aldershot: Ashgate.

Sheptycki, J. (forthcoming) 'Brand Interpol', in S. Hufnagel (ed.) *A Question of Trust: Socio-legal Imperatives in International Police and Justice Cooperation*, Oxford: Hart.

Sherman, L. (2009) 'Evidence and Liberty: The Promise of Experimental Criminology', *Criminology and Criminal Justice*, 9(1): 5–28.

Singer, P. (2004) *One World: The Ethics of Globalization*, New Haven: Yale University Press.

Sklair, L. (2009) 'The Transnational Capitalist Class and the Politics of Capitalist Globalization', in S. Dasgupta and J.N. Pieterse (eds) *The Politics of Globalization*, London: Sage, 82–97.

Stone, C.E. and Ward, H.H. (2000) 'Democratic Policing: A Framework for Action', *Policing and Society*, 10(1): 11–47.

Wilkinson, R.G. and Pickett, K. (2009) *The Spirit Level: Why More Equal Societies Almost Always Do Better*, London: Allen Lane.

# Index

Please note that page numbers relating to Notes will be denoted by the letter 'n' and note number following the note. Page references to Figures will be in **bold**, while those for Tables will be *italics*.

CPSIA information can be obtained
at www.ICGtesting.com
Printed in the USA
LVOW13*1443111217

559403LV00010B/200/P

9 780415 715331